D1035940

Indirect Perception

MIT Press/Bradford Books Series in Cognitive Psychology
Stephen E. Palmer, editor

A Dynamic Systems Approach to Development: Applications, edited by Linda B. Smith and Esther Thelen (1993)

A Dynamic Systems Approach to the Development of Cognition and Action, edited by Esther Thelen and Linda B. Smith (1994)

Cognition and the Visual Arts, by Robert L. Solso (1994)

Indirect Perception, edited by Irvin Rock (1996)

Indirect Perception

Edited by Irvin Rock
With a foreword by Stephen E. Palmer

A Bradford Book
The MIT Press
Cambridge, Massachusetts
London, England

© 1997 Massachusetts Institute of Technology

All rights reserved. No part of this book may be reproduced in any form by any electronic or mechanical means (including photocopying, recording, or information storage and retrieval) without permission in writing from the publisher.

This book was set in Palatino by Asco Trade Typesetting Ltd., Hong Kong.

Printed and bound in the United States of America.

Library of Congress Cataloging-in-Publication Data

Indirect perception / edited by Irvin Rock : with a foreword by
   Stephen E. Palmer.
      p.   cm. – (MIT Press/Bradford Books series in cognitive
   psychology)
   "A Bradford Book."
   Includes bibliographical references (p.   ) and index.
   ISBN 0-262-18177-0 (hardcover : alk. paper)
      1. Perception. 2. Schemas (Psychology) 3. Gestalt psychology.
   I. Rock, Irvin. II. Series.
   BF311.I46   1996
   153.7–dc20   96-26924
                                                        CIP

Contents

Series Foreword

This series presents definitive works on cognition viewed from a psychological perspective, including undergraduate and graduate textbooks, reference works, research monographs, and edited volumes. Among the wide variety of topics addressed are perception, attention, imagery, memory, learning, categorization, language, problem solving, thinking, and cognitive development. Although the primary emphasis is on presenting psychological theories and findings, most volumes in the series are interdisciplinary, attempting to develop important connections between cognitive psychology and the related fields of anthropology, computer science, education, linguistics, neuroscience, and philosophy.

Stephen E. Palmer

Foreword: The Legacy of Irvin Rock

Stephen E. Palmer

This volume represents what is almost certain to be the last published statement by Irvin Rock on global perceptual theory. I believe it is an especially fitting culmination of his long and distinguished career for several reasons that I hope to make clear in this foreword. Along the way, I will mention some of the important contributions he has made during this career and place them in a historical context relevant to the subject matter of this book.

Irvin Rock is a global theorist in the grand tradition of the truly great perceptionists, such as Hermann von Helmholtz, Max Wertheimer, and James J. Gibson. Like them, he grapples with the big, important issues of perceptual theory, ones that bear importantly on the answer to Koffka's (1935) famous question: Why do things look as they do? This volume is based on one of these big questions: Is perception a "direct" process in which our experiences result simply from extracting information from retinal stimulation, as Gibson proposed, or is it an "indirect" process in which experiences are derived by inference in a layered, hierarchical system of interpretations, as Helmholtz maintained? Rock's answer in this book is that perception is indirect, at least in the sense that some conscious perceptions are caused by other prior conscious perceptions rather than being directly and independently determined by retinal stimulation.[1]

Rock's reasons for believing this are largely empirical rather than theoretical. Unlike some theorists, Rock pays close attention to a broad range of experimental evidence in evaluating theoretical claims. For him, theory and experiment always go hand in hand: theories are proposed in the service of explaining or predicting empirical results, and experiments are performed in the service of testing theories. This approach is well represented in this volume. In the first chapter, which is new, Rock lays out the theoretical issues underlying what he refers to as indirect perception. The rest of the volume is then devoted to presenting detailed evidence in support of the indirect view. It is not incidental that Rock himself is an author or co-author of most of the reprinted articles, for he has done more work on this topic than anyone else. Just as surely, however, it is not simply a collection of Rock's "greatest hits," but a careful selection of articles that he believes provide convincing evidence for indirect perception. Although Rock has authored or co-authored most of these articles, several were written by others, usually including one or more of his students, colleagues, or friends.

The interplay between theory and experiment is absolutely essential in understanding Rock's approach to perceptual science. As I will explain shortly, he is one of the few theorists to have significantly changed his mind about the nature of perception due to experimental results. He was trained in the Gestalt tradition and began his career following this line of theorizing. But in the course of his many perceptual experiments, he began to see that his results were more in line with the Helmholtzian idea of perception as unconscious inference. Rock later extended this theoretical position in important ways, developing his own unique version in response to his own experimental results, some of which surprised him. The product is a rich and interesting view of perception that is remarkably modern, despite its roots in Helmholtz's ideas from more than a century ago. Perhaps the fullest statement of his position is contained in his classic 1983 book, *The Logic of Perception*, which I heartily recommend to the interested reader for more information. This volume is in many ways its successor, updating both Rock's theoretical ideas and the evidence supporting his indirect view of perception.

A Brief History of Perceptual Theory

The reader's appreciation of this volume and its implications will be enhanced by understanding something about the history of perceptual theory and Rock's place within it. Those who already possess such an understanding may safely skip this foreword, which constitutes an extremely brief primer on modern psychological theories of perception.

There are essentially three different approaches to perceptual theory that are serious candidates for a metatheoretical framework within which detailed accounts of perception have been proposed (see Rock 1983, chap. 2). In historical order, they are the *inferential approach* initially formulated by Helmholtz, the *organizational approach* proposed by Gestalt psychologists, and the *ecological approach* advanced by Gibson. I should say at the outset that although these positions are often treated as though they are mutually exclusive, it is not clear whether they are truly incompatible or, if they are, in precisely what ways. They are often used to address quite different perceptual problems, and they certainly bear complex and highly debatable relations to one another, enough to have fueled many heated controversies over the years.

The Inferential Approach
The inferential approach, due initially to Helmholtz ([1867] 1962), proposes that perception is fundamentally a thoughtlike (or "ratiomorphic") process. The perceiver is given the spatiotemporal pattern of stimulation on the retina and must "infer" what environmental situation or event is most likely to have produced that retinal stimulation. Inferential theorists assume that the pair of 2-D images on the retina is informationally inadequate to uniquely determine the 3-D array of objects in space that produced them. Their reasoning is that information is irretrievably lost in going from the 3-D world to any 2-D projection of it. To fill the gap, they hypothesize that the observer somehow *adds information* from internal sources, what in modern parlance would be called "heuristic assumptions." In essence, the inferential approach hypothesizes that observers make very rapid and unconscious inferences based jointly on optical information in their retinal images and internally stored knowledge of the likelihood of various real-world situations given particular kinds of image structure. (This probabilistic internal knowledge is generally thought to be derived from past experience of the individual perceiver, but it could also be innately determined by evolutionary learning of the entire species.) When the internal knowledge they add is correct and appropriate to the situation—as it usually is—perception will be veridical. When it is incorrect or inappropriate, however, perception will be illusory, often in quite predictable ways. This ability to predict both accurate and illusory perceptions is one of the great strengths of inferential theories.

To understand the kind of explanations offered within an inferential framework, consider the image displayed in figure F.1A. Nearly everyone perceives two squares, one behind the other, as depicted in figure F.1B by the gray lines indicating hidden edges. But notice that the image doesn't actually contain two squares. There are two regions, and one of them is indeed a square, but the other is actually L-shaped, as shown in figure F.1C. Why, then, do people perceive two squares arranged in depth rather

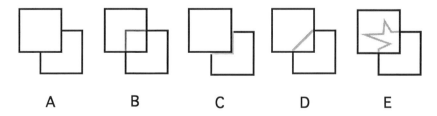

A   B   C   D   E

Figure F.1
Possible completions of a partly occluded object. Gray lines in B–E indicate hidden contours in the scene depicted in A.

than a square and L-shaped figure abutting each other in the same plane? And even if the square is perceived as in front of another object that is partly occluded, why is the second shape perceived as a square rather than a pentagon as shown in figure F.1D, or the irregular shape depicted in figure F.1E, or any of an infinite number of other alternatives? Helmholtz's answer was that the perception of one square occluding the other is achieved because this is *the most likely real-world situation* that would project this image to the retina. The "mosaic" interpretation (fig. F.1C) is unlikely because of the precise alignment required for the two sets of edges to exactly coincide as they do in figure F.1A. No such precision of alignment is required if one object is in front of and occludes the other. Some further explanation is required to account for why the occluded shape is seen as square, however. Again, likelihood provides a plausible answer. The alternative shapes for the farther object are less likely than the square because they are less frequently seen. Thus, the criterion of maximizing likelihood in Helmholtzian theories of unconscious inference accounts nicely for the visual completion of such partly occluded objects. Whether it is true or not is another matter.

The inferential approach to perceptual theory is closely related to modern computational theories of vision (e.g., Marr 1982). The connection lies principally in the assumption that the perceptual problem is generally underconstrained—that is, that the 3-D world cannot be uniquely recovered from a pair of 2-D images—and that its solution must therefore make use of heuristic assumptions of some sort. The kind of inferences derived by computational theories are not generally generated by symbolic logic, as one might expect from calling them "inferences," but by complex numerical calculations, sometimes carried out in neural networks. Still, the general thrust of such models is very much in the spirit of Helmholtz's formulation: to infer the most likely environmental situation that might have given rise to the optical structure of the image. Although current computational theories are still a long way from achieving this goal, enough progress has been made that it appears to be a viable approach.

The Organizational Approach
The organizational approach, developed initially by Gestalt psychologists (most notably Max Wertheimer, Kurt Koffka, and Wolfgang Köhler), also proposes that perceivers add something to the inadequate pattern of retinal stimulation, but it claims that these contributions are based on evaluating the *intrinsic structure* of alternative interpretations rather than on evaluating their likelihood or probability. Gestalt theorists assume that the initial retinal representation is essentially unstructured and that any and all organization within the experienced percept is therefore the result of processes occuring within the visual nervous system. Whereas Helm-

holtz proposed that the visual system arrived at a perception by selecting the most *likely* (i.e., most probable) interpretation consistent with the retinal image, Gestalt theorists proposed that perception was determined by selecting the "best" interpretation (i.e., the one with the simplest, most regular, most symmetrical structure). When the real-world situation is in fact the simplest, most regular, and symmetrical possibility consistent with the retinal image—as it often is—the Gestalt view predicts veridical perception. In other cases, it predicts illusory perceptions.

Organizational theories offer a slightly different explanation of the perception of visual completion illustrated in figure F.1 than do inferential theories, one based on "figural goodness" (in German, "gut Gestalt"). Gestalt theorists would claim that the perception of a second square arises because it is "better" than the alternatives in the sense of being simpler, more regular, and more symmetrical. In the particular case shown, simplicity alone is sufficient to account for the perception: the square in figure F.1B has only four sides, whereas the L-shaped region in figure F.1C has six, the pentagon in figure F.1D has five, and the complex polygon in figure F.1E has still more. Note that explanations in terms of likelihood and simplicity coincide whenever the most likely interpretation is also the "best" in terms of figural goodness. Since this is often the case, these theories are often difficult to distinguish. (The interested reader is referred to Pomerantz and Kubovy's [1986] review for a full discussion of this and related issues concerning theories of perceptual organization.)

Although the organizational approach was once a major force in perceptual theory, several problems have eroded its popularity. One is that for many years no formal theories were available to determine what organization was best. This led to a disturbing circularity: what is perceived is the best alternative, but what is best could only be determined by what was perceived. More recently, however, formal versions of organizational theory have been developed that overcome this problem to a large extent (e.g., Leeuwenberg 1971; Van der Helm and Leeuwenberg 1991). A second problem was (and is) the Gestalt insistence that perception depends importantly on the *global* structure of the stimulus. They maintained that "the whole is different from the sum of its parts" in ways that implied that perception could never be understood in terms of simply putting together local bits of visual information. This holistic claim conflicts with the analytic tradition of western science and is not readily assimilated into it. Yet another problem is that many psychologists (erroneously) believe Gestalt theory to have been empirically disproven. This misconception arose because Köhler made a bold physiological conjecture that perceptual organization might arise through dynamic interaction of electromagnetic force fields in the brain (e.g., Köhler and Wallach 1944). When this idea was discredited by experimental results (e.g., Lashley, Chow, and Semmes 1951;

Sperry and Milner 1955), many researchers generalized the conclusion beyond Köhler's physiological conjecture to the more abstract and general Gestalt hypotheses about the nature of organizational processing. This inference is unwarranted because the abstract theoretical proposals of Gestalt theory might be correct even if Köhler's conjecture is not. Indeed, some of these abstract aspects of Gestalt theory are quite compatible with modern neural network models of brain function (see Palmer 1995; Rock and Palmer 1990), which are very much alive and thriving.

The Ecological Approach
The ecological approach of James J. Gibson (1950, 1966, 1979) takes a radically different viewpoint. It assumes that all the information necessary for veridical perception is available in the dynamic array of light that stimulates the retina. Perhaps Gibson's greatest contributions to the field of perception were his demonstrations that optical information is incredibly rich in global structure and that this structure strongly constrains our perceptions of the environment in lawful ways. He discovered a large number of spatial and spatiotemporal patterns of optical structure that provide information about the layout of surfaces in the visible environment, including texture gradients, motion gradients, and the accretion and deletion of texture, to name just a few. Indeed, Gibson believed that optical structure constrained perception so strongly that no contribution by the observer was necessary. He therefore rejected the idea that perception required unconscious inferences based on prior knowledge because all the necessary information is contained in the dynamic flux of optical information available to observers as they actively explore their environments. His theory of ecological optics therefore emphasized the informational structure of optical events on the retina rather than how the brain processes that information. As one writer aptly put it, Gibson's approach was "Ask not what's inside your head, but what your head's inside of" (Mace 1977).

Ecological theorists would offer a different kind of explanation for the perception of two squares in figure F.1A. To begin, they would claim that the perception of the two squares is uniquely determined by the optical information available. What might this information be? If the observer were actively exploring the environment, as ecological theorists assume is generally the case, and if the two objects were separated in depth, information about their relative distance from the observer and occlusion of the farther surface by the closer one would arise from the accretion and deletion of texture on the farther object by the edges of the nearer object (Gibson 1979). As the farther object is progressively disoccluded, more of its straight edges would be revealed, and the extrapolation of these straight edges would imply that the farther object is indeed a square. But this scenario cannot account for the perception of figure F.1A as a picture of such a situation, or indeed for the perception of two squares actually pasted together, because observer motion in these cases provides no information from textural occlusion/disocclusion and because the same perception arises even when the observer doesn't move. Here ecological theorists must rely on the informational value of the so-called T-junctions that occur when one object's edge disappears behind another (e.g., Kellman and Shipley 1991). T-junctions generally imply occlusion, and if the visual system assumes that the occluded "stem" of the T continues behind the occluding edge with the same curvature as the visible portion, then the occluded object would uniquely be a square.[2]

Gibson was aware that the brain somehow had to "pick up" the information in the optical stimulus in order for it to be useful to the observer, but he said very little about the processes that might accomplish this. Perhaps to emphasize his rejection of the idea that observers contribute to perception by unconscious inference as Helmholtz hypothesized, Gibson referred to his proposals as a theory of *direct perception*. He was not very explicit about defining direct perception precisely, but he clearly meant to contrast it with Helmholtz's view that perception is mediated by internal knowledge. Gibson also avoided saying very much about how direct perception might actually occur in the brain except by a broad analogy. He suggested that structures in the brain *resonate* to optical information, much as a tuning fork resonates to a particular frequency of acoustic vibration. Thus, when the appropriate optical structure is present in the stimulus, a particular brain mechanism would respond by firing, thereby indicating the presence of that structure in the perception.

Modern computational theorists owe a significant debt to Gibson's ecological approach, although this fact is not widely acknowledged. Many computationalists—especially since the mathematically sophisticated contributions by Marr, Horn, Binford, Koenderink, and others—work initially at an abstract level by analyzing the relation between the optical structure of images and the environmental situation that produced it. In fact, they look for information that would constrain the mapping from image to environment, just as Gibson advocated in his ecological approach. Many computationalists part company with Gibson, however, over two of his closely related claims: that optical information alone is sufficient to recover the environmental scene and that perception is therefore direct and unmediated. Explicit rejections of Gibson's approach appeared in Marr's (1982) influential book, *Vision*, and in Shimon Ullman's widely read (1980) article, "Against Direct Perception." Both analyzed Gibson's views from a computational standpoint and found them unacceptable. The numerous commentaries that followed Ullman's article provide a broad sampling of diverse viewpoints—pro, con, and in between—on Gibson's proposals to which the interested reader is referred.

Rock's Views on Perceptual Theory

Perhaps the greatest and longest-standing intellectual passion of Rock's professional career has been trying to understand visual perception at the global level of these large-scale theoretical approaches. He pursued this quest by questioning the logical consistency of existing perceptual theories, by performing experiments to test their predictions, and by extending these theories into new and uncharted territory.

From Gestalt to Unconscious Inference

Rock's particular perspective on the three theoretical approaches described above is unique. His earliest theoretical leanings were toward the organizational approach, shaped substantially by his training at the hands of several distinguished Gestalt psychologists, including Hans Wallach, Mary Henle, Solomon Asch, and Martin Scheerer. Perhaps for this reason Rock is often mistakenly believed by some to be theoretically allied with the Gestalt organizational position, even today. Although he has remained sympathetic to certain Gestalt ideas about the nature of perceptual organization and problem solving throughout his career, his major theoretical alliance changed over the course of many years of study. As he explored human perception experimentally, his findings slowly convinced him that something akin to unconscious inference was a better overall framework for perceptual theory than the Gestalt approach. By the 1970s Rock had become one of the strongest advocates of inferential theory and had contributed significantly to its development. His last public lecture, given as part of the Distinguished Psychologists lecture series at the University of California, Berkeley (December 1994), provided incontrovertible evidence of this theoretical conversion process. He related a personal history of the empirically driven evolution of his theoretical ideas in a talk entitled, "On Changing One's Perception of Perception."

Although there are several other prominent theorists who have argued for an inferential theory of perception in one form or another—most notably Julian Hochberg and Richard Gregory—it is Rock who has written most extensively and persuasively on this perspective. *The Logic of Perception* is perhaps the single most important statement of this approach since the writings of Helmholtz ([1867] 1962). It is certainly the most thorough analysis of its merits relative to those of competing perspectives. Rock has also written numerous chapters in edited books that argue cogently for an inferential approach, including "In Defense of Unconscious Inference" (Rock 1977) in Epstein's excellent book, *Stability and Constancy in Visual Perception*, and "The Logic of *The Logic of Perception*" (Rock 1993), to name just two.

Rock's eclectic brand of inferential theory is somewhat different from Helmholtz's, having been enriched by the subsequent proposals and discoveries of organizational and ecological theorists like the Gestaltists and Gibson, as well as by Rock's own contributions. His general theoretical framework is that perception is essentially a problem-solving process, and he borrowed heavily from Gestalt writings on problem solving (e.g., Duncker 1945). The problem, as Helmholtz realized, is to determine what situation in the external world might have produced the pattern of optical stimulation that the retina records. Unlike Helmholtz, however, Rock seldom invokes either the likelihood principle or past experience. Rather, the visual system solves this problem by making inferences, by proposing hypotheses, and by testing them, much as scientists do in constructing and testing theories to account for observed data.

Many of Rock's elaborations of this basic framework have since become central tenets of modern computational theories of vision, although they are seldom recognized as such. Among his most important theoretical contributions are the following:

1. *Propositional Descriptions.* One of Rock's significant theoretical proposals was the idea that perceptions are essentially propositional descriptions of objects (e.g., Rock 1973). This idea has been formalized by others as the hypothesis that object perceptions can be represented as hierarchical structural descriptions, probably the most widely held position about the nature of shape representation (e.g., Marr and Nishihara 1977; Palmer 1975).

2. *Frames of Reference.* Another important insight Rock had early on was that these shape descriptions were constructed relative to a perceptual frame of reference (e.g., Rock 1973). Although he borrowed this idea from earlier Gestalt theorists (e.g., Duncker 1929; Asch and Witkin 1948), his application of it to shape description foreshadowed later computational theories that emphasized the importance of local and global coordinate systems (e.g., Marr and Nishihara 1977; Palmer 1975, 1989).

3. *Avoidance of Coincidence.* More recently, Rock (1983) began to realize the importance of the fact that the visual system abhors solutions that rely on coincidence. In the Gestalt principle of good continuation, for example, vision prefers to interpret two edges that are aligned as due to their being part of the same object rather than as an accident of a particular viewpoint. In computational vision, the same idea has been proposed and extended by Lowe (1985) in terms of the visual system preferring "nonaccidental properties" that arise from "general perspective."

4. *Stimulus Conformity and Stimulus Support.* Rock believed that the ultimate solution to the perceptual problem posed by the retinal image is

subject to two critical constraints. First, the solution must *conform to the pattern of retinal stimulation* in the sense of being compatible with it. For example, one does not perceive the partly occluded object in figure F.1A as triangular because that is geometrically incompatible with the given retinal image. Second, every aspect of the solution must be *supported by some aspect of the stimulus*. For example, one does not perceive a completely occluded circle behind the closer square in figure F.1A because there is no stimulus support for this logical possibility.

5. *Initial versus Preferred Perceptions*. Perhaps most relevant to this particular volume, Rock distinguished between earlier (*initial*) and later (*preferred*) perceptions. In many cases, people first perceive a solution that is close to the pattern of stimulation literally given on the retina, but later achieve a "better" perception that supersedes and dominates the first. An example would be the completion of partly occluded objects (see figure F.1) where the initial very fleeting perception might be of a mosaic of regions as given in the image, but the preferred perception is of one object being farther away and partly covered by the nearer object (cf. Sekuler and Palmer 1992).

Through these and other theoretical contributions, Rock has fleshed out and extended inferential theories beyond Helmholtz's original formulation. Rock's version is consistent with Helmholtz's at its core, but the rest is decidedly modern in thrust and points the way toward computational (or information-processing) models of vision.

Direct versus Indirect Perception
As Rock states in his book, *The Logic of Perception*, the problem-solving approach to perception implies a hierarchy in which certain perceptions must be achieved before others are possible.

> Enough examples have been given to make it evident that perception is often based upon, preceded by, or at least affected by another perception. In fact, if we consider all the categories analyzed here, virtually all the phenomena of object and event perception would seem to have been included.... The phenomena discussed in this chapter are entirely compatible with a cognitive theory of the kind developed in the previous chapters. Solving the problem of what object or event is producing the proximal stimulus takes time and generally entails a sequence of steps. In that respect, the theory subscribes to the major tenet of the contemporary approach of information processing. There is no difficulty with instances in which one step in the sequence itself has the status of a percept. (Rock 1983, 299)

In this book, Rock makes the argument that if such sequences of conscious perceptions exist, they constitute a form of *indirect perception* to be contrasted with Gibson's notion of direct perception. His reasoning is that because the later, higher-level percept is mediated by the earlier one, rather than being determined directly by higher-order retinal structure in the optical stimulus, it is not direct and unmediated as Gibson proposed. Moreover, it is not just that one particular pattern of stimulation leads to the final result, but that *any* pattern producing the required earlier perception leads to it. For example, if a certain perception of grouping depends on the prior perception of a certain depth arrangement, then any retinal event leading to that depth perception—be it due to binocular disparity, motion parallax, linear perspective, or whatever—will also cause that perception of grouping. Thus, to the extent that perceptions truly depend on other perceptions and not just on the particular pattern of stimulation that caused it, Gibson's claim of direct perception would be undermined.

But to what extent *is* it true? This is an empirical question, one that cannot be resolved simply by logical arguments about the relative merits of different theories. A great believer in the ability of careful experiments to decide between alternative theories, Rock marshals a considerable body of evidence to support his contention that at least some perceptions are indeed determined by other perceptions. By and large, Rock lets the evidence speak for itself. His new introductions to the selections set the stage for the experiments and sometimes explain the logic behind them, but allow the reader to draw his or her own conclusions based on the data.

What the results of these experiments generally show is that one aspect of perception is strongly dependent on a prior aspect of perception. The perceived shape of an object depends on its perceived orientation (rather than its retinal orientation); the perceived grouping of objects depends on their perceived proximity, lightness, and shape (rather than their retinal proximity, luminance, and shape); the perceived lightness of a surface depends on its perceived illumination (rather than its retinal luminance); and so forth. Is this unequivocal evidence of a hierarchy of perceptions, one determining another, as Rock suggests? Or might the same results also be consistent with a direct perception scheme in which each aspect of perception is determined independently from higher-order structure in retinal stimulation, as Gibson maintained?

The difficulty with the account in terms of direct perception is that in certain cases, the same stimulus information can lead to different perceptions of one property, B, when nothing changes but the observer's perception of another property, A. If observers view figure F.2, for example, they generally perceive its shape to be that of an upright diamond. If they are then told to imagine it as having been tilted clockwise by 45 degrees, so that the upper right segment is its top, they then perceive its shape to be square *as soon as they perceive its orientation as tilted*. This is just one

Figure F.2
The ambiguous square/diamond. The shape of this figure can be perceived either as an upright diamond or a square tilted by 45 degrees.

example, but it is a particularly good one precisely because the change in perceived shape can occur in the absence of any change other than that of the perceived orientation of the figure. The difficulty for direct perception is that it does not explain the dependencies that exist between the perception of orientation and the perception of shape.

Notice first that the stimulus information is exactly the same for both perceptions. This is a problem for any purely stimulus-based theory because differences in perceptions are supposed to be caused by differences in retinal information. When the retinal information is the same, the perception should be the same. A direct perception theorist might try to counter this objection by claiming that these different perceptions result simply from the resonation of different brain mechanisms to different aspects of retinal information, but there are problems here too. There is surely no difficulty with there being more than one brain mechanism that can resonate to different aspects of the structure of a single image, just as more than one tuning fork can resonate to different components of a complex acoustic waveform. To be concrete, let us suppose there is a separate brain mechanism, A1, for perceiving the vertex as the top and another, A2, for perceiving the upper right segment as the top. Further, suppose there is a separate mechanism, B1, for perceiving its shape as a diamond and another, B2, for perceiving its shape as a square. But why shouldn't both mechanisms A1 and A2 resonate at once? Or mechanisms B1 and B2? Given that both sorts of information are available in the image, some mechanism is needed to explain why both corresponding resonators do not respond at the same time. And even if this mutual exclusivity were somehow explained, there is still the further problem of why A1 resonating should lead necessarily to B1 resonating rather than B2, and why A2 resonating should lead to B2 resonating rather than B1. These causal dependencies seem to require additional structure in the system, such as A1's resonance *causing* resonance in B1, and A2's resonance *causing* resonance in B2. But this is precisely the kind of causal scheme postulated by Rock in his hierarchical problem-solving theory in which one perception is mediated by another. Many of the facts recounted in this volume are therefore difficult to reconcile with a direct view of perception.

Experimental Contributions
Most of the research articles Rock has collected here are ones of which he is an author, often together with one or more of his students and/or colleagues. The articles thus provide a glimpse of Rock's creativity and brilliance as an experimentalist. His empirical contributions over the years have been varied and broad, astonishingly so in light of the modern tendency to specialize in increasingly narrow fields. He has made landmark contributions to the understanding of perceptual adaptation, perceptual organization, perceptual constancy of size, shape, orientation, position, and lightness, shape perception, motion perception, visual dominance, attention, and learning. Not all of these fields are represented in this volume, of course, but several of them are. In the course of these investigations, he pioneered a number of ingenious experimental techniques that enabled him to investigate important theoretical issues such as the existence of perception-perception causal chains. Theoretically driven ingenuity is indeed one of the hallmarks of Rock's empirical work. First, he thinks of an important theoretical question, often one so basic that others have not even recognized that it existed. Then he figures out how to test it, frequently inventing some clever new method or measure in order to do so. Sometimes the actual manipulation is extremely simple. It appears that merely asking the question in the right way shows him how to find the answer.

For example, consider Rock and Brosgole's (1964) elegant experiment on grouping by proximity. Prior research had shown that, all else being equal, closer objects tend to group together (Wertheimer [1923] 1950). But nobody had ever asked whether the "proximity" involved was determined by the perception of their relative distances in tridimensional space or by the relative distances in the bidimensional space of the retinal image. Everyone else seemed to *assume* it was retinal distance that mattered, but Rock raised the question and then saw how to answer it. He and Brosgole simply showed observers rectangular arrays of luminous beads in an otherwise dark room that were either presented in the frontal plane or tilted in depth (see figure F.3) and asked whether they perceived them as grouped into rows or columns. When seen in the frontal plane, the beads grouped into columns because they were closer together vertically than horizontally (see figure F.3A), as predicted by both the retinal and phenomenal state of affairs. When tilted by a sufficient amount, as shown in figure F.3B, however, the predictions of the two definitions of proximity diverged.

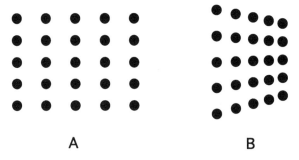

A   B

Figure F.3
Stimuli used by Rock and Brosgole (see chapter 3) to examine whether grouping is based on
retinal or perceived proximity.

Retinal proximity predicted a change to grouping by rows as the foreshortening due to tilting the display in depth reduced the horizontal distances on the retinal image. Phenomenal proximity, however, predicts no
such change in grouping. As long as depth perception is accurate, the
beads will be seen as closer together vertically in 3-D space and continue
to be seen as grouped into columns.

Rock and Brosgole first showed that tilting the array did not change
the perceived organization as long as observers had sufficient information
to perceive depth accurately. Then they also showed that if the relative
spacing of the objects is *misperceived* due to lack of sufficient depth information (e.g., viewing the array with just one eye) or due to the break-
down of depth perception under extreme conditions (e.g., large angles of
tilt), perceived grouping does switch to rows. This shows how one perception (experienced 3-D proximity) can determine another (experienced
grouping). If grouping had turned out to be governed by retinal proximity rather than by perceived 3-D proximity, Gibson's claim of direct perception would have been supported because perceived grouping would
not have been mediated by the prior perception of relative proximity, but
determined directly from retinal structure. This was not what Rock and
Brosgole found, however, and so the inference of indirect perception of
grouping via perceived proximity is warranted.

Many of the experiments reported in this volume can also be viewed
from a slightly different perspective to shed light on what Rock and I
have called the "levels question" (Palmer and Rock 1994). The focal issue
of the levels question is where various processes occur in the stream of
visual processing. In the case of Rock and Brosgole's (1964) experiment,
for example, the question is at what level of visual processing does perceptual grouping occur? Is it a relatively early process that operates at the
level of the 2-D retinal image, or a relatively late one that operates at the

level of the 3-D percept? As we have already said, the results show that grouping is determined by perceived proximity in 3-D space. We therefore conclude that grouping cannot be an exclusively early process, but must either occur relatively late or both early and late. Rock and I have now asked the levels question in several studies about several different visual features, many of which are reprinted in this volume. The general presupposition before the studies were performed was that the early retinal factor governed the phenomenon. In fact, the answer has almost always turned out to be that it is the later, perceived value of the feature that matters (Palmer and Rock, forthcoming).

Some Personal Remarks

I would be remiss in writing a foreword to this final book of Rock's without making a few more personal comments about Irv,[3] for he is unique in several important ways that are not captured by the purely intellectual description given above. As my colleague Alison Gopnik so eloquently put it, Irv is about as close to the Platonic ideal of a research scientist as one is ever likely to meet. I want to explain why I feel this is such an apt characterization of Irv for reasons quite independent of his many important contributions to the literature on visual perception.

One is that Irv is a warm, caring, and wonderful human being in both his professional and personal life. He is intellectually humble and unpretentious to a degree that is almost unheard of among academicians of his stature. The reason, I think, is that he has never lost his childlike curiosity in trying to solve the puzzles of perception. As a result, he is far more interested in trying to reach the truth about perception than in playing intellectual games of one-upsmanship or increasing his own reputation at someone else's expense.

A second observation is that he is one of the most talented and beloved mentors I have ever had the pleasure of knowing. Among his students are a large number of well-known and highly regarded perceptionists, including William Epstein, Alan Gilchrist, Lloyd Kaufman, Arien Mack, and Sheldon Ebenholtz, as well as a number of promising younger investigators who have yet to make their mark. In addition, he has collaborated with and enriched the intellectual lives of a number of younger colleagues who, although not technically his students, have learned a great deal about perception from interacting with him, collaborating with him, and studying his work. Although this group is too large to list exhaustively, it includes Walter Gerbino, Alison Gopnik, Michael Kubovy, Theodore Parks, William Prinzmetal, Dennis Proffitt, V. S. Ramachandran, and myself.[4] It is noteworthy that when Rock gave what turned out to be his final public lecture in December 1994 at Berkeley, a number of his former students, colleagues, and admirers came from considerable distances to attend, including several from the East Coast. That is the sort of admiration and devotion Irv inspired in others, both for his impressive scientific contributions and for his consummate humanity.

A third quality Rock possesses that sets him apart is his complete and utter devotion to his work. After his formal retirement from Rutgers University in 1987 at age 65, he came to the University of California at Berkeley as an Adjunct Professor of Psychology where he made important contributions for almost a decade. Despite formidable health problems that would have sidelined a less dedicated scientist, he set up and maintained a very active laboratory at Berkeley. The rate at which he published research papers and book chapters seemed, if anything, to increase as the years progressed. He actively supervised graduate students, taught graduate lecture courses, participated fully in the intellectual functions of both the Psychology Department and the Institute of Cognitive Studies, and made himself generally available to any colleague who requested his assistance. When he discovered his illness in January 1995, he worked full speed for as long as he could to complete several projects, including an important new research monograph with Arien Mack on their recent experiments on the role of attention in perception (Mack and Rock, forthcoming) as well as this volume on indirect perception. But even these last two books will not be his final publications, for at the time of his death he was collaborating with several colleagues on projects that are currently in progress.

Visual perception will be a less exciting field without the innovative presence of Irvin Rock, and those of us who worked with him during his long and productive career will miss him deeply. His brilliant theorizing, ingenious experiments, and careful interweaving of the two are a rare combination indeed. But his ideas will surely live on in his published work, and his approach will be carried on by the students, colleagues, and friends who have been touched by his greatness.

Notes

1. By "perception" I mean (as does Rock) a conscious experience based on sensory processes rather than just any type of sensory-based representation, which might be conscious or not. Thus, saying that some perceptions are caused by other perceptions cannot be supported simply by pointing to the fact that all conscious visual perceptions are derived from a retinal representation for the simple reason that people do not experience their retinal images (i.e., retinal images do not count as perceptions because they are not conscious). The fact that the perceived shape of an object depends on its perceived orientation *does* imply perception-perception dependency, however, because the perception of orientation is quite conscious and perceived shape depends on it.

2. I have tried to construct this explanation according to ecological principles, but the reader may have noticed the language of inferential theory creeping in nevertheless: "the extra-

polation of these straight edges would imply that the farther object is square," "T-junctions imply occlusion...," and "if the visual system assumes that...." My problem in avoiding this kind of language is that, unlike Gibson, I do not see how the perception of the farther square can be uniquely specified by the optical information. Some kind of informational contribution of the observer seems required to arrive at the perception of the farther square, and "assumptions" and "inferences" seem the most natural way to talk about it. The only alternative I can see is resorting to "brain talk" about the activity of neural circuits that implement these operations. Gibson's framework allows this option through his "resonance" metaphor for brain mechanisms, as explained in the paragraph that follows.

3. In this section of personal remarks I refer to Rock as "Irv" because that is how I and the people I mention all know him. It would seem stilted and artificial to call him anything else in these contexts.

4. Indeed, I learned more about perception from interacting with Irv than I did in all my formal training in psychology. He spent a sabbatical year at Berkeley when he was finishing *The Logic of Perception*. I read a chapter each week and discussed it with him, ostensibly to provide him with suggestions. This I did to the best of my ability, but the primary outcome of the enterprise was to educate me in the issues of classical perception at the hands of a master perceptionist. I have always been grateful for this experience, which I now realize was unique and one of the most important opportunities of my professional life. Among other things, it laid the groundwork for Irv's eventual decision to come to Berkeley after retiring from Rutgers and for our later collaboration on a number of joint experimental and theoretical papers.

References

Asch, S. E., and H. A. Witkin. 1948. Studies in space orientation: I. Perception of the upright with displaced visual fields. *Journal of Experimental Psychology* 38:325–27.

Duncker, K. 1945. On problem solving. *Psychological Monographs* 58:1–112.

Gibson, J. J. 1950. *The perception of the visual world*. Boston: Houghton Mifflin.

Gibson, J. J. 1966. *The senses considered as perceptual systems*. Boston: Houghton Mifflin.

Gibson, J. J. 1979. *The ecological approach to visual perception*. Boston: Houghton Mifflin.

Helmholtz, H. von. [1867] 1962. *Treatise on physiological optics*, vol. 3. Translated from the German by J. P. C. Southall. New York: Dover.

Kellman, P. J., and T. F. Shipley. 1991. A theory of visual interpolation in object perception. *Cognitive Psychology* 15:141–221.

Köhler, W., and H. Wallach. 1944. Figural aftereffects: An investigation of visual processes. *Proceedings of the American Philosophical Association* 88:269–357.

Koffka, K. 1935. *Principles of Gestalt psychology*. New York: Harcourt, Brace, and Company.

Lashley, K. S., K. L. Chow, and J. Semmes. 1951. An examination of the electrical field theory of cerebral integration. *Psychological Review* 58:123–36.

Leeuwenberg, E. L. J. 1971. A perceptual coding language for visual and auditory patterns. *American Journal of Psychology* 84:307–50.

Lowe, D. G. 1985. *Perceptual organization and visual recognition*. Boston: Kluwer.

Mace, W. M. 1977. Gibson's strategy for perceiving: Ask not what's inside your head but what your head's inside of. In *Perceiving, acting, and knowing*, edited by R. Shaw and J. Bransford. Hillsdale, NJ: Erlbaum.

Mack, A., and I. Rock. Forthcoming. *Inattentional blindness: Perception without attention*. Cambridge, MA: MIT Press.

Marr, D. 1982. *Vision*. San Francisco: Freeman.

Marr, D., and Nishihara, H. K. 1977. Representation and recognition of the spatial organization of three-dimensional shapes. *Proceedings of the Royal Society of London (Series B)* 200:269–94.

Palmer, S. E. 1975. Visual perception and world knowledge: Notes on a model of sensory-cognitive interaction. In *Explorations in cognition*, edited by D. A. Norman and D. E. Rumelhart, 279–307. San Francisco: Freeman.

Palmer, S. E. 1989. Reference frames in the perception of shape and orientation. In *Object perception: Structure and process*, edited by B. Shepp and S. Ballesteros, 121–63. Hillsdale, NJ: Erlbaum.

Palmer, S. E. 1995. Gestalt psychology redux. In *Speaking minds*, edited by P. Baumgartner and S. Payr, 156–76. Princeton, NJ: Princeton University Press.

Palmer, S. E., and I. Rock. 1994. Rethinking perceptual organization: The role of uniform connectedness. *Psychonomic Bulletin and Review* 1:29–55.

Palmer, S. E., and I. Rock. Forthcoming. Perceptual grouping: It's later than you think.

Pomerantz, J., and M. Kubovy. 1986. Theories of perceptual organization. In *Handbook of perception and human performance*, vol. 2, edited by K. R. Boff, L. Kaufman, and J. P. Thomas, 36-1–36-46. New York: Wiley.

Rock, I. 1973. *Orientation and form*. New York: Academic Press.

Rock, I. 1977. In defense of unconscious inference. In *Stability and constancy in visual perception: Mechanisms and processes*, edited by W. Epstein, 321–73. New York: Wiley.

Rock, I. 1983. *The logic of perception*. Cambridge, MA: MIT Press.

Rock, I. 1986. The description and analysis of object and event perception. In *Handbook of perception and human performance*, vol. 2, edited by K. R. Boff, L. Kaufman, and J. P. Thomas, 33-1–33-71. New York: Wiley.

Rock, I. 1993. The logic of *The logic of perception*. *Italian Journal of Psychology* 20:841–67. (Volume honoring G. Kanisza, edited by P. Legrenzi.)

Rock, I., and L. Brosgole. 1964. Grouping based on phenomenal proximity. *Journal of Experimental Psychology* 67:531–38.

Rock, I., and S. E. Palmer. 1990. The legacy of Gestalt psychology. *Scientific American* 262 (December): 84–90.

Sekuler, A. B., and S. E. Palmer. 1992. Visual completion of partly occluded objects: A microgenetic analysis. *Journal of Experimental Psychology: General* 121:95–111.

Sperry, R. W., and N. Milner. 1955. Pattern perception following insertion of mica plates into visual cortex. *Journal of Comparative and Physiological Psychology* 48:463–69.

Ullman, S. 1980. Against direct perception. *Behavioral and Brain Sciences* 3:373–415.

Van der Helm, P. A., and E. L. J. Leeuwenberg. 1991. Accessibility: A criterion for regularity and hierarchy in visual pattern codes. *Journal of Mathematical Psychology* 35:151–213.

Wertheimer, M. [1923] 1950. Untersuchungen zur Lehre von der Gestalt. II. *Psychologische Forschung* 4:301–50. Partial translation in *A sourcebook of Gestalt psychology*, edited by W. D. Ellis, 71–81. New York: The Humanities Press.

Part I
On Direct Perception

Introduction

In this section, I introduce the reader to the thesis that perception may, more often than not, be indirect. By "indirect" I mean that perception is based on prior perceptions, implying a perception–perception chain of causality. There is, first, a chapter I have written to introduce this volume. Second, there is a chapter by William Epstein on percept–percept couplings in which he considers the general thesis of the dependency of one percept on another and its relation to the Gibsonian thesis that perception is a direct "response" to the visual stimulus. He argues forcefully that there is no philosophical reason to deny causal-role status to a percept in its determination of another percept. Toward the end of providing experimental evidence in support of the percept–percept chain, Epstein marshals an impressive body of work.

Some of this evidence comes up later in the volume, but some does not, so Epstein's chapter provides an opportunity to cover evidence that would not otherwise be included given the already long list of chapters.

Finally, Epstein makes the case that the existence of percept–percept couplings is congenial to a computational or constructivist theory of perception, and potentially embarrassing to a direct theory. He writes, "If one percept is contingent or conditional on another, then the cardinal tenet of direct theory cannot be sustained" (9). The constructive process operates on perceptual representations to generate new perceptual representations. That is the heart of the matter.

Chapter 1
The Concept of Indirect Perception
Irvin Rock

Over a lifetime of research I have often had reason to ask a question about the immediate determinant of a particular perceptual phenomenon. The reason was that the meaning of the determinant under study was ambiguous. The first time I ran across this question concerned the altered appearance of objects and their consequent loss of recognizability when their orientation in a frontal plane was changed. The ambiguity concerned the meaning of "orientation." Was it the altered orientation of the object's image on the retina that mattered or the altered orientation of the object as it was perceived in the scene? Ordinarily, of course, both of these changes occur concomitantly, but I realized that they could be separated. One way of doing so was to require an observer to view a novel object from a tilted or inverted orientation (of the whole body or just the head), after having previously seen it from an upright position. Given information from gravity or from the visual frame of reference, the location of an object's top, bottom, and sides would appear unchanged in the scene, but the orientation of its retinal image would undergo a change. Conversely, one could tilt the object in the second viewing by the same angle as the body or head was tilted. In this case, the orientation of the object in the environment would change (and presumably would be perceived to do so), but the orientation of the retinal image would not.

My colleagues and I performed experiments along these lines to ascertain which meaning of orientation was relevant to the effect: the retinal or the phenomenal. The results of the experiments are described in chapter 9 and need not be discussed here except to say that what mattered for shape recognition was phenomenal orientation. It turned out that this same question could be asked about any number of other phenomena because a similar ambiguity arises in trying to understand perceptual organization, the perception of shape (apart from the effect of orientation on shape), the nature of masking, the perception of lightness, the perception of motion, and the perception of illusions. Each of these topics is addressed in a part of this volume.

Given the emergence of a clear question in science, curiosity alone is a sufficient reason for pursuing it and, at the beginning, I was driven to a large extent by curiosity. However in each case, I also realized that the answer to the retinal/phenomenal question had important theoretical consequences. Consider the ambiguity that arises in the case of perceptual grouping. The Gestaltists proposed a number of "laws" of grouping, concerning why certain elements grouped with one another. One such law was that of proximity: all else being equal, elements that are nearer to one another than others would group into larger structures. This was taken to mean that the corresponding retinal images of the elements in the array, being more proximal to one another—and thus projecting representations to regions of the visual cortex that were nearer to one another, relatively speaking—tended to attract one another more strongly than cortical representations that were farther apart. This was the Gestalt view, although the Gestaltists were not explicit about it beyond the just-mentioned brain metaphor, because they were unaware of the retinal-phenomenal ambiguity.

The ambiguity arises when one realizes that the elements whose retinal images are closer to one another are also usually *perceived* to be closer together. The "law" could therefore be reformulated as follows: elements *perceived* to be closer together than others tend to be grouped into larger structures (for example, into columns or rows). Now, although it isn't obvious when the array is in the frontal plane that the perception of proximity entails more or different processing than just the proximity given by the projection of their images to the visual cortex, the fact is that such further or different processing is implicated. To make this clear, imagine the array of elements to be small objects (e.g., tiny spheres) in a rectangular lattice such that they are closer together vertically than horizontally. When viewed head-on in the frontal plane, the observer tends to see columns rather than rows. Suppose now one views the entire array from the side so that, by virtue of perspective foreshortening, the projection of the spheres to the retina (and cortex) is altered. If one is far enough to the side, the sphere's images will be closer together horizontally (see figure F.3). However, given adequate depth perception leading to constancy (i.e., veridical perception), the relative position of the spheres vis-a-vis one another will continue to appear as it did when viewed from directly in front. If so, the spheres would still appear to be closer together vertically, and thus one would continue to perceive columns rather than rows. This would occur as long as constancy held and the correct "law" of proximity is the reformulated one based on *perceived* proximity.

This experiment was performed by Brosgole and myself (see chapter 3). The results implicate perceived or phenomenal proximity rather than retinal proximity, as was the case for perception of shape after changes in perceived versus retinal orientation. The same question has now been asked about other Gestalt principles of grouping, and analogous experiments have been performed with the same general result: grouping appears to be governed by perceived rather than retinal factors. Chapters 3, 4, and 5 describe these experiments.

Why is the realization of this ambiguity and a clarification of the question it poses important? The answer is that it tells us about the level or stage of processing that underlies the phenomenon of grouping by proximity. At the time of Wertheimer's classic paper on the laws of grouping in 1923, questions about "level" were rarely, if ever, asked. It was with the later advent of information processing as an approach to perception and cognition that such questions became central. However, it was implicit for Gestalt psychology that perceptual grouping occurred at a very early stage of processing because, until the scene before us became organized, no further perception could occur. The achievement of discrete, segregated units in the field was held to be the end product of organization, and thus organization was the sine qua non for all subsequent perception.

Interestingly enough, in the years that followed Wertheimer's publication, the assumption that grouping occurred at a very early stage remained an article of faith by subsequent investigators and later was explicitly stated by those favoring an information-processing approach. The interest had shifted to attention, and it was held that perceptual grouping was *pre*-attentive. It was argued that attention required the prior phenomenal existence of units in the field to which it could be deployed or not, as the case may be (e.g., Neisser 1967; Treisman 1986).

However, given the findings that grouping conforms to *perceived* structure and therefore must emerge at a later stage following depth perception and constancy operations, important new questions arise. Given the logical argument that perceptual organization *must* occur at an early stage on the one hand and, given the *finding* that Gestalt grouping does *not* occur at an early stage on the other, then what principle or principles govern initial perceptual organization? Do the Gestalt laws play any role in the final organization of the scene or are they mere laboratory epiphenomena? The entire question of grouping has to be reopened and reexamined, as Palmer and Rock (1994a, 1994b) have recently done.

So here we see, in one example at least, the importance of (1) recognizing that there is an ambiguity in the meaning of a determinant (in this case "proximity"), (2) attempting to disambiguate the meaning, and (3) attempting to clarify the process underlying the phenomenon in question. Clearly the "retinal" answer to the question points in one theoretical direction and the "phenomenal" answer points in a very different theoretical direction.

I will give only one other example here of the retinal-phenomenal ambiguity in the determination of a phenomenon in order to bring out the theoretical importance of knowing the answer. It concerns the perception of lightness: the appearance of surfaces along the white-gray-black continuum. For roughly the last half century most investigators of this topic have been favorably disposed to the theory that it is not the absolute intensity of light (or luminance) reflected by a surface that governs its apparent lightness, but the ratio of the intensities from adjacent regions (e.g., Land 1977; Wallach 1948). This theory seemed to explain not only lightness perception, but also lightness constancy: the fact that the apparent lightness of a surface does not change with increments or decrements of the intensity of light that illuminates the surface. Since such changes of overall light intensity typically affect adjacent regions equally, the ratio of the light they reflect remains more or less constant despite widely varying levels of illumination.

The ambiguity in this case concerns the meaning of "adjacency." Adjacency could mean the contiguity of the retinal images of two (or more) regions. However, it could also mean the *perceived* contiguity of the regions giving rise to these retinal images. The two meanings of adjacency can be teased apart, although, more often than not, it is true that two adjacent retinal regions will result from two regions in the environment that are adjacent to one another. However, one has only to think of separating the regions in depth to realize that such spatially separated regions can still project to the retina in such a way as to be side by side, so to speak.

It makes a good deal of intuitive and theoretical sense to believe that the ratio of the luminance of two adjacent *retinal* regions would determine perceived lightness and therefore, lightness constancy, whether or not they are reflected from environmentally adjacent regions. A priori, it does not seem very likely that the ratio of *phenomenally* adjacent regions would have any such effects merely because they *appear* to be next to one another. Be that as it may, as suggested above, one can easily create a situation in which region 1 is at a different depth or in a different depth plane than region 2 while their retinal images are nonetheless adjacent. In this case we can arrange to have retinal adjacency but not phenomenal adjacency as shown in figure 1.1.

It has been found that when such an arrangement is created and one allows the difference in depth or planarity to be perceived, the luminance ratio between regions 1 and 2 no longer governs perceived lightness. By the simple maneuver of eliminating cues to depth, while holding everything else about the display and the observer's position constant, a drastically different outcome regarding perceived lightness occurs because now the two regions *are* perceived to be phenomenally adjacent. Experiments of this kind will be described in chapter 22 of this volume (and see Gilchrist 1980) so no further discussion is required now except to emphasize that here again it is the phenomenal factor, not the retinal, that matters.

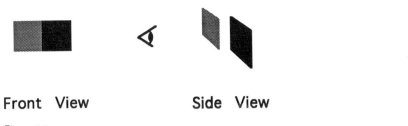

Front View   **Side View**

Figure 1.1
Retinally adjacent regions can be either phenomenally adjacent or separated in depth.

What is the importance of realizing the ambiguity of "adjacency"? The theoretical implications are profound. If what matters for the determination of perceived lightness by the ratio of the luminances of adjacent regions is that the *retinal images* of these regions be adjacent, one kind of theory is implicated. In fact, based on this interpretation of adjacency (which has been implicit or explicit for well over a century), one might think that a process of lateral inhibition between retinally adjacent regions is responsible for the outcome (e.g., Cornsweet 1970). Indeed *contrast* has been explained in terms of lateral inhibition, and as the luminance of region 1 increases when it is seen in sunlight instead of shadow, the luminance of region 2 increases equally, and thus its lateral inhibition of region 1 increases. Thus the net change in rate of firing of neurons from region 1 would be said to remain about the same. Hence constancy! Other such lower-level or sensory kinds of theory of lightness constancy are also possible. But if what matters is that the adjacency must be *phenomenal*, then a very different kind of theory seems required, one that is more central and that entails cognitive operations. For example, the particular lightness of each region must be inferred by where its luminance stands relative to that of other regions, particularly relative to the region of highest luminance that is taken to be white and thus serves as an anchor for the various regions of differing luminance (see Gilchrist 1995).

So much for illustrations of ambiguity concerning the meaning of a determinant of a particular perceptual phenomenon and for why resolving that ambiguity is so important. As can be seen from these illustrations and many others to be discussed in this volume, however, the ambiguity is generally resolved in favor of the phenomenal rather than the retinal aspect of the stimulus conditions. This fact has further, deep implications that form the central thesis of this volume. If it is the *perceived* character of the stimulus array that matters in regard to the phenomenon under consideration—be it perceived orientation, perceived proximity, perceived adjacency, or whatever—then such perception becomes an earlier stage of processing that culminates in a later, final perception. Perceived orientation is the precondition for perceived shape, perceived proximity is the precondition for the perception of grouping by proximity, perceived adjacency is the precondition for the perception of lightness, and so forth.

Such conclusions are important because they show that *one perception depends upon another, prior perception*. We thus have a perception → perception chain of causation which means, among other things, that the final perception, the one we are generally seeking to explain, is *indirect*. It cannot be said to be the *direct* result of a proximal stimulus, as James J. Gibson (1950, 1966, 1979) maintained, no matter how complex or higher-order we take that proximal stimulus to be. As to a possible philosophical objection to the claim that one perception can cause another, there is a simple rejoinder. The initial perception is itself caused by events occurring in the brain (although at this stage of our knowledge of the brain we usually don't know precisely what neurophysiological process accounts for it), and so is the final perception for that matter. So the perception → perception chain of causality can be translated to a brain-event-1 → brain-event-2 chain of causality. No philosophical problems are entailed by this formulation of the "indirect perception" thesis because all the events in question are ordinary physical processes.

However, this translation into talk about brain events should not be taken to weaken the claim I am making here. One might want to argue that the claim simply reduces to the argument that a somewhat longer, more complex sequence of brain events underlies (or causes) a particular perception than has heretofore been recognized for the phenomenon under consideration. But that would be to miss the point. The first brain event in the sequence is the neural correlate of the initial percept; the second brain event is the neural correlate of the final percept. They are qualitatively and ontologically distinct events. Moreover, one must not forget about the intentional "content" if one chooses to translate the argument about a perception → perception chain of causation into the language of neurophysiology. So, for example, if the initial perception is one of the phenomenal orientation of an object, then that "content" must somehow be represented by the initial brain event; the same holds true for the "content" of the later perception of the object's shape and its representation in the second brain event.

That the content of the initial perception is crucial—rather than a particular pattern of sensory stimulation—is seen by the fact that there are often many routes to its achievement. For example, if the perceived orientation of an object is the important first stage in the achievement of its unique phenomenal shape, then we need to recognize that there are various stimulus conditions or proximal stimuli that can lead to that perceived orientation. The direction of gravity alone can be responsible because experiments have shown that a luminous object in an otherwise dark room will (1) appear to have a top, bottom, and sides as governed by gravity, and (2) appear to have a shape that is, in part, a function of (1). The visual frame of reference alone can be responsible for the outcome because experiments have shown a powerful effect on perceived orientation (and therefore on perceived shape) of a large tilted frame even while gravity remains unchanged. Egocentric visual coordinates can lead to these effects too because a change of an object's orientation in a *horizontal plane* (which eliminates gravitational information), viewed through a circular aperture that eliminates external reference frames, will lead to an altered perception of its top and bottom, and therefore to an altered perception of its shape.

A similar argument holds for cases where the perceived depth of an object is the first step in the perception of some other property such as grouping or lightness. There are many different kinds of cues to depth, and it is easily shown that one can be substituted for another to achieve the initial percept. So, in summary, it is not appropriate or parsimonious to reduce perception to some proximal stimulus, as theorists favoring a direct theory of perception might wish to do, since what matters is the phenomenally perceived property, however that may be achieved.

A possible criticism of the claim presented here of one perception depending upon a prior perception is that the two perceptions may be temporally co-occurring rather than successive. In the case of lightness perception as affected by perceived adjacency in the third dimension, for example, one might argue that all one is entitled to say is that a given depth perception *is intimately associated with* a given lightness perception rather than that a given depth perception *causes* a given lightness perception. However, if the claim I am making were only one of association, then a form of symmetry should follow:[1] manipulating perceived lightness should be just as likely to yield changes of perceived depth as manipulating perceived depth should yield changes of perceived lightness. Yet that is not generally the case. If one introduces stereoscopic information that two regions are not in the same plane, change in the perceived lightness of one or both regions will occur; however, introducing a change in the perceived lightness of two such regions does not usually affect or create perceived depth. To be sure, there are cases where luminance differences based on attached shadows can create an impression of depth, as in the homogeneous surface lightness of a sculpture or a crumpled handkerchief. But here it is luminance differences that have the effect on perceived depth, not perceived lightness differences.

In other examples, irreversibility of the chain of causation is even clearer. Does it make sense to say that the achievement of grouping determines the perception of proximity or similarity? Does it make sense to say that certain perceived distortions in the size and shape of a three-dimensional wire cube, when the cube rotates (or we walk around it), cause perceptual reversal to occur? Rather, it is well known that these distortions occur because the perceived reversal of the cube necessitates a reinterpretation of the sizes and shapes of the retinal images of the cube. Ordinarily the far face yields a smaller image than the near face and is corrected for appropriately on the basis of perceived depth. When a regular cube is seen with reversed depth, the face yielding the *larger* image is perceived as farther away, so that constancy operations enlarge this face even more, yielding the perception of a highly irregular cube.

Finally, it would seem that even if, despite my arguments above, one could not establish a unidirectional sequence of events, it remains indisputable that a complex interactive relationship must obtain between a certain perceived character of the proximal stimulus and a further perception. Given the evidence to be presented in this volume, it is simply not possible to argue that perception is *direct*, if one takes this to mean the determination of perception by the proximal stimulus without mediating perceptual events.

Two Kinds of Indirect Perception

There seems to be another kind of indirect perception that ought to be distinguished from the kind I have been discussing thus far. In the kind I have been discussing, the two perceptions that occur are not on different levels or stages of processing, nor do they imply a lower-level–higher-level sequency. They have equal status. Thus, for example, grouping per se is not a higher stage of processing than perceived proximity or similarity. In such situations grouping *depends* upon or makes use of perceived proximity or similarity. Moreover, the occurrence of the first perception does not lead automatically to the second perception. The first perception is a necessary condition for the occurrence of the second, but it isn't a sufficient condition.

So, for example, achieving the perception of the directional coordinates of an object does not, ipso facto, lead to the perception of the object's phenomenal shape. It is a necessary step because assigning such coordinates differently will give rise to a very different phenomenal shape. But without focusing attention on the object, no consciously perceived shape may occur at all. On the other hand, the awareness that an object is present and the awareness of where its top and bottom are, no doubt do occur without focused attention.

The other kind of indirect perception refers to instances in which the final experience is the end result of a two-stage sequence. The existence of the first stage is in part speculative because often one is not fully aware of it. A good example of this kind of indirectness is amodal completion. In figure 1.2 one sees a circle, part of which is occluded by a square per-

Figure 1.2
Amodal completion of a circle partly occluded by a square.

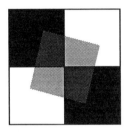

Figure 1.3
Phenomenal translucency of a square region through which a black and white checkerboard is perceived.

ceived to be in front of it. I have suggested elsewhere that, prior to the occlusion/completion perception, another occurs—however fleetingly—in which one sees literally what is represented in the figure: namely, a three-quarter circle adjacent to a rectangle in a kind of mosaic arrangement. There is now some experimental evidence supporting the existence of this literal stage (e.g., Gerbino and Salmaso 1985; Sekuler and Palmer 1992).

Another example of this kind of indirectness of perception is that of phenomenal translucency. In figure 1.3 one perceives a checkerboardlike background of black and white regions with a tilted translucent square in front, through which one also sees the background. But, prior to that perception, another may occur in which the tilting square consists of four different regions of differing perceived lightness. Because this perception correlates perfectly with the differing luminances in the entire figure, I have suggested that in this case as well, one might describe it as "literal." By way of contrast, the amodal completion in figure 1.2 and the translucency "solution" in figure 1.3 are more creative and depart from the proximal stimulus in a one-to-one correspondence. I have suggested the terms *world mode* or *constancy mode* to describe these presumably later perceptions.

I imagine the reader can appreciate that the sequence from perception 1 to perception 2 in these last examples is different from the sequence of two perceptions discussed throughout the early part of this chapter. But how to characterize the difference? First, the sequence in these examples represents two perceptions arising from the same proximal stimulus, which therefore can be characterized as ambiguous. Second, in these new examples, the transition is from a lower-level, earlier-stage processing to a higher-level, deeper, final stage of processing. In fact, once the world mode perception occurs—in cases where it did not do so immediately—it is more or less irreversible. It is all but impossible not to see it this way just as it seems to be psychologically irreversible not to recognize, let us say, a word, even though it must be the case that there was a moment in time prior to recognition in which it was not yet identified. There clearly is a strong *preference* for the world mode solution. However, I hasten to add that such a preference does not rule out the occurrence of the literal mode stage *along with* the world mode stage. So, for example, in perceiving the amodally completed circle in figure 1.2, one can continue to be aware that the circle is not completely visible in the retinal image.

There is much more that can be said about this second kind of sequence from one perception to another, but hopefully what I have said will suffice to distinguish it from the first kind of sequence. Yet it seems correct to say that in both cases, perception is indirect. In the first case—let us call it type A—the indirectness comes about because it is simply not the proximal stimulus per se that can be said to yield the perception we are trying to explain. That stimulus must first give rise to a certain perception, be it of orientation, of proximity, of depth, etc., before the final perception can be expected to occur. The second kind of indirectness—call it type B—comes about because some ambiguous stimuli are first perceived on the basis of their literal correspondence to the proximal stimulus. However, that perception or "solution" is inadequate for some reason, so that perception is superceded. (Notice that being *superceded* is not the same as being *replaced* because the prior interpretation still exists.) One reason for the inadequacy of the first perception is that that perception requires acceptance of a coincidental or accidental relation between the proximal stimulus and the state of affairs in the world. But to pursue this important question would carry us too far afield.

Although the focus of this book concerns type A indirectness and virtually all the examples to be covered are of this type, it was important to make the distinction to avoid possible confusion. However, the realization that there is type B indirectness certainly strengthens the main thesis—namely that perception, more often than not, cannot be understood as a direct "response" of the visual system to the proximal stimulus. In fact, it becomes a challenge to find examples in which perception is direct, and having found them—assuming they exist—to ask what they have in common.

Note

1. I wish to thank Steve Palmer for pointing out the importance of asymmetries of this sort in establishing perception-perception causal chains.

References

Cornsweet, T. N. 1970. *Visual perception.* New York: Academic Press.

Gerbino, W., and D. Salmaso. 1985. Un analisi processuale del completamento amodule. *Giornale Italiano de Psichologia* 12:97–121.

Gibson, J. J. 1950. *The perception of the visual world.* Boston: Houghton Mifflin.

Gibson, J. J. 1966. *The senses considered as perceptual systems.* Boston: Houghton Mifflin.

Gibson, J. J. 1979. *The ecological approach to visual perception.* Boston: Houghton Mifflin.

Gilchrist, A. 1980. When does perceived lightness depend on perceived spatial arrangement? *Perception & Psychophysics* 28:527–38.

Gilchrist, A. 1995. Local and global processes in surface lightness perception. *Perception & Psychophysics* 57:125–35.

Land, E. 1977. The retinex theory of color vision. *Scientific American* 237:108–28.

Neisser, U. 1967. *Cognitive psychology.* New York: Appleton-Century-Crofts.

Palmer, S. E., and I. Rock. 1994a. Rethinking perceptual organization: The role of uniform connectedness. *Psychonomic Bulletin and Review,* 1(1): 29–55.

Palmer, S. E., and I. Rock. 1994b. On the nature and order of organizational processing: A reply to Peterson. *Psychonomic Bulletin and Review* 1:515–19.

Sekuler, A. B., and S. E. Palmer. 1992. Visual completion of partly occluded objects: A microgenetic analysis. *Journal of Experimental Psychology: General* 121:95–111.

Treisman, A. 1986. Properties, parts, and objects. In *Handbook of perception and human performance,* vol. 2, edited by K. R. Boff, L. Kaufman, and J. P. Thomas, 35-1–35-70. New York: Wiley.

Wallach, H. 1948. Brightness constancy and the nature of achromatic colors. *Journal of Experimental Psychology* 38:310–24.

Wertheimer, M. 1923. Untersuchungen zur Lehre von der Gestalt. II. *Psychologische Forschung,* 4:301–350. Partial translation in *A sourcebook of Gestalt psychology,* edited by W. D. Ellis, 71–81. New York: The Humanities Press, 1950.

Chapter 2
Percept–Percept Couplings
William Epstein

Introduction

Is perception direct or mediated? This question has lately been the focus of lively debate between advocates of J. J. Gibson's approach to visual perception (Gibson 1966, 1979; Turvey 1975, 1977; Shaw and Bransford 1977; Reed 1987) and advocates of a constructivist or computational approach (Fodor and Pylyshyn 1981; Rock 1977; Gogel 1979; Ullman 1980). The debate does not turn exclusively on consideration of experimental data; in particular, the argument is laced with epistemological and logical concerns. Given the aspirations of J. J. Gibson to do ontology, epistemology, and psychology, it is entirely appropriate that these concerns enter into the debate. Nevertheless, laboratory investigators will look to experimental data to help decide the issue. Among the relevant experiments are those which purport to exhibit linkages among percepts in the organization of the visual world. Hochberg's (1974) term "percept–percept coupling" will be adopted to refer to instances in which organization of the perceptual world seems to include links between percepts. Linkages between percepts have been reported in a wide variety of experimental contexts. The experiments which are summarized in the next section illustrate the type of observations which imply the existence of percept–percept couplings and suggest the diversity of experimental contexts which have supplied these observations.

Illustrative Experiments

Induced Motion and Perceived Distance (Gogel and Koslow 1972)
If a stationary point of light is observed in a luminous frame in otherwise dark surroundings, setting the frame in motion will induce the stationary point to appear to move in a direction opposite to the physical movement of the frame. In a variant of the standard arrangement Gogel and Koslow

Originally published in *Perception* 11 (1982): 75–83. Reprinted with permission.

(1972) presented the stationary point in a dual frame context with the two frames moving in opposite phase, i.e., when the near frame moved left the far frame moved to the right. Manipulation of stereopsis was used to make the stationary point appear to be in the plane of the near frame, in a plane midway between the two frames, or in the plane of the far frame. Gogel and Koslow found that the direction of perceived motion of the point was determined by the direction of movement of the frame which was perceptually coplanar with the point. (At the midway position the direction of induced movement was not regularly related to either frame movement direction.) Gogel and Koslow conclude:

> One perception, the perception of the depth relation between the frame and the point of light affected another perception, the perception of the motion of the point of light." (P. 213)

Metacontrast, Masking and Perceived Depth Separation (Lehmkuhle and Fox 1980)
Metacontrast masking refers to the detrimental interactions that occur between spatially adjacent contours. In the typical arrangement all components of the display are arranged in the same plane. Lehmkuhle and Fox (1980) examined the effect of *apparent* separation in depth between target and mask on masking function. The target (Landolt C) and the mask (annulus) were generated stereoscopically with the use of dynamic random-dot color stereograms and were viewed by the anaglyph technique. Binocular disparity was varied by manipulating the delay between the onset of one dot in relation to the onset of its correlated dot of the other color. This procedure allowed Lehmkuhle and Fox to introduce a wide range of differences of perceived separation in depth without creating proximal differences significant to contour formation. Lehmkuhle and Fox (1980) found that perceived depth separation significantly affected masking:

> When the position of the target remains fixed in space and the mask is displaced in depth from the target, so that the mask appears farther away from the observer than does the target, masking declines with increasing depth separation ... it is an outcome difficult to accommodate within models of visual masking based on the concept of lateral inhibition. (P. 619)

Perceived Lightness and Perceived Spatial Arrangement (Gilchrist 1977)
There is universal agreement that luminance ratios count prominently in determining perceived lightness. But in what space are we to locate the surfaces which contribute the interacting luminances? The question escapes notice under standard laboratory conditions because under these

conditions distal, proximal, and perceived spatial arrangements are per-fectly correlated. However, these arrangements have been decorrelated by Gilchrist (1977, 1980) with striking results. Gilchrist manipulated depth information so as to cause a target to appear coplanar with either one or the other of two surroundings of objectively different luminance. Although the retinal luminances and thus the luminance ratios were the same for both perceived spatial organizations, the perceived lightness of the target differed greatly for the two conditions of perceived coplanarity. Gilchrist (1977) concludes:

> ... perceived lightness of a surface can vary from white to black depending merely on its perceived spatial position, without any significant change in the retinal array.... If the perceived light-nesses of surfaces depend on their perceived location in space, depth processing must occur first and be followed by the determination of surface lightness. That is, processing is initiated by a pattern of intensity differences on the retina; then the nervous system uses various depth cues to construct a spatial model to fit the retinal pat-tern. As this spatial model is completed, lightnesses are assigned to the various surfaces in accord with the coplanar ratio principle. (Pp. 186–187)

Perceived Depth and Perceived Motion in Uniform Flow Fields (McConkie and Farber 1979)
Relative optical motions are effective carriers of information concerning spatial layout. McConkie and Farber (1979) presented a computer-gen-erated display consisting of two superimposed sets of dots moving in opposite horizontal directions across a CRT screen. The dots within each set moved at a uniform speed and were viewed monocularly under direc-tions to fixate the center of the display. Observers reported the direction of perceived depth (separation between the sets) and then adjusted the angular speed of one of the moving dot fields to match the speed of the field moving in the other direction. McConkie and Farber found that the variable field was consistently adjusted to a higher speed than the standard when it appeared farther away than the standard in depth and to a lower speed when it appeared nearer. A striking aspect of this finding is that the display was bistable. Some observers consistently perceived one of the sets as more distant while other observers consistently perceived the alternate set of moving points as more distant. (Both fields were in fact located in the plane of the CRT screen.) Accordingly, it would be impossible to predict the relative perceived speed of the two fields of dots without knowing their relative perceived distance. McConkie and Farber (1979) conclude:

the results of experiments 1 and 2 verify the existence of a coupling or linkage among apparent relative speeds of the fields, apparent direction of drift of the fixation target, and perceived internal depth relations. (P. 502)

Alternate Solutions to Kinetic Stimulus Transformations (Rock and Smith 1981)
A luminous line oscillating in the frontal plane behind an invisible rectangular aperture in otherwise dark surroundings will undergo continuous and concurrent changes in length and angle. These optical transformations are known to elicit perception of a line of constant length rotating in depth (Wallach and O'Connell 1953; Braunstein 1976). But if the edges of the rectangular aperture are made visible the appearance of the line is altered: the line will appear to be oscillating in the frontal plane with its endpoints occluded by the opaque screen (Rock and Smith 1981, experiment 1). If, without changing the motion of the line or the dimensions of the rectangular aperture, the aperture is made to appear to be a rectangular surface, the appearance of the line is altered again: the line will appear to be oscillating on a figural region and changing in length (Rock and Smith 1981, experiment 2). The results were replicated with subjective contours replacing real contours in the formation of the visible aperture or figural region. Rock and Smith (1981) conclude that perceiving depth in the presence of optical transformations is not a case of direct perception. Instead there is a

> *link* between perceiving figures with such contours and the perception of the oscillating line ... the perception of the aperture or the opaque figure occurs first, indeed before the line is set in motion ... it is that perception which then sets the stage for how the oscillating line will be perceived ... the perception of the latter is logically dependent upon the perception of the former. If that illusory-contour perception does not occur ... then there would be little reason to expect any outcome other than the kinetic-depth solution in all conditions. What is important here theoretically is that there are occasions, of which this is one, where one perception is a function of or is logically dependent upon another perception. (P. 26)

Space-Time Relationship in Apparent Motion (Attneave and Block 1973)
Korte (1915) postulated that an increase in temporal separation between two alternating stimuli must be accompanied by an increase in spatial separation in order that apparent movement can occur. A number of observations suggest that the spatial separation in Korte's law should be taken as perceived separation rather than distal or proximal stimulation. An experiment by Attneave and Block (1973) supports this suggestion.

Attneave and Block presented pairs of successive stimuli in the objective frontal plane for monocular viewing. In the control condition the pairs, separated either by 4 or 8 cm, were embedded in a pictorial representation of a frontal surface, i.e., a zero perspective gradient. In the experimental condition the pair, separated objectively by 4 cm, was embedded in a perspective representation of a surface oriented in an oblique plane. The effect of perspective was to make the latter pair appear to lie in a plane in depth separated by an interspace greater than 4 cm. In fact, the mean judgment of the interspace was $3 \cdot 32$ cm for the apparent frontal-parallel pair and $4 \cdot 5$ cm for the apparently slanted pair. The principal question was whether the phenomenally greater spatial separation would require significantly longer temporal separation to produce optimal apparent movement. The answer was affirmative for every one of the subjects. Attneave and Block noted that the increase in temporal separation was 27% of the difference between the temporal separations required by the 4 and 8 cm control pairs. This effect was consistent with the magnitude of overestimation of the spatial separation. Attneave and Block (1973) conclude:

> the representation of distances in three-dimensional space is antecedent to the occurrence of apparent movement [and the data] support the view that an approximately isotropic model of physical space is constructed internally and that apparent movement is based on events within this analog model. (Pp. 306, 301)

Relevance for Theory

The observation that percepts are coupled is congenial to the computational or constructivist theory of perception.[1] According to this brand of theory the perceptual world is the product of a series of computational or reasoning-like operations which operate on sensory input. For example, in perceiving shape-at-a-slant the visual system allegedly combines a representation of projective shape with a representation of rotation in depth, i.e., perceived slant, to compute, infer or construct a best-fitting model (percept) of the distal shape–slant configuration. The data that are entered into this construction are themselves constructions or coded representations. For example, registered projective shape and perceived slant are entered into the computational algorithm, not unprocessed visual angle and binocular disparity. The constructive process operates on perceptual representations to generate new perceptual representations. An explicit working out of this form of explanation has been represented by Rock (1977).

On the other hand, percept–percept couplings are a potential embarrassment for direct theory. The data seem to implicate causal relations among percepts in the organization of the visual world. If one percept is conditional on another then the cardinal tenet of direct theory cannot be sustained. The percept in question will have been removed from direct control by information in stimulation. Advocates of direct theory require an alternative interpretation of the concurrent percepts which retains the direct link between information in stimulation and perception.

A clue can be found in J. J. Gibson's (1979) reinterpretation of the invariant relationships proposed by the taking-into-account theory (Epstein 1973, 1977) of the perceptual constancies. As one example, to explain size constancy, the taking-into-account theory posits that perceived size is a function of the product of perceived distance and visual angle. Note that this hypothesis links two percepts causally. In commenting on this hypothesis Gibson (1979) offers the following sharply contrasting interpretation: Perceived size is a function of higher order variables of stimulation, e.g., the amount of surface texture occluded by the object:

> ... both size and distance are perceived directly. The old theory that the perceiver *allows* for distance in perceiving size of something is unnecessary. The assumption that the cues for distance *compensate* for the sensed smallness of the retinal image is no longer persuasive ... the old puzzle of the constancy of perceived size at different distances does not arise. (P. 162)

Note the principal characteristics of Gibson's model of size perception: (a) there is no perceptual representation of size correlated with the retinal size of the object; (b) perceived size and perceived distance are independent direct functions of information in stimulation; (c) perceived size and perceived distance are not causally linked, nor is the perception of size mediated by operations combining information about retinal size and perceived distance. The correlation between perceived size and perceived distance is attributed to the correlation between the specific variables of stimulation which govern these percepts in the particular situation. Extending the foregoing argument to the general class of percept–percept couplings the advocate of direct theory would aver that the couplings do not reflect causal connections between percepts. Instead the percepts in question are concurrent but independent perceptual covariants of correlated variables of stimulation.

The Case for the Causal Interpretation

In this section objections and questions pertaining to the causal interpretation of percept–percept couplings will be examined. At the outset let us explicitly recognize that the proposition under examination is *not* that all instances of percept–percept coupling require a causal interpretation. A number of familiar cases readily yield to the correlational interpretation. For example, the stereoscopic specific shape and the apparent depth separation between figure and ground which are elicited by random-element stereograms are coupled but not causally linked. These perceptual features are independent percepts coordinate with overlapping variables of the stereoscopic input. It is not intended to deny the plausibility of the correlational account in every case. This disclaimer notwithstanding, it would be telling for the current version of direct theory if even a single instance of causal linkage between percepts is convincingly demonstrated.

One concern with the causal interpretation arises from the very notion of perceptual interactions. While it is obvious that a physical event may cause either a mental event or another physical event, the proposal that one mental event can interact causally with another is discomforting. Perhaps this concern can be allayed by a review of the standard criterion for attribution of causal relations: If under certain circumstances perceiving variations of X is causally related to perceiving variations of Y, and if X and Y had *not* been so related but circumstances were otherwise changed, the observer would still have been perceiving variations of X but not be perceiving variations of Y, then perceiving X is conditional and causally prior to perceiving Y. The key which unlocks the relationships of causality, partial correlation, and precedence is the counterfactual conditional: if the percepts have not been causally linked then sometimes variations of Y but not variations of X. There is no compelling reason to suppose that the causal interpretation of perceptual relations cannot be subject to this test. It should be noted that, since the correlational interpretation asserts that percepts X and Y will be coupled only when the link is supported by shared information, it does not find instances of the counterfactual conditional to be contradictory. That is, the correlational interpretation does not suppose that when Y is perceived, X must also be perceived.

As a general rule, the case for causality does not rest exclusively on a test of the counterfactual conditional. Attribution of causality is on firmer ground when a coherent theoretical model of the linkages provides guidelines for testing the putative causal link. Consider again the perceptual experience associated with viewing random-element stereograms. Specific shape, e.g., a square, and spatial separation between figure and ground are plausibly construed as concurrent but not causally related responses to binocular disparity. Suppose as Gulick and Lawson (1976, chapter 10) have done, we ask next about the perceived size of the stereoscopically generated square. We find that perceived relative size varies as a function of stereopsis. The stereoscopic square appears relatively diminished for crossed disparity and relatively enlarged for uncrossed disparity and the magnitude of the size difference is a function of the degree of disparity. Should perceived size be added to perceived shape and depth to comprise a triplet of concurrent but otherwise unrelated percepts? Or should perceived size variations be tied to the variations of relative depth elicited by stereopsis?

The answer will depend on an assessment of the following premises:

(a) There is no known direct correlation between disparity and size.
(b) If perceived size and perceived distance were not in fact causally related it is highly unlikely that variations of perceived size would be observed.
(c) There is a general theoretical model of size perception which explicitly links perceived size to perceived depth.
(d) The model specifies how perceived size should change with changes in perceived depth.
(e) The observed changes of retinal size are in the direction predicted by the model.

In relation to this latter point, note that the correlational interpretation does not provide an explanation of the systematic and lawful relation between the supposedly independent percepts. Returning to the example involving concomitant perceived motion, it has been found that the velocity of the apparent motion varies in direct proportion to the variations of perceived distance. This relationship can be assimilated; indeed, it is required by the computational theory. On the rival account the lawful relationship between the percepts may be explicable in principle but the burden of explanation has not been taken up by critics of the notion that percepts are causally linked. Merely referring the concurrent perceptual changes to concurrent changes of stimulation is a form of hand-waving unless there is a basis in the analysis of ecological optics which lends specificity to the explanation or there is independent experimentation which exhibits the alleged psychophysical relations.

Another concern with the causal interpretation is aroused by the fact that the hypothetical causal relations between percepts often are bidirectional or at least that the direction of the causal flow may vary under different conditions. Thus Gilchrist (1980, pp. 534–535) describes circumstances under which perceived lightness depends on perceived depth and circumstances under which perceived depth depends on perceived lightness. Instances of bidirectionality are common in analyses of the relationship between perceived size, S', and perceived distance, D'. On one occasion, D' is said to determine S' and on another occasion S' is said to determine D'. Indeed in some cases causal flow in both directions may be observed under a single set of circumstances [e.g., see Kaufman and Rock's (1962) analysis of the Moon Illusion].

According to the standard analysis of causality to say that percept Y is caused by percept X is to say that percept Y is conditional on the *prior* occurrence of percept X. However, it should be noted that directionality is an attribute of the causal relation. Directionality is not an inherent property of the event X. Consider a fanciful case. No one has witnessed a single instance of a telephone ringing preceding (causing) the action of the telephone dial. Nevertheless, this does not reflect a special efficacy inherent in dialing which dictates that the direction of conditionality should be from dialing to ringing. Directionality is a property of the telephone system, not of dialing, and the system could be modified by an eccentric engineer to be bidirectional. In this eventuality, observing that sometimes ringing is followed by dial movement and at other times dialing is followed by ringing would not require that we abandon the claim that the two events are causally linked. With similar reasoning applied to percept–percept couplings, bidirectionality does not mitigate against a causal interpretation. Admittedly, bidirectionality is more plausible when a model of the process renders bidirectionality intelligible. The point of this argument is that bidirectionality is not incompatible with a causal interpretation of the percept–percept couplings.

Finally, we turn to the claim implicit in the causal interpretation that the coupled data are not unprocessed optical variables; instead the coupled data are perceptual representations, that is, the optical input is encoded into the language of perceptual experience. As illustration, in the case of perceived size-at-a-distance, it is perceived distance that is entered into the computational process, not motion parallax or accommodative convergence. In the case of Rock and Smith's (1981) analysis of the kinetic-depth effect it is *perceived contour* independently of the particulars of the stimulus configuration which enters in the determination of the effect.

The principal support for the claim that the causally coupled events are in fact percepts is provided by the evidence of the intersubstitutability or functional equivalence of optical inputs. In examining the determinants of percept Y, e.g., perceived lightness, if a number of optically independent but functionally equivalent variables are introduced individually, e.g., stereopsis and interposition, and these variables are known to produce comparable variations of percept X, e.g., perceived relative distance, and if these latter variables also induce comparable effects on percept Y (perceived lightness), then the perceptual representation (perceived relative distance) rather than particular optical input (stereopsis and interposition) is implicated on the percept–percept coupling. [These manipulations actually have been executed by Gilchrist (1980) who has drawn the same conclusion.]

Deployment of this logic may be clarified by the following application. As we move about the environment, objects in the scene appear to be stationary despite the fact that the image of any object in the scene slides across the retina. Direct theory has a ready explanation of this fact:

During movement, the point's relation to the arrangement as a whole remains unaltered; in short, *nonmovement* of the point is specified by an invariant arrangement in the ordinal pattern. (Turvey 1977, p. 7)

A contrasting computational interpretation may be traced to Helmholtz. In its original formulation this interpretation attributed perceived stationarity to a comparison between the efference copy of the head/eye movement, i.e., central record of the command to the musculature, and the reafferent optical motion. But more recent work (Gogel 1977, 1979; Gogel and Tietz 1974; Hay and Sawyer 1969, Wallach et al. 1972) has added an element to the computational theory by showing that *perceived* depth is entered into the calculation.

Consider the following hypothetical experiment. Suppose a stationary point is presented to an observer who views the point while moving the head through a designated arc. The point is embedded in a field-filling frontal-parallel display designed to be equivalent to the projection of a regularly textured surface at a 45° rotation-in-depth about its vertical axis. Of course, varying the location of the point in the display will not significantly alter the objective distance of the point from the eye. Nevertheless, the perceived distance of the point will be affected, appearing more distant when it is superimposed on phenomenally more distant parts of the phenomenally rotated surface, and appearing relatively nearer when it is superimposed on the phenomenally nearer parts of the surface. Let us stipulate that in the former condition the point appears to be at a distance greater than the true distance, and under the latter condition it appears at a distance less than the true distance. Under these circumstances head movement will be accompanied by perceived motion of the point, the direction of perceived movement being opposite to the direction of head movement in the former case and in the same direction as movement of the head in the latter case.

This hypothetical experiment, adapted from Gogel's research, is offered as support for the proposition that perception of stability is linked to perception of distance. However, taken alone, the experiment cannot establish this conclusion since the argument may be made that the appearance of movement and the differences in direction are due solely to the differences in optical input which necessarily accompany the manipulation of perceived distance. Testing the intersubstitutability of optical inputs can resolve the matter. For the particular hypothesis under consideration other optical variables are needed which (a) are recognized as independent determinants of perceived distance and (b) are generally believed to exploit different aspects of depth-correlated stimulation. Manipulation of oculomotor and motion parallax cues are two variables that satisfy these requirements. Both of these variables have been identified by independent experiments as effective determinants of perceived relative distance and the two trade on variables of optical input that differ from each other and from the effective stimulus variation (texture, gradient, perspective) in the principal experiment. If the effects of manipulations of accommodation, convergence, and motion parallax on concommitant perceived motion are similar in direction and magnitude to the effects associated with the variations in the first experiment, then the set of experimental operations converge to support the hypothesis that a representation of distance is involved in the computational process. In fact, experiments by Gogel and Teitz (1973, 1974, 1977, 1979) exhibit this very result, leading Gogel (1979) to stipulate

> ... the existence within the visual system of a stable relation between perceived concommitant motion (W'), perceived change in direction (ϕ') per unit of sensed head motion (K') and perceived distance (D'). The relation between these variables, ... $W' = K' - \phi D'$ ... is a perceptual equation to be distinguished from a psychophysical equation that relates only a single perceptual dimension to physical stimuli. (Pp. 10—11)

Conclusion

The theory of direct perception (Gibson 1950, 1966, 1979) makes a strong appeal to our taste for economy of explanation. In an age when cognitive psychologists vie in elaborating complex mental structures and operations, Gibson promises that the psychology of perception can do without recourse to anything more than direct accessing, "picking up" of information in stimulation. The analogy certainly is imperfect; nevertheless Gibson's stance puts one in mind (sic!) of Watson's S-R psychology. In their eschewal of mediating events and their emphasis on stimulus control (for Gibson, information in stimulation) Gibson and Watson are kindred spirits. In offering his theory in his customary straightforward uncomprising style Gibson has performed an incalculable service which may merit him a place in the history of twentieth century psychology rivalling Watson's. Nevertheless, it is unlikely that advocates of the theory of direct perception will succeed in converting the unbelievers until they address the facts of perception accumulated over the decades by investigators outside the fold. Among these facts, the occurrence of percept—percept coupling needs early attention.

Note

1. The interpretation and analysis which follows should not be attributed to any of the investigators whose work was summarized in the preceding section.

References

Attneave F., Block G., 1973 "Apparent movement in tridimensional space" *Perception & Psychophysics* **13** 301–307.

Braunstein M. L., 1976 *Depth Perception Through Motion* (New York: Academic Press).

Epstein W., 1973 "The process of 'taking-into-account' in visual perception" *Perception* **2** 267–285.

Epstein W., 1977 "Historical introduction to the constancies" in *Stability and Constancy in Visual Perception: Mechanisms and Processes* Ed. W. Epstein (New York: John Wiley).

Fodor J. H., Pylyshyn Z. W., 1981 "How direct is visual perception? Some reflections on Gibson's 'ecological approach'" *Cognition* **9** 139–196.

Gibson J. J., 1950 *The Perception of the Visual World* (Boston, MA: Houghton Mifflin).

Gibson J. J., 1966 *The Senses Considered as Perceptual Systems* (Boston, MA: Houghton Mifflin).

Gibson J. J., 1979 *The Ecological Approach to Visual Perception* (Boston, MA: Houghton Mifflin).

Gilchrist A. L., 1977 "Perceived lightness depends on perceived spatial arrangement" *Science* **195** 185–187.

Gilchrist A. L., 1980 "When does perceived lightness depend on perceived spatial arrangement?" *Perception & Psychophysics* **28** 527–538.

Gogel W. C., 1977 "An indirect measure of perceived distance from oculomotor cues" *Perception & Psychophysics* **21** 3–11.

Gogel W. C., 1979 "The common occurrence of errors of perceived distance" *Perception & Psychophysics* **25** 2–11.

Gogel W. C., Koslow M., 1972 "The adjacency principle and induced movement" *Perception & Psychophysics* **11** 309–314.

Gogel W. C., Tietz J. D., 1973 "Absolute motion parallax and the specific distance tendency" *Perception & Psychophysics* **13** 284–292.

Gogel W. C., Tietz J. D., 1974 "The effect of perceived distance on perceived movement" *Perception & Psychophysics* **16** 70–78.

Gogel W. C., Tietz J. D., 1977 "Eye fixation and attention as modifiers of perceived distance" *Perceptual and Motor Skills* **45** 343–362.

Gogel W. C., Tietz J. D., 1979 "A comparison of oculomotor and motion parallax cues of egocentric distance" *Vision Research* **19** 1161–1170.

Gulick W. L., Lawson R. B., 1976 *Human Stereopsis: A Psychophysical Approach* (New York: Oxford University Press).

Hay J., Sawyer S., 1969 "Position constancy and binocular convergence" *Perception & Psychophysics* **5** 310–312.

Hochberg J., 1974 "Higher-order stimuli and inter-response coupling in the perception of the visual world" in *Perception: Essays in Honor of J. J. Gibson* Eds. R. B. MacLeod, H. L. Pick (Ithaca, NY: Cornell University Press).

Kaufman L., Rock I., 1962 "The moon illusion" *Science* **136** 953–961.

Korte A., 1915 "Kinematoskopische Untersuchungen" *Zeitschrift für Psychologie* **72** 193–296.

Lehmkuhle S., Fox R., 1980 "Effect of depth separation in metacontrast masking" *Journal of Experimental Psychology: Human Perception and Performance* **6** 605–621.

McConkie A. B., Farber J. M., 1979 "Relation between perceived depth and perceived motion in uniform flow fields" *Journal of Experimental Psychology: Human Perception and Performance* **5** 501–508.

Reed E. S., 1987 "Why do things look as they do? A review of J. J. Gibson's *The Ecological Approach to Visual Perception* in *Cognitive psychology in question* Eds. A. Costall, A. Still (New York: St. Martin's Press).

Rock I., 1977 "In defense of unconscious inference" in *Stability and Constancy in Visual Perception: Mechanism and Processes* Ed. W. Epstein (New York: John Wiley).

Rock I., Smith D., 1981 "Alternative solutions to kinetic stimulus transformations" *Journal of Experimental Psychology: Human Perception and Performance* **7** 19–29.

Shaw R., Bransford J., 1977 "Introduction: psychological approaches to the problem of knowledge" in *Perceiving, Acting and Knowing* Eds. R. Shaw, J. Bransford (Hillsdale, NJ: Lawrence Erlbaum).

Turvey M., 1975 "Perspectives in vision: conception of perception" in *Reading, Perception and Language* Eds. D. Duane, M. Rawson (Baltimore, MD: York).

Turvey M., 1977 "Contrasting orientations to the theory of visual information processing" *Psychological Review* **84** 67–88.

Ullman S., 1980 "Against direct perception" *Behavioral and Brain Sciences* **3** 373–381.

Wallach H., O'Connell D. N., 1953 "The kinetic depth effect" *Journal of Experimental Psychology* **45** 205–217.

Wallach H., Yablick G. S., Smith A., 1972 "Target distance and adaptation in distance perception in the constancy of visual direction" *Perception & Psychophysics* **12** 139–145.

Part II
Perceptual Organization

Introduction

The reader will recall that in chapter 1, I pointed out that there is an ambiguity about the determining factors of perceptual grouping. Thus, for example, proximity can be defined on the basis of the relative *retinal* locations of images of the elements with respect to one another, or it can be defined in terms of the *perceived* proximity of the elements to one another. In this section I will present the evidence from several investigations that strongly support the conclusion that it is the *perceived* property that matters for grouping. This research spans a period of fifty years because the work of Olson and Attneave (1970) and of Rock and Brosgole (see chapter 3) was preceded by that of Corbin (1942).

By way of introduction, a few general comments may be useful here. Suppose, having shown the crucial role of the *perceived* property—for example, proximity—one wanted to know if grouping based on that perceptual property is preceded by grouping based on the retinally defined property at an earlier stage of processing. To investigate this possibility, one might want to decrease the time allowed for the achievement of grouping. In that way, epigenetically, one might reveal such an earlier stage. However, such a reduction in exposure time would probably result in a loss of depth perception of the grouping pattern. If so, the grouping would be based, not on a purely retinal state of affairs, but on a *different perceived* state of affairs—namely, a different slant of the array. Within such a flattened array, closer retinal proximities are associated with closer perceived proximities. So a different grouping might be achieved, but it would be based on a different perceived state of affairs rather than the retinal state of affairs. In the extreme case, the array would be perceived as in the frontal plane, thus completely confounding the retinal and phenomenal properties. It may therefore be impossible to answer this question, at least by experiments that potentially degrade constancy operations.

There are a few studies, not covered by the chapters included here, that might be said to call into question the major conclusion we draw about the determinants underlying grouping. For example, there was an early investigation by Olson and Attneave (1970) of texture segregation. Short line elements in one quadrant of a circular display differed in orientation from that of such elements in the rest of the display. Vertical (V) and horizontal (H) elements are more quickly discriminated from one another than are oblique left and oblique right oriented elements although the angular difference is the same, 90 degrees in both cases. That leads to faster detection of the different quadrant for the V and H condition. But what should we expect if the observer views the array with his or her head tilted 45 degrees? Now the environmentally defined V and H elements become retinally oblique, and the environmentally defined oblique elements become retinally vertical and horizontal.

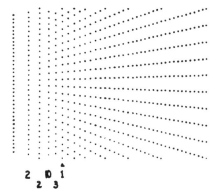

Figure II.1
Dot patterns. The number under a column indicates the frequency with which the column was chosen as the inflection point of the surface. Pointer shows locus of equal spacing between columns and radii, measured at middle radius.

The results were mixed with regard to the central issue, for the retinally defined V and H elements led to the shortest quadrant segregation time, but the difference was not at all as great as when the subject is upright. There is clear evidence that the *perceived* V and H difference leads to faster response times than does the *perceived* oblique difference. So the investigators concluded that both levels, retinal and phenomenal, play a role in grouping. However, one problem with this particular method is that at this time we do not know whether the basis of texture segregation is grouping by similarity of elements *or* the local differences between elements it borders. See Julesz (1981). The recent work of Nothdurft (1992) has thrown this question wide open. At any rate, if it is a matter of the detection of borders by feature contrast, then the issue of segregation via retinal *or* perceived *similarities* does not arise. Why the discrimination of local differences in orientation ought to be quicker as a function of retinal rather than perceived orientation is not at all obvious.

There is another earlier study by these investigators (Attneave and Olson, 1966) in which grouping patterns similar to those employed by Rock and Brosgole (see chapter 3) were presented to subjects. However, the patterns of interest consisted of elements aligned so as to group and to converge at a distance (see figure II.1). So the patterns were stimuli that, via perception, were themselves cues to depth. The authors claim that the patterns organize into the radial lines via proximity grouping which, contrary to Rock and Brosgole's findings and claim, is based on a lower retinally based level of proximity. Then, once organized in this way, prior to depth perception, the perceived lines can have other consequences. They point up the difference in conclusions between the two investigations: in

Rock and Brosgole's study, grouping is based on phenomenal proximity and the phenomenal proximity is based on binocular depth perception; in Attneave and Olson's study, proximity grouping occurs *prior* to depth perception.

There may be some confusion here. In Attneave and Olson's study, one starts with an array of dots that group into radial lines via proximity (and good continuation, I hasten to add). That grouping is based on the perceived proximity of the elements in a frontal plane which, given that perceived plane at the outset, is a function of retinal proximity of the elements. Once that grouped array of lines is achieved, no doubt very rapidly, it is, as a whole, a perspective cue to depth. It, therefore, appears to recede in depth, and it has a consequence that dot elements at the end of the converging lines, if spaced equidistantly from one another, lead to the perseveration of the grouping for about two columns beyond the equidistance point. In Rock and Brosgole's study, perception of the slanted array via binocular disparity gives rise to the impression of the array sloped in the third dimension. But, to repeat, the perceived depth in turn leads to the *perception* of certain proximities that govern the grouping.

Beck (1975) also carried out an experiment on grouping line elements as a function of constancy. An array of line elements of varying orientation was viewed both when the array was vertical (i.e., in the frontal plane) and when it was tilted backward in three-dimensional space. As in the experiments described in this section, the question was whether grouping would be governed by the retinal or perceived aspect of the elements (in this case, their orientation). When the array is slanted backward, the retinal orientation of the elements changes, but if constancy holds, and if it is their perceived orientation that matters, slanting the array should have no effect, at least up to the point that constancy no longer obtains. That last caveat may be crucial. Under the conditions of slant of the array about a horizontal (X) axis, constancy does seem to fall off, at least to this observer. However, there were other complexities of this experiment, because varying the slant of the array introduced a number of other unwanted changes, each of which required a separate control. These complexities make it hard to evaluate the results of the experiment.

However, in the light of the *entire evidence* now available, as presented in the following chapters, the conclusion about the crucial role of the *perceived* property of elements, in contrast to their retinal properties, seems warranted. And this, in turn, is what leads me to speak of the indirectness of perception in the case of grouping. First, we must achieve the *perception* of the properties of the elements, their relative proximities, their lightnesses, their amodal shapes, etc. Then one relates these perceived element properties to one another and achieves groupings following the Gestalt principles as here reformulated.

Not discussed in these chapters is the question of the role of attention in grouping. For some time it has been assumed that grouping is preattentive and that it is based on an organization resulting from the application of Gestalt principles (e.g., Neisser 1967; Treisman 1986). There is now evidence to the contrary, however (Mack and Rock, forthcoming; Ben-Av, Sagi, and Braun 1992). Grouping seems to require attention, at least grouping based on aggregating separate elements in patterns like those typically used to demonstrate Gestalt principles. This finding dovetails with the conclusion drawn here about the level at which grouping occurs. If grouping is based on the *perceived* properties of the elements, then one would hardly expect it to be preattentive and, given the new evidence, apparently it is not.

References

Attneave, F., and R. K. Olson. 1966. Inferences about visual mechanisms from monocular depth effects. *Psychonomic Science* 4:133–34.

Beck, J. 1975. The relation between similarity grouping and perceptual constancy. *American Journal of Psychology* 88:397–409.

Ben-Av, M. B., D. Sagi, and J. Braun. 1992. Visual attention and perceptual grouping. *Perception & Psychophysics* 52:277–94.

Corbin, H. H. 1942. The perception of grouping and apparent movement in visual depth. *Archives of Psychology*, no. 273.

Julesz, B. 1981. Textons: The elements of texture perception and their interactions. *Nature* 290:91–97.

Mack, A., and I. Rock. *Inattentional blindness: Perception without attention*. Forthcoming. Cambridge, MA: MIT Press.

Neisser, U. 1967. *Cognitive psychology*. New York: Appleton-Century-Crofts.

Nothdurft, H. C. 1992. Feature analysis and the role of similarity in preattentive vision. *Perception & Psychophysics* 52:355–75.

Olson, R. K., and F. Attneave. 1970. What variables produce similarity grouping? *American Journal of Psychology* 83:1–211.

Treisman, A. 1986. Properties, parts, and objects. In *Handbook of perception and human performance*, vol. 2, ed. K. R. Boff, L. Kaufman, and J. P. Thomas, 35-1–35-70. New York: Wiley.

Chapter 3

Grouping and Proximity

Irvin Rock and Leonard Brosgole

The grouping of stimuli on the basis of proximity is one of the major Gestalt laws of the spontaneous organization of the visual field. Presumably, more proximal stimuli on the retina yield stronger forces of attraction between their corresponding loci of excitation in the brain than less proximal stimuli. However, it has not been demonstrated that it is the anatomical closeness within the proximal stimulus array which governs grouping. The only investigator who ever raised this question was Corbin (1942), who speculated that grouping may be accomplished on the basis of the perceived spatial relations between the points in a stimulus array, and that this phenomenally perceived proximity and retinal proximity, although usually coinciding, can be experimentally separated and thrown into conflict.

Corbin's method was to present an array of illuminated points in the dark seen as columns when in the frontal plane. A gradual lateral tilting of the stimulus configuration into the third dimension progressively foreshortened the horizontal distance between the columns as projected to the retina. Corbin reasoned that under monocular viewing the amount of tilt required to produce a shift from a grouping of columns to one of rows could be predicted in accordance with the actual projection of the image on the retina. Under conditions where the oblique plane of the points was made visible, however, the perceived distance between the columns should remain more or less constant, and a grouping of rows should never be seen despite the severity of stimulus tilt—i.e., if grouping is based upon the *perceived* distance between points.

Since a significantly greater tilt was required to produce a shift in the perceived organization when O could see the slant of the array of points, but a shift under these conditions nevertheless did occur, Corbin concluded that both retinal proximity and phenomenally perceived proximity play an equally important role.

Originally published in *Journal of Experimental Psychology* 67, 6 (June 1964): 531–538, under the title "Grouping Based on Phenomenal Proximity." Reprinted with permission.

The following experiments represent an attempt to expand upon and refine Corbin's procedure. We hypothesized that if grouping is based upon phenomenally perceived proximity, the shift that Corbin obtained might have been due to the falling off of constancy, not to a limitation of the phenomenal factor in grouping. In order to test this hypothesis, we included a measure of constancy at various angles of stimulus tilt, which Corbin had not done.

Experiment I

Method

Apparatus. The apparatus consisted of luminously painted glass spheres of $\frac{5}{16}$ in. in diameter, strung vertically and presented in a dark room. They were 3 in. apart vertically and 4 in. apart horizontally so that when in the frontal plane all *O*s would see columns. The spheres were strung to a frame (30 in. in height and 40 in. in width) which could be swiveled about a vertical axis at its right end so that the array could be presented at any angle from frontal-parallel (0°) to 90° if desired. The degree of slant could be read off directly from a protractor mounted to the frame. In order to eliminate the contour formed by the total array of points as a factor which might affect constancy, *S*s viewed the array through a 9-in. diameter circular aperture placed in front of it. Thus, regardless of the angle of the frame behind the aperture, *S* saw the array within a circular region.

Procedure. Observations were made under monocular conditions and binocular conditions in a totally dark room. The monocular condition was always presented first, since otherwise a memory effect yielding some degree of constancy might have carried over from the binocular condition and spuriously obtruded itself.

The *S* was seated 10 ft. from the array. His head was centered in relation to the circular aperture. Following dark adaptation, and using either his left or right eye, *S* was asked to respond to each stimulus presentation in terms of whether he saw columns or rows. The instructions depicted the experiment as being one of esthetic judgment. It was explained that the luminous dots could be seen to fall either into columns, going up and down, or rows, going across, and that it was *S*'s initial impression to each presentation that was desired. The array was presented at 0, 25, 30, 35, 40, 45, 50, 55, 60, 65, 70, and 75° of tilt in a prearranged random order. After each judgment, *S* closed his eyes and the aperture was covered by a shield while *E* changed the angle of tilt. In this way *S* could not see the array being tilted. (Corbin's procedure was to permit *O* to rotate the array until he reported it was just as easy to see columns as rows. This method tends to encourage the operation of sets and expectations—for example, the perceived grouping at the outset may carry over and affect the grouping at a later moment. Also, searching for the point where it "is just as easy to see columns as rows" may entail a difficult judgment about equivalence.) Following the monocular grouping judgments, the array was again presented; now at 0, 25, 35, 45, 55, 65, and 75° of tilt in a pre-arranged random order and a distance judgment was obtained. The E specified two columns (those closest to the axis of rotation) and O was to note the horizontal distance between them. The array was then covered and O indicated when a $\frac{1}{4}$ in. wide variable luminous horizontal line, located at a distance of 10 ft., appeared equal in length to the column separation. Only one grouping and extent estimate was requested per degree of tilt in each of the two conditions. For the distance judgments, ascending and descending trials were counterbalanced for the various angles of tilt. Following the distance judgments, the entire procedure was repeated using binocular vision.

Subjects.   Nine males and six females ranging in age from 15 to 57 served as Ss. The majority, however, were high school students. Their mean age was 23.3 yr. All were naive as to the purpose of the experiment.

Results
Despite the random order of presentation, Ss were consistent in that they did not reverse their reported grouping at angles beyond the point at which they shifted to rows. Under monocular vision Ss saw the array as columns until, on the average, it was tilted back to an angle of 43.0°. By trigonometric computation, the retinal separation horizontally between points would equal the vertical separation at 41.4°. Hence, the result shows little evidence of any constancy effect, as expected. Under binocular vision, on the other hand, the average position at which the shift occurred was 53.3°, a value significantly different from the monocular value at the .01 level of confidence. Figure 3.1 shows the number of Ss seeing a column organization at the different tilts for monocular and binocular vision. It may be noted that whereas almost all Ss in the monocular condition had switched to rows by 45°, only one S in the binocular condition had done so.

The distance measures correspondingly showed a continuous and significant decrease for each successive increment of tilt from 0° to 75° under monocular observation (see fig. 3.2). (The average of the SDs for the seven different tilts of the array was .47 in.) For binocular observation they did not show any appreciable change until the array was tilted back

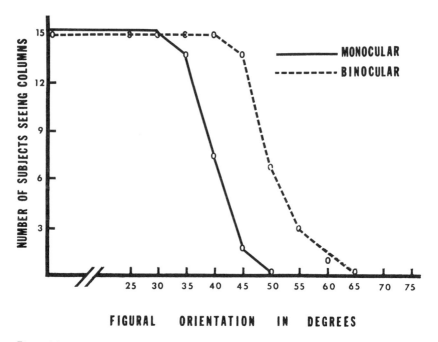

Figure 3.1
Number of Ss seeing columns at each orientation of the array: Exp. I.

to 55° or more. (The average of the SDs for the seven tilts was .65 in.) (It will be noted that the average perceived distance between columns is 3.1 in.—binocular—or 3.4 in.—monocular—even at 0° whereas the objective distance between column dots was previously stated to be 4 in. The discrepancy is partly due to the fact that the objective distance is given center-to-center whereas the judgments are no doubt made interior-to-interior. The latter distance measures 3.7 in. In addition there is probably some illusion of magnitude involved wherein the thin luminous line appears longer than an equivalent separation between the columns of dots.)

It is clear that with binocular vision Ss were to some extent able to take slant into account in perceiving the distance between columns. The fact that constancy falls off at 55° suggests that the lateral distance between points is no longer *perceived* to be greater than the vertical distance between them. This would lead to the prediction that a grouping shift would occur at about this point. This is precisely what happened. Hence one cannot say that the shift presents evidence that retinal proximity as a determinant begins to become effective at certain angles of tilt as Corbin contended.

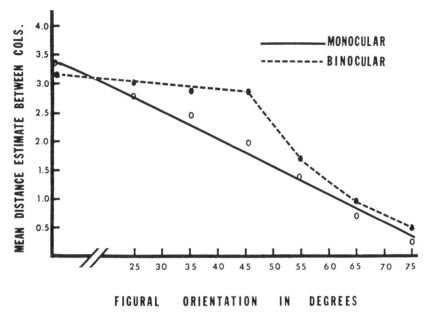

FIGURAL   ORIENTATION   IN   DEGREES

Figure 3.2
Mean distance estimate between columns at each orientation of the array: Exp. I.

Experiment II

Method

Procedure. The procedure was the same as in Exp. I except for the following three modifications:

1. In order to increase the constancy effect still further under binocular viewing, Os were permitted to view the array without the circular aperture in front of it.

2. In order to determine at what point the perceived distance between the columns equaled that between the rows, distance judgments were obtained for the vertical separation as well as for the horizontal. This necessitated the adding of an adjustable luminous vertical line to the apparatus. At each angle of tilt, then, a horizontal and vertical distance judgment was obtained. The two judgments for each angle of tilt were separated in time as part of a prearranged randomized order.

3. The order of presentation of the monocular and binocular conditions was counter-balanced between Ss. Although there was good reason to avoid presenting the monocular condition second in Exp. I, the criticism could be made that the results for the binocular condition were influenced by practice or the like.

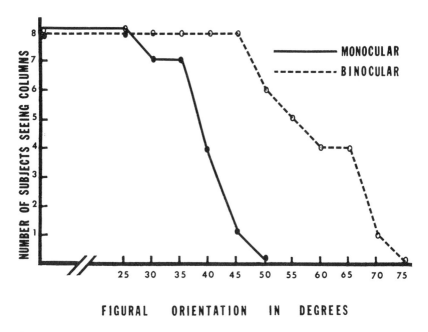

FIGURAL   ORIENTATION   IN   DEGREES

Figure 3.3
Number of Ss seeing columns at each orientation of the array: Exp. II.

Subjects. Eight naive Ss, five males and three females, served as Ss. Their mean age was 25.0 yr.

Results

The effects disclosed by the first experiment were magnified through the adoption of the modified procedure. Whereas under monocular viewing a mean of 41.9° of rotation was required to produce the transformation in figural organization, 62.5° was necessary in the binocular condition. This difference was significant beyond the .01 confidence level. Figure 3.3 gives the results for grouping.

As to the effect of order, although there only were four Ss in each sub-group, certain differences seem to be suggested. When the monocular condition was first, the shift occurred on the average at 43.75° while the shift in the binocular condition which followed was at 68.75°. When the binocular condition was first, the shift occurred at 56.25° and the shift for monocular viewing was at 40°. Thus both orders yield a large difference between monocular and binocular viewing, but the monocular-binocular order yields a greater difference. Comparing the two conditions which came first with one another reveals an appreciable difference, but the two conditions which came second show a difference of 28.75° in the average

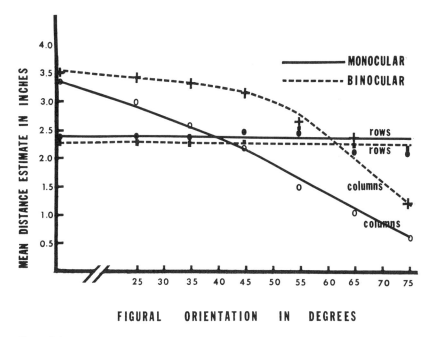

Figure 3.4
Mean distance estimates between columns and between rows at each orientation of the array: Exp. II.

point of shift. It is not clear why the difference is exaggerated when the monocular and binocular conditions are second, but it would seem to be due primarily to the greater effectiveness of binocular viewing when it comes second.

As in the first experiment, constancy was found to prevail only under binocular viewing. Figure 3.4 gives the results of distance judgments. (The average of the SDs for the seven tilts of the array for monocular viewing was .52 in. and for binocular viewing it was .48.) It is clear that under monocular viewing the distances between columns were estimated more or less in accord with visual angle, as was the case in Exp. I. (As a matter of fact the distance judgments under monocular viewing in both experiments fell off at a rate somewhat greater than would be predicted on the basis of visual angle.) Under binocular viewing the distance between columns did not show any appreciable departure from perfect constancy until at least 55°. (In general the tendency toward constancy was stronger in Exp. II than Exp. I for the more extreme tilts.) The Wilcoxon signed-ranks test was used for executing a series of multiple comparisons following the disclosure of significant main effects by the

Friedman two-way analysis of variance. The .01 confidence level was pre-established as the region for the rejection of the null hypothesis. It was determined that under monocular viewing there was a significant decrement in the magnitude of the estimates for all tilts of the array 35° or more from those offered at 0° of tilt. Also there was a significant decrement in the distance estimates for virtually every successive increment in the tilt of the array. On the other hand, only the estimates at 75° of tilt in the binocular condition differed significantly from those at 0°.

The distance between rows for monocular or binocular vision remained fairly constant throughout (note that the average distance is less than the true value of 3 in.) As can be seen, the two monocular curves cross at approximately 40° indicating that at this angle the points were perceived as equidistant in each direction and this corresponds closely with the point of shift in grouping. For binocular vision, the points were, on the average, perceived as equidistant in each direction at 62°, since the two binocular curves cross at about this point. This coincided with the point of shift in grouping. It is of significant import that not one S under either of the two conditions had shifted to a grouping of rows so long as the horizontal separation was perceived to be greater than the vertical extent.

To summarize these findings, whereas tilt produced a marked and continued degeneration of horizontal extent judgments in the monocular condition, constancy prevailed in the binocular condition in that the perception of distance was veridical throughout a considerable range of tilts of the array. These differences in the perception of spatial relations coincided with predicted differences in grouping.

Discussion

The results of both experiments are clear in showing that grouping is not based on the retinal distance between points. The principles of grouping play an important role in Gestalt theory. It was on the basis of these autochthonous principles that the field was held to become structured into discrete and segregated entities. Since an attempt was made at offering an alternative to empiricism, it became necessary to specify completely objective unifying factors, such as proximity or similarity. Prior to any experience, then, these objective factors must operate because they determine the way in which the field will be organized. It, therefore, now comes as quite a challenge to this approach to discover that, at least in the case of one grouping factor, it is not the contiguity of elements within the proximal stimulus that governs the perceptual outcome. Rather, grouping appears to be based upon perceived proximity which is itself the outcome of complex organizational processes involving the central integration of information about distance. The fact that Gestalt theorists played such an important role in promulgating the notion of perceptual constancy should not be allowed to confuse the present issue. When the array is tilted, the dots along the rows could be perceived to be farther apart than those along the columns because of constancy, but this does not require that O must see columns. In other words, regardless of how the spacing of the dots is perceived, the grouping should still be based on proximity between the elements in the retinal image according to the Gestalt notion of grouping.

We are left with an intriguing problem. Why should grouping occur on the basis of experienced proximity rather than retinal contiguity? One answer is that we learned that stimuli which appear closer together are usually part of a common unit—i.e., grouping by proximity may be based on past experience as suggested by Brunswik and Kamiya (1953). If so, it would be paradoxical in that the grouping principles were intended as an alternative to theories which explain organized perception on the basis of past experience. Of course, the problem remains of explaining how the common unit is itself perceived as a unit in the first place.

Needless to say, it is quite possible that other principles of grouping are also based on phenomenal rather than objective factors. For example, elements which are perceived as similar may be seen as part of one unit regardless of whether the corresponding proximal stimulus elements on the retina are objectively similar. It is not too difficult to imagine how this could be tested. The same is true for certain other grouping principles.

The findings concerning grouping are similar in certain important respects to those reported recently by Rock and Ebenholtz (1962) on stroboscopic movement. These authors raised the question whether the necessary conditions for stroboscopic movement entail change of location of the stimulus on the retina (as had been assumed to be the case) or change in the phenomenal location of the stimulus. They found the latter to be the necessary condition—apparent movement is seen even where there is no change in the locus of retinal stimulation so long as the stimulus is located in two separate places in space. Concerning both studies the question may be raised as to how "phenomenal" proximity or "phenomenal" location can be held to play a causal role in perception. The answer would have to be that the brain processes underlying such experience mediate the perceptual outcome. Nevertheless, it is useful to speak of "phenomenal" factors since there may be various stimulus conditions which would lead to the same outcome provided they share the feature of yielding the same experienced spatial relations. It is these experienced spatial relations—not spatial relations given in the retina—that seem to be crucial. In the case of stroboscopic movement, at least two different stimulus conditions yielded phi, although neither involved change of the retinal locus of the stimulus. Furthermore, if it should turn out to be correct that we have learned to see stroboscopic movement or learned to group by proximity, then it follows that the first step in the process is perceiving certain spatial relations. Hence for the time being, it is convenient to refer to the necessary stimulus conditions in phenomenal terms. Ultimately we shall want to go beyond this way of specifying the conditions.

Note

The authors wish to express their appreciation to John Ceraso for his helpful suggestions during the course of this study.

References

Brunswik, E., and Kamiya, J. Ecological cue-validity of "proximity" and of other gestalt factors. *Amer. J. Psychol.*, 1953, **66**, 20–32.

Corbin, H. H. The perception of grouping and apparent movement in visual depth. *Arch. Psychol., N. Y.*, 1942, No. 273.

Rock, I., and Ebenholtz, S. Stroboscopic movement based on change of phenomenal rather than retinal location. *Amer. J. Psychol.*, 1962, **75**, 193–207.

Chapter 4
Grouping and Lightness

Irvin Rock, Romi Nijhawan, Stephen E. Palmer, and Leslie Tudor

Introduction

It is now widely acknowledged that a precondition for the perception of the world of objects and events is a process of organization in the visual system. As Gestalt psychologists pointed out, there is no more a priori affinity within the light that reaches the retina from a single external object than there is from light some of which emanates from within that object and some of which emanates from elsewhere. Thus the experience of the world as consisting of discrete and separate things is an achievement that typically (but not always) corresponds accurately to the actual presence of separate things in the real world.

It is also widely accepted that, at least on a descriptive level, the Gestalt laws of grouping (Wertheimer 1923) and the related law about figure–ground organization (Rubin 1921) give an account of how such organization might be achieved. Elements within the proximal stimulus are presumably grouped with one another on the basis of factors such as their relative proximity and similarity to one another, the extent to which they are smooth or "good" continuations of one another, whether or not they move in the same direction with the same speed as one another, and the like. Stimuli tend to be seen as figure rather than as ground if they are surrounded, symmetrical, or convex regions, and the like.

However, if these laws indeed account for the parsing of the field into things and non-things, they have been assumed to operate at a very early stage of processing, prior to the allocation of attention and prior to further processing that will yield constancy of object properties such as size, shape, lightness, and the like. This follows because attention and constancy mechanisms are believed to presuppose the prior existence of discrete entities or candidate objects on which to operate. But the stage at which grouping occurs is an empirical question subject to experimental analysis.

Originally published in *Perception* 21 (1992): 779–789, under the title "Grouping Based on Phenomenal Similarity of Achromatic Color." Reprinted with permission.

In one such study on the role of proximity in grouping, Rock and Brosgole (1964) elaborated on an earlier experiment by Corbin (1942), the latter being the first investigation with which we are familiar ever to consider the question of "level" in perceptual grouping. The basic plan was first to arrange luminous beads on invisible strings such that the beads were nearer to one another vertically than horizontally. When the array was seen in the subject's frontal plane, columns rather than rows were therefore perceived. Then the array was tilted about a vertical axis and placed at various slants such that the foreshortening between columns led to changes in the relative retinal proximity of beads along the horizontal dimension compared with the vertical dimension. Thus if grouping were based on proximity defined at the level of the retina, at some degree of tilt of the array—beyond approximately 41°—grouping should have shifted from columns to rows.

The result was that, under conditions of binocular viewing, grouping did not shift to rows until the array was tilted by such a large angle that constancy failed, namely beyond 55°. Constancy here refers to the perceived separation between beads along the horizontal axis, and separate measurements of it were obtained. However, under conditions of monocular viewing, where there were few if any effective cues to depth within the array, grouping shifted from columns to rows at about the point at which the projected horizontal separation between beads equaled the vertical separation, i.e., at a tilt of 43°. The perceived separation between beads also became equal at about this point under monocular conditions.

Thus it would seem from these results that either it is perceived proximity (rather than retinal proximity) among elements that governs grouping, or, at the very least, when the perception of relative proximity differs from retinally defined relative proximity, the former supersedes the latter as the principle of grouping. We can assume that in the monocular condition of this experiment subjects perceived the array in a frontal plane regardless of its objective tilt, and the constancy measures bear this out. [See the equidistance tendency described by Gogel (1965)]. This is similar to the state of affairs that obtains in Wertheimer's demonstrations of proximity in a drawing: Retinal proximity and perceived proximity are necessarily confounded.

From the results of Rock and Brosgole (1964) one might reasonably conclude that grouping occurs at a later, post-constancy stage of processing and is not based on the state of affairs at the retinal level. However, there is other evidence to which we refer in section 4.4 suggesting that the story may be more complex.

The experiments we now describe bear on the issue of grouping based on similarity of neutral color when some elements in an array are lighter or darker gray than others. This leads to a strong grouping effect when all

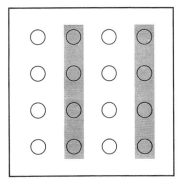   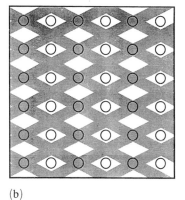

(a)   (b)

Figure 4.1
The arrays used by Tudor in preliminary experiments. Shadows were cast along columns (or
rows) of gray spots (a). This altered their luminance but not their perceived lightness since
the shadows were perceived as shadows, although this is not entirely the case in this picture.
In a second experiment a crisscross pattern of diagonal shadows was used (b); this favored
neither columns nor rows but did alter the luminance of all spots in adjacent columns. (After
Tudor 1987.)

other grouping factors, such as proximity, are neutralized. However, there
are two ways of looking at differences in neutral color. A light-gray element yields a retinal image of greater luminance than a darker one. But it
is also perceived as lighter and could be seen as such even if it were in
dimmer illumination. In fact, the illumination could be adjusted so that the
lighter element would yield an image of the same luminance as a darker
element in stronger illumination. So the question to be resolved by
experiment is whether grouping is based on the similarity of luminance at
the retinal (or proximal) level, or on the similarity of perceived lightness
at the distal (or constancy) level.

In a preliminary experiment, Tudor (1987) cast shadows over rows or
columns of gray circular spots on a white background as a means of varying luminance while holding perceived lightness constant. But the elongated shadow itself tended to induce grouping in the direction of its long
axis, perhaps by virtue of common region (Palmer 1992)—(see figure
4.1a). To eliminate this unwanted factor, in a second preliminary experiment, Tudor introduced a crisscross pattern of diagonal shadows across
the entire array and this pattern favored neither columns nor rows—(see
figure 4.1b). All spots were the same shade of gray. Grouping in this
experimental condition was compared with grouping in two control conditions: in one, no shadows were introduced, and in the other, the spots
that were shadowed in the experimental condition were darker gray.

These darker gray spots had the same luminance as the shadowed spots in the experimental condition. A number of patterns were used in all three conditions, which varied the ratios of proximities between columns and rows, pitting lightness (luminance) against proximity.

The result was that the grouping achieved in the experimental or shadowed condition was virtually identical to that achieved in the control conditions in which all spots were unshadowed and the same shade of gray, whereas both of these conditions yielded grouping different from that achieved when alternate rows or columns were different shades of gray. Thus it appears that grouping of this kind occurs on the basis of perceived lightness and not on the basis of luminance at the level of the retina.

However, there are two shortcomings of this method. One is that the crisscross pattern is confusing and tends to obfuscate grouping into columns or rows. A second is that, for reasons to be explained, we wanted to include a control condition that simulated the luminance ratios in the shadow condition, but did not contain shadows. To do so requires the introduction of a dark strip behind a series of elements, which, needless to say, would have even more of an unwanted effect on grouping than did the elongated shadow referred to above in the first preliminary experiment. In fact, Tudor (1987) tried this out in the first preliminary experiment and obtained precisely this unwanted outcome. The current method overcomes both of these shortcomings.

Experiment 1: Cast Shadow

Method

Subjects. Nine students at the University of California at Berkeley participated. They were all naive concerning the theoretical issues under study.

Stimuli and Procedure. The essential idea of the method was to introduce the shadow along a column of small square elements (as in the first preliminary experiment described by Tudor) but its elongated direction was orthogonal to the grouping that was expected to occur. Thus, as shown in figure 4.2a, given five columns of squares equidistant from one another, the question posed was whether the middle shadowed column would group with the columns on the left or on the right. If a shadow cast vertically on the middle column has the effect of creating a vertical grouping within the column it is presumably irrelevant with respect to the horizontal grouping of that column.

To address the critical question of whether grouping occurs on the basis of perceived lightness or on the basis of physically measurable lumi-

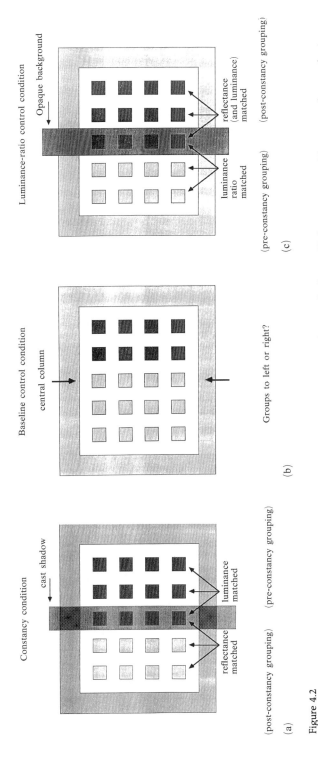

Figure 4.2

The arrays used in the present work. In the experimental array (a) a shadow is cast over the central column of light-gray squares. This creates the same luminance for these squares as for the darker ones on the right. However, it is unlikely that the reader will achieve constancy in this picture as did the subjects and thus perceive the shadowed squares as the same lightness as the light-gray square. In the baseline control array (b) the squares in the central column have the same reflectance values as the corresponding ones in (a). In the luminance-ration control array (c) the ratio of luminance of squares to background is the same in the central column as in the two columns on the left. To achieve this outcome, darker squares were used in the central column on a dark-gray strip. These match the lightness of the squares on the right. However, the reader may perceive the central square as somewhat lighter than those on the right, as did the subjects. The luminance of the central column matches exactly the luminance of the squares and surrounding shadow in the experimental array (a).

nance at the retinal level, the reflectance of the squares in the two columns to one side, let us say the right, matched the lower luminance of the shadowed squares in the middle column. However, the reflectance of the middle-column squares equaled that of the squares in the two columns on the other side, let us say the left. If constancy prevailed, these middle-column squares would appear the same lightness as those having the same reflectance, despite the presence of the shadow. Therefore, if grouping occurs on the basis of luminance, the middle column of squares should group with the columns of squares of equal *luminance* on the right; if grouping occurs on the basis of perceived lightness, the squares in the middle column should group with the squares of equal *reflectance* on the left.

To prepare the subject for the task on the critical trials, the two possible groupings of the middle column were first explained and demonstrated to them. It was illustrated first with gray squares as elements containing either vertical or horizontal yellow lines. Three columns on one side, e.g., on the right, had squares with horizontal lines and two columns on the other side, e.g., the left, had squares with vertical lines. The next illustration contained an array of three columns of red squares and two columns of green squares. In addition, a vertical rectangle (green) was placed behind the middle (red) column. Subjects were told that their task was to say "left" or "right" indicating to which side the middle column seemed to group or belong. It was explained that the grouping was to be on the basis of the squares themselves not on anything surrounding them, such as the green rectangle behind the red squares. Thus in these illustrations the grouping of the middle column was unambiguous.

After these instructions and the two illustrations, a series of six arrays of elements, each of five columns (as in the two illustrative arrays), was presented. Three of these six arrays were critical in that they concerned the property of lightness under investigation. One was the experimental array in which the middle column of gray squares was shadowed (figure 4.2a) as already explained. The second was a baseline control array containing three columns of light-gray squares and two of dark-gray squares, as in figure 4.2b. The reflectance values of these squares were the same as in the experimental array, the only difference being that the central column was not shadowed. This array should provide a baseline of grouping against which to compare responses to the other two critical arrays. We assumed that all subjects would group the middle column with the lighter two columns since these squares match on the basis of both luminance and perceived lightness.

The third critical array was the "luminance-ratio" control (figure 4.2c) mentioned briefly above. The rationale for this requires more detailed explanation. Assuming that in the experimental shadowed array the middle column is grouped with the columns containing the lighter (reflectance-matched) gray squares, it can be argued that the basis for such grouping is not perceived lightness after the achievement of constancy, but the ratio of the luminance of the squares to that of the immediately surrounding background. The luminance ratio of the shadowed squares to their immediate background (which is also shadowed) will be the same as that of the lighter squares to their background. After all, the shadow across the middle column does not alter the luminance ratio between squares and their background.

The rationale for this control may seem puzzling because it is now widely believed that the basis of lightness constancy, when a shadow is cast over a given surface and its surround, is precisely the preservation of the luminance ratio of that surface to its surround (Wallach 1948). However, there is now good reason to believe that this ratio will yield constancy if and only if the edge of the shadow is interpreted by the perceptual system as a shadow edge—i.e., as due to a change in illumination. If it is instead interpreted as a reflectance edge, then constancy will not be achieved (Gilchrist et al. 1983; Gilchrist 1988). Therefore, what we sought to investigate in the luminance-ratio control array was whether a column of squares whose luminance ratio to their background is the same as that of the light-gray squares to their background, but that nonetheless do not appear phenomenally the same shade of gray as those lighter squares, will or will not group with columns of those lighter squares, as they (presumably) will in the experimental, shadow, condition.

We achieved this control condition by placing a dark-gray strip of paper behind the middle column of squares. The squares had the same reflectance as the dark-gray squares in the adjacent columns, as illustrated in figure 4.2c. The luminances of the squares and background strip in the middle column of this array precisely matched those of the squares and background in the middle column of the experimental shadowed array (shown in figure 4.2a). However, the edge of the strip did not look like a shadow because the strip extended beyond the cardboard containing the square elements and occluded the border, and possibly also because its edge was sharp rather than gradual as in the penumbra of the shadow in the experimental condition. It looked like a reflectance edge, which in fact it was. Hence, the darker strip and central squares did not appear to have the same lightness as the rest of the background and the squares to the left, in contrast to the experimental display for which constancy prevailed. [The exact conditions necessary for the perceptual system to discriminate between reflectance and shadow edges are not fully known (see Gilchrist et al. 1983), but for our purposes this is not essential. What matters is that we were able to create conditions where the edge in question looked like a shadow edge in our experimental condition, and thus yielded constancy, yet looked like a reflectance edge in our luminance-ratio control condition.]

Since the luminance of the middle squares in this second control array was the same as that of the squares in the experimental, shadowed array (which in turn were matched to the darker squares in the columns on the other side), the reflectance of these middle-column squares in the luminance-ratio condition was in fact the same as that of the darker squares. So the question arises whether they appeared to be the same lightness as the darker squares. The answer is that they did not; they appeared slightly lighter. The reader may perceive this in figure 4.2c. This is no doubt the result of simultaneous contrast, because the middle squares are on a darker background (namely the strip) than the squares in the adjacent columns.

Let us return to the sequence of the six arrays. The three critical arrays (the experimental and two control arrays) were presented within a sequence of six arrays in the first, fourth, and sixth positions. However, which of the three appeared in which of these positions was random. The second, third, and fifth arrays were fillers selected from the following unambiguous arrays: three columns of squares and two of triangles; three columns of yellow squares and two of blue; three columns of squares with holes in the center and two columns of squares without such holes. These noncritical arrays were always shown in this order. For both the critical and the noncritical arrays, the three-column–two-column arrangement was equally often in one orientation as in its mirror image.

Each array consisted of elements, generally squares, 2.5 cm × 2.5 cm, separated vertically and horizontally by 2.5 cm. There were four such elements in each of five columns. The elements were mounted on sheets of thick paper, 30.5 cm wide × 22.9 cm high; the reflectance value of the paper was 9.5 (90%) on the Munsell scale and its luminance value was 2.07 cd m^{-2}. These sheets were in turn mounted in the centers of cardboard sheets (71.1 cm × 55.9 cm), the reflectance value of which was 8.0 (59.1%) on the Munsell scale and the luminance value was 1.20 cd m^{-2}. The cardboard sheets had holes at the top so that they could be easily mounted on hooks on the wall. For the first (baseline) control array the luminance of the lighter squares in the three columns was 1.6 cd m^{-2}; the luminance of the darker squares in the remaining two columns was 0.35 cd m^{-2}. In terms of reflective values, these squares were 8.5 (68.4%) and 4.75 (17.6%) on the Munsell scale respectively. For the experimental condition, the array was the same as the one just described except that the shadow cast along the middle column rendered the luminance of these squares (which were of the same reflectance as the lighter squares) to be the same as that of the darker squares rather than as that of the lighter squares. The shadow was produced by a vertical strip of cardboard suspended between a single incandescent 40 W bulb and the array. The power output of the bulb happened to be very close to giving a luminance match between the dark squares and the shadowed squares. A finer adjustment of this was achieved by reducing the current to the bulb. The sides of the bulb were covered with black paint so as to minimize stray light which would otherwise reflect off the walls of the room. This was done to meet the single-light-source requirement as far as possible. The bulb was 155 cm behind the strip, which in turn was 15.2 cm from the array hung on the wall. For the second (luminance-ratio) control array, darker squares were placed on a dark-gray strip (30.5 cm × 5.1 cm) orientated vertically in the region of the middle column. The luminance of these squares was also 0.35 cd m^{-2} and that of the strip was 0.46 cd m^{-2}. The reflectance value of the strip was 5.5 (24.6%) on the Munsell scale. As noted above, the strip extended beyond the border of the cardboard sheet.

The observer viewed the arrays through an opening in a partition placed 61 cm from the arrays on the wall. The opening, large enough to allow binocular viewing, was occluded between exposures of each array. When the experimenter had removed the preceding array and replaced it by the appropriate one in the series, the occluding cardboard was removed and the next array exposed. No time limit was imposed, but virtually all subjects responded within a few seconds, usually less than five. The subject responded "left" or "right," meaning that the central column appeared to group with or "belong" with the columns on the left or right.

Results. Grouping for the three noncritical unambiguous arrays was always as expected and will not be considered further. For the baseline control array consisting of three columns of light-gray squares and two of darker-gray squares, grouping was also as would be expected under these unambiguous conditions for all nine subjects. For the experimental shadowed condition, seven of the nine subjects (78%) grouped the shadowed column with the lighter squares in the adjacent columns and two (22%) grouped the shadowed column with the darker squares in the adjacent columns on the opposite side. For the luminance-ratio control array containing the dark-gray strip, all nine subjects (100%) grouped the control squares with the dark-gray squares of equal absolute luminance. In other words, changing the background edges of the vertical rectangular region from illumination to reflectance edges reversed perceived grouping for the majority of the subjects despite the equality of the ratio of square to background in the middle column and the lighter-gray squares in the adjacent columns. This occurred despite the fact already noted that, by virtue of contrast, the central dark-gray squares on the darker-gray strip in the luminance-ratio control condition looked somewhat lighter than the dark-gray squares in the adjacent columns which were not on a strip.

Experiment 2: Transparency

Method

We sought another method to investigate the same question, namely whether grouping is based on similarity of luminance as projected to the retina, similarity of perceived lightness based on some constancy operation, or possibly on the equivalence of luminance ratios between element and background rather than on constancy per se. A method that will allow this question to be tested is based on perception of phenomenal transparency. Under certain conditions when one views a surface through a partially transparent (translucent) filter, the surface nonetheless is perceived veridically with respect to its reflectance or color. However, the luminance of that surface is also lowered by the filter.

Subjects.   Nine new subjects were recruited; all were naive about the theoretical issues under study.

Stimuli and Procedure.   The method and procedure were essentially the same as in experiment 1 with respect to the arrays, the instructions, the procedure, and task. The two control arrays were the same as in experiment 1 except that the specific luminance values differed from those of experiment 1 but within experiment 2 they corresponded to one another and to the experimental, transparency array, analogously to experiment 1. The experimental transparency array was created by suspending a narrow, 29.0 cm × 4.5 cm neutral-density strip 15.2 cm in front of the array mounted on the wall such that from the position of the observer it was seen to be in front of the squares in the middle column only. It was 137.2 cm from the opening through which the subject looked.

The reflectance values of the light-gray and dark-gray squares in the baseline control and experimental arrays were the same as in experiment 1. Their luminance values were 49 cd m^{-2} and 13 cd m^{-2} respectively. The luminance of the light-gray squares in the middle column as viewed through the filter was 13 cd m^{-2} and thus matched that of the dark-gray squares. The luminance values of the background sheets of thick paper and the cardboard sheets were 62 cd m^{-2} and 34.5 cd m^{-2} respectively. The reflectance value of the strip used in the luminance-ratio control condition was 5.5 (24.6%) on the Munsell scale and its luminance, which matched that of the region surrounding the squares in the middle column in the experimental array, was 15.3 cd m^{-2}.

With binocular vision, the filter strip was perceived to be well in front of the array in the experimental condition. Consequently a relative unambiguous constancy effect occurred. The light-gray squares in the middle column seen through the transparency strip appeared to be about the same lightness as the squares of the same reflectance seen in the adjacent columns. Figure 4.2 can serve again to illustrate the three conditions of experiment 2.

Results.   The results were even clearer than those of experiment 1. In the baseline control array all subjects grouped the squares in the central column with those of the same lightness in adjacent columns. In the experimental transparency array all subjects did the same thing, indicating that the altered luminance due to the translucent filter had no effect. In the luminance-ratio control array all subjects reversed their grouping; they saw the control column of squares as belonging with the dark-gray squares in the columns on the other side. Thus, despite the equivalent luminance ratio of squares to backgrounds of the middle-column squares and the light-gray squares in the adjacent columns, all subjects grouped on the basis of the reflectance of the squares themselves when they viewed this array.

Discussion

The results of both experiments indicate that grouping by similarity of neutral gray color is based on perceived lightness after the achievement of constancy, and not on the luminance of the elements at the level of the proximal stimulus. The experiments also rule out an explanation based on ratio of luminance at the level of the proximal stimulus. Such ratios can be regarded as a higher-order attribute of the proximal stimulus such as has been advocated by Gibson (1950, 1966). Of course, even if that proved to be the relevant variable in defining similarity of neutral color, it would not follow that grouping per se was explainable in terms of a higher-order attribute or direct perception theory. Grouping is the kind of process for which advocates of direct perception find no need.

   In any event, by ruling out the luminance explanation and the ratio-of-luminances explanation of the similarity underlying grouping in our experiments, we are left with the post-constancy achievement of particular phenomenal shades of gray as the basis of grouping. This is not to deny that an explanation in nonphenomenological language cannot be realized eventually. Indeed the research of Gilchrist on lightness perception and related phenomena has provided a good account of the kinds of processes underlying the perception of lightness and lightness constancy (Gilchrist 1979, 1988). But whatever these processes may be, we now have to accept the fact that grouping such as we have examined here does not occur until that stage or level of processing at which constancy is achieved.

This conclusion fits the one we drew in the introduction in describing the experiment by Rock and Brosgole (1964) on grouping by proximity. It only partially fits the findings of Olson and Attneave (1970) on the question of whether texture segregation, based on the different orientation of line elements in one quadrant of an array, results from the retinal or perceived orientation of these elements. Both factors seem to be implicated. Moreover, in a study by Beck (1975) in which the grouping of line elements by similarity was investigated, the same question of whether grouping is based on retinal or perceived orientation of elements led him to conclude that it was retinal orientation that mattered.

On the other hand, some as yet unpublished findings from our laboratory further support the conclusion that grouping occurs at a stage beyond that of the retinal input. These findings are derived from experiments in which the simple method of separating the planes in the third dimension in which the elements to be grouped are phenomenally located was used (Palmer 1992; Palmer and Rock 1994; Palmer, Neff, and Beck 1996). In these examples it is not so much the achievement of constancy that matters, as it is just the achievement of differential phenomenal depth. But the achievement of that depth and its utilization in grouping does imply that grouping in these cases does not occur exclusively at the very early stage of processing, as was previously assumed.

There is, therefore, a respectable amount of evidence indicating that grouping based on the Gestalt principles occurs at a relatively late level of processing. One should not then jump to the conclusion that grouping occurs only at this relatively late, post-constancy level. A more cautious—and correct—formulation would be to say simply that *grouping is affected by the perceived properties of the distal object*. One way in which this might happen is indeed if grouping occurs only at a relatively late post-constancy level. (Call this the "late only" hypothesis.) But it is also possible that grouping based on the perceived properties of the distal object merely supersedes a previously achieved grouping based on the 2-D properties of the proximal stimulus. (Call this the "both early and late" hypothesis.) How could these two hypotheses be discriminated experimentally?

One might think that this could be accomplished by presenting displays such as we used in our experiments for a very brief period, perhaps followed by a pattern mask. The underlying idea is that such a brief exposure would directly tap the initial preconstancy representation. After all, it is widely believed that image shape and size information can be extracted rapidly and simultaneously over the entire visual array (Beck 1967; Treisman and Gelade 1980; Julesz 1981), whereas perceptual constancy requires focal attention and a certain amount of additional processing time to achieve (Epstein and Lovitts 1985; Epstein and Broota 1986;

Epstein and Babler 1989, 1990; Epstein et al. 1992). By restricting the presentation time, one might be able to study the organization of the early pre-constancy representation. Then, assuming that the processing of achromatic color follows a similar two-stage scheme, the "both early and late" hypothesis predicts that grouping performance should change dramatically under brief presentation conditions, favoring the grouping alternative based on similarity of image luminances rather than that based on similarity of perceived lightnesses (as we found at long exposures in the experiments reported here).

Although such experiments could certainly be carried out, the difficulty arises in the theoretical interpretation of their results. Suppose that when the critical array is presented for 150 ms or less, subjects group the shadowed central column according to luminance information. Does this fact demonstrate that there is an initial pre-constancy grouping based on luminance information? The key question turns out to be whether brief presentations actually tap the hypothesized pre-constancy representation or not. The luminance-based result is clearly compatible with this possibility, but it can be equally well predicted from the "late only" hypothesis. One need only assume that brief presentation causes the late, post-constancy representation to be constructed without constancy processes having had sufficient time to complete their task. Thus according to the "late only" hypothesis grouping on brief-exposure trials would not be based on *luminance* information at all, but on nonveridically perceived *lightness*. Hence one might easily obtain the result predicted by the "both early and late" hypothesis without it being correct: grouping might well occur only at the late level, but appear to be based on some earlier stage if its information is passed on to later levels without achieving full constancy. We therefore find it difficult to imagine an experiment that would succeed in disentangling these two hypotheses.

In any event, the important problem that now is revealed by our findings and conclusions is this: If the Gestalt laws do not adequately explain the organization and parsing of the visual field at the earliest stage of processing, and if some organization, logically speaking, must be assumed to occur at that early stage, then what principles explain it? We suggest, as a tentative answer (Palmer and Rock 1994), that organization of the field occurs at an early stage on the basis of a new principle, namely *uniform connectedness*. We suggest that regions of interconnected uniform stimulation, such as spots, lines, or larger areas, are interpreted by the perceptual system as signifying a single unit.

Note

This research was supported in part by the following grants: a Research Scientist Award MH 00707 from NIMH to Irvin Rock, Grant MH 46141 from NIMH to Stephen Palmer and Irvin Rock; Grant BNS from NSF to Stephen Palmer; Grant MH 42573 from NIMH to Arien Mack and Irvin Rock. Concerning this last grant, we acknowledge our indebtedness to Arien Mack for her contributions to the formulation of the research proposal, in part bearing on the issue of stages of processing in perceptual organization. We thank Jacob Beck, Alan Gilchrist, John Harris, Michael Kubovy, and an anonymous reviewer for their helpful suggestions about the manuscript.

References

Beck J., 1967 "Perceptual grouping produced by line figures" *Perception & Psychophysics* **2** 491–495.

Beck J., 1975 "The relation between similarity grouping and perceptual constancy" *American Journal of Psychology* **88** 397–409.

Corbin H. H., 1942 "The perception of grouping and apparent movement in visual depth" *Archives of Psychology* **273**.

Epstein W., Babler T., 1989 "Perception of slant-in-depth is automatic" *Perception & Psychophysics* **45** 31–33.

Epstein W., Babler T., 1990 "In search of depth" *Perception & Psychophysics* **48** 68–76.

Epstein W., Babler T., Bownds S., 1992 "Attentional demands of processing shape in three-dimensional space: Evidence from visual search and precuing paradigms" *Journal of Experimental Psychology: Human Perception and Performance* **18** 503–511.

Epstein W., Broota K. D., 1986 "Automatic and attentional components in perception of size at a distance" *Perception & Psychophysics* **40** 256–262.

Epstein W., Lovitts B., 1985 "Automatic and attentional components in shape at a slant" *Journal of Experimental Psychology: Human Perception and Performance* **11** 355–366.

Gibson J. J., 1950 *The Perception of the Visual World* (Boston, MA: Houghton Mifflin).

Gibson J. J., 1966 *The Senses Considered as Perceptual Systems* (Boston, MA: Houghton Mifflin).

Gilchrist A., 1979 "The perception of surface blacks and whites" *Scientific American* **240** 112–126.

Gilchrist A., 1988 "Lightness constancy and failures of constancy: A common explanation" *Perception & Psychophysics* **43** 415–424.

Gilchrist A., Delman S., Jacobson A., 1983 "The classification and integration of edges as critical to the perception of reflectance and illumination" *Perception & Psychophysics* **33** 425–436.

Gogel W., 1965 "Equidistant tendency and its consequences" *Psychological Bulletin* **64** 153–163.

Julesz B., 1981 "Textons, the elements of texture perception and their interactions" *Nature (London)* **290** 91–97.

Olson R. R., Attneave F., 1970 "What variables produce similarity grouping?" *American Journal of Psychology* **83** 1–12.

Palmer S. E., 1992, "Common region: A new principle of perceptual grouping" *Cognitive Psychology* **24** 436–447.

Palmer S. E., Neff J., Beck D., 1996 "Late influences on perceptual grouping: Amodal completion" *Psychonomic Bulletin and Review* **3** 75–80.

Palmer S. E., Rock I., 1994 "Rethinking perceptual organization: The role of uniform connectedness" *Psychonomic Bulletin and Review* **1** 29–55.

Rock I., Brosgole L., 1964 "Grouping based on phenomenal proximity" *Journal of Experimental Psychology* **67** 531–538.

Rubin E., 1921 *Visuell wahrgenommene Figuren* (Copenhagen: Gyldenalske Boghandel) [Reprinted as "Figure and ground" in *Readings in Perception* Eds. D. C. Beardslee, M. Wertheimer (Princeton, NJ: Van Nostrand, 1958) pp. 194–203.]

Treisman A., Gelade G., 1980 "A feature-integration theory of attention" *Cognitive Psychology* **12** 97–136.

Tudor L., 1987 *Levels of Processing in Perceptual Organization* MA thesis, Rutgers University, New Brunswick, NJ.

Wallach H., 1948 "Brightness constancy and the nature of achromatic colors" *Journal of Experimental Psychology* **38** 310–324.

Wertheimer M., 1923 "Untersuchungen zur Lehre von der Gestalt, II" *Psychologische Forschung* **4** 301–350.

Chapter 5

Grouping and Amodal Completion

Stephen Palmer, Jonathan Neff, and Diane Beck

In 1923 Max Wertheimer called attention to the previously unappreciated problem of perceptual organization. Simply stated, the problem is that because the objects of phenomenal perception are not given in any simple way in the retinal image, they must be an achievement of the visual nervous system. This raised the question of what features in the retinal image cause the visual system to organize it into the objects people experience perceptually. Wertheimer took the initial step of identifying a number of important factors that have come to be known as the "Gestalt laws of grouping," although "principles of grouping" is perhaps a more appropriate description. Among the principles Wertheimer demonstrated were proximity, similarity (of color, size, orientation, etc.), closure, continuity, and common fate (Wertheimer 1923). To this list, recent demonstrations have added the factors a common region (Palmer 1992) and element connectedness (Palmer and Rock 1994).

Surprisingly few modern theorists have attempted to locate grouping process within the context of a temporally ordered theory of vision. Among those who have, grouping generally has been considered a "low-level" process that works on some relatively "early" image-based representation prior to the achievement of constancy and the operation of attention (e.g., Beck 1975; Hochberg 1971; Marr 1982; Neisser 1967; Treisman 1986).[1] The logic of this early approach to grouping is fairly persuasive and goes as follows. The image must be organized into discrete units before any later process can operate that requires such units as input. If grouping is the process that provides these discrete units, and if the operations underlying perceptual constancy presuppose such units, then grouping must operate before perceptual constancy. This early view of grouping was implicit in Wertheimer's original discussion and appears to represent conventional wisdom on the level at which grouping occurs.

As airtight as the early argument may appear logically, other theorists have argued that grouping may occur relatively late in perceptual

Originally published in *Psychonomic Bulletin and Review* 3 (1996): 75–80, under the title "Late Influences on Perceptual Grouping: Amodal Completion." Reprinted with permission.

processing, after constancy has been achieved and attentional has been deployed (e.g., Barrow and Tenenbaum 1978; Mack, Tang, Tuma, Kahn, and Rock 1992; Palmer and Rock 1994). The problem with the early argument is that it rests on two rather dubious assumptions: (1) that the discrete elements are derived from an unorganized image by grouping operations, and (2) that perceptual constancy requires the results of such grouping operations. Palmer and Rock (1994) have argued against the first assumption by pointing out that the kind of grouping Wertheimer (1923) actually demonstrated *presupposes* the existence of the to-be-grouped elements rather than providing an explanation. This exposes a processing gap between the unstructured image and the formation of elements from which the groups are to be constructed. To fill it, Palmer and Rock proposed that two processes were required: (1) an organizational principle, which they called "uniform connectedness" (UC), that designates a set of connected regions of roughly constant or slowly varying sensory qualities, and (2) figure-ground organization to determine which of the UC regions constitute figural objects rather than background. Both sorts of processes must operate *prior to* grouping operations because they are required to divide the unsegmented image into the figural elements that are then grouped into higher-order elements according to Wertheimer's principles.

Palmer and Rock (1994) also questioned the second assumption that grouping is required for constancy processing. In support, they pointed to a number of computational theories of depth and constancy processing that appear to operate quite independently of standard grouping operations. There are influential theories of stereoscopic depth interpretation, for example, that operate on ungrouped input from single receptors (e.g., Marr and Poggio 1977) or simple line and edge detectors (e.g., Marr and Poggio 1979). There are even theories that work on an image-based representation that is not divided into discrete elements of any type, relying instead on the output of local spatial frequency filters (e.g., Jones and Malik 1992). Thus it appears questionable to assume that grouping *must* occur prior to higher-level, postconstancy representations. The question remains: does it?

The level at which grouping processes operate is ultimately an empirical question, but answering it requires special conditions not present in standard demonstrations. The problem is that uniformly illuminated, flat, pictorial displays viewed in the frontal plane completely confound retinal and perceived properties. To examine the possibility that grouping occurs after constancy processing, one must employ more complex viewing conditions that separate retinal and perceived levels of representation, such as using depth and illumination effects to decouple them.

The first well-controlled experiment to explicitly examine the levels question concerned grouping by proximity. Rock and Brosgole (1964) investigated whether the distances that govern proximity grouping are defined in the two-dimensional image plane or in perceived three-dimensional space. They constructed a two-dimensional rectangular array of luminous beads that could be presented to observers in a dark room either in the frontal plane (perpendicular to the line of sight) or slanted in depth so that the horizontal dimension was foreshortened to a degree that depended on the angle of slant. The beads were actually closer together vertically than horizontally, so that when they were viewed in the frontal plane, observers always reported seeing them organized into columns rather than rows.

The crucial question was how the beads would be grouped when the observer saw the same lattice slanted in depth so that the beads were retinally closer together in the horizontal direction, but perceptually closer together in the vertical direction. When observers viewed this display binocularly, so that they had good depth information, they reported seeing the beads organized into vertical columns, just as in the frontal viewing condition. This result clearly supports the hypothesis that grouping occurs after constancy due to stereoscopic depth perception. At extreme slants, observers did report seeing the beads organized into rows, but Rock and Brosgole also showed that this occurred precisely when constancy broke down, leading to the erroneous perception that the beads were closer horizontally than vertically.

Thus, Rock and Brosgole (1964) found that grouping occurred on the basis of perceived three-dimensional proximity rather than two-dimensional retinal proximity. These results therefore support the hypothesis that grouping occurs relatively late in processing, at least after binocular depth information has been incorporated and perception is (approximately) veridical. Analogous conclusions have been drawn for grouping by the newly reported factors of common region (Palmer 1992) and element connectedness (Palmer and Rock 1994), because both grouping factors depend strongly on stereoscopic depth perception. What matters is the enclosure and the connectedness of elements in perceived three-dimensional space rather than in two-dimensional retinal space.

Recent experiments by Rock, Nijhawan, Palmer, and Tudor (1992) have extended the conclusion that grouping occurs after perceptual constancy to include lightness constancy. They investigated whether the important factor in similarity grouping based on achromatic color is the retinally measured *luminance* of the grouped elements or their phenomenally perceived *lightness* after lightness constancy has been achieved. The methods devised for these experiments are closely related to the present study.

Rock and his colleagues examined the role of lightness constancy in grouping using cast shadows and translucent overlays to decouple retinal luminance and perceived lightness. Observers were shown displays containing five columns of squares and were asked to report whether the central column appeared to group with the columns on the right or on the left. In the baseline control condition, only the reflectance of the central squares was varied by using different shades of gray paper. The central squares clearly grouped to the left with the squares having both the same retinal luminance and the same perceived lightness.

The crucial constancy display was carefully constructed so that the central squares were identical in reflectance to the squares on one side— that is, they were made of the same shade of gray paper—but were seen behind a strip of translucent, neutral-gray plastic. Under these conditions, the luminance of the central squares was identical to that of the squares on the other side. Thus, if grouping were based on relatively early processing of image structure, the central squares should be grouped with the luminance-matched ones. If it were based on relatively late processing after transparency perception had been achieved, they would group with the reflectance-matched ones.

The results supported the postconstancy grouping hypothesis: similarity was based on the perceived lightness of the squares rather than on their retinal luminance. A control condition that eliminated perceived transparency showed that this result was not due simply to grouping based on ratios of retinal luminances. All luminances in this control display were the same as in the original experiment except for those at the borders, where complete occlusion by the central gray strip blocked the perception of transparency, resulting in the perception of dark gray squares on top of a lighter gray background strip. In this case, all observers grouped the central column of squares with the dark ones, opposite to the grouping obtained in the transparency condition. Another experiment showed that the same results occurred when luminance and lightness were decoupled by casting a shadow across the central column of elements instead of hanging a plastic strip in front of them. Observers reported that the shadowed squares in the central column grouped with the reflectance-matched ones rather than with the luminance-matched ones. Thus, these results also demonstrate relatively late influences on similarity grouping.

This experiment extends this line of inquiry to another process that is often assumed to occur relatively late: namely, amodal completion of partly occluded objects. It is well known that if observers see a simple object partly occluded by another, there is a strong tendency to perceive its shape as completed amodally (i.e., without direct stimulus support from any sensory modality) behind the occluding object. It is also widely believed that this process must be a relatively late one, occurring after the determination of relative depth relations among objects based on the "pictorial" cue of interposition or occlusion. The present question is whether grouping by shape similarity will be determined by the retinal shape of uncompleted elements or by the perceived shape of completed elements. If grouping occurs entirely before completion, shape similarity should be governed by the retinal shape of the uncompleted elements. If it occurs after completion or if it is an extended process that has some component after completion, then grouping should be determined by the perceived shape of the elements as completed behind the occluding object.

This question is addressed using methods similar to those developed by Rock et al. (1992). In each display, the question is whether the central column of half circles groups with the other half circles on one side or with the whole circles on the other side in displays like those shown in figure 5.1. When there is no bar in the display (figure 5.1E), grouping is clearly governed by simple shape similarity: the central row of half circles groups strongly and unambiguously with the other half circles.[2] The crucial question is what happens with a comparable display in which the central half circles can be perceived as amodally completed whole circles behind an occluding bar, as shown in figure 5.1A. A precompletion view of grouping predicts that the central elements will group with the half circles on the right because that is their retinal shape; a postcompletion view predicts that they will group with the full circles on the left because that is their perceived shape. The vast majority of observers of this demonstration agree that they group with the whole circles, supporting the postcompletion view.

But even if the central column is grouped with the full circles, as predicted by the postcompletion view, there is an ambiguity of interpretation due to the presence of the occluding rectangle because it divides the elements into two regions. Palmer (1992) has recently shown that "common region" is a powerful factor in grouping, and so might determine the outcome in the completion demonstration (figure 5.1A). Predictions based on similarity of completed shape and on common region are therefore confounded in this demonstration display.

To disentangle these two grouping effects, a study was undertaken in which the factors of common region and shape similarity were orthogonally combined. Figure 5.1 shows the 2 × 2 design. Note first that all the figures in the middle column are half circles on the retina.[3] Effects of amodal completion on grouping should be evident in differences between the top (A and B) and bottom (C and D) displays because they differ only in the contiguity of the rectangular strip with the straight side of the central half circles. If completion does not affect grouping, the displays in the top

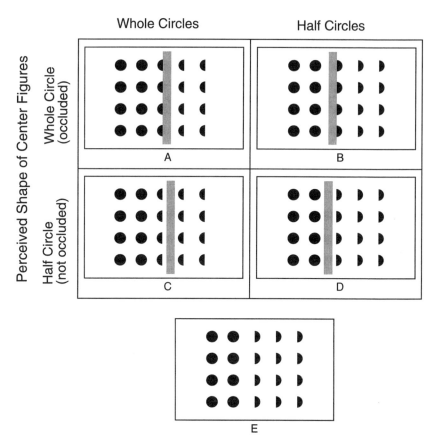

Shape of Figures in Common Region

Whole Circles   Half Circles

Perceived Shape of Center Figures

Whole Circle (occluded)

Half Circle (not occluded)

A

B

C

D

E

Figure 5.1
The design of the present study. The factors of amodal completed shape and common region were orthogonally combined in displays A–D to study their independent effects and possible interaction. Display E shows a control condition in which the bar is not present.

row would produce the same results as the ones below it. Effects of common region should be evident in differences between the left (A and C) and right (B and D) displays because they differ only in the location of the occluding strip and the associated direction of the straight side of the half circles. If common region does not affect grouping, the displays in the left column should produce the same results as those to its right. The orthogonal design also allows the possible interaction of these two factors to be examined.

Method

Subjects
The subjects were thirteen females and eight males who were students at the University of California at Berkeley. They were volunteers recruited in the lobby of the psychology building and were given a candy bar for their participation.

Stimuli
The stimuli consisted of four types of experimental displays and four types of control displays. The eight experimental stimuli were the four displays shown in figures 5.1A–D, plus their mirror reversals. The control stimuli consisted of similar displays (in both mirror-image versions) containing (1) three columns of half circles and two of whole circles (figure 5.1E), (2) three columns of whole circles and two of half circles, (3) three columns of horizontal bars and two of vertical bars, and (4) three columns of squares and two of circles. Images of all experimental displays were mounted on 5 × 8-inch index cards. A blue strip of construction paper was pasted onto the cards where the gray rectangle is shown in figure 5.1 to maximize the impression of occlusion. (Blue paper was used simply to make the occluding strip obviously different in color from the array of black figures.) Two copies of each of these displays were constructed for a total of thirty-two stimulus cards.

Procedure
Subjects were asked to sort the cards according to whether they perceived the middle column as grouped with the columns to the right or left of it. They were told to place the cards in the right stack if the middle column grouped to the right and in the left stack if it grouped to the left. Subjects were then given four practice trials consisting of the four unambiguous control displays described above. The experimenter placed the first card in its appropriate pile and all but one of the subjects sorted the remaining three practice stimuli as expected. During the experiment proper, all

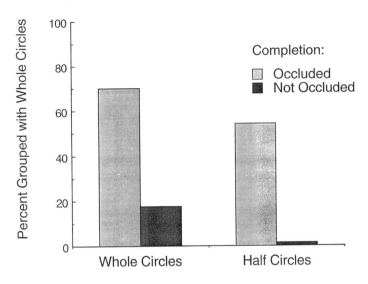

Figure 5.2
The results of the present study. Average percentage of subjects who grouped the central elements with the whole circles as a function of display type (see figure 5.1).

subjects sorted all thirty-two cards into the same two piles. The control stimuli were randomly intermixed with the experimental stimuli containing the occluding strip. Some subjects specifically asked about the occluder (because there was no occluder in the control stimuli used in the practice trials), to which the experimenter replied that the strip was part of the display and that the subject's task was still to decide whether the middle column grouped to the left or right. The deck of cards was shuffled prior to being used for another subject.

Results

One of the twenty subjects was eliminated because he gave inappropriate responses to several of the unambiguous control displays. Figure 5.2 shows the percentage of subjects who grouped the central half circles with the whole circles as a function of whether they were occluded or not (the amodal completion manipulation) and whether they were on the same or different side of the rectangular strip from the other columns of whole circles (the common region manipulation). There was a large effect due to similarity of the amodally completed shape, with the central figures being 54 percent more likely to be grouped with the whole circles when they were occluded by the rectangular strip than when they were not ($F(1, 19) = 36.01$, $p < .001$). There was also a main effect due to common region, with the central figures being 16 percent more likely to be grouped with the whole circles when they were on the same side than when they were on the opposite side ($F(1, 19) = 4.64$, $p < .05$). As the graph suggests, these two factors did not interact ($F < 1$).

Discussion

The results show quite clearly that perceptual grouping is affected by similarity of amodally completed shape as well as common region.[4] From this we infer that grouping either occurs after the processes that support visual completion or is a temporally extended process that includes components following or concurrent with completion. These results are thus compatible with those cited previously as showing that grouping involves the *perceived* rather than the *retinal* state of affairs (Palmer 1992; Palmer and Rock 1994; Rock and Brosgole 1964; Rock et al. 1992). As such, they reinforce the conclusion that grouping has relatively late components. Given the general consensus that completion is a fairly complex process involved in the construction of depth interpretations (e.g., Kellman and Shipley 1991), they extend the current line of evidence against the view that grouping occurs only early in perception.

There is an alternative to the conclusion that grouping occurs later than previously believed, however: completion might actually occur earlier than previously believed. He and Nakayama (1992) have suggested as much based on their conclusion that completion occurs prior to pop out. This ambiguity highlights a logical difficulty with drawing firm conclusions about how early or late a given process is by the method used here. If a stimulus manipulation associated with process X (say, completion) influences a response associated with process Y (say, grouping), all that can actually be concluded is that X occurs before or contiguous with Y. If such a result is found surprising given current theoretical assumptions about the temporal location of X and Y in visual processing, it can lead equally well to the conclusion that Y is later than previously assumed, that X is earlier, or both. We favor the conclusion that grouping occurs later than generally has been assumed largely because of the converging evidence reviewed in the introductory remarks: grouping is influenced by *many* different factors that were previously thought to affect perception relatively late in processing. One could equally well conclude that all of these processes occur earlier than previously assumed, but if enough such processes are claimed to be earlier, at some point the net effect is the same as saying that grouping is later than previously assumed.

The conclusion that grouping is a relatively late process raises a fairly important problem, however. If grouping occurs relatively late in visual processing, is it not logically necessary for there to be *some* organizational process at an early stage to support stereoscopic depth interpretation, lightness constancy, and visual completion, to name just a few of the important processes that have traditionally been presumed to depend on the results of early grouping processes? There seem to be two general possibilities. One is that essentially the same grouping principles operate both before and after constancy, with only the representations on which they operate being different. The other is that although constancy and completion processes may require *some* form of perceptual organization—for example, Palmer and Rock (1994) suggest lines, edges, and uniformly connected regions—this organization may be very different from the results of the kind of grouping processes discussed by Wertheimer. It might even be the case that processing local image information is sufficient to support these higher-level visual processes without any traditional grouping operations at all. Luminance edges, lines, blobs, and terminators at specific retinal locations such as those proposed in Marr's (1982) "primal sketch" and the output of local spatial frequency filters (e.g., Malik and Perona 1990; Jones and Malik 1992) are two possible candidates for constructing such a preconstancy representation. If such representations are sufficient for achieving constancy, the sort of grouping Wertheimer investigated might indeed occur *only* at some relatively late stage.

One potential difficulty for this "late-only" approach in the present results is the fact that subjects grouped the occluded circles with the full circles only 70 percent of the time, even when both completion and common region biased them toward this outcome. If grouping occurs *only* after completion, it seems that this datum should be much closer to 100 percent. To explain the discrepancy, one would have to claim that the cues for completion were weak in the present stimuli for some reason.[5] Although this is certainly a logical possibility, it seems more plausible that the discrepancy arises from a residual tendency toward grouping on the basis of uncompleted retinal shape.

This conjecture is consistent with the alternative view that grouping happens both early and late (Palmer and Rock 1994). Early grouping at the image-processing level would provide a preliminary organization that could be used to bootstrap the higher-level processes involved in constancy. The results of these processes could then modify the provisional two-dimensional organization that resulted from image-based grouping processes to conform to the perceived, postconstancy properties. In this case, the postconstancy grouping process would have to overcome the results of preconstancy grouping, and this might explain why the probability of grouping the occluded circles with the whole circles never reached 100 percent.

If grouping occurs both before and after constancy and completion processing, there are two quite distinct ways in which this might happen. The most obvious possibility is that grouping might take place in two distinct stages, one preceding and the other following constancy operations. However, grouping could also be a single process within a processing cascade (e.g., McClelland 1979), one that begins prior to constancy operations, but receives feedback from these later operations whose results are able to alter the grouping derived initially just from bottom-up information. (See Palmer and Rock 1995 for more discussion of this possibility.)

Although distinguishing among these possibilities is clearly an empirical problem, it is not obvious how to obtain definitive experimental evidence. One possibility is to use masking displays to terminate processing prior to constancy operations. Another is to use "deadline" response procedures to force subjects to respond before constancy operations are finished. But neither procedure can easily distinguish between the major alternatives. For the sake of argument, let us suppose that such procedures showed "early" organizational effects consistent with image-based features rather than perceived structure. At first blush, this might seem to indicate an early component to perceptual grouping. Further reflection suggests a second possibility, however. The same results could occur if there were *no* early grouping process, simply because a late grouping process cannot reflect constancy processing when there is insufficient time for that processing to be completed. The late grouping process would then merely be working with incompletely processed preconstancy information that had effectively "passed through" the constancy process unaltered. Because of this theoretical ambiguity of interpretation, we have not carried out such experiments. Other techniques we have not yet considered might yield more definitive results, however.

In any case, there is one conclusion from the present results that remains unquestionable: grouping is not a simple, early process that works only on properties of image-based representations. Rather, it is a much more sophisticated process, one that incorporates the results of pictorial depth perception, occlusion, and amodal completion as well as stereoscopic depth perception and lightness constancy.

Notes

Reprints should be requested from Stephen E. Palmer, Psychology Department, University of California, Berkeley, CA, 94720.

This research was supported in part by a National Institute of Mental Health grant 1-RO1-MH46141 to the first author jointly with Irvin Rock.

We wish to thank Irvin Rock, Nicola Bruno, James Cutting, Wendell Garner, James Pomerantz, and Johan Wagemans for their helpful comments on prior drafts of this chapter.

1. Although processes in vision can surely be located within a temporal continuum from very early to very late, we dichotomize the level at which grouping occurs in different theories into "early" versus "late" for simplicity. We take the dividing point to be the level at which constancylike operations occur—including perception of depth, occlusion, and completion—because such operations would appear to mark the change from a 2-D image-based representation to a 3-D environment-based one. In Marr's (1982) theory, for example, the primal sketch is clearly early by our criteria, and the "3-D volumetric description" clearly late, with the "2.5-D sketch" somewhere in between. We acknowledge that the early/late dichotomy is not as sharp as we would like due to the fact that constancy is not a unitary process, but a large collection of different operations that may take place at somewhat different times during visual processing. Still, we find the early/late distinction a simple and useful one.

2. Although only this version of the half circle control condition was included in the original experiment, a subsequent study was performed using both this display and one in which the half circles faced in the opposite direction (i.e., with their flat sides away from the circles). No differences were found between these two versions, suggesting that it is not a major factor in the experimental results.

3. The occluded circles appear to be slightly larger than the unoccluded ones due to an illusion in perceiving amodally completed figures. Kanizsa (1975) has shown that figures completed behind an occluder are perceived as measurably larger than equivalent control figures, presumably because they are seen to extend behind the occluder.

4. Although the effect of completed shape was substantially greater than than of common region, it is difficult to conclude anything from this fact. The problem is that the strength of both factors can vary over a substantial range depending on how they are operationalized. Which factor is strongest in any given experiment therefore may depend on the specific conditions employed. In the present experiment, the shape difference between circles and half circles is rather strong (compared with the difference between, say, squares and half squares) and the common region differences due to a single strip between regions are rather weak (compared with, say, borders that completely enclose two different regions).

5. We decided to paste the blue strips of construction paper abutting the half-circular central elements for precisely this reason: we wanted the information for occlusion to be as clear and unambiguous as possible. The thickness of the paper helped to create the impression that it was in front of and covering the visible half circles.

References

Barrow, H. G., and J. M. Tenenbaum. 1978. Recovering intrinsic scene characteristics from images. In Computer vision systems, edited by A. Hanson and E. Riseman, 3–26. New York: Academic Press.

Beck, J. 1975. The relation between similarity grouping and perceptual constancy. American Journal of Psychology 88:397–409.

He, Z. J., and K. Nakayama. 1992. Surfaces versus features in visual search. Nature 359:231–33.

Hochberg, J. 1971. Perception: I. Color and shape. In Experimental psychology, edited by J. W. Kling and L. A. Riggs, 395–474. New York: Holt, Rinehart & Winston.

Jones, D., and J. Malik. 1992. A computational framework for determining stereo correspondence from a set of linear spatial filters. In Proceedings of Second European Conference on Computer Vision, edited by G. Sandini, 395–410. Sanat Margherita Ligure, Italy: Springer Verlag.

Kanisza, G. 1975. Amodal completion and phenomenal shrinkage of visual surfaces. *Italian Journal of Psychology* 2:187–95.

Kellman, P. J., and T. F. Shipley. 1991. A theory of visual interpolation in object perception. *Cognitive Psychology* 23:141–221.

Mack, A., B. Tang, R. Tuma, S. Kahn, and I. Rock. 1992. Perceptual organization and attention. *Cognitive Psychology* 24:475–501.

Malik, J., and P. Perona. 1990. Preattentive texture discrimination with early vision mechanisms. *Journal of the Optical Society of America* A7:923–32.

Marr, D. 1982. *Vision.* San Francisco: Freeman.

Marr, D., and T. Poggio. 1977. Cooperative computation of stereo disparity. *Science* 194:283–87.

Marr, D., and T. Poggio. 1979. A computational theory of human stereo vision. *Proceedings of the Royal Society of London (Series B)* 204:301–28.

McClelland, J. L. 1979. On the time relations of mental processes: An examination of systems of processes in cascade. *Psychological Review* 86:287–330.

Neisser, U. 1967. *Cognitive Psychology.* New York: Appleton-Century-Crofts.

Palmer, S. E. 1992. Common region: A new principle of perceptual grouping. *Cognitive Psychology* 24:436–47.

Palmer, S. E., and I. Rock. 1994. Rethinking perceptual organization: The role of uniform connectedness. *Psychonomic Bulletin and Review* 1:29–55.

Palmer, S. E., and I. Rock. 1995. On the nature and order of perceptual organization: A reply to Peterson. *Psychonomic Bulletin and Review* 1:515–19.

Rock, I., and L. Brosgole. 1964. Grouping based on phenomenal proximity. *Journal of Experimental Psychology* 67:531–38.

Rock, I., R. Nijhawan, S. Palmer, and L. Tudor. 1992. Grouping based on phenomenal similarity of achromatic color. *Perception* 21:779–89.

Treisman, A. 1986. Properties, parts, and objects. In *Handbook of perception and human performance,* vol. 2, edited by K. R. Boff, L. Kaufman, and J. P. Thomas, 35-1–35-70. New York: Wiley.

Wertheimer, M. 1923. Untersuchungen zur Lehre von der Gestalt. II. *Psychologische Forschung* 4:301–50. Partial translation in *A sourcebook of Gestalt psychology,* edited by W. D. Ellis, 71–81. New York: The Humanities Press, 1950.

Part III
Shape

The message in all the chapters in this part is this: Perceived shape is a mental construction based on the perceived location of its regions relative to one another. Perceived shape is, therefore, indirect in the sense that processes must first occur that lead to the perceived location of the parts or regions that will form the boundaries of the object. We should distinguish "region" from "part" because not all objects have specifiable subparts. An outline square can be divided into distinct parts (i.e., its four sides) but a circle cannot. However, a circle does have an outer boundary, and that boundary can be regarded as consisting of various regions. So, for a figure like a circle with the smoothly changing directions of its boundary, it is the collective aggregation of these perceived directions that forms the basis for perceiving its overall shape.

Of all the studies included in this part, the research by myself and Christopher Linnett, described in chapter 6, most directly manipulates the perceived direction of the subparts that make up the figures investigated. This is done by presenting the parts *over time* and requiring eye movements that place these parts in locations on the retina that, if seen simultaneously, would give rise to an entirely different shape from that objectively presented on the computer screen. However, if constancy of direction prevails for these same parts such that their location is veridically perceived, then collectively they constitute the shape that was actually presented. In this investigation, therefore, it is beyond dispute that the phenomenal shape is the indirect consequence of the prior perception of the location of its parts.

These results dovetail nicely with the argument made repeatedly by Julian Hochberg (1968, 1981, 1982) to the effect that, to be perceived, shape requires successive eye movements and the spatiotemporal integration of the sequence of images stimulating the fovea. (This presumes that little useful information is picked up from regions of the figure that do not fall on the fovea). Thus, according to this view, we must achieve an integration of parts of objects all the time in daily life by a process similar to the one subjects employ in this investigation.

The message in the next two chapters is similar to that in chapter 6: namely, that phenomenal objects can be synthesized from regions presented piecemeal over time. This is achieved by a method known as anorthoscopic perception, in which either a figure moves behind a narrow stationary aperture or the narrow aperture moves in front of a stationary figure (Rock 1975). Only a small region of the figure is therefore visible at any time. If one can be sure that the aperture is not displacing over the retina—as has now been ascertained to be the case—then the perception of the figure in its entirety cannot be explained by the extended image of the figure being "painted" across the retina over time. Rather, it would seem necessary to conclude that the anorthoscopic percept is the end result of synthesizing a continuous set of directions into an overall shape.

Chapter 7 contains a discussion of the entire problem of anorthoscopic perception, which includes far more than just the question of perceiving shape by integrating perceived directions. There is the prior question of why we see a shape being revealed over time instead of a visible element bobbing up and down within a narrow slit, which is literally the stimulus the eye directly receives. Perceptual processes of problem solving are alleged to be necessary, and many unanswered questions about such problem solving remain.

Chapter 8 seeks to show, using a variation of the anorthoscopic paradigm, that a shape can be "created" even when the element visible through the slit is not displaced at all. This phenomena is called induced shape because an impression of motion in the opposite direction in the aperture and its opaque surround is induced by the motion of a textured background. It is one of those phenomena—as is anorthoscopic perception per se—that needs to be seen to be fully appreciated. Unfortunately, this is not possible in static illustrations such as the ones provided in this chapter.

The next several chapters all bear on the role of orientation in the perception of shape. As noted in chapter 1, orientation affects shape in establishing which parts of the object are located at the top, bottom, left, and right. These "sides" of the object are given by information concerning what is up and down in the environment and not by what is up and down in the retinal image of the object. Thus, the first step for the observer is to establish these reference directions through orientation constancy operations. Only then can the assignment of these perceived directions affect phenomenal shape. So here again, the perception of shape is indirect. The logic and evidence for these conclusions is presented in chapter 9.

A second article in this series (chapter 10) deals with the perception of symmetry about a vertical axis. It is known that when the axis is vertical, the perception of symmetry is strong whereas it is not evident that phenomenal symmetry occurs at all, at least spontaneously, when the axis of symmetry is horizontal or oblique. At any rate, the by now familiar question arises: is it perceived or retinal verticality that is relevant? This chapter by myself and Leaman presents evidence that resolves the question and discusses the implications.

Chapter 11 reports a similar, but much more recent study concerning another phenomenon of orientation perception. Ferrante, Gerbino, and Rock (chapter 11) studied the perception of the right angle. Right angles that are upright—that is, the sides of which are vertical and horizontal—appear immediately as right angles. One can easily discriminate between a right angle and slightly lesser or greater angles, such as 88 or 92 degrees. But if the angle is oblique, such that its symmetrical axis is vertical rather than either of its sides, then it does not look like a right angle, and the above discriminations are not easily made. The chapter describes experiments that separate the perceived vs. the retinal orientation of the right angle because the effect of uprightness of the angle—an instance of the oblique effect (Appelle 1972)—could be based on either of these factors. This particular effect could be rooted in basic sensory properties of the visual system, such as the larger distribution of neurons sensitive to the vertical and horizontal orientation of contours and edges with respect to the retina. If so, we would expect the effect to be a class 1 oblique effect following the classification suggested by Essock (1980). But it could also be a class 2 oblique effect in which the effect reduces to the initial perception of the angle's sides as vertical and horizontal in the environment. If so, the phenomenal right angle is a derivative of the perceived orientations of its parts and not simply a "good Gestalt" of the whole figure.

In a final part of this section on the perception of shape are a few chapters that fit better here than elsewhere, although the first of these is not concerned with the perception of shape, but rather with the possibly deeper issue of the perception of objects. It concerns masking or, more precisely, backward pattern masking. When a figure is followed more or less immediately by another figure or a pattern that overlaps it, usually line by line, the initial figure is not perceived or it is not adequately perceived. Ordinarily, the mask is superimposed on the locus of regions occupied by the figure or target. One would think this to be a plausible way to proceed if one wants to achieve the interference or masking effect.

However, this typical procedure leaves unclarified the question of whether the masking has its effect because its retinal image is superimposed over the retinal image of the target, as is plausible, or possibly because its perceived location in the world is exactly where the target had appeared to be. A priori, this would seem to be unlikely. As the reader knows full well by now, these two meanings of "superimposed" can be separated, in this case by requiring the subject to track a moving dot. This can result in the placement of the location of the mask vis-a-vis the target anywhere one chooses and allow separating the mask from the target in retinal or phenomenal space. The surprising result is described by Charles White in chapter 12. It would seem that even an effect heretofore thought of as low level and sensory may be indirect. First one must achieve the veridical perception of a mask's direction based on constancy operations of direction before interference from a mask can occur. Both target and mask must appear in the same *subjective* direction, not merely the same objective location, because the investigator first notes and then follows up on the fact that there is some loss in directional constancy.

White also investigated backward masking in relation to retinal or phenomenal location of the mask when the changed location of the mask is achieved by saccadic rather than pursuit eye movements. Here the result is the opposite to what occurs with pursuit eye movement. The retinal location is what matters. White speculates that the different outcomes for the two kinds of eye movement can be understood in terms of the functional significance for vision of these two oculomotor systems. In tasks like reading, which entails a series of saccades, one wants what one is now fixating to be seen optimally, and the rest of the text to be suppressed. That means that whatever is foveal at time 2 will be in the same retinal location as something else that stimulated it at time 1. It makes sense for that prior stimulation to be masked, which is what occurs with saccadic eye movement (i.e., *retinal* masking). For smooth pursuit eye movements, however, the main function would appear to be maintaining foveal fixation of a target. That calls for effective masking of the background and thus depends upon target and background appearing in the same place. That, in turn, would enhance the visibility of the target that is pursued.

Further evidence along this line was provided by Lehmkuhle and Fox (1980) who varied the stereoscopic distance between the plane of the target (a Landolt C with a gap) and the plane of the mask. The effect of masking clearly declined with increasing separations in depth, although there was a curious asymmetry in result depending upon whether the mask was in front of or in back of the target. At any rate, we have here further evidence that it is the identity of the *perceived* (rather than retinal) location of target and mask that matters for backward masking. Since, once again, depth must first be achieved (in this case by stereopsis), in order for the observer to assign contours to differing planes in depth, then masking can hardly be the direct, sensory process it has previously been believed to be.

In a final chapter in this section an investigation is described that concerns an aspect of symmetry other than verticality. It concerns the fact that the two "halves" of a figure about the axis of symmetry look similar or identical. One might say that the appearance of equality about the y axis is the reason why the figure looks symmetrical. Once again, however, one can inquire whether it may not be the perception of equality of halves that matters for symmetry, but simply the fact that the retinal images on the two sides of the axis *are* identical. Ordinarily both of these are true when the perception of symmetry is examined.

To separate them Janet Szlyk and her coinvestigators slanted the figures in depth, about an environmentally vertical axis (see chapter 13). This has the effect of foreshortening the projection of the figure along the horizontal direction, but of foreshortening the more distant half of the figure more than the nearer half. Thus, symmetry on the retina is no longer present. Given constancy of shape, however, the two halves may be perceived to be equal. In the investigation, the shape of the figure is manipulated as is both the shape of the two halves of the figure and the perception of its slant. The results once again show the indirectness of the process: First, via constancy operations, one achieves either an equality or inequality of the two halves of the figures; then one either perceives symmetry or asymmetry depending upon the figure and whether depth perception is or is not allowed.

References

Appelle, S. 1972. Perception and discrimination as a function of stimulus orientation: The "oblique effect" in man and animals. *Psychological Bulletin* 78:266–78.

Essock, E. A. 1980. The oblique effect of stimulus identification considered with respect to two classes of oblique effects. *Perception* 9:445–49.

Hochberg, J. 1968. In the mind's eye. In *Contemporary theory and research in visual perception*, edited by R. N. Haber, 309–31. New York: Holt.

Hochberg, J. 1981. Levels of perceptual organization. In *Perceptual organization*, edited by M. Kubovy and J. R. Pomerantz, 255–78. Hillsdale, NJ: Erlbaum.

Hochberg, J. 1982. How big is a stimulus? In *Representation and organization in perception*, edited by J. Beck, 95–144. Hillsdale, NJ: Erlbaum.

Lehhmkule, S., and R. Fox. 1980. Effect of depth separation on metacontrast masking. *Journal of Experimental Psychology: Human Perception and Performance* 6:605–21.

Rock, I. 1975. *An introduction to perception.* New York: Macmillan.

Chapter 6

Shape and the Retinal Image

Irvin Rock and Christopher M. Linnett

Introduction

It has been assumed that processing the shape of an object begins with, or is based on, the shape of its retinal image. Of course, we do not mean to imply that the processing underlying the perception of shape is nothing more than the transmission of the image to the visual cortex. It is now generally believed that images are encoded by neural mechanisms that respond to extended stimulation of receptive fields such as contours or edges (Hubel and Wiesel 1962) or specific spatial frequencies (Campbell and Robson 1968; De Valois et al. 1979). Nonetheless, these mechanisms are presumably grounded in the *location* of the retinal stimulation, and it is well known that these neural mechanisms in the visual cortex are retinotopically organized.

Thus it still seems correct to say that the shape of the image on the retina ought to play a fundamental role in the perception of shape. Why else would an eye have evolved in which the shape of the retinal image is a faithful representation of the shape of the external object—at least in the case of surfaces normal to the line of sight—and why else would a neuroanatomical system have evolved which preserves the spatial relationships of the retinal image via retinotopic mapping in the projection of fibers to the visual cortex? To put the matter in the form of a rhetorical question, would shape be veridically perceivable if the retinal image bore no geometrical correspondence whatever to the external object it represented? When an object is slanted into the third dimension, the situation is acknowledged to be more complicated, and it is assumed that constancy mechanisms correct for the distortion of the shape of the image projected to the retina. But even here the process is thought to begin with the shape of the image on the retina, and information about depth presumably leads to a correction of the image-implied shape.

We shall restrict our analysis here to the case of two-dimensional objects in the frontal plane. The main point we wish to make is that there

Originally published in *Perception* 22 (1993): 61–76, under the title "Is a Perceived Shape Based on Its Retinal Image?" Reprinted with permission.

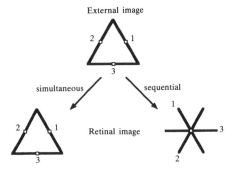

Figure 6.1
Two possible retinal images from viewing a triangle. The triangle composite on the left is the result of simultaneously viewing all three sides of the triangle. The asterisk composite on the right is the result of sequentially fixating the center of one side of the triangle at a time.

are two possible bases for shape perception under such conditions, which are virtually always confounded: one is the shape of the retinal image and the other is the shape based on information concerning the relative location of the parts of the object. When we see a shape such as a triangle, it is always the case that a triangular image stimulates the retina; it is also the case that we have information about the actual location of the parts of the triangle relative to one another. The latter information derives primarily from the perceived radial direction of these parts with respect to the observer. To make this clear by example, imagine that, instead of holding the eyes still, one fixates successively on the center of each side of the triangle. Assume further that only the fixated sides will enter into the processing of the triangle as a whole. Under such conditions the retinal image of the three successively fixated sides forms an image of an asterisk, not a triangle (see figure 6.1). However, given the mechanism by which eye position is taken into account in assessing the direction of a fixated point, each such central point of the three sides of the triangle should be correctly localized in space. This process has been referred to as compensation, corollary discharge, or constancy of direction. In short, the information is available that these three fixated points are locations differing from one another and that the sides of which they are the centers are arranged in a triangular configuration.

Therefore, we may perceive the triangular shape not because it happens to yield a composite triangular image, but because we veridically perceive the relative location of its sides based on information from eye position. In the ordinary case, when we see the triangle in its entirety based on a single fixation, the same argument holds. Here the veridical location of the three sides in space is given by the single position of the eyes in relation to the location of the retinal images of the three sides. The theoretical issue can be thought of in terms of the level or stage of processing that underlies shape perception. If the processing of shape begins directly with the shape of the retinal image, then the stage or level of processing is a relatively early one. But if the processing of shape does not begin until the locations of the parts of the object are perceived, which in turn depends upon a constancy mechanism, then shape perception is clearly based on a relatively late stage or higher-level operation.

Ordinarily, these two possible bases of shape perception are confounded. But it is possible to separate them if the parts of a figure are presented successively and the observer is required to move his or her eyes as each part is presented, as in the example given above.[1] The parts must be presented successively, and rapidly enough to allow a synthesis of the parts into a composite phenomenal shape, but not so rapidly that the eyes cannot make the required movements in time to change fixation. We achieved these conditions by requiring the subject to track a rapidly moving target point as it traced out a circular path, with smooth-pursuit eye movements—rather than saccadic eye movements (which we had tried in pilot experiments). During the tracking, line components of figures were flashed in particular locations so that, were they all seen simultaneously, they would have constituted a particular composite shape on the computer screen. However, by virtue of the eye movement, the relative locations of these components on the retina created an entirely different composite shape—the retinal image. The speed of presentation, though, was not fast enough to create the impression of a composite shape that appeared to be simultaneously present.

Were the screen and/or other objects in the scene visible, the location of each component of the figure could have been perceived based on its position relative to the screen or to other objects. But in the dark such object-relative information was not available and the only basis for the localization of components was subject-relative, which in turn was based on eye position. Because our experiment was conducted in the dark, when we refer to a composite shape on the computer screen, we do so simply as a convenient and unambiguous way of describing the composite of the figure as it would in fact be seen on the screen were all its components visible simultaneously. This configuration is also the composite based on relative locations with respect to the observer.

We also separated the relative retinal locations of the parts of a figure from their perceived relative locations in space by using a moving frame of reference. In this case it was not necessary to require the subjects to move their eyes while the parts of the figure were successively flashed.

Method

Subjects
Eleven subjects participated in the experiment, all but two of whom were paid for their time. None knew about the hypothesis under investigation, although all had some background in psychology.

Apparatus and Stimuli
The component contours of shapes were presented successively via an IBM AT personal computer connected to two monitors. The stimulus monitor was a Sony Trinitron 13-inch color monitor driven by the AT&T TARGA-16 color graphics board. Each contour was briefly presented; this was followed by an interstimulus interval (ISI) before the presentation of the next component.

The rationale for determining the ISIs and "on" times was as follows. We wanted the cycle of presentation of all components of a figure to be as brief as possible so that the phenomenal impression of a figure, albeit successively presented, would be as close as possible to one in which all components were seen simultaneously. But a constraint was the time required to track the moving fixation target. In those conditions in which the fixation target moved, it did so counterclockwise in a circular path with a diameter of 5.6 deg of visual angle (3.25 cm). We wanted accurate tracking in which the eyes kept pace with the moving target and we found the maximum speed for such tracking to be slightly less than 1 revolution per second. We wanted the "on" time to be as brief as possible, with the constraint that it would be long enough for the component to be clearly visible. An "on" time of 67 ms was found to be the best. To avoid smearing of a component across the retina, the fixation target actually stopped briefly during the presentation of the component. The stoppage of motion of the target during these 67 ms gave a slightly jerky impression to the smooth circular motion of the target. It did not seriously interfere with smooth tracking. We alerted subjects to the fact that these brief pauses would happen during their tracking of the target and it did not present a problem.

The total revolution time was therefore the sum of the "on" times and ISIs: 1390 ms and 1270 ms for shapes with three and four components, respectively. The ISIs for the three-component figures were 397 ms; for the four-component figures they were 251 ms. The three-component figures were a triangle and an asterisk, the four-component figures were a square and a cross. The cross had two components, but was treated as having four, like the square, so when the target rotated, four line presentations occurred during one revolution. The sequence of the components was repeated five times, and the interval between the last component of one series and the first component of the next series was equal to the ISI.

The room was totally dark for all conditions. The target was a red square and the contour components of the figures were bright white lines on a dark computer screen. To render the monitor screen invisible, the subjects viewed through several sheets of red acetate filter such that only the target and figure components were visible. We made the target red so that through the red filter it would appear dim and thus contrast with the bright lines, but would still be clearly visible on the dark background. Everything appeared as shades of red through the filter. Given the dark-field conditions, the *only* basis for the perceived location of contour components was the relation between image location and eye position. Information as to the location of components with respect to the screen and to objects in the room was not available, and there was no lingering phosphor illumination from the previous line presentation at the time of the current line presentation.[2] In this sense the experiment was conservative because veridical perception of the relative location of components depended entirely on the mechanism underlying constancy of direction, entailing information about eye position.

The subject sat at a distance of 33 cm from the monitor screen, and used a chin rest. The moving fixation target was a small square (0.24 cm on each side) which subtended a visual angle of 0.4 deg. The triangle and asterisk figure components subtended angles of 9.5 deg long and 0.3 deg wide (5.52 cm × 0.16 cm), and the cross and square figure components were each 5.5 deg long and 0.3 deg wide (3.20 cm × 0.16 cm).

In all conditions the subjects reported on the shape of the composite of the components by selecting one of four alternative shapes presented on the computer screen. Subjects were instructed to give a verbal signal after the end of the five cycles to indicate that they were ready for the recognition test to appear; this gave them a brief pause to contemplate the shape of the composite figure. The four alternative shapes are shown in figure 6.2; their sizes were the same as those of the stimuli presented. They were arranged on the screen in two rows of two, and the location of each was randomized across conditions and subjects. The rationale for the construction of the set of choice patterns was as follows. It included the figure which was correct if all parts had been on simultaneously and their relative directions accurately perceived. It also included the figure which would be generated by the locations of the successive components in the composite retinal image. The other two figures were compromises between these two extreme alternatives, with one being more similar to the figure that was successively presented on the screen and one being more similar to the figure that was successively presented on the retina.

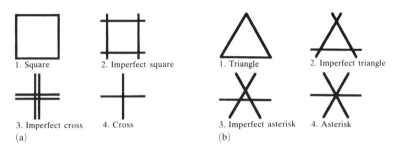

1. Square   2. Imperfect square   1. Triangle   2. Imperfect triangle

3. Imperfect cross   4. Cross   3. Imperfect asterisk   4. Asterisk
(a)   (b)

Figure 6.2
Response choices shown to subjects in all conditions. (a) Choices for the square and cross
figures. (b) Choices for the triangle and asterisk figures.

Procedure

All subjects were first given practice trials in the most difficult condition,
namely the one in which they had to track the target that moved in a circular path (condition 2). The tracking task was first explained to them.
They were told to accurately track the target in its circular path, given the
brief haltings of the target, while the figure components flashed at their
various locations. Subjects were given a demonstration of the rotating
target alone, and then four practice trials with each figure once. In a trial,
the target made five revolutions alone and then five revolutions with presentation of the figure components. Next, the appropriate recognition test
was given, and the subject selected the composite which looked most
like the one presented sequentially. Subjects were told to base their selection on the spontaneous impression of how the sequence of components
would look if they were all visible at the same time, without thinking
about what the figure could or should be.

Afterimage Procedure

After these practice trials an afterimage procedure was run to test a subject's tracking accuracy and improve it through more practice if necessary.
The purpose of this test was to determine the composite of the sequence
of contour components on the retina—the afterimage. If subjects did not
track with reasonable accuracy, then the interpretation of the experimental results would be very different. Imagine the case where a subject
did not track at all. The retinal image and the perceived location of the
figure components relative to one another would be the same. So we
needed evidence about the success of tracking. Eye-movement recordings
would have been difficult to obtain under our dark-field conditions and
would have lengthened the time of the experiment greatly. The afterimage method yielded the same knowledge in a much simpler way.

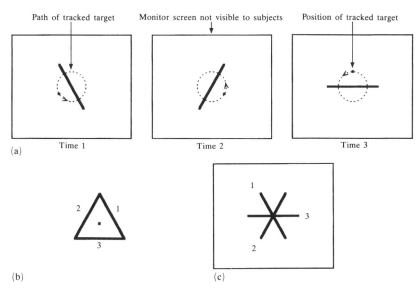

Figure 6.3
(a) A schematic representation of the afterimage procedure and condition 2 which involved tracking of a revolving target. The figure shows the conditions for producing an after-image of a triangle when the composite of an asterisk is displayed successively on the screen. The component contours flashed when the target was in the positions indicated in the three time frames. (b) The composite image on the retina. (c) The composite in relation to the screen; this is also the composite percept based on the phenomenal directions of each contour with respect to the subject, and would be seen if the eyes remained stationary.

For every subject, we presented the asterisk figure sequentially with the subject tracking the target. In this condition the target was magenta and the line components of the figure white. No red filters were used so that luminance was increased. The luminance of the magenta target was 31.0 cd m^{-2} and the luminance of the white contours was 99.5 cd m^{-2}. For the asterisk, each component flashed when the target was peripheral to the center of one of the contours, with the result that the retinal image of the composite was that of a triangle (see figure 6.3). In pre-testing with other observers we found that a negative afterimage of the entire figure was indeed established from the sequential presentation and remained present phenomenally, albeit briefly and weakly, at the end of the five cycles of the figure presentation. The subjects viewed the afterimage by closing their eyes for a few seconds immediately after the presentation, and then opening them and looking at the still dim computer screen. The afterimage looked like a figure with dark lines. If and only if the subject tracked the target would the afterimage look like a triangle. Otherwise it would look like an asterisk. As many trials were given to each subject as were necessary for him or her to achieve the appropriate afterimage, and occasionally a few more.

Results of the Afterimage Procedure. Every subject was able to see an afterimage of the composite of the successive contour components. By the end of the afterimage trials all subjects achieved either a perfect or imperfect triangle afterimage (figure 6.2b, 1 or 2) indicating that they were tracking with either perfect or near perfect accuracy. The number of trials required to achieve this perception varied from one to eight; even those subjects who tracked accurately on the first trial were given one or two more trials. By the last trial, all subjects succeeded in seeing at least the imperfect triangle.

We interpret the results to mean that many subjects could not track the moving target with perfect accuracy and instead tended to track in a path of a diameter slightly less than the one in which the target actually moved. This corresponds with the finding of Fujii (1943) and Coren et al. (1975). However, even an imperfect-triangle afterimage is one that implies rather good tracking. Therefore we assumed that the composite retinal image created by tracking was one that was radically different from the composite percept generated by the perceived location of the component contours relative to one another—in the case of the afterimage trials, an asterisk.

Having completed the afterimage trials the subjects participated in each of the four conditions of the experiment. For purposes of clarity we shall describe each of those conditions and give the results separately. The order of the conditions was randomized between subjects, and each subject was shown each of the four figures in each condition in a random order.

Condition 1: Fixation of a Stationary Target

This condition was a control designed to establish just how accurately subjects could perceive the composite configuration created by the successive presentation and select the correct figure from among the four alternatives offered in the test. Subjects maintained fixation on a stationary centrally located target. The target was red and the line components were white (to make them maximally brighter than the target), but through the filter everything appeared in shades of red and differed only in luminance. The luminances through the filter were 0.5 cd m^{-2} for the target and 2.6 cd m^{-2} for the line components. Since the eyes were presumably stationary, the configuration of component images on the retina should have been the same as the configuration based on the *perceived* location of these components relative to one another. Therefore the pre-

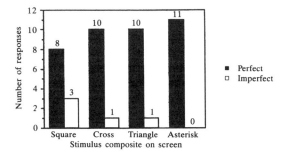

Figure 6.4
Results of condition 1 which involved fixation of a stationary target. In this condition the composite in relation to the monitor screen is the same as the composite retinal image.

diction was that subjects would perceive the configuration veridically, i.e., as if all the components were seen on the screen simultaneously. But there might have been some lack of precision in the perception of the configuration simply because the contours were not seen simultaneously. Thus, for example, when a triangle pattern was displayed, a subject might have been uncertain that the end points of each contour met precisely with one another. In that event the subject might have chosen the imperfect triangle rather than the perfect triangle (i.e., figure 6.2b, 2 instead of 1). It was important to assess such errors in evaluating the results of the other conditions.

Results
Subjects had little difficulty in integrating the successive components into a composite percept. In the 44 trials (eleven subjects, four figures per subject), 39 responses were perfectly correct. The other 5 responses were selections of the imperfect version of the composite (figure 6.2a, 2 and 3 for the square and cross, and figure 6.2b, 2 and 3 for the triangle and asterisk, respectively). Figure 6.4 shows the results for each figure separately. The few selections of the imperfect version tell us that even under these ideal conditions there was still some error. No statistical analyses were performed in this and the subsequent experiments reported here because an appropriate test could not be found, and further, the significance of the pattern of results from all four conditions is, in a sense, more of a qualitative than quantitative nature.[3]

The reader may wonder whether any afterimage, such as was generated in the condition testing for afterimages, was generated in this or in any of the other conditions to be described. If this were so the afterimages could obviously interfere with the purpose of the experiment. In fact, no afterimages were visible in any of the four conditions of the experiment, because subjects viewed the presentations through red filters which lowered the luminance of the display considerably. More objective evidence on this question is based on a consideration of conditions 2 and 4. If an afterimage were present in those conditions, and, as is plausible, the subjects based their recognition choices on it, they would choose figures based on the composite retinal image rather than on the composite based on the relative location of the parts. As will be seen, however, this was not what the majority of subjects did.

Condition 2: Tracking a Moving Target

As already explained briefly, in this condition the subjects tracked the moving target while also noting the shape of the configuration of component contours. They had already been given practice in this condition and the afterimage results indicated that each subject could perform the task. They were told that the path of motion of the target would be circular but slightly jerky because the target would stop momentarily as each component contour was flashed (see figure 6.3). The target was red and the contours were white, as in condition 1.

At the end of the ten cycles of the moving target (five alone and five with component presentation) subjects were shown the four choices in the test pattern. By tracking the target, there were now two possible bases for choice for the subjects on the test. They could choose the configuration that corresponded to the retinal image created. In the case of the asterisk figure, for example, that would mean choosing either the triangle pattern or imperfect triangle pattern (figure 6.2b, 1 or 2, respectively). Or the subjects could choose the configuration that corresponded to the arrangement of the components relative to one another as they appeared on the monitor screen. In the case of the asterisk figure, that would mean choosing the asterisk or imperfect asterisk pattern (figure 6.2b, 4 or 3, respectively). The logic of the possible choices in the test for the triangle, square, and cross figures was the same.

Results

Overall, subjects chose the test pattern that corresponded to the composite on the screen 19 times (e.g., the perfect triangle when a triangle was presented, the perfect cross when a cross was presented, and so on). They chose the test pattern that corresponded to a hypothetical imperfect composite on the screen 14 times (e.g., the imperfect triangle when a triangle was presented, and so on). They chose the test pattern that was closer to the retinal-image composite 10 times, and the alternative that perfectly matched the retinal-image composite once. For the asterisk, for example, these choices correspond to figure 6.2b, 4, 3, 2, and 1, respectively. Figure 6.5 gives a figure-by-figure analysis, with the results shown sepa-

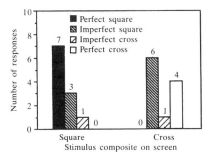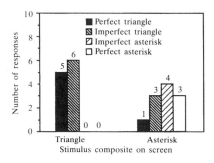

Figure 6.5
Results of condition 2. In this condition the composite in relation to the monitor screen is different from the composite retinal image.

rately for the square and cross figures, and for the triangle and asterisk figures. When a square stimulus was presented, it tended to be perceived as a square (or imperfect square) and when a triangle stimulus was presented, it tended to be seen as a triangle (or imperfect triangle), and so on. Had the composite percepts been based on the retinal state of affairs, when a square stimulus was presented it would have tended to be perceived as a cross (or an imperfect cross), and when a triangle stimulus was presented it would have tended to be perceived as an asterisk (or an imperfect asterisk), and so on.

There were errors, however, and subjects often chose the imperfect rather than the perfect figure in the test corresponding to the composite that had been presented sequentially, as can be seen in figure 6.5. But this is not surprising for several reasons. One is that some errors of this kind were made in condition 1. To perceive the correct alternative requires the precise match up of end points or central regions. However, there were admittedly more "imperfect" selections in condition 2 than in condition 1. Another reason for this outcome was the difficulty of the task. It is not easy to track the circular path of the target on the one hand and note the shape of the composite configuration on the other. Still, if one adds together the selections which were either perfect or imperfect representations of the stimulus composite on the monitor screen, the results are 33 of these selections versus only 11 selections based on either the perfect or imperfect retinal-image composites. Thus 75% of the selections were based primarily on how the component contours were *perceived* to fit together and only 25% on how their retinal images fit together.

Condition 3: Tracking a Moving Target within a Moving Square Frame

This condition is based on the possibility that the perceived location of the components of a configuration vis-à-vis one another might be determined by where these components were perceived to be located with respect to a frame of reference. A contour that has a certain location relative to a reference frame might well appear to be conjoined with other contours on the basis of their locations relative to that frame of reference into a composite shape. This might occur even though the location of each of these contours with respect to the observer and to the monitor screen would yield an entirely different composite shape. Reference-frame effects have been shown to be important with respect to phenomena such as motion (Duncker 1929), orientation of the vertical of space (Asch and Witkin 1948a, 1948b; Witkin and Asch 1948; Di Lorenzo and Rock 1982), orientation and form (Rock 1973), and so forth. For a review of such effects and their theoretical implications, see Rock (1990).

In this condition, a square outline and the target at its center traveled together in a circular path on the screen at the same rate as the target alone had traveled in condition 2. This was the only change from condition 2. The square frame was 11 cm on each side and subtended a visual angle of 18.6 deg at the distance at which the subject sat. The target and the frame were red, the figural lines were white. The procedure used in this condition creates a conflict between what one ought to perceive based on the location of the component contours on the retina as well as their location with respect to the frame of reference on the one hand, with what one ought to perceive based on their location with respect to the screen or the observer on the other hand. In other words, the retinal image is the same as the frame-of-reference figure, and these are in conflict with the composite figure on the screen. If, for example, the components would create an asterisk on the screen, the subject's retinal image would be a triangle, as in condition 2, and the components with respect to the frame of reference would also form a triangle. The situation is shown schematically in figure 6.6. Thus here the prediction based on the retinal state of affairs was the same as the one based on the phenomenal state of affairs *if and only if* the latter was primarily governed by the stimulus relationships of contours with respect to a moving frame of reference. Otherwise one might have expected the results to parallel those of condition 2 because there the potential conflict was between the retinal state of affairs and the phenomenal one, in which the latter was based on directions perceived with respect to the subject and, as we have seen, this latter percept dominated.

An interesting feature of this procedure is that the subjects found it much easier to track the moving target than they did in condition 2. That is, the circular motion of the reference frame, with the target at its center, helped subjects to track the target. We do not know whether this kind of effect is known to investigators who work on eye movements—one possibility is that it is due to a boost from optokinetic nystagmus—but it

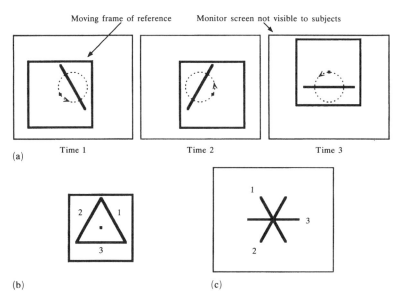

Figure 6.6
(a) A schematic representation of condition 3 which involved tracking of a revolving target and frame of reference. The figure shows the successive presentation of the components of a triangle with respect to the frame of reference. The component contours flashed when the target and frame were in the positions indicated in the three time frames. (b) The configuration created with respect to the moving frame of reference and also the composite created on the retina. (c) The composite created on the screen, which is the composite with respect to the observer.

certainly made the task in this condition easier for subjects. This is the reason why we did not feel it necessary to give subjects practice on this task, concentrating all the practice trials instead on the procedure to be used in condition 2. Subjects were first shown the target and the frame revolving without any contour presentations as a demonstration before the actual trials. In a trial the target and frame made five cycles alone and then five cycles with the component contour presentations.

Results
Of the 44 trials, 41 resulted in a selection of a figure that was the correct composite of the contours in relation to the frame of reference (which was the same as the composite with respect to the retinal image). The majority of these were perfect representations but 10 were selections of the imperfect ones. Were it not for the effect of the frame of reference, the results would have been very different, judging by the results of condition 2 in which no frame of reference was present; in condition 2 selections were made primarily on the basis of how the component contours fit together

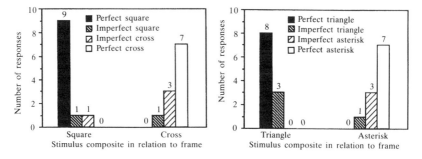

Figure 6.7
Results of condition 3. In this condition the composite in relation to the frame of reference is the same as the composite retinal image, and both are different from the composite in relation to the monitor screen.

in relation to the observer. Figure 6.7 gives the results for each figure, the square and cross, and the triangle and asterisk.

Condition 4: A Displacing Square Frame without Tracking

The purpose of this condition was to determine the power of the moving frame in establishing the phenomenal location of the components of a configuration even when the retinal image *and* the location of the components with respect to the subject indicated a different configuration. Here the subject was instructed to hold his or her eyes stationary. In this condition a particular image should be created on the retina. This image, together with the perceived location of the components with respect to the subject, should both indicate one particular shape of the configuration. On the other hand, since the square frame changed positions, the perceived location of components with respect to the frame should indicate a different shape of the configuration. The retinal image and the composite on the screen are then the same and both are in conflict with the figure in relation to the frame of reference. The situation is shown schematically in figure 6.8.

In this condition, the frame of reference did not follow a circular path; instead it flashed at the appropriate locations for component presentations. These locations of the frame were the same as those in condition 3 at the time the component contours flashed. The square frame of reference was 16.3 deg of visual angle (9.68 cm) on each side. The frame was white, and appeared at each location for either one-third or one-quarter of the cycle time. The white figural component appeared at the same time as the frame but was on for only 33 ms. This shorter "on" time was used mainly to prevent apparent motion. The ISI between component presentations

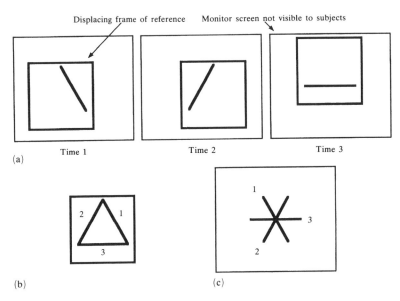

(a) Time 1   Time 2   Time 3

(b)   (c)

Figure 6.8
(a) A schematic representation of condition 4 which involved a displacing frame of reference and no target. The figure shows the successive presentation of the components of a triangle with respect to the frame of reference. The component contours flashed once in each of the three positions of the frame of reference. (b) The configuration created with respect to the displacing frame of reference. (c) The composite created on the screen, which is both the composite on the retina and with respect to the observer.

was 373 ms when the figure had three components, and 334 ms when the figure had four components. Total time for one cycle was thus 1220 ms for three components and 1470 ms for four components.

We did not require the subject to fixate a stationary target in this condition because we believed that a fixation target would allow for relational information at odds with that of the moving frame. Instead we first showed the subject a white fixation target in the center of the screen and requested that he or she maintain that fixation when the target went off, as it did when the five-cycle trial began a moment later. We assumed that the subjects followed these instructions, although we cannot prove it. The subjects were selected graduate students and members of the faculty; even if they had tried to track the frame, their resulting composite would have been very irregular. Assuming that they maintained fixation, this condition was a rather strong test of the possible role of a reference frame in determining the perceived location of contours seen within it and, therefore, ipso facto, in relation to one another. After all, there are two reasons for perceiving the composite shape otherwise—both the composite retinal image and the composite created by the perception of the direction of

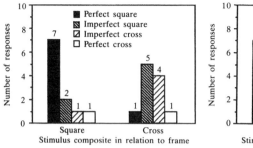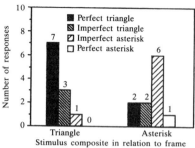

Figure 6.9
Results of condition 4. In this condition the composite in relation to the frame of reference is different from the composite retinal image and from the composite in relation to the monitor screen. The latter two are the same.

each contour relative to the subject ought to lead to one shape. Only the relation of contours to the reference frame ought to lead to the opposite shape, that is a triangle if an asterisk composite is presented (or vice versa) and a cross if a square is presented (and vice versa).

Our expectations for this condition were limited because reference frame effects are known to be limited when they do not serve as world surrogates (compare the rod and frame effect with the rather complete determination of the upright when an observer is inside a tilted room [Witkin 1949]). Even the Kopfermann (1930) effect, in which shapes such as squares and diamonds are seen within a tilted rectangle, is limited in its effectiveness: the diamond now does look more or less like a square but the square does not look like a diamond as it should if the frame of reference completely determined the outcome. Nonetheless, the effect in our experiment was strong.

Results
The results indicate that in 31 of the 44 trials (70.5%), subjects selected a test figure that was either the perfect or imperfect composite based on the relation of the parts to the frame of reference. In 9 trials the selection was the imperfect retinal-image composite or the composite appearing on the screen, and in 4 trials the selection was the perfect retinal composite or composite on the screen. Figure 6.9 gives the results for each figure, the square and cross, and the triangle and asterisk.

Discussion

Our results indicate that overall, across all three experimental conditions, a phenomenal shape was based on integration of the perceived locations of its parts relative to one another rather than directly from their relative retinal location, whether the perceived location was based on egocentric radial direction (as in condition 2) or in relation to a frame of reference (as in conditions 3 and 4). Of these two bases of perceived location the frame of reference determinant seemed to be the stronger. Of course, we cannot demonstrate this conclusion in the case where all parts are simultaneously visible as in the ordinary conditions of form perception in daily life. But we have separated the two possible bases of component integration in daily life by separating the stimulation of the parts over time. The phenomenal end product of the experience of the composite shape in our experiments was similar to the case in which the composite shape is seen simultaneously.

In those conditions in which the target is tracked along a circular path, we assume that a compensation or constancy process occurs such that the location of the line components with respect to the observer is perceived veridically. To put it differently, we assume that these locations will not be perceived solely on the basis of their corresponding retinal locations. There appears to be unanimous agreement that constancy of location or direction occurs with saccadic eye movements but there has been some disagreement about whether or not it occurs in the case of smooth-pursuit or tracking eye movements. Stoper (1967, 1973) maintained that compensation does not occur in the latter case but Mack and Herman (1973, 1978) and Honda (1985, 1990) found that it does, albeit incompletely. Festinger et al. (1976) and Holtzman et al. (1978) reported an extreme departure from constancy based on underestimation of velocity of eye movement. However, these investigations concerned tracking of linear motion, not circular motion such as we employed here. Circular motion entails constantly changing direction and this information is probably available and used. In our experiment this information may also have been supplemented by the three or four brief pauses of the moving target. In any event, our results clearly imply position constancy.

The results of some recent research in which saccadic eye movement was required have demonstrated that observers can integrate the location of points from different fixations into a world-centered representation of simple geometric shape despite the entirely different near-foveal location of the points on the retina (Hayhoe et al. 1991). This finding parallels ours with smooth-pursuit eye movement. Hayhoe et al. also found that the continued presence of a stationary reference point improved performance appreciably, thus demonstrating object-relative as well as subject-relative determination of the spatial integration. This finding parallels ours in which a frame of reference was found to play a fundamental role in the integration of shape.

Results of research on anorthoscopic perception also support the conclusion that phenomenal shape is based upon a process of integrating the information about the location of the parts of an object with respect to one another. When a figure moves behind a narrow slit in an opaque surface (or the slit moves over a stationary figure) so that only part of the figure is visible at any instant, one nonetheless tends to perceive the figure in its entirety even though there is no spreading of the image of the figure over the retina (Parks 1965; Hochberg 1968; Fendrich and Mack 1980; Rock 1981; Rock et al. 1987). In the case where the slit moves over the figure and the observer tracks the slit, the directions of the successive parts of the figure are perceived on the basis of eye position just as in condition 2 of our experiment. The interesting difference, though, between the two paradigms is that in condition 2 an extended retinal image was created that was different from the shape perceived, whereas in the moving-slit anorthoscopic procedure essentially no extended image at all is created. In the case where the figure moves behind a stationary slit, the successive parts of the figure all appear in the same egocentric direction, namely straight ahead in the slit, so that a process of taking account of eye position in arriving at the veridical perception of the locations of the parts cannot explain the outcome. Rather it seems necessary to assume that the perceived motion of the elements of the figure within the slit enables the perceptual system to reconstruct the shapes of the figure on the basis of the sequence of arrival of these elements in the slit. But here again there is no extended image of the figure as long as the observer fixates the slit. So this evidence supports the evidence we present here.

There is another line of evidence that fits with the conclusion we have drawn, namely, that often in daily life or in experiments it is necessary to change one's fixation from one part of a figure to another to perceive its shape. This is because much of the figure not currently being fixated is far from the fovea and thus is poorly resolved and a change of fixation is required to bring it to the fovea. Julian Hochberg has emphasized this point repeatedly (Hochberg 1968, 1981, 1982). The components of a figure thus fixated successively over time are hardly in the appropriate places on the retina to make up a composite image that corresponds at all to the shape of the figure. Thus an integration based on *perceived* location would have to occur very much along the lines that our evidence here suggests. Assuming that the general shape of the figure would still be detectable even if much of it were off fovea at any one moment, the purpose of the successive fixations would be more in the nature of sharpening the perceptions of the off-foveal regions rather than creating them out of whole cloth. After all, there still is an extended image of the figure present in each position of the eye. That being the case, the evidence we present here more directly challenges the assumption that perceived shape derives directly from the shape of the retinal image of an object, than does the argument that changing fixations are required to perceive shapes. In any event these two kinds of evidence, anorthoscopic perception and the need for successive fixations in viewing shapes, certainly dovetail with the evidence we present here.

If indeed, as our evidence suggests, the manner in which the component parts of a form are assembled is based not on how they fit together on the retina, as has always seemed a reasonable assumption, but on how they fit together in perceived space, then form perception becomes a much more complicated process than we have heretofore assumed. Of course it is true that in daily life both modes of assemblage of parts are available since typically a figure or object is present simultaneously in its entirety. So one might think that the two modes of assembly of a composite form work cooperatively, but there is little support for this conclusion in our data. If both modes of assembly were important, there would have been many more cases in our data where such assembly was based on the retinal state of affairs. As it is, most cases seem to suggest assembly on the basis of perceived location of components relative to one another, and the fact that the choices were often not quite perfect representations of the composites presented can be explained in other ways, as we have done above.

Therefore it would seem that the stage at which the perception of shape occurs is relatively *late*, since it depends upon the prior achievement of constancy of direction. This conclusion is similar to one that can be drawn from various lines of evidence bearing on another problem that is relevant to shape perception, namely that of perceptual grouping. Grouping, or perceptual organization, is clearly a necessary precondition for the perception of the shape of an object. However, one might ask whether the Gestalt laws of grouping such as proximity or similarity operate on the basis of the retinal state of affairs or on the perceived state of affairs. Several converging lines of evidence suggest that it is the perceived state of affairs that matters (Rock and Brosgole 1964; Olsen and Attneave 1970; Palmer 1992; Rock et al. 1992; Palmer et al. 1996; Palmer and Rock 1994; but see Beck 1975).

Notes

This research was supported by Research Scientist Award KO5 MH00707 to Irvin Rock and NIMH grant 42573 jointly to Arien Mack and Irvin Rock. We thank Stephen Palmer, Arien Mack, Martin Banks, Geoffrey Keppel, and Julian Hochberg for their comments on the manuscript.
1. Other investigators have used the method of the successive rather than the simultaneous presentation of the parts of a figure, but their purposes were quite different from the one

described here [see MacFarland (1965), Julesz (1967), Palmer (1977), and Thompson and Klatzky (1978)]. Moreover, and more importantly, they were not concerned as we are with the analytical question of separating the retinal location of a part from the perceived location with respect to the figure as a whole. Hence they did not require the subjects to move their eyes between successive presentations of the parts of the figure.

2. We measured the decay of the phosphor illumination after the offset of a contour presentation using a photocell connected to an oscilloscope. The photocell was attached to the monitor screen and a white patch was flashed for 67 ms. Even without the filter the phosphor decay was very steep. After only 4 ms from offset the residual energy level had nearly returned to the baseline level of the monitor's black background. Therefore, because the ISI was either 251 ms or 397 ms, there would be no physical trace of the previous contour, which could have provided relative spatial information, at the time of the current contour presentation.

3. The chi-square test was not appropriate because every condition involved obtaining more than one response from each subject, and chi-square can not be used with repeated measures. An analysis of variance could have been performed on this type of data but the results would not have been very informative. The same is true for correlation statistics. Other statistics were reviewed but none seemed appropriate, so we decided that it was better to let the reader look at the percentages and view the whole pattern of data in the graphs, rather than to apply an inappropriate and possibly misleading statistic.

References

Asch S. E., Witkin H. A., 1948a "Studies in space orientation: I. Perception of the upright with displaced visual fields" *Journal of Experimental Psychology* **38** 325–327.

Asch S. E., Witkin H. A., 1948b "Studies in space orientation: II. Perception of the upright with displaced visual fields and with body tilted" *Journal of Experimental Psychology* **38** 455–477.

Beck J., 1975 "The relation between similarity grouping and perceptual constancy" *American Journal of Psychology* **88** 397–409.

Campbell E. W., Robson U. G., 1968 "Application of Fourier analysis to the visibility of gratings" *Journal of Physiology (London)* **197** 551–566.

Coren S., Bradley D. R., Hoenig P., Girgus J., 1975 "The effect of smooth tracking and saccadic eye movements on the perception of size: The shrinking circle illusion" *Vision Research* **15** 49–55.

De Valois R., De Valois K., Yund E. W., 1979 "Response of striate cortex cells to gratings and checkerboard patterns" *Journal of Physiology (London)* **291** 483–505.

Di Lorenzo J., Rock I., 1982 "The rod and frame effect as a function of righting the frame" *Journal of Experimental Psychology: Human Perception and Performance* **8** 536–546.

Duncker K., 1929 "Über induzierte Bewegung" *Psychologische Forschung* **12** 180–259.

Fendrich R., Mack A., 1980 "Anorthoscopic perception occurs with retinally stabilized stimulus" *Investigative Ophthalmology and Visual Science, Supplement* **19** 166.

Festinger L., Sedgwick H. A., Holtzman J. D., 1976 "Visual perception during smooth pursuit eye movements" *Vision Research* **16** 1377–1386.

Fujii E., 1943 "Forming a figure by movements of a luminous point" *Japanese Journal of Psychology* **18** 196–232.

Hayhoe M., Lachter J., Feldman J., 1991 "Integration of form across saccadic eye movements" *Perception* **20** 393–402.

Hochberg J., 1968 "In the mind's eye" in *Contemporary Theory and Research in Visual Perception* Ed. N. Haber (New York: Holt) pp. 309–331.

Hochberg J., 1981 "Levels of perceptual organization" in *Perceptual Organization* Eds. M. Kubovy, J. R. Pomerantz (Hillsdale, NJ: Lawrence Erlbaum) pp. 255–278.

Hochberg J., 1982 "How big is a stimulus?" in *Organization and Representation in Perception* Ed. J. Beck (Hillsdale, NJ: Lawrence Erlbaum) pp. 191–217.

Holtzman J. D., Sedgwick H. A., Festinger L., 1978 "Interaction of perceptually monitored and unmonitored efferent commands for smooth pursuit eye movements" *Vision Research* **18** 1545–1555.

Honda H., 1985 "Spatial localization in saccade and pursuit-eye movement conditions: A comparison of perceptual and motor measures" *Perception & Psychophysics* **38** 41–46.

Honda H., 1990 "The extraretinal signals from the pursuit-eye movement system: Its role in the perceptual and egocentric localization systems" *Perception & Psychophysics* **48** 509–515.

Hubel D. H., Wiesel T. N., 1962 "Receptive fields, binocular interaction and functional architecture in the cat's visual cortex" *Journal of Physiology (London)* **160** 106–154.

Julesz B., 1967 "Some recent studies in vision relevant to form perception" in *Models for the Perception of Speed and Visual Form* Ed. W. Wathen-Dunn (Cambridge: MIT Press) pp. 136–154.

Kopfermann H., 1930 "Psychologische Untersuchungen über die Wirkung zweidimensionaler Darstellungen körperlicher Gebilde" *Psychologische Forschung* **13** 293–364.

MacFarland J. H., 1965 "Sequential part presentation: A method of studying visual form perception" *British Journal of Psychology* **56** 439–446.

Mack A., Herman E., 1973 "Position constancy during pursuit eye movement: An investigation of the Filehne illusion" *Quarterly Journal of Experimental Psychology* **25** 71–84.

Mack A., Herman E., 1978 "The loss of position constancy during pursuit eye movements" *Vision Research* **18** 55–62.

Olsen R., Attneave F., 1970 "What variables produce similarity grouping?" *American Journal of Psychology* **80** 1–21.

Palmer S. E., 1977 "Hierarchical structure in perceptual representation" *Cognitive Psychology* **9** 441–474.

Palmer S. E., 1992 "Common region: A new principle of perceptual grouping" *Cognitive Psychology* **24** 436–447.

Palmer S. E., Neff, J., Beck, D., 1996 "Late influences on perceptual grouping: Amodal completion" *Psychonomic Bulletin and Review* **3** 75–80.

Palmer S. E., Rock I., 1994 "Rethinking perceptual organization: The role of uniform connectedness." *Psychosonomic Bulletin and Review* **1** 29–55.

Parks T., 1965 "Post-retinal visual storage" *American Journal of Psychology* **78** 145–147.

Rock I., 1973 *Orientation and Form* (New York: Academic Press).

Rock I., 1981 "Anorthoscopic perception" *Scientific American* **244**(3) 145–153.

Rock I., 1990 "The frame of reference" in *The Legacy of Solomon Asch: Essays in Cognition and Social Psychology* Ed. I. Rock (Hillsdale, NJ: Lawrence Erlbaum) pp. 243–268.

Rock I., Brosgole L., 1964 "Grouping based on phenomenal proximity" *Journal of Experimental Psychology* **67** 531–538.

Rock I., Halper F., Di Vita J., Wheeler D., 1987 "Eye movement as a cue to figure motion in anorthoscopic perception" *Journal of Experimental Psychology: Human Perception and Performance* **13** 344–352.

Rock I., Nijhawan R., Palmer S. E., Tudor L., 1992 "Grouping based on phenomenal similarity of achromatic color" *Perception* **21**(6) 779–789.

Stoper A. E., 1967 *Vision during Pursuit Movement: The Role of Oculomotor Information* Doctoral dissertation, Brandeis University, Waltham, MA.

Stoper A. E., 1973 "Apparent motion of stimuli presented stroboscopically during pursuit movement of the eye" *Perception & Psychophysics* **13** 201–211.

Thompson A. L., Klatzky R. L., 1978 "Studies of visual synthesis: Integration of fragments into forms" *Journal of Experimental Psychology: Human Perception and Performance* **4** 244–263.

Witkin H. A., 1949 "Perception of body position and of the position of the visual field" *Psychological Monographs* **63** (7, whole No. 302).

Witkin H. A., Asch S. E., 1948 "Studies of space orientation: IV. Further experiments on perception of the upright with displaced visual fields" *Journal of Experimental Psychology* **38** 762–782.

Chapter 7
Anorthoscopic Perception
Irvin Rock

How one visually perceives the shape of things is an old topic in experimental psychology, but it is still not well understood. In some ways the eye is like a camera, in that an object of a certain shape gives rise to an image of the same shape on the surface of the retina. The simple analogy breaks down, however, in situations where the presence of such an image is neither sufficient nor necessary to account for the perceived shape. In order to learn more about the perceptual process investigators over the years have devised a variety of laboratory techniques. My colleagues and I at the Institute for Cognitive Studies of Rutgers University have recently concentrated on a method that calls for viewing a figure in successive sections through a narrow slit. In recognition of the unusual nature of this experimental arrangement we have adopted the 19th-century term anorthoscopic ("abnormally viewed") to characterize perception in such cases.

One of the first problems to arise with the eye-as-camera analogy is that it does not take account of the question of how the components of the retinal image are organized. Consider an array of three dots that are not in a line. They will be seen as the corner points of a triangle only if they are grouped into one unit by the perceptual system; in the presence of other dots their triangularity may be less evident. Even a well-known figure composed of lines may not be recognized if the perceptual system associates the lines with other lines to form different groupings. Then there is the matter of organizing a pattern into figure and ground: a familiar shape may not be perceived—even though an image of that shape is present on the retina—if some other part of the field of view is taken to be the figure.

Another problem is that of orientation. If one misperceives where the top, bottom and sides of a figure are, the mere presence of its image on the retina does not ensure that the figure will be recognized. The orientation of a figure in the third dimension can also be a factor in the

Originally published in *Scientific American* 244, 3 (1981): 145–153. Reprinted with permission.

perception of form. For example, a circle viewed obliquely projects an elliptical image on the retina, but it may nonetheless appear to be circular under the right conditions.

All these examples indicate that the existence of an accurate retinal image is not a sufficient explanation of the perception of a form. Other factors must be invoked. Indeed, an accurate retinal image is sometimes not a necessary factor. It can easily be shown that if only parts of a figure are present, other parts may be perceived as if they too were present. Consider a simple line drawing of two rectangles, one of which appears to overlap and occlude the other; the figure may be seen as two complete rectangles even though the image of one is incomplete. In other cases contours (called subjective or illusory contours) are seen in spite of the absence in the retinal image of the abrupt transition from light to dark that is usually considered the stimulus for a perceived contour [see "Subjective Contours," by Gaetano Kanizsa; *Scientific American*, April, 1976].

In the last two examples at least some of the contours of the figure are present in the retinal image. In other experiments one can perceive a form without any contour in the retinal image. With the aid of a stereoscopic viewer a random distribution of graphic elements can be presented to each eye separately in such a way that no figure is visible with either eye alone. If a cluster of the elements in the display presented to one eye is shifted horizontally with respect to the same cluster in the display presented to the other eye, however, the perceptual system may detect the similarity of the two clusters and infer that there is a shape either in front of the rest of the display or behind it. Here the perceived shape emerges not from retinal-image contours present in each eye but from the boundaries of a region the perceptual system infers is an entity in the scene [see "Experiments in the Visual Perception of Texture," by Bela Julesz; *Scientific American*, April, 1975].

Another example has a closer connection with my own recent work. Suppose a luminous point traverses a path in a dark room and an observer is instructed to track it with his eyes. The image of the point would always fall at about the same place on the retina (namely the fovea), but the viewer would nonetheless perceive the shape of the path. This impression would be very close to the perception of a form, and yet there would be no extended image on the retina corresponding to the path of the point. When Fred Halper and I tried this simple experiment in our laboratory at Rutgers, we found that observers do as well in apprehending the shape of such a path as they do when they keep their eyes still, so that the image of the point does move across the retina.

One might still argue that the perception of a path is not the same as the perception of a shape. After all, one sees a contour in the latter case,

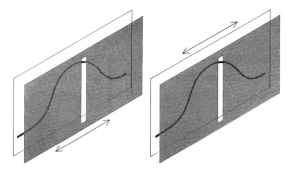

Figure 7.1
Anorthoscopic presentation is an abnormal method of visual stimulation adopted by the author and his colleagues to test the retinal-painting hypothesis, which holds that an image is spread over the retina one area at a time. The technique calls for viewing successive sections of a figure through a narrow slit. Two experimental conditions are possible: either a slit moves in front of a stationary figure (*left*) or a figure moves behind a stationary slit (*right*).

not just a moving point. With a small change in the experimental procedure, however, there is a way to achieve a strong impression of a shape. Instead of a dark room and a moving point, the observer is presented with a narrow slit in an opaque surface moving across a line drawing of a figure [see fig. 7.1]. If the observer tracks the slit closely, the slit stimulates only a narrow strip on the retina and the image of the visible portion of the figure accordingly moves up and down within this retinal strip. Alternatively, the figure can be moved back and forth behind a stationary slit; if the eyes of the observer in this case remain stationary, fixating the slit, the slit again stimulates only a narrow strip on the retina. At no time in either case is there an image on the retina that resembles the shape of the figure. Nevertheless, under these conditions we find that figures are easily perceived.

In the 19th century several investigators, including Joseph Plateau, Fritz Zöllner and Hermann von Helmholtz, employed a similar arrangement to study certain visual phenomena. They referred to their procedure as anorthoscopic presentation, presumably because it was a nonstandard method of visual stimulation. The experimental device called the anorthoscope consisted of two disks mounted axially one behind the other. The disks could rotate at different speeds and in opposite directions. The observer viewed figures on the rear disk through slits in the front disk, thereby perceiving certain illusory distortions of the figures.

This early work was apparently forgotten until 1965, when it was rediscovered by T. E. Parks of the University of California at Davis. Both in the 19th century and after the rediscovery a controversy arose over how to interpret the effect. Helmholtz and others thought an extended image of the figure behind the slit is always imprinted on the retina. This interpretation has since come to be known as the "retinal painting" hypothesis, since it is based on the assumption that an image is spread over the retina one area at a time. Where the slit moves in front of a stationary figure, retinal painting would require the observer to keep his eyes stationary and not track the slit. Where the figure moves behind a stationary slit retinal painting would require the observer to move his eyes back and forth. Helmholtz argued that the observer might not always know whether his eyes were still or moving.

If the retinal-painting hypothesis is correct, the perception of form under such conditions would hardly be surprising. An extended retinal image of a figure would then be present in both of the cases cited above, and the only difference between perception in the abnormal viewing situation and in the normal situation would be that in anorthoscopic viewing the image would be created in segments presented successively rather than simultaneously. Moreover, because the sensory cells of the retina tend to continue discharging for a short time after the stimulation has ended (a phenomenon known as neural persistence), the image presented in successive segments would not be significantly different from an image formed all at once, assuming that the successive presentations were fast enough. The observer would therefore be expected to perceive the entire anorthoscopic image as if it had been established normally.

To evaluate the retinal-painting hypothesis one needs to know exactly what the eyes of the observer are doing during an anorthoscopic presentation. In our experiments, therefore, we usually make videotape recordings of the observer's eyes during the presentation. In one test Joseph Di Vita and I had observers view curved-line figures that were approximately five and a half inches long through a slit an eighth of an inch wide from a distance of two and a half feet. Either the figure moved back and forth through five cycles or the slit did. The speed of the figure or the slit was one pass (that is, one half cycle) per second, which was lower than the speed adopted by other investigators of anorthoscopic perception. Eye recordings indicated at every moment the direction of gaze with respect to the display. The observer was told to press a switch only during the periods when a figure was perceived behind the slit. The signal was recorded with the videotaped record of eye movement.

When the slit was stationary, the data showed that by and large observers kept their eyes still whether or not they were told to do so and whether or not they were given a point on the slit to fixate. Of course, the eyes did not remain perfectly stationary, but the occasional small, rapid motions to one side or the other (known as saccadic eye movements) were not sufficient to account for the perception of form. The observers did not always perceive a figure, but there were many times when they did and when their eyes were more or less stationary.

These findings were recently confirmed by Robert Fendrich and Arien Mack of the New School for Social Research. In their experiment the image of the display was stabilized in such a way that even if the eyes moved, the image of the slit would not be displaced across the retina. Nevertheless, their observers also perceived a figure moving behind the slit.

When the slit in our experiments moved over a stationary figure, the observers typically moved their eyes along with the slit. There was usually a lag, however, with the slit quickly getting a little ahead of the eyes and remaining ahead until it reached its terminal position, whereupon the eyes quickly caught up. It was nonetheless clear that the image of the slit did not move far enough over the retina to explain the perception of form; indeed, the retinal image did not even move consistently in the right direction. In this situation a figure was almost always perceived, and its size was perceived more or less correctly.

Other experiments done in our laboratory and elsewhere indicate that the only way the anorthoscopic effect could result from retinal painting would be if the image of the slit were to move over the retina very quickly. Only at a speed approaching five sweeps per second, or five times the speed we typically employ, could neural persistence account for the impression of a whole figure. Moreover, in the moving-figure condition retinal painting would have to be based on eye movements, and therefore the eyes would have to move back and forth at a rapid rate. Observers are unable to move their eyes that fast.

On the basis of this and other evidence we conclude that retinal painting is not a sufficiently general explanation of anorthoscopic perception. What then is the basis of form perception in experiments of this kind? Consider again the tracking of a luminous point in a dark room. Although the image of the point does not move over the retina, the perceptual system does receive information about the path of the point, because the eyes must move to track it. The perceptual system takes into account the position of the eyes in judging, from the retinal stimulus, the location of the point in space. Thus the perceived path of the point is derived from the set of perceived locations of the point as it moves.

Generalizing this argument to all form perception, one can say that when an extended image of a figure is present on the retina, the observer perceives each point of the figure as being in a certain place. Hence one might suppose the perceived shape is the result of a mental synthesis of the perceived locations of all the points constituting the shape. This process might be organized hierarchically, with points synthesized into lines

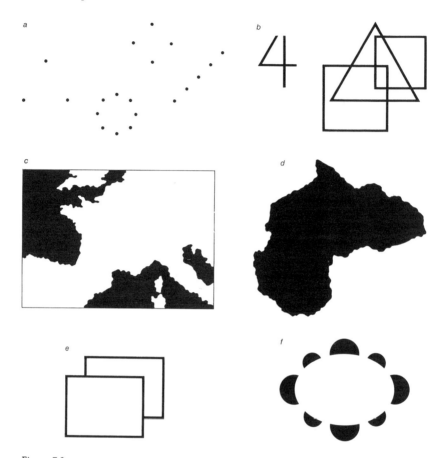

Figure 7.2
Limited role of the retinal image in the visual perception of form is illustrated by means of six examples. In *a* the three dots at the left are seen as the corner points of a triangle only if they are organized into one unit by the perceptual system; in the presence of other points (*right*) the triangle may not be perceived. In *b* the numeral 4 (*left*) will not be seen as such if the perceptual system associates its constituent lines with other lines to form different groupings (*right*). In *c* the familiar shape of western Europe will not be perceived if the background (in this case the surrounding bodies of water) is taken to be the figure. Similarly in *d* the continent of Africa may not be recognized if one is not aware that the top of the figure (that is, north) is to the left. These four examples show that the mere presence of a particular retinal image is insufficient to account for what is perceived. In *e* two rectangular shapes, one shape overlapping and occluding the other, may be seen as two complete rectangles even though one is actually incomplete. In *f* a subjective (or illusory) contour is readily perceived even in the absence of the abrupt light-dark transition that is usually considered the stimulus for the perception of contours. The last two examples reveal that an accurate or complete retinal image is not necessary to explain what is perceived.

and the placement of lines with respect to one another synthesized into figures. If it is, it might be the set of perceived locations that is important about a retinal image of a figure. In other words, perhaps the role of the retinal contours of a figure is to establish a set of locations that together yield a form.

The same argument can be applied to anorthoscopic perception. The perceptual system integrates the information about the locations of the parts of the figure as they appear successively through the slit. When the slit moves over a stationary figure, the visible element at one end of the figure is characterized as, say, "at the bottom of the slit and to the left," whereas a moment later the visible element is characterized as "higher in the slit and straight ahead." Integrating the directions leads to the perception of an oblique line sloping upward to the right. Therefore both anorthoscopic perception and normal form perception can be said to entail an integration of all given locations of parts of a figure with respect to one another into a description of the whole.

This explanation turns out to be incomplete for several reasons. First, direction with respect to the observer is given directly in the moving-slit condition but not in the moving-figure condition. In the latter case the slit remains stationary and straight ahead. Where then does the information come from that the successively revealed parts of the figure are in different places? Apparently it must first be hypothesized that something is moving behind the slit. Once that idea is entertained, the temporal succession of stimuli can be converted into a spatial configuration. Next, as in the moving-slit condition, the perceptual system can integrate the sequence of stimuli into a shape based on the set of directions of the parts with respect to one another.

Our analysis suggests another reason the location-synthesis hypothesis does not tell the whole story. Often observers do not perceive a figure in the anorthoscopic display. This result must be related in some way to the kind of figure we employ, because other investigators have not reported such failures. We have deliberately chosen figures with several distinctive features: they are single lines and are shaped so that only one figure element at a time is visible in the slit; they are fairly smooth curves rather than patterns with abrupt changes in direction; they are continuous lines rather than dotted or broken; they do not depict familiar objects. Others have employed figures such as squares, circles and ellipses or outline drawings of familiar objects such as animals.

We consider our kind of figure to be ambiguous in that the anorthoscopic display of it could logically represent either an element moving vertically in a slit or an extended figure being revealed through the slit. Therefore we reasoned that we could investigate what factors are important in figure perception, since a figure is not always perceived. Our guiding hypothesis has been that figure perception under anorthoscopic conditions is based on an unconscious process of problem solving. Even before any location-synthesis activity begins, the perceptual system must hypothesize that there is an extended figure behind the slit and that it is being revealed in successive sections.

To clarify this hypothesis consider what would be seen if the figure were made luminous and were viewed in a dark room, so that the slit was not visible. In the stationary-slit condition all the observer would see would be a point of light moving up and down. In the moving-slit condition the observer would see a moving point of light traversing a path. In neither case would one describe the percept (the perceived entity) as an extended figure. Thus it seems the observer must realize that the momentary view is through a narrow slit and that the remainder of the figure is hidden by an opaque surface. Unlike problem solving as an act of thought, problem solving in perception requires support from the stimulus. To perceive a figure anorthoscopically it is not enough to know one is looking through a slit; the slit must be seen.

Under certain conditions the observer may even "invent" a slit when none is visible. Fendrich and Mack have found that if a circle is moved behind an invisible slit and the appropriate suggestion is made, observers who at first see the visible parts of the circle moving vertically later perceive a figure moving horizontally behind an illusory slit. Their experiment provides a good example of how the perceptual system tends to rationalize a solution adopted by the problem-solving faculty if the stimulus does not fully support it.

Not only must the slit be seen; the visible portion of the figure must also extend fully across it. To clarify this point Alan L. Gilchrist and I devised a technique for stimulating anorthoscopic presentation. Instead of a figure behind the slit, there was only a small line segment drawn on transparent plastic. The plastic was attached by thin rods to a set of rollers that rode on a cam not visible through the slit; the cam had the shape of the figure to be simulated [see fig. 7.3].

Under some conditions simulation with this instrument leads to figure perception. In this instance, however, we widened the slit so that the visible line segment did not fill it but rather was isolated within it. Although the segment moved vertically and changed its slope just as it had when the slit was narrower, a figure was never perceived. The stimulus apparently violated the logic of the solution: that one was viewing a continuous figure being revealed through the slit.

Consider next the kind of figure displayed behind the stationary slit. If the figure is an oblique straight line and the ends do not pass across the

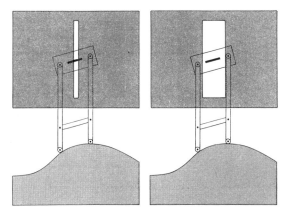

Figure 7.3
Simulation technique was devised by the author and one of his colleagues, Alan L. Gilchrist, to investigate the phenomenon of anorthoscopic perception. Here the technique is used to verify that for a figure to be perceived under anorthoscopic conditions the visible portion of the figure must be seen to extend across the slit from one side to the other. A small line segment drawn on a piece of transparent plastic is attached by thin rods to a set of rollers that ride on a cam not visible through the slit. The visible part of the line segment moves up and down and simultaneously changes its slope just as the visible part of an actual line figure would. When the slit is narrower than the length of the line segment, a figure is often perceived (*left*). When the slit is wider than the line segment, however, the figure is never perceived (*right*).

slit (which is about a sixteenth of an inch wide and is viewed from a distance of about three feet), the stimulus consists of a line segment undergoing vertical displacement. This stimulus could result from either of two physical events: a segment moving up and down at a uniform speed or an oblique line moving back and forth horizontally at a uniform speed.

Under such conditions of ambiguity Hans Wallach of Swarthmore College long ago demonstrated that the shape of the aperture has an important influence on what is perceived. There is a strong tendency to perceive the line as moving parallel to the long axis of the aperture, probably because with a narrow slit there is no information to suggest any change in the identity of the segment. Accordingly we have found that under such conditions an extended, moving figure is never perceived.

Suppose the figure is a curved line but the conditions of presentation are otherwise the same. Here the only new factor is that the visible segment accelerates and decelerates as it moves vertically. Ann Corrigan and I have found that this information does not alter the outcome. All observers perceive a vertically moving segment, not a figure.

Next suppose the width of the slit is increased to an eighth of an inch. Under these conditions we found that the slope of the visible segment

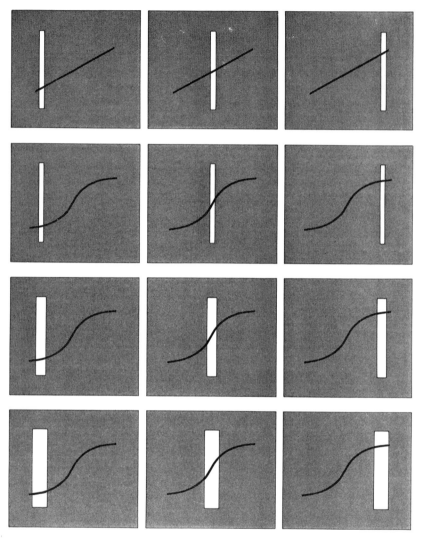

Figure 7.4
Strong tendency to perceive an anorthoscopically displayed line figure as a line segment undergoing vertical displacement rather than as a horizontally revealed continuous line is demonstrated in four display sequences, each sequence representing three successive times. When an oblique straight line is displayed anorthoscopically (*top*), it never appears to be an extended, moving figure, presumably because there is no hint of any change in the segment's identity. When a curved-line figure is presented under the same conditions (*second from top*), the visible segment accelerates and decelerates as it moves vertically within the slit, but this additional information does not seem to change the perception. Even when the width of the slit is doubled, so that the slope and the change in the slope of the visible segment are detectable (*third from top*), most observers still do not perceive a figure. Only when the slit is widened still further, so that the curvature and the change in the curvature become detectable (*bottom*), is a figure perceived. All the figures were viewed from about three feet away.

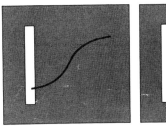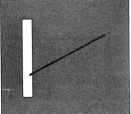

Figure 7.5
Appearance of the end points of a line in the slit of an anorthoscopic display may aid in the perception of a shape, but this factor by itself does not seem to be adequate to shift the balance in favor of figure perception. An oblique straight line still tends to be perceived as a vertically displacing line segment even when its end points are visible (*left*). A curved line with its end points visible, on the other hand, is more likely to be seen as a figure (*right*).

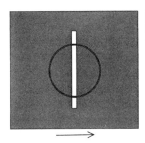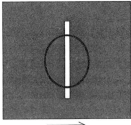

Figure 7.6
Compression effect is often observed in anorthoscopic displays in which the figure moves behind a stationary slit. The perceived figure, in this case a circle (*left*), is typically compressed along its axis of motion, forming what appears to be a vertically elongated ellipse (*right*).

and the change in the slope can be detected through the slit. Even with this information, however, and the correlated vertical acceleration and deceleration of the segment, most observers still do not perceive a figure. Hence one might conclude that the tendency noted by Wallach for a segment to maintain its identity is so strong that it will do so even if the segment appears to tilt back and forth as it rises and falls.

Only when the slit is widened still further, so that the curvature and the change in the curvature become detectable through the slit, does the balance shift in favor of figure perception. Why this is true is not yet clear, although several possibilities come to mind. One might speculate that the acceleration of a line segment upward just as its slope is tilting toward the vertical and just as its curvature is changing appropriately would represent too much of a coincidence if there were no extended curved line behind the slit. A moving-figure solution explains why these features vary together in this way, and the perceptual system tends to seek such solutions and to reject percepts that postulate mere coincidental variations.

Alternatively, one might say that the notion of a line segment moving vertically while simultaneously tilting and changing its curvature is a very complex perception. A moving figure is a simpler perception, and it has been argued that the perceptual system prefers the simplest description consistent with the stimulus. Moreover, one might speculate that the combination of changes, including changes of curvature, is recognizable to the perceptual system on the basis of past experience as the combination produced by an object passing behind a narrow aperture.

There are other kinds of information in the display that can affect the outcome. Allowing the ends of the figure to be seen through the slit may lead to the perception of a shape. Clearly when the ends are visible, there is a moment of unambiguous information to the effect that something is moving across the slit, not along it. One might think of this information as a cue that suggests the figure hypothesis, but in itself the information does not seem to be adequate; an oblique straight line still tends to be seen as a vertically moving segment except for the brief time when the end points are in view. When such end-of-line information is coupled with change-of-slope information, however, the balance is often shifted toward figure perception. Perhaps the reason is that a perceived change of slope tends to support the hypothesis triggered by seeing the ends of the line. The kind of unambiguous information given by the end points may be present throughout a figure if it has sharp discontinuities or changes in the direction of contours.

There is another factor we have found to be important. If the observer knows the display may represent a figure behind a slit, he is more likely to perceive it. Ordinarily merely knowing something (for example knowing that an illusion is an illusion) does not affect what one perceives, but in this case it does. Even with prior knowledge the conditions must be favorable for form perception. Such knowledge has no effect if the slope of the line segment never changes or if the figure is luminous and viewed in the dark so that the slit is not visible.

Our research on the characteristics of the display that govern the perceptual outcome bears on the question of whether the anorthoscopic effect is genuinely perceptual when retinal painting is ruled out. Several investigators have contended that when only part of the figure is seen at any moment, the impression one has of the whole figure is more a matter of knowing it is present than a result of true form perception. Only if one sees the whole figure at once, they say, should the experience be described as form perception.

In my opinion there is a confusion here that can be traced to a theoretical preconception. If one believes form perception presupposes an extended retinal image all of whose parts are present simultaneously, then of course the anorthoscopic effect cannot be perceptual when retinal painting is ruled out. There is no reason, however, to equate form perception with simultaneity. Hearing a melody or a spoken sentence is certainly perceptual, even though what is perceived is extended over time. Only if the figure or the slit were moved very slowly might it be appropriate to say that one fails to perceive the figure although one knows it is there. Analogously, one might block the perception of a melody by separating the tones by extremely long intervals.

The fact is that those who have experienced the anorthoscopic effect in the laboratory are sure it is a perceptual phenomenon. One reason for the certainty is undoubtedly the clear differences that are observed under the different conditions. Hence the failures become very important. Observers may know that a figure is being presented, but they never perceive it unless the conditions allow. In other words, there are cases where it is appropriate to say the observer knows a figure is being presented but does not perceive it; these cases, in contrast, make it clear that the other cases are perceptual. Moreover, there are many instances where perception shifts from one possibility to the other during the presentation; such a reversal under ambiguous conditions is one of the hallmarks of the perceptual process.

There is one peculiarity of anorthoscopic presentation I have not yet mentioned. When the slit is stationary and the figure is moving, the perceived figure is generally distorted; typically it is compressed along the axis of its motion. Thus a circle may look like an ellipse with its longer axis vertical. What is responsible for this effect? Advocates of the retinal-painting hypothesis have suggested that the distortion results from the failure of the observer to move his eyes in perfect synchrony with the figure. If the eye movement fell short of either the speed or the amplitude of the figure motion, the image painted on the retina would be compressed, and that could nicely account for the distortion.

An experiment carried out in 1967 by Stuart M. Anstis and Janette Atkinson of the University of Bristol tends to support this hypothesis. They introduced a moving target (a point of light) that the observer had to track back and forth. By varying the speed of the target point with respect to the speed of the figure, Anstis and Atkinson were able to "paint" a retinal image of the figure that varied in shape. For example, if the moving figure was a circle and the tracking target moved at half speed, the image spread over the retina would be an ellipse whose vertical axis was twice as long as its horizontal axis. If the figure moved to the

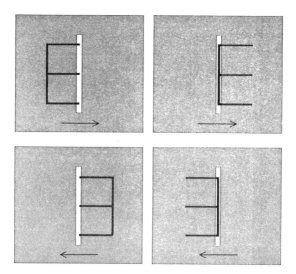

Figure 7.7
Perceived figure is reversed if an observer misjudges the direction of its motion behind a
stationary slit. In this experimental setup the letter *E* appears if the direction of motion of the
figure is correctly perceived to be toward the right (*top*), but the reversed figure Ǝ is seen if
the direction of motion is mistakenly interpreted to be toward the left (*bottom*).

right as the tracking target moved to the left, the image created would be
the reverse of the one yielded by ordinary perception. The observers
reported seeing figures whose shapes corresponded precisely with the
retinal image established.

This finding puzzled my colleagues and me for some time because we
had good reason to doubt that the retinal-painting hypothesis accounts
for the anorthoscopic effect or for these perceptual distortions. Ultimately
we devised an alternative explanation that seems to fit the facts better. To
understand the explanation one must first consider more carefully the
perception of figure motion when the slit is stationary and the figure is
moving. According to the retinal-painting hypothesis, what should be
seen is the whole figure within a large rectangular opening; the rectangle
represents the image of the slit, which should also be painted on the
retina. That is not what is seen. What is seen is a figure moving behind
the narrow slit.

The question is: What determines the perceived speed of the figure?
Given the narrowness of the slit, information about the speed of the
figure can hardly be conveyed accurately by the brief passage of distinguishable contour components across the slit. Moreover, with the
figures we employ there are no distinguishable components except at the
ends. Therefore the speed of the figure is at best ambiguously repre-

sented. The perceived length of the figure depends entirely on its perceived speed, at least according to the problem-solving interpretation of anorthoscopic perception. Since the commonest outcome when there is no tracking target is one of perceived compression, we conclude that the speed is underestimated. We do not know why this is so, but it is important to keep in mind that there is no reason to expect accurate speed perception either.

When a tracking target is introduced, the perceptual system seems to assume that the figure is moving at the speed of the target. One can formulate a general hypothesis that eye movement is a cue to figure motion under anorthoscopic conditions. Given this cue, the perceived speed of the figure is doubled when the target moves at twice the figure speed and is reduced by half when the target moves at half the figure speed. Since the apparent length of the figure depends on how far it seems to move behind the slit during the interval between the appearance of one end and the appearance of the other end, the distortion found by Anstis and Atkinson is explained. It results from a mental construction of length derived from the apparent speed of the figure and not directly from a distorted retinal image.

To provide evidence for our interpretation Di Vita, Halper, Deborah Wheeler and I did an experiment in which observers viewed a curved-line figure moving behind a slit at a certain speed and at the same time tracked a target dot. In effect we repeated the Anstis-Atkinson experiment but with our kind of figure. There was an important addition to the procedure as well. The observer not only indicated the perceived length of the figure (by adjusting a shadow-casting device that varied the length of a replica of the figure while holding its height constant) but also told us whether the speed of the figure appeared to be equal to, less than or greater than that of the moving target. Observations were made at several target speeds: equal to the speed of the figure, half the speed of the figure, twice the speed of the figure and the same speed as the figure but in the opposite direction. There was also a condition of free viewing, with no moving target present.

Whenever a target was tracked, all observers perceived a figure, whereas in the free-viewing condition none did. We deliberately made the slit very narrow in this experiment (a sixteenth of an inch), which we knew would eliminate the anorthoscopic effect under the more usual no-tracking condition.

The first point to be made about the results is that tracking is an important determinant of the anorthoscopic figure percept. We believe the major reason for this is that movement of the eyes provides an effective cue that a figure is moving back and forth behind the slit. Moreover, such

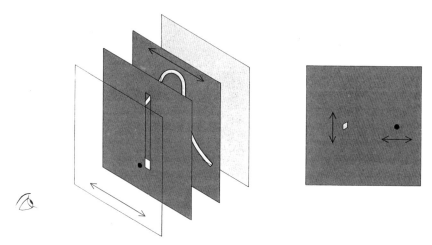

Figure 7.8
Multiple surfaces were employed by the author and his colleagues in one of their control experiments on anorthoscopic perception. The first surface in front of the viewer is a transparent sheet of plastic on which a luminous tracking target (*colored dot*) is mounted; this sheet moves back and forth. The next surface is an opaque, stationary card with a vertical slit. The third surface is an opaque card with a cutout stencil of the test figure; this surface also moves back and forth. The back surface is a translucent sheet of plastic that diffuses the light from the battery of lamps behind it. The panel at the right shows what the viewer sees when the experiment is carried out in a dark room: a horizontally moving luminous tracking target and a line segment that appears to be moving vertically (or almost vertically). A moving figure is not seen under these experimental conditions because the slit is not perceived. When the same display is employed but the figure is instead drawn on the third surface and the room lights are on, a moving figure is always seen by the viewer.

a cue specifies the figure's speed, whereas without it the speed is indeterminate. It would be difficult to arrive at a figure percept of a definite length with the speed indeterminate. Virtually all the observers reported that the speed of the figure was the same or almost the same as that of the target regardless of the actual speed of each. As for the perceived length of the figure, if the actual length is assumed to be 1, the perceived length was .77 when the two speeds were the same, 1.65 when the target speed was twice that of the figure and .50 when the target speed was half that of the figure.

When the figure moved in one direction and the target in the opposite direction at the same speed, all observers perceived the figure as the mirror image of its true shape. For this test we employed an asymmetrical figure and had each observer make a rough sketch of what he perceived. The outcome was what one would predict on the basis of the reversed image painted over the retina, but it was also what we predicted from our eye-movement cuing hypothesis. Not only was the speed of the figure behind the slit ambiguous; its direction was too. For example, if the letter E was the figure and it moved to the right, the end points of its three horizontal prongs would be revealed first. If the figure seemed to be moving to the left but the end points of the prongs still appeared first and were followed by the vertical contour of the E, the figure would have to be a left-right reversed figure: Ǝ. That the direction of motion was mistakenly perceived in this way is borne out by the incorrect response of all those observers who perceived the reversed figure when they were asked its direction of movement.

In this last experiment the tracking of a moving target has the effect of spreading the image of the figure over the retina. Although we have rejected the hypothesis that the image thus painted is the direct cause of anorthoscopic form perception and of the observed distortions, there is one aspect of the results that suggests an important role of the extended image. The figure percept is clearer and more similar to ordinary form perception under these conditions than it is when the eyes are stationary while viewing the stationary slit. We have found a similar result when, in the moving-slit condition, a stationary point is introduced and the observer fixes his gaze on it. Here too the image is spread over the retina, whereas in tracking the moving slit there is no such extended image. In both cases when such an image is present, an observer rarely fails to perceive a figure even if the conditions are otherwise poor for the anorthoscopic effect.

We call the improvement in anorthoscopic perception that can be attributed to an extended retinal image the facilitation effect. Apparently the perceptual system finds it easier to integrate the successive slices of the figure into a whole form when the slices are spread across the retina than when they all fall on one vertical strip. Although the extended image can thereby facilitate the anorthoscopic effect, it does not directly cause it. Reasons for this conclusion have been given above, and in addition it is supported by certain further control experiments.

In one of these experiments the figure was a horizontal straight line, and the observer tracked a target moving at the same speed as the figure. Although an image of the figure was spread over the retina, no observer perceived a figure. Instead the visible segment of the line seemed to be part of the slit and there was no impression of anything moving (except the target dot). We can only conclude that without some vertical displacement of the contour there is no reason for the perceptual system to infer that an extended figure is moving behind the slit; hence the extended image, although present, is not integrated into a mentally constructed form.

In another control experiment the figure consisted of a cutout stencil of a curved figure, which was illuminated from behind. A luminous target dot was also provided, and the display was viewed in an otherwise dark room. When the observer tracked the moving target, an image of the bright line was spread over the retina. Nevertheless, no figure was perceived. Rather, the visible segment of the figure, which was essentially a small point of light, appeared to move up and down, although its path seemed to be slightly tilted from the vertical.

Since tracking has the effect of spreading the image of the visible fragment over the retina, the failure to obtain a figure percept in this case shows dramatically how the anorthoscopic effect depends on the perception of the slit as an opening in an opaque surface. Only then is there the needed support for the mental construction of an extended figure.

In any event there seem to be two factors that combine to make the anorthoscopic perception of form particularly successful when a moving target is tracked. Eye movement serves as a cue that a figure is moving at right angles to the slit and imparts an unambiguous speed to the figure. The formation of an image spread over the retina facilitates the integration of the figure. Perhaps it is this facilitation that has led some investigators to subscribe to the retinal-painting hypothesis.

In conclusion, I have argued that the perception of form can be understood as a process of integrating information about the location of the parts of a figure with respect to one another (provided the parts are organized into one unit and are interpreted as figure rather than as ground). Physical contours or their representations in the retinal image are not necessary as long as some kind of information indicates where the boundaries of a figure are. Consequently anorthoscopic presentation of a figure one part at a time can yield form perception even though no extended image of the whole figure appears on the retina at any one time.

Because the anorthoscopic display is ambiguous and does not necessarily represent an occluded figure, however, the achievement of a form percept entails a process of problem solving. The presence of a region seen as a narrow aperture in a surrounding opaque surface is indispensable, and the stimulus must have certain other properties as well if perception of a figure is to be the preferred solution. Where a figure moves behind a stationary slit the perceptual system must also infer the figure's speed and direction in order to reconstruct its length and shape.

If this interpretation of the events that follow viewing an anorthoscopic display is correct, the perception of form is a process much closer to the cognitive level than has heretofore been recognized. It cannot be explained as a direct outcome of the physiological processing of contours stimulating the retina.

Chapter 8
Induced Form
Irvin Rock and Alan L. Gilchrist

If a figure is moved behind a narrow stationary slit or if a slit is moved over a stationary figure, under certain conditions the observer perceives an extended figure (Zöllner, 1862; Helmholtz, 1962; Parks, 1965; Haber and Nathanson, 1968; Anstis and Atkinson, 1967; Rock and Halper, 1969; Rock and Sigman, 1973). Two kinds of explanations have been proposed for this effect. According to the retinal-painting hypothesis, an extended image of the figure is created by virtue of eye movements. This implies that the observer moves his eyes in the case of the moving-figure paradigm and holds his eyes still in the case of the moving-slit paradigm. It further implies that neural persistence converts the temporally successive retinal "slices" into a simultaneous extended neural representation of the figure. If this hypothesis is correct, form perception under such conditions is neither surprising nor theoretically significant.

According to the other hypothesis, the effect can occur without an extended image of the figure and, therefore, without the eye movements necessary to produce such an image. Rather, the impression of an extended figure is held to result from a process of synthesizing the set of phenomenally perceived locations of the momentarily visible element into a unified form. If one views form perception under the more typical conditions of a simultaneously extended image as the result of a "description" of the entire set of locations of the constituent parts of a figure relative to one another rather than as the result of some other process (such as the discharging of a set of neural contour detectors), then form perception under the special conditions of successive exposure is not as anomalous as it might first seem to be.

The crucial point about the second hypothesis is that information be provided concerning the *phenomenal* locations of the parts of the figure relative to one another. With the eyes stationary, such information is ordinarily provided by the varying locations within the retinal image,

Originally published in *The American Journal of Psychology* 88 (1975): 475–482. Reprinted with permission.

with each retinal locus serving as a local sign of a particular field location. But since the same retinal locus can signify various phenomenal locations for various positions of the eyes, the perception of an extended figure in the moving-slit paradigm is to be expected, according to the second explanation, even when the eyes accurately track the moving slit. Such figure perception in the case of the moving-figure paradigm is less easily explained, since with the eyes held still, neither varying retinal location nor varying eye position occurs. One must therefore assume that the perceptual system infers that each successive view of the figure represents a neighboring spatial "slice" of the figure—that the varying phenomenal locations are arrived at from the succession of locations within the narrow slit (for example, the leftmost region is below the central region, which in turn is above the rightmost region).

Another determinant of perceived location is the position of a stimulus object relative to another object serving as frame of reference. Thus, induced movement can be understood as an impression that an object has changed its location although relative to the observer it has not changed its direction. It would seem to follow that an impression of an extended figure could result from viewing an element through a slit when the slit does not objectively move but only appears to do so via induced movement. The purpose of the experiment reported here was to demonstrate that such an effect occurs, thereby supporting the second type of explanation of the perception of a figure seen through a narrow slit.

To illustrate the method, consider the conditions present when a vertical slit is actually passing over a simple, wavy-line type of figure. That part of the line figure which is visible through the slit can be said to displace up and down within the slit. At the same time, the slit is seen to move left and right. To create an illusory equivalent of these conditions, the opaque rectangle containing the slit is placed against a background of textured wallpaper. When this background, which thus serves as a frame of reference for the opaque rectangle, is moved left and right, it makes the rectangle (containing the slit) appear to move in the opposite direction. Furthermore, both the background and the rectangle are moved together up and down so as to produce the necessary vertical displacement in the visible element of the figure seen through the slit (see figure 8.1). Thus, except for changes of slope, the visible element maintains a stationary location. Therefore, to the extent that the observer fixates the element, the retinal image of the "figure" is never more than a rather small spot. If a line figure is perceived under these conditions, it is a percept of form induced by the movement of the background, and we therefore refer to it as induced form.

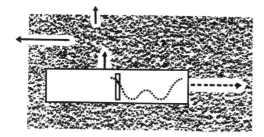

Figure 8.1
A schematic of the induced-form paradigm: the solid arrows indicate objective movement; the dashed arrow, the induced impression of movement; the dotted line, the induced form.

Method

Display

A video tape of the display was made. The display was viewed by the observer on a television screen at a distance of 6 ft. The slit measured $\frac{5}{16}$ by $2\frac{3}{4}$ in. on the screen and the rectangle $3\frac{3}{4}$ by 14 in. Since the wallpaper background displaced $5\frac{3}{4}$ in. in one horizontal pass and since the rectangle and wallpaper together displaced $1\frac{3}{4}$ in. vertically, the size of the induced form if perceived without distortion would be $5\frac{3}{4}$ in. wide by $1\frac{3}{4}$ in. high. The shape of the induced form is shown in figure 8.1.

Procedure

Four different conditions were employed, each with separate observers. In the *experimental condition (induced form)*, the observers were shown the induced-form paradigm via television for approximately 20 sec (about 17 apparent passes of the slit over the figure, since the background moved back and forth at a rate of about 1.2 sec per pass).

In *control condition 1 (blank field)*, the observers could see only the element, as it existed in the experimental condition, but on an otherwise blank, homogeneous background. Neither the slit, nor the opaque rectangle, nor the background pattern was visible. This was viewed for approximately 20 sec.

In *control condition 2 (moving slit)*, for purposes of comparison, the observers were shown a television picture of an opaque rectangle with a slit that *did* pass over the figure. With the exception of this difference, the features of this condition paralleled those of the experimental condition: the shape of the figure was the same, as were the speed and displacement of rectangle relative to background, the presence of a background pattern, and so on. In this condition, however, only the opaque rectangle moved and it moved only horizontally; the background pattern was stationary.

The procedure here, therefore, is essentially that employed by Rock and Halper (1969).

In *control condition 3 (moving figure)*, the observers were shown a television picture of the figure moving behind a *stationary* slit. Other than the fact that here the slit was stationary and the figure moved, viewing conditions were similar to those in the experimental condition and in control condition 2 (moving slit): the same figure was used, its speed was the same as that of the slit in those conditions, and the same background pattern was present. However, in this condition, only the figure moved and it moved only horizontally; the opaque rectangle and background pattern were stationary. The procedure here, therefore, is essentially that employed by Parks (1965) and others.

In each condition, the procedure consisted of several steps. First, the moving display was shown for 20 sec. Second, the observer was simply asked to describe what he had seen. If his description was in any way ambiguous, he was questioned further. Third, he was asked to draw a diagram of whatever he reported seeing in the slit. Finally, he was given a recognition test containing the correct figure and five similar ones. In addition, for the observers in the experimental condition, eye movements were carefully monitored and the observers were asked what the slit appeared to be doing.

Observers

The observers were college students who were naive with respect to the phenomenon under study. Altogether, 40 observers were tested, 10 in each condition.

Results

It was generally quite clear what the observers perceived and their drawings seemed to clear up any ambiguities in their verbal descriptions. The main concern here is whether they perceived an extended line figure or a small element moving vertically within the slit. The results for the four conditions were as follows.

Of the 10 observers in the *experimental condition*, 6 perceived a line figure revealed by an apparently moving slit. They reported that the slit appeared to be moving over a stationary figure. The remaining observers had the impression of an element moving up and down a horizontally moving slit.[1] In other words, all observers were subject to induced movement but not all to induced form.

None of the observers in *control condition 1 (blank field)* perceived a line figure revealed by the moving slit. Rather, they perceived a small stationary rectangular spot that appeared to tilt slightly clockwise and counterclockwise.

Of the 10 observers in *control condition 2 (moving slit)*, 4 perceived a line figure revealed by the moving slit. The others had the impression of an element moving up and down a horizontally moving slit.

Of the 10 observers in *control condition 3 (moving figure)*, 7 perceived a line figure moving behind a stationary slit. The others had the impression of an element moving up and down a stationary slit.

Concerning eye movement in the experimental condition, the only condition in which that was investigated in this study, the majority of observers had the impression they were tracking the phenomenally moving (but objectively stationary) slit. Yet, within the limits of accuracy permitted by unaided monitoring of their eyes by the experimenter, on the whole the observers' eyes remained stationary. In support of this finding is the result of video recordings of eye position for two observers during their inspection of the moving display. The recordings were made by means of a closeup lens. An enlarged picture of the eye in which the pupil's diameter measured approximately $4\frac{1}{2}$ in. was visible on the television screen, so that even small eye movements would be readily seen. No detectable eye movement occurred for these two observers, both of whom nonetheless experienced an extended line figure.

The results of the recognition test were not particularly revealing. This test was given only to those observers who reported perceiving a line figure, since it would make no sense to the other observers. Of those 6 observers in the experimental condition, 3 identified the correct test figure and 2 selected a very similar figure. For control condition 2 (moving slit), no observer was correct, but 1 selected a very similar alternative. For control condition 3 (moving figure), 1 observer was correct and 4 selected very similar alternatives. It must be borne in mind, however, that figures perceived through a narrow slit are often distorted in length, a distortion which may explain the relatively poor performance in the recognition test.

Discussion

The main finding was of induced form. While the number of observers in each condition was small, so that final conclusions about differences or the lack of them between conditions are not possible, the result in the experimental condition is typical of what we have found in our laboratory over a period of several years in research on figure perception through a narrow slit; namely, that a majority of the observers perceive a line figure and a minority perceive an element moving up and down the slit.

Can the perception of form in the experimental condition be explained on the basis of the retinal-painting hypothesis? In order for an extended image of the induced figure to be formed, the observers would have to move their eyes not only horizontally but vertically as well, since the element visible through the slit is stationary. It is not clear why an observer would tend to move his eyes this way. If he attempted to track the slit in its horizontal excursions, which *would* be understandable, he would in fact have to hold his eyes still, since the opaque rectangle does not move horizontally. It is interesting to note in this connection that most observers in the experimental condition did have the impression they were moving their eyes in tracking the slit. In any event, monitoring of eye position indicated essentially no eye movements by these observers. It is relevant at this point to note that there is now considerable evidence that retinal "painting" is neither a necessary nor sufficient explanation of form perception in the moving-slit paradigm (Rock and Halper, 1969; Rock and Sigman, 1973) and some evidence to this effect in the moving-figure paradigm (Parks, 1970).

In some respects, the induced-form paradigm is similar to the moving-figure paradigm. In both cases, the slit is stationary, at least in the horizontal direction, and so no horizontally extended retinal image of a figure is formed (unless the eyes move). Therefore, some might be inclined to argue that it is unnecessary to believe there is a unique effect justifying the name "induced form." But the fact is that the stimulus conditions are different in the two cases, the only similarity being in the fact that in both cases the slit does not displace horizontally. Moreover, phenomenally these two effects are quite different. In one case (induced form), the observer has the impression a moving slit is passing in front of a stationary figure, whereas in the other case (moving figure), he has the impression a figure is passing behind a stationary slit.[2] There are probably also certain measurably different effects of these stimulus conditions, such as those concerning distortion. The moving-figure paradigm almost always results in a substantial phenomenal compression of the figure along the direction of motion. We do not have the impression that this is true in the induced-form paradigm, although as yet we have no quantitative data to support this assertion. Distortion in the moving-slit paradigm occurs only when the observer tracks the slit (as was established in an unpublished study by Koncsol and Rock, in 1972).

We therefore conclude that induced form provides evidence that a sufficient basis for the perception of an extended figure is information concerning the set of phenomenal locations of parts of a figure relative to one another. An extended (and simultaneous) retinal image is not a necessary basis for the perception of an extended figure. That not all observers perceived a figure in the induced-form condition of the present experiment can be understood in much the same way that such a result can be understood for all cases of form successively revealed through a narrow slit. The proximal stimulus is ambiguous in that it could result either from an element displacing vertically within the slit *or* from a figure being successively revealed. The former outcome implies an identity of the element regardless of its vertical position. The latter outcome implies a change of identity; that is, the element is construed to represent different portions of an object. Since there seems to be a preference for no change of identity (Wallach, 1935; Wallach, Weisz, and Adams, 1956), other factors must enter in to shift the preference toward change of identity. Sight of the ends of the figure through the slit and visible changes of slope are no doubt such factors, but in addition, other information that supports the perceptual hypothesis of a figure partially occluded and successively revealed through a slit is relevant (Rock and Sigman, 1973).

Notes

This research was supported by a Public Health Service Research Scientist Award to the first author. Received for publication October 7, 1974.
1. Since this effect is best appreciated when directly experienced, we will make available a section of video tape to the interested reader on request.
2. Because of this difference, one might understandably claim that in the moving-figure paradigm, the observer moves his eyes back and forth *once he is aware a figure is displacing* horizontally, in order to track some point in the figure. But in the induced-form paradigm, the figure is phenomenally stationary, so that no such tendency to track should be elicited.

References

Anstis, S. M., and Atkinson, J. 1967. Distortions in moving figures viewed through a stationary slit. *American Journal of Psychology* 80:572–585.

Haber, R. N., and Nathanson, L. S. 1968. Post-retinal storage? Some further observations on Park's camel as seen through the eye of a needle. *Perception and Psychophysics* 3:349–355.

Helmholtz, H. von. 1962. *Treatise on physiological optics*, trans. J. C. Southall, vol. 3, p. 251.

Parks, T. E. 1965. Post-retinal visual storage. *American Journal of Psychology* 78:145–147.

Parks, T. E. 1970. A control for ocular tracking in the demonstration of post-retinal visual storage. *American Journal of Psychology* 83:442–444.

Rock, I., and Halper, F. 1969. Form perception without a retinal image. *American Journal of Psychology* 82:425–440.

Rock, I., and Sigman, E. 1973. Intelligence factors in the perception of form through a moving slit. *Perception* 2:357–369.

Wallach, H. 1935. Über visuell wahrgenommene Bewegungsrichtung. *Psychologische Forschung* 20:325–380.

Wallach, H., Weisz, A., and Adams, P. A. 1956. Circles and derived figures in rotation. *American Journal of Psychology* 69:48–59.

Zöllner, F. 1862. Über eine neue art anorthoskopischer Zerrbilder, *Poggendorff's Annalen der Physik und Chemie* 117:477–484.

Chapter 9
Orientation and Form
Irvin Rock

Many common experiences of everyday life that we take for granted present challenging scientific problems. In the field of visual perception one such problem is why things look different when they are upside down or tilted. Consider the inverted photograph [see fig. 9.1]. Although the face is familiar to most Americans, it is difficult to recognize when it is inverted. Even when one succeeds in identifying the face, it continues to look strange and the specific facial expression is hard to make out.

Consider also what happens when printed words and words written in longhand are turned upside down. With effort the printed words can be read, but it is all but impossible to read the longhand words [see fig. 9.2]. Try it with a sample of your own handwriting. One obvious explanation of why it is hard to read inverted words is that we have acquired the habit of moving our eyes from left to right, and that when we look at inverted words our eyes tend to move in the wrong direction. This may be one source of the difficulty, but it can hardly be the major one. It is just as hard to read even a single inverted word when we look at it without moving our eyes at all. It is probable that the same factor interfering with the recognition of disoriented faces and other figures is also interfering with word recognition.

The partial rotation of even a simple figure can also prevent its recognition, provided that the observer is unaware of the rotation. A familiar figure viewed in a novel orientation no longer appears to have the same shape [see figs. 9.3, 9.4]. As Ernst Mach pointed out late in the 19th century, the appearance of a square is quite different when it is rotated 45 degrees. In fact, we call it a diamond.

Some may protest that a familiar shape looks different in a novel orientation for the simple reason that we rarely see it that way. But even a figure we have not seen before will look different in different orientations [see fig. 9.5]. The fact is that orientation affects perceived shape, and that

Originally published in *Scientific American* 230, 1 (1974): 78–85, under the title "The Perception of Disoriented Figures." Reprinted with permission.

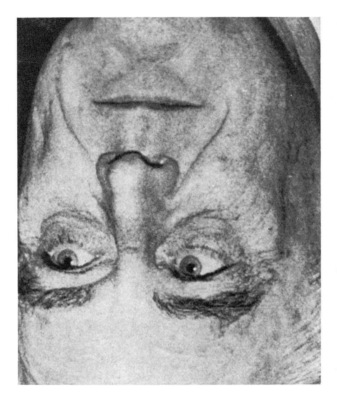

Figure 9.1
Inverted photograph of a famous American demonstrates how difficult it is to recognize a familiar face when it is presented upside down. Even after one succeeds in identifying the inverted face as that of Franklin D. Roosevelt, it continues to look strange.

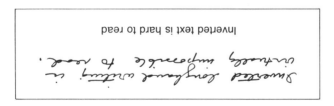

Figure 9.2
Inverted words are difficult to read when they are set in type, and words written in longhand are virtually impossible to decipher. The difficulty applies to one's own inverted handwriting in spite of a lifetime of experience reading it in the normal upright orientation.

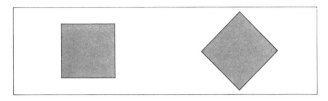

Figure 9.3
Square and diamond are two familiar shapes. The two figures shown here are identical; their appearance is so different, however, that we call one a square and the other a diamond. With the diamond the angles do not spontaneously appear as right angles.

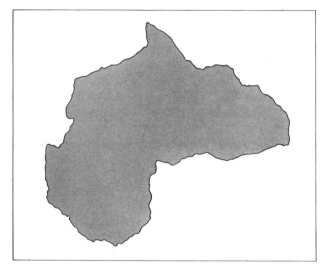

Figure 9.4
"Unfamiliar" shape shown here becomes a familiar shape when it is rotated clockwise 90 degrees. In a classroom experiment, when the rotated figure was drawn on the blackboard, it was not recognized as an outline of the continent of Africa until the teacher told the class at the end of the lecture that the figure was rotated out of its customary orientation.

the failure to recognize a familiar figure when it is in a novel orientation is based on the change in its perceived shape.

On the other hand, a figure can be changed in various ways without any effect on its perceived shape. For example, a triangle can be altered in size, color and various other ways without any change in its perceived shape [see fig. 9.6]. Psychologists, drawing an analogy with a similar phenomenon in music, call such changes transpositions. A melody can be transposed to a new key, and although all the notes then are different, there is no change in the melody. In fact, we generally remain unaware of

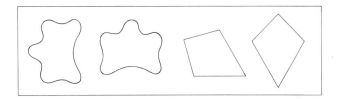

Figure 9.5
Novel or unfamiliar figures look different in different orientations, provided that we view them naïvely and do not mentally rotate them. The reason may be the way in which a figure is "described" by the perceptual system. The figure at the far left could be described as a closed shape resting on a horizontal base with a protrusion on its left side and an indentation on its right side. The figure adjacent to it, although identical, would be described as a symmetrical shape resting on a curved base with a protrusion at the top. The second figure from the right could be described as a quadrilateral resting on a side. The figure at the far right would be described as a diamondlike shape standing on end.

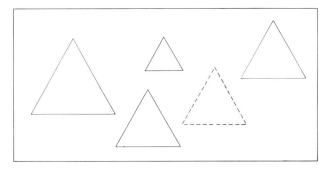

Figure 9.6
Alteration in size, color, or type of contour does not change the perceived shape of a triangle. Even varying the location of the triangle's retinal image (by looking out of the corner of your eyes or fixating on different points) does not change perceived shape.

the transposition. Clearly the melody derives from the relation of the notes to one another, which is not altered when the melody is transposed. In much the same way a visual form is based primarily on how parts of a figure are related to one another geometrically. For example, one could describe a square as being a four-sided figure having parallel opposite sides, four right angles and four sides of equal length. These features remain unchanged when a square is transposed in size or position; that is why it continues to look like a square. We owe a debt to the Gestalt psychologists for emphasizing the importance in perception of relations rather than absolute features.

Since a transposition based on rotation also does not alter the internal geometric relations of a figure, then why does it look different in an altered orientation? At this point we should consider the meaning of the term orientation. What changes are introduced by altering orientation? One obvious change is that rotating a figure would result in a change in the orientation of its image on the retina of the eye. Perhaps, therefore, we should ask why different retinal orientations of the same figure should give rise to different perceived shapes. That might lead us into speculations about how the brain processes information about form, and why differently oriented projections of a retinal image should lead to different percepts of form.

Before we go further in this direction we should consider another meaning of the term orientation. The inverted and rotated figures in the illustrations for this article are in different orientations with respect to the vertical and horizontal directions in their environment. That part of the figure which is normally pointed upward in relation to gravity, to the sky or to the ceiling is now pointed downward or sideways on the page. Perhaps it is this kind of orientation that is responsible for altered perception of shape when a figure is disoriented.

It is not difficult to separate the retinal and the environmental factors in an experiment. Cut out a paper square and tape it to the wall so that the bottom of the square is parallel to the floor. Compare the appearance of the square first with your head upright and then with your head tilted 45 degrees. You will see that the square continues to look like a square when your head is tilted. Yet when your head is tilted 45 degrees, the retinal image of the square is the same as the image of a diamond when the diamond is viewed with the head upright. Thus it is not the retinal image that is responsible for the altered appearance of a square when the square is rotated 45 degrees. The converse experiment points to the same conclusion. Rotate the square on the wall so that it becomes a diamond. The diamond viewed with your head tilted 45 degrees produces a retinal image of a square, but the diamond still looks like a diamond. Needless to say, in these simple demonstrations one continues to perceive correctly where the top, bottom and sides of the figures are even when one's posture changes. It is therefore the change of a figure's perceived orientation in the environment that affects its apparent shape and not the change of orientation of its retinal image.

These conclusions have been substantiated in experiments Walter I. Heimer and I and other colleagues have conducted with numerous subjects. In one series of experiments the subjects were shown unfamiliar figures. In the first part of the experiment a subject sat at a table and simply looked at several figures shown briefly in succession. Then some of the subjects were asked to tilt their head 90 degrees by turning it to the side and resting it on the table. In this position the subject viewed a series of

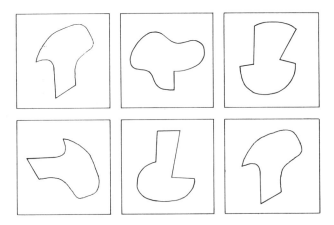

Figure 9.7
Rotation of retinal image by tilting the head 90 degrees does not appreciably affect recognition of a novel figure (*figure at top left*). Subjects first viewed several novel targets while sitting upright. Then they were shown a series of test figures (*all others*) and were asked to identify those they had seen before. Some subjects tilted their head 90 degrees; others viewed the test figures with their head upright. Tilted-head subjects failed to recognize figures that were retinally "upright" (for example figure at bottom left) about as much as upright viewers did (to whom such figures were not retinally upright). Tilted-head subjects recognized environmentally upright figures (*bottom right*) as often as upright viewers did.

figures [see fig. 9.7]. Most of the figures were new, but among them were some figures the subject had seen earlier. These figures were shown in either of two orientations: upright with respect to the room (as they had been in the first viewing) or rotated 90 degrees so that the "top" of the figure corresponded to the top of the subject's tilted head. The subject was asked to say whether or not he had seen each figure in the first session. He did not know that the orientation of the figures seen previously might be different. Other subjects viewed the test figures while sitting upright.

When we compared the scores of subjects who tilted their head with subjects who sat upright for the test, the results were clear. Tilted-head subjects recognized the environmentally upright (but retinally tilted) figures about as well as the upright observers did. They also failed to recognize the environmentally tilted (but retinally upright) figures about as often as the upright subjects did. In other words, the experiments confirmed that it is rotation with respect to the up-down and left-right coordinates in the environment that produces the change in the perceived shape of the figure. It is not rotation of the retinal image that produces the change, since altering the image's orientation does not adversely affect recognition and preserving it does not improve recognition.

Figure 9.8
Figures with intrinsic orientation appear to have a natural vertical axis regardless of their physical orientation. A region at one end of the axis is perceived as top.

Figure 9.9
Impression of symmetry is spontaneous only when a figure is symmetrical around a vertical axis. Subjects were asked to indicate which of two figures (*middle and right*) was most like the target figure (*left*). The figure at right was selected most frequently, presumably because it is symmetrical around its vertical axis. If the page is tilted 90 degrees, the figure in the middle will now be selected as being more similar to the target figure. Now if the page is held vertically and the figures are viewed with the head tilted 90 degrees, the figure at right is likely to be seen as being the most similar. This suggests that it is not the symmetry around the egocentric vertical axis on the retina but rather the symmetry around the environmental axis of the figure that determines perceived symmetry.

In another experiment subjects viewed an ambiguous or reversible figure that could be perceived in one of two ways depending on its orientation. For example, when one figure that looked like a map of the U.S. was rotated 90 degrees, it looked like the profile of a bearded man. Subjects were asked to rest their head on the table when viewing the ambiguous figures. The question we asked ourselves was: Which "upright" would dominate, the retinal upright or the environmental upright? The results were decisive. About 80 percent of the subjects reported seeing only the aspect of the ambiguous figure that was environmentally upright, even though the alternative was upright on their retina [see fig. 9.10].

Why does the orientation of a figure with respect to the directional coordinates of the environment have such a profound effect on the perceived

Figure 9.10
Ambiguous figures can be perceived in different ways depending on the orientation assigned
to them. Figure at left can look like the profile of a man's head with a chef's hat (*top left*) or,
when rotated 90 degrees, like a dog (*bottom left*). Figure at right can look like the profile of a
bearded man's head (*top right*) or like a map of the U.S. (*bottom right*). When subjects with
their head tilted 90 degrees to one side viewed these ambiguous figures (*direction of subject's
head is shown by arrow*), they preferentially recognized the figure that was upright in the environment instead of the figure that was upright on the retina.

shape of the figure? The answer I propose is that perceived shape is
based on a cognitive process in which the characteristics of the figure are
implicitly described by the perceptual system. For example, the leftmost
shape in fig. 9.5 could be described as a closed figure resting on a horizontal base with a protrusion on the figure's left side and an indentation
on its right side. The colored figure to the right of it, although it is identical and only rotated 90 degrees, would be described quite differently,
as being symmetrical with two bumps on the bottom and with left and
right sides more or less straight and identical with each other. I am not
suggesting that such a description is conscious or verbal; obviously we
would be aware of the descriptive process if it were either. Furthermore,
animals and infants who are nonverbal perceive shape much as we do. I
am proposing that a process analogous to such a description does take
place and that it is not only based on the internal geometry of a figure but
also takes into account the location of the figure's top, bottom and sides.
In such a description orientation is therefore a major factor in the shape
that is finally perceived.

From experiments I have done in collaboration with Phyllis Olshansky
it appears that certain shifts in orientation have a marked effect on perceived shape. In particular, creating symmetry around a vertical axis

where no symmetry had existed before (or vice versa), shifting the long axis from vertical to horizontal (or vice versa) and changing the bottom of a figure from a broad horizontal base to a pointed angle (or vice versa) seemed to have a strong effect on perceived shape. Such changes of shape can result from only a moderate angular change of orientation, say 45 or 90 degrees. Interestingly enough, inversions or rotations of 180 degrees often have only a slight effect on perceived shape, perhaps because such changes will usually not alter perceived symmetry or the perceived orientation of the long axis of the figure.

There is one kind of orientation change that has virtually no effect on perceived shape: a mirror-image reversal. This is particularly true for the novel figures we used in our experiments. How can this be explained? It seems that although the "sides" of visual space are essentially interchangeable, the up-and-down directions in the environment are not. "Up" and "down" are distinctly different directions in the world we live in. Thus a figure can be said to have three main perceptual boundaries: top, bottom and sides. As a result the description of a figure will not be much affected by whether a certain feature is on the left side or the right. Young children and animals have great difficulty learning to discriminate between a figure and its mirror image, but they can easily distinguish between a figure and its inverted counterpart.

Related to this analysis is a fact observed by Mach and tested by Erich Goldmeier: A figure that is symmetrical around one axis will generally appear to be symmetrical only if that axis is vertical. Robin Leaman and I have demonstrated that it is the perceived vertical axis of the figure and not the vertical axis of the figure's retinal image that produces this effect. An observer who tilts his head will continue to perceive a figure as being symmetrical if that figure is symmetrical around an environmental vertical axis. This suggests that perceived symmetry results only when the two equivalent halves of a figure are located on the two equivalent sides of perceptual space.

If, as I have suggested, the description of a figure is based on the location of its top, bottom and sides, the question arises: How are these directions assigned in a figure? One might suppose that the top of a figure is ordinarily the area uppermost in relation to the ceiling, the sky or the top of a page. In a dark room an observer may have to rely on his sense of gravity to inform him which way is up.

Numerous experiments by psychologists have confirmed that there are indeed two major sources of information for perceiving the vertical and the horizontal: gravity (as it is sensed by the vestibular apparatus in the inner ear, by the pressure of the ground on the body and by feedback from the muscles) and information from the scene itself. We have been able to demonstrate that either can affect the perceived shape of a figure.

A luminous figure in a dark room will not be recognized readily when it is rotated to a new orientation even if the observer is tilted by exactly the same amount. Here the only source of information about directions in space is gravity. In a lighted room an observer will often fail to recognize a figure when he and the figure are upright but the room is tilted. The tilted room creates a strong impression of where the up-down axis should be, and this leads to an incorrect attribution of the top and bottom of the figure [see "The Perception of the Upright," by Herman A. Witkin; *Scientific American,* February, 1959].

Merely informing an observer that a figure is tilted will often enable him to perceive the figure correctly. This may explain why some readers will not perceive certain of the rotated figures shown here as being strange or different. The converse situation, misinforming an observer about the figures, produces impressive results. If a subject is told that the top of a figure he is about to see is somewhere other than in the region uppermost in the environment, he is likely not to recognize the figure when it is presented with the orientation in which he first saw it. The figure is not disoriented and the observer incorrectly assigns the directions top, bottom and sides on the basis of instructions.

Since such knowledge about orientation will enable the observer to shift the directions he assigns to a figure, and since it is this assignment that affects the perception of shape, it is absolutely essential to employ naïve subjects in perception experiments involving orientation. That is, the subject must not realize that the experiment is concerned with figural orientation, so that he does not examine the figures with the intent of finding the regions that had been top, bottom and sides in previous viewings of it. There are, however, some figures that seem to have intrinsic orientation in that regardless of how they are presented a certain region will be perceived as the top [fig. 9.8]. It is therefore difficult or impossible to adversely affect the recognition of such figures by disorienting them.

In the absence of other clues a subject will assign top-bottom coordinates according to his subjective or egocentric reference system. Consider a figure drawn on a circular sheet of paper that is lying on the ground. Neither gravity nor visual clues indicate where the top and bottom are. Nevertheless, an observer will assign a top to that region of the figure which is uppermost with respect to his egocentric coordinate reference system. The vertical axis of the figure is seen as being aligned with the long axis of the observer's head and body. The upward direction corresponds to the position of his head. We have been able to demonstrate that such assignment of direction has the same effect on the recognition that other bases of assigning direction do. A figure first seen in one orientation on the circular sheet will generally not be recognized if its ego-centric orientation is altered.

Now we come to an observation that seems to be at variance with much of what I have described. When a person lies on his side in bed to read, he does not hold the book upright (in the environmental sense) but tilts it. If the book is not tilted, the retinal image is disoriented and reading is quite difficult. Similarly, if a reader views printed matter or photographs of faces that are environmentally upright with his head between his legs, they will be just as difficult to recognize as they are when they are upside down and the viewer's head is upright. The upright pictures, however, are still perceived as being upright even when the viewer's head is inverted. Conversely, if the pictures are upside down in the environment and are viewed with the head inverted between the legs, there is no difficulty in recognizing them. Yet the observer perceives the pictures as being inverted. Therefore in these cases it is the orientation of the retinal image and not the environmental assignment of direction that seems to be responsible for recognition or failure of recognition.

Experiments with ambiguous figures conducted by Robert Thouless, G. Kanizsa and G. Tampieri support the notion that retinal orientation plays a role in recognition of a figure [see fig. 9.16]. Moreover, as George Steinfeld and I have demonstrated, the recognition of upright words and faces falls off in direct proportion to the degree of body tilt [see fig. 9.11]. With such visual material recognition is an inverse function of the degree of disorientation of the retinal image. As we have seen, the relation between degree of disorientation and recognizability does not hold in cases where the assignment of direction has been altered. In such cases the greatest effect is not with a 180-degree change but with a 45- or 90-degree change.

The results of all these experiments have led me to conclude that there are two distinct factors involved in the perception of disoriented figures: an assignment-of-direction factor and a retinal factor. I believe that when we view a figure with our head tilted, we automatically compensate for the tilt in much the same way that we compensate for the size of distant objects. An object at a moderate distance from us does not appear small in spite of the fact that its retinal image is much smaller than it is when the object is close by. This effect usually is explained by saying that the information supplied by the retinal image is somehow corrected by allowing for the distance of the object from us. Similarly, when a vertical luminous line in a dark room is viewed by a tilted observer, it will still look vertical or almost vertical in spite of the fact that the retinal image in the observer's eye is tilted. Thus the tilt of the body must be taken into account by the perceptual system. The tilted retinal image is then

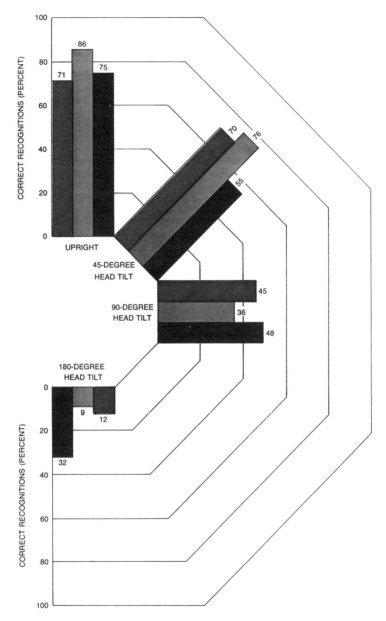

Figure 9.11
Recognition of certain kinds of visual material decreased almost in direct proportion to the degree of head tilt of the observer. In a series of experiments the number of correct recognitions of faces (*dark gray*), written words (*gray*) and fragmented figures (*black*) were recorded for various degrees of head tilt. Subject saw several examples of each type of test material in each of the head positions. For this visual material recognition is an inverse function of the degree of disorientation of the retinal image.

Figure 9.12
Single letter that is tilted can be easily identified once it is realized how it is oriented. A strangeness in its appearance, however, remains because the percept arising from the uncorrected retinal image continues to exist simultaneously with the corrected percept.

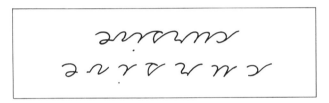

Figure 9.13
Inverted longhand writing is difficult to decipher because many inverted units resemble written upright letters. For example, an inverted *u* will look like an *n* and an inverted *c* like an *s*. Moreover, the connection between letters leads to uncertainty about where a letter begins and ends. Several inverted units can be grouped together and misperceived as an upright letter. Separating the inverted letters makes them easier to decipher.

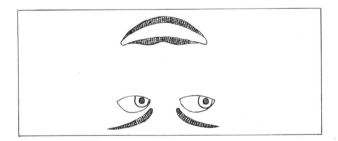

Figure 9.14
Inverted facial features are difficult to interpret because while attention is focused on correcting one feature other features remain uncorrected. For example, one might succeed in correcting the eyes shown here so that they are perceived as gazing downward and leftward, but at that very moment the mouth is uncorrected and expresses sorrow rather than pleasure. Conversely, one might correct the mouth and misperceive the eyes.

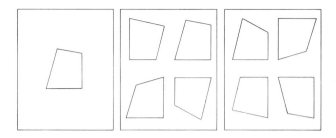

Figure 9.15
Multiple items were found to have an adverse effect on recognition of even simple figures. Subjects sitting upright viewed the target (*left*). Then they were briefly shown test cards, some of which contained the target figure (*middle*) and some of which did not (*right*). The subjects were to indicate when they saw a figure that was identical with the target figure. Half of the test cards were viewed with the head upright and half with the head inverted. Recognition was poor when inverted subjects viewed the test cards. In other experiments with a single test figure head inversion did not significantly affect recognition.

Figure 9.16
Ambiguous faces are perceived differently when their images on the retina of the observer are inverted. If you hold the illustration upright and view it from between your legs with your head inverted, the alternative faces will be perceived even though they are upside down in terms of the environment. The same effect occurs when the illustration is inverted and viewed from an upright position. Such tests provide evidence that figures such as faces are recognized on the basis of their upright retinal orientation.

corrected, with the result that the line is perceived as being vertical. Just as the correction for size at a distance is called size constancy, so can correction for the vertical be called orientation constancy.

When we view an upright figure with our head tilted, before we have made any correction, we begin with the information provided by an image of the figure in a particular retinal orientation. The first thing that must happen is that the perceptual system processes the retinal image on the basis of an egocentrically assigned top, bottom and sides, perhaps because of a primitive sense of orientation derived from retinal orientation. For example, when we view an upright square with our head tilted, which yields a diamondlike retinal image, we may perceive a diamond for a fleeting moment before the correction goes into operation. Head orientation is then automatically taken into account to correct the perception. Thus the true top of the figure is seen to be one of the sides of the square rather than a corner. The figure is then "described" correctly as one whose sides are horizontal and vertical in the environment, in short as a "square." This correction is made quickly and usually without effort. In order to describe a figure the viewer probably must visualize or imagine it in terms of its true top, bottom and sides rather than in terms of its retinal top, bottom and sides.

If the figure is relatively simple, the correction is not too difficult to achieve. If we view an upright letter with our head tilted, we recognize it easily; it is of interest, however, that there is still something strange about it. I believe the dual aspect of the perception of orientation is responsible for this strangeness. There is an uncorrected perception of the letter based on its retinal-egocentric orientation and a corrected perception of it based on its environmental orientation. The first perception produces an unfamiliar shape, which accounts for the strange appearance of the letter in spite of its subsequent recognition. In our experiments many of the figures we employed were structurally speaking equivalent to letters, and in some cases we actually used letters from unfamiliar alphabets.

With a more complex figure, such as an inverted word or an upright word viewed by an inverted observer, the corrective mechanism may be entirely overtaxed. Each letter of the word must be corrected separately, and the corrective mechanism apparently cannot cope simultaneously with multiple components. It is true that if an observer is given enough time, an inverted word can be deciphered, but it will never look the same as it does when it is upright. While one letter is being corrected the others continue to be perceived in their uncorrected form. There is a further difficulty: letter order is crucial for word recognition, and inverting a word reverses the normal left-to-right order.

The recognition of inverted longhand writing is even more difficult. When such writing is turned upside down, many of the inverted "units" strongly resemble normal upright longhand letters. Moreover, since the letters are connected, it is difficult to tell where one letter ends and another begins. Separating the letters of the inverted word makes recognition easier. Even so, it is all too easy to confuse a *u* and an *n*. This type of confusion is also encountered with certain printed letters, namely, *b* and *q*, *d* and *p* and *n* and *u*, although not as frequently. In other words, if a figure is recognized on the basis of its upright retinal-egocentric orientation, this may tend to stabilize the perception and block the correction process. The dominance of the retinally upright faces in figure 9.16 probably is an effect of just this kind.

There may be a similar overtaxing of the corrective mechanism when we view an inverted face. It may be that the face contains a number of features each of which must be properly perceived if the whole is to be recognized [see "The Recognition of Faces," by Leon D. Harmon; *Scientific American*, November, 1973]. While attention is focused on correcting one feature, say the mouth, other features remain uncorrected and continue to be perceived on the basis of the image they form on the retina. Of course, the relation of features is also important in the recognition of a face, but here too there are a great number of such relations and the corrective mechanism may again be overtaxed.

Charles C. Bebber, Douglas Blewett and I conducted an experiment to test the hypothesis that it is the presence of multiple components that creates the difficulty of correcting figures. Subjects were briefly shown a quadrilateral figure and asked to study it. They viewed the target figure with their head upright. Then they were shown a series of test cards each of which had four quadrilateral figures. The test cards were viewed for one second, and the subjects were required to indicate if the target figure was on the card.

The subjects understood that they were to respond affirmatively only when they saw a figure that was identical with the target figure both in shape and in orientation. (Some of the test figures were similar to the target figure but were rotated by 180 degrees.) Half of the test cards were seen with the subject's head upright and half with the subject's head inverted. It was assumed that the subject would not be able to correct all four test figures in the brief time that was allowed him while he was viewing them with his head down. He had to perceive just as many units in the same brief time while he was viewing them with his head upright, but he did not have to correct any of the units. We expected that target figures would often not be recognized and that incorrect figures would be mistakenly identified as the target when the subjects viewed the test cards with their heads inverted.

The results bore out our prediction. When multiple components have to be corrected, retinal disorientation has an adverse effect on recognition. The observer responded to twice as many test cards correctly when he was upright than he did when he was inverted.

As I have noted, when we look at figures that are difficult to recognize when they are retinally disoriented, the difficulty increases as the degree of disorientation increases. Why this happens may also be related to the nature of the correction process. I suggested that the observer must suppress the retinally (egocentrically) upright percept and substitute a corrected percept. To do this, however, he must visualize or imagine how the figure would look if it were rotated until it was upright with respect to himself or, what amounts to the same thing, how it would look if he rotated himself into alignment with the figure. The process of mental rotation requires visualizing the entire sequence of angular change, and therefore the greater the angular change, the greater the difficulty.

As every parent knows, children between the ages of two and five seem to be quite indifferent to how a picture is oriented. They often hold a book upside down and seem not at all disturbed by it. On the basis of such observations and the results of some early experiments, many psychologists concluded that the orientation of a figure did not enter into its recognition by young children. More recent laboratory experiments, however, do not confirm the fact that children recognize figures equally well in any orientation. They have as much difficulty as, or more difficulty than, adults in recognizing previously seen figures when the figure is shown in a new orientation. Why then do young children often spontaneously look at pictures upside down in everyday situations? Perhaps they have not yet learned to pay attention to orientation, and do not realize that their recognition would improve if they did so. When children learn to read after the age of six, they are forced to pay attention to orientation because certain letters differ only in their orientation.

In summary, the central fact we have learned about orientation is that the perceived shape of a figure is not simply a function of its internal geometry. The perceived shape is also very much a function of the up, down and side directions we assign to the figure. If there is a change in the assigned directions, the figure will take on a different perceptual shape. I have speculated that the change in perceived shape is based on a new "description" of the figure by the perceptual system. The directions assigned are based on information of various kinds about where the top, bottom and sides of a figure are and usually do not depend on the retinal orientation of the image of the figure. When the image is not retinally upright, a process of correction is necessary in order to arrive at the correct description, and this correction is difficult or impossible to achieve in the case of visual material that has multiple components.

All of this implies that form perception in general is based to a much greater extent on cognitive processes than any current theory maintains. A prevailing view among psychologists and sensory physiologists is that form perception can be reduced to the perception of contours and that contour perception in turn can be reduced to abrupt differences in light intensity that cause certain neural units in the retina and brain to fire. If this is true, then perceiving form results from the specific concatenation of perceived contours. Although the work I have described does not deny the possible importance of contour detection as a basis of form perception, it does suggest that such an explanation is far from sufficient, and that the perception of form depends on certain mental processes such as description and correction. These processes in turn are necessary to account for the further step of recognition of a figure. A physically unchanged retinal image often will not lead to recognition if there has been a shift in the assigned directions. Conversely, if there has been no shift in the assigned directions, even a very different retinal image will still allow recognition.

Chapter 10
Symmetry
Irvin Rock and Robin Leaman

In discussing the problem of phenomenal similarity, Goldmeier (1) demonstrated that symmetry was a very important aspect of a form's appearance, particularly symmetry about the vertical and horizontal axes. A form which is symmetrical about these axes will look quite different from one which is roughly the same shape but which is modified so as to be asymmetrical. Moreover, symmetry about a vertical axis is more effective in this respect than about a horizontal axis.

To prove this, Goldmeier performed an experiment in which a figure which was both vertically and horizontally symmetrical was to be compared with two modified versions of it, one preserving the vertical symmetry only, and the other the horizontal symmetry only. (See fig. 10.1.) The preference was clearly for the vertically symmetrical version; that is to say, the observers regarded it as more similar to the original. The other version—asymmetrical about the vertical axis—looks quite different from the original.

This fact can be observed in daily life. Vertically symmetrical figures do look symmetrical, whereas the symmetry is often not noticed in horizontally symmetrical figures (as, for example, an object and its mirror image in a lake).

The question arises whether Goldmeier's effect depends upon symmetry about an axis of the image which is vertical on the retina or about an axis perceived as phenomenally vertical regardless of the orientation of the retinal image; "vertical" and "horizontal" are here ambiguous terms. It is possible to tease apart these two meanings, by having the observer tilt his head in relation to what he perceives to be the figure's vertical axis. One of the authors has shown by this technique that, in general, the apparent changes that occur when a form is disoriented are due primarily to phenomenal and not retinal disorientation (2, 3). For example, it can be shown that a square looks like a diamond when it is tilted 45 degrees, not

Originally published in *Acta Psychologica* 21 (1963): 171–183, under the title "An Experimental Analysis of Visual Symmetry." Reprinted with permission.

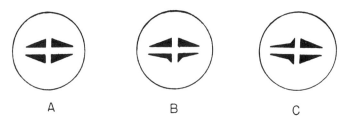

A   B   C

Figure 10.1
Goldmeier's Figure. A. Standard which is symmetrical about the vertical and horizontal axis.
B. Comparison figure symmetrical about vertical axis. C. Comparison figure symmetrical
about horizontal axis. If the page is turned 90 degrees, C rather than B would be regarded as
more similar to A.

because its image becomes a "diamond," but because its main axes assume
a new orientation in relation to the perceived "up" and "down" of space.
When the head is also tilted 45 degrees, the figure still looks like a diamond although the image is now once more a "square." Conversely, an
upright square still looks like a square when viewed with the head tilted
45 degrees although its image is now a "diamond." Thus, without instruction or information to the contrary, we tend to assume spontaneously
that a figure is upright in regard to the main directions of space and this
phenomenal orientation has been shown to be the important factor. If it is
seen again in a different orientation in the environment it will often not
be recognized as the same, even when it preserves the same orientation in
relation to the retina that it had previously. Conversely if it remains
upright in phenomenal space it will easily be recognized even if its orientation on the retina is changed. These findings are in contradiction to
those reported with familiar figures by Köhler (1940) and by Thouless
(1947).[1] However, just as it is possible, with a certain attitude, to see a
diamond as a tilted square, so it is possible, within certain structural limitations, for other forms to be seen as having a phenomenal top and
bottom divorced from that given by the up and down of our spatial
framework. This can be done by inducing a set to see a particular region
of the figure as its top (or in certain cases by familiarity with figures such
as faces or letters, where we know which portion is the top).[2]

    Since Goldmeier's finding is an orientation effect, we can ask these same
questions concerning it: Does the greater saliency of vertical symmetry
depend upon this axis being vertical in relation to the retina or upon it
being perceived as vertical in relation to the phenomenal up and down of
space? A further question is whether it is possible to divorce the phenomenal orientation of the figure from the up and down of space by inducing
a set.

Figure 10.2
The four additional figures used in this study. A in each case is the standard, B the vertically symmetrical comparison figure and C the horizontally symmetrical comparison figure. When the figures are presented at right angles to the position shown here, C becomes the figure with vertical symmetry.

Procedure and Results

Two experiments, employing 20 adult subjects each, were performed. Goldmeier's figure and four new ones, each of which was symmetrical about both axes, were shown.

Figure 10.2 shows the four new figures and the two comparison objects for each, one of which is symmetrical about the vertical axis only, and one of which is symmetrical about the horizontal axis only.[3] After viewing each original figure for five seconds, the subject was shown its two comparison figures simultaneously—in the same orientation as the original—and asked to indicate which of the two seemed to be more similar to the original. The left-right position of the two alternatives for a figure was counterbalanced. In order to control for factors other than symmetry which might influence a choice (such as the possibility that one comparison figure was more drastically altered than the other), after the subject had made judgments for the five figures, the entire series was presented again with the cards turned 90 degrees. A choice based on vertical symmetry would require the subject to switch his preference of alternatives and now choose as most similar the comparison figure which was before rejected. The figures were presented first in the orientation shown in figures 10.1 and 10.2 for half the subjects and in the 90 degrees tilted position first for the other half. Since analysis of each figure indicated no such absolute preferences, the data from both runs were combined. For the first 10 subjects of both experiments a choice of "neither" was allowed. In the last 10, a choice was forced. For the first 10 subjects the order of the five figures was varied randomly. For the last 10 they were presented in a fixed sequence. To minimize any memory effects a time interval of one week elapsed between each condition and the next. The control condition was presented first for all subjects, while the order of the two experimental conditions following it was counterbalanced. The 20 subjects of exp. I were shown the figures under each of the following three conditions. The results will be given separately for each.

Experiment I

Control Condition.   The figure's main axes were aligned with the vertical and horizontal directions of space and the subject was upright. (Shown schematically in fig. 10.3a) The subject was told explicitly that the figures were all upright. He was first shown an arrow, pointing upward, and told, "I am going to show you some figures and I want you to try to see them as if they were upright like this arrow, so that their tops are here (pointing) and their bottoms are here (pointing)." He was next shown a sequence of three familiar figures, simply drawn, each clearly upright and each containing a main axis that is obviously vertical: a tree, a man, and a crucifix. As each of these figures was presented, the student was asked, "What is this? Where is the top of this figure?" After the three figures were all shown, the subject was told, "You notice all these figures are upright. I am going to show you some new, unfamiliar figures, that are also upright, just like the ones you have seen. Take a good look at each one, and then point out the top of the figure." Each original design was then presented, and when the subject had indicated the location of its apparent "top," after completion of its five-second exposure, the original was removed and the comparison figures presented for judgment of similarity. Aside from these instructions to the subject, the situation is like Goldmeier's. Following the presentation of all five figures in one orienta-

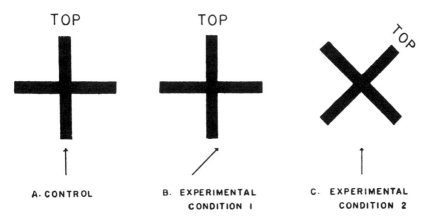

TOP   TOP

A. CONTROL   B. EXPERIMENTAL   C. EXPERIMENTAL
                       CONDITION I   CONDITION 2

Figure 10.3
Schematic illustration of the three conditions of experiment I. The figure represents the environmental orientation of the vertical and horizontal axes of the standard and comparison figures in each condition. The arrow represents the position of the subject's head in each condition. The word "top" refers to the position that the subject was instructed and set to see as the top of the figure.

tion, the five were shown again with figures rotated 90 degrees. Thus all data for one condition was secured before going on to the next condition.

Results: For the five figures, the 20 subjects selected the vertically symmetrical alternative 159 times, and the horizontally symmetrical alternative 37 times, a highly significant difference. In four instances, the subject was unable to choose. This result simply confirms and extends Goldmeier's findings with the new figures, and sets the stage for the following variations.

Experimental Condition 1. Here the subject's head was tilted 45 degrees clockwise (for half the subjects) or counterclockwise (for the remaining half). The figures remained in the same position as for the control series. The subject was reminded that the figures were still upright as before and was given again the initial series of familiar figures (fig. 10.3b). Under this condition, neither symmetrical axis of a figure is horizontal or vertical on the retina. Phenomenally, however, the vertical axis is aligned with the visual frame of reference as well as the direction of gravity.

Results: 146 choices were of the vertical alternative and 51 of the horizontal, a highly significant difference. In three instances, the subject was unable to choose. This result is similar to that in the first condition where the head is upright, demonstrating that the phenomenal factor alone can produce an effect which is about as strong, even though neither comparison figure should be favored from the standpoint of symmetry with respect to a vertical retinal direction.

Experimental Condition 2. Here the subject remained upright, while the axes of the figure were tilted 45 degrees (clockwise or counterclockwise). The subject was instructed that the figure was thusly tilted (fig. 10.3c), and was presented with the initial familiar figures tilted to this degree, otherwise following the same procedure as before.

This experiment puts to a very stringent test the hypothesis that the crucial factor in Goldmeier's effect is the symmetry about a *phenomenally* vertical axis. Here the phenomenally induced orientation of a figure is in conflict both with its retinal orientation and with an orientation that might be given by the directions of space. The axes of the figures are neither retinally vertical and horizontal nor aligned with the major axes of space, so that there should not be any effect at all, but for the influence of the special instructions which were designed to give a particular phenomenal orientation to the figure.

In fact, as will be noted below, with different instructions concerning where the top of the figure was, one does *not* get any effect in this situation (compare exp. II, control condition).

Results: Under this condition, the subjects made 129 choices favoring the phenomenal vertical of the figure and 68 favoring the horizontal, a highly significant difference. In three instances the subject was unable to choose.

For all three conditions, all five figures were found to show the effect and virtually every subject reflected the group tendency. It is perhaps worth mentioning at this point, that this effect occurs without the subject being in any way aware of what it is that determines his selection, or that he is behaving consistently with respect to any determinant. Symmetry is never mentioned and, as far as could be determined, did not enter as a conscious basis of choice.

Experiment II
To further test the role of the phenomenal orientation of a figure in producing the Goldmeier effect, exp. II was designed. (There were two subgroups of 10 subjects each, treated slightly different as described above for exp. I.) The subjects in this experiment were instructed, in each of the three conditions, to see as the phenomenally vertical axis, one of the *diagonal* axes of each figure. That is, the top of the figure, as seen, lay between the two symmetrical axes. The subjects in these experiments were shown initial familiar figures tending to have an X-like character in their normal upright orientation: a windmill, a railroad-crossing sign, and a butterfly with spread wings. As in exp. I, subjects indicated the perceived orientation of each original figure by pointing out where its "top" was seen to lie.

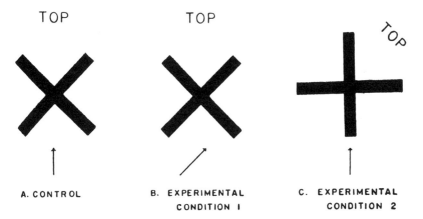

TOP   TOP

A. CONTROL   B. EXPERIMENTAL   C. EXPERIMENTAL
                       CONDITION I   CONDITION 2

Figure 10.4
Schematic illustration of the three conditions of experiment II.

Control Condition. Under the first condition, the subject was upright and was instructed to see each figure as upright, although its symmetrical axes were tilted 45 degrees [clockwise or counterclockwise (fig. 10.4a)]. Thus, except for the difference of instructions concerning the phenomenal orientation of the figures, the viewing conditions were exactly the same as for exp. I subjects in their second experimental condition. Since there was now no symmetry which could be designated as vertical by any criterion, and since there was symmetry about *each* of the diagonals of the standard, there was no reason to expect any clear-cut preference.

Results: A preference for alternatives preserving symmetry on the left diagonal was made in 90 cases, and on the right diagonal in 92 cases. In 18 instances, subjects were unable to choose, a much larger number than in exp. I. Further analysis of individual results failed to show any consistency of preference for one diagonal rather than the other. These results form the baseline for evaluating the results of the next two conditions.

Experimental Condition 1. Next, the subject's head was tilted 45 degrees clockwise or counterclockwise, and the figures remained as before with their symmetrical axes tilted 45 degrees (fig. 10.4b). Again the subject was instructed to see each figure as before, upright, with the phenomenal top lying midway between the two symmetrical axes. The familiar figures were presented in upright orientation. Under these conditions, neither symmetrical axis of a figure is phenomenally vertical, but one of them will present an image that is vertical on the retina.

Results: Subjects chose the alternative having a retinally vertical symmetry 92 times, while there were 94 choices of retinally horizontal symmetry,

Table 10.1
Choices of vertically or horizontally symmetrical comparison figures ($N = 20$ in each experiment)

	Control			Experimental condition 1			Experimental condition 2		
	V†	H	N	V	H	N	V	H	N
experiment I	159	37	4	146	51	3	129	68	3
%	79.5	18.5	2	73	25.5	1.5	64.5	34	1.5
experiment II	90*	92**	18	92	94	14	100	90	10
%	45	46	9	46	47	7	50	45	5

* left diagonal;   ** right diagonal.
V = vertical, H = horizontal, and N = neither.
† The meaning of "vertical" and "horizontal" differs in the various conditions; see text.

and 14 failures to make a choice. That is, retinal orientation alone was ineffective.

Experimental Condition 2. Finally, the subjects were shown the figures with the symmetrical axes vertical and horizontal in space and the subject himself upright (fig. 10.4c). This is like the control situation originally given in exp. I, which produced such a strong effect. There was one difference, however. In this case, the subject was instructed to see each figure as if it were tilted 45 degrees (clockwise or counterclockwise) retaining the same phenomenal top, bottom, and sides that he had perceived before. He received the initial familiar figures thusly tilted. The phenomenally vertical axis was then diagonal to either symmetrical axis. This experiment was something of a long shot because, as given, one symmetrical axis is here vertical both retinally and spatially. Therefore only the set induced by the instructions and familiar figures could eliminate the effect.

Results: 100 choices of the vertically symmetrical alternative, and 90 of the horizontal, an insignificant difference and strikingly different from the 159 to 37 choice made by the subjects of exp. I, control condition, under similar viewing conditions. In 10 instances no choice was made. Table 10.1 summarizes the results for exp. I and II. In exp. I the Goldmeier effect was shown to occur in *the absence of* symmetry about a vertical retinal axis; in exp. II it was shown to be absent in *the presence of* such symmetry.

By using the same subjects in all three conditions in exp. I it was possible to take advantage of the consistent set to see the figures in their "cross" orientation (+). Having established this set in the control condition, it was easy to continue it in experimental condition 1 even though the subject's head was now tilted. Similarly it made it more likely that he would see the figure in this way in experimental condition 2 despite the fact that here the figure was tilted in space. Following the same reasoning the subjects of exp. II were also used for all three conditions, where, in each case, it was desired that they see the figures in the "X" orientation. It might be argued that this procedure leads to a possible influence of the earlier conditions on the later ones since the same subjects are used in all three. That is, the subject might make a selection based on what he had selected in a previous condition, a memory effect. This is highly unlikely because the first, second, and third conditions are each separated by a week. Furthermore, each figure is shown twice in each condition by turning it 90 degrees. A symmetry response, therefore, requires selection of different comparison figures on the two presentations. Since the figures would appear at least somewhat similar in each orientation, and considering that five figures are involved, it would be difficult for the subject to recall his own response in each case even if he wanted to. Thus it is difficult to imagine how experience in an earlier condition could produce any consistent bias in a later condition. As a check on this possibility the data of the last 10 subjects of exp. II were examined. In this experiment the Goldmeier effect was not operating so that no general factor determined the subject's choices as in exp. I. Hence any tendency to choose a comparison figure on the basis of what had been selected in a previous condition should be clearly revealed. There were altogether 109 cases where subjects selected the same comparison figure in experimental condition 1 or 2 as he did in the control condition; there were 91 cases where they selected the other comparison figure. There were 57 "same" choices and 43 "different" ones in the transition from experimental condition 1 to experimental condition 2. Thus it is clear there is no significant tendency for a subject to perseverate in his selection from condition to condition.

There is one final point to be made. The experiment was designed in such a way that subjects in exp. I were expected in all three of their conditions to obtain the effect; conversely, subjects in exp. II were expected not to obtain the effect. These expectations were met. One may then raise the question of a sampling error here. Perhaps by chance, subjects in exp. II were just not susceptible to Goldmeier's effect. Of course, this is not very plausible with randomly selected samples of this size; but as a further check, 6 of the subjects of exp. II were located again and given the first (control) condition for exp. I. Under this condition, the symmetrical axes are aligned with the environment and the subject is upright. Where these subjects had before, under instructions to see the figures as tilted, shown a 32 to 28 preference for the vertically symmetrical alternative, now under instructions to see the figure as upright, they preferred the vertically symmetrical figure 45 times, the horizontal only 15. This finding also bears on the question raised in the previous paragraph. These subjects obviously did not perseverate in particular figural selections from exp. II to exp. I.

Discussion

These results present further evidence that orientation plays a role in form perception primarily in relation to the influence that the directions "top," "bottom," and "sides" have on phenomenal shape. The orientation of the image per se (and therefore of the pattern of excitation in the cortex) does not seem to be the critical factor here in contradiction to the findings of Köhler and others.

The results are also of interest in relation to the problem of symmetry as such. Not only is symmetry more salient about a vertical · axis, but it would seem that this is the only orientation in which a symmetrical figure will spontaneously be perceived as symmetrical. We have performed some preliminary experiments in which figures, symmetrical about one axis only, are shown in various orientations. Each is presented in only one orientation and it is assumed to be upright in space. The same subjects are asked to report whether or not each figure appears symmetrical. For the most part only when the axis is vertical is a figure perceived as symmetrical.

If perceived symmetry of a figure depends on the figure's apparent orientation, what does this imply for classical Gestalt theory? One would think that a symmetrical pattern would look symmetrical regardless of its orientation, if the important factor is the distribution of figural forces in a homogeneous medium. Or if cognizance is taken of the fact that orientation is an important factor in perceiving symmetry, one would think Gestalt theory would have to maintain that the vertical orientation in the cortex for some reason yields a more symmetrical distribution. But here we have shown that the vertical orientation that is implicated in symmetry does not refer to a retinal-cortical direction but to a phenomenal direction. This fact does not seem compatible with Gestalt thinking on the subject.

We are, therefore, left with an intriguing problem. The impression of symmetry in visual perception seems to depend on seeing the objectively similar halves as "sides," i.e., left and right sides with respect to a vertical axis. Since "left" and "right" do not necessarily refer to anatomical left and right (in the retina and cortex) there can be no simple neurophysiological explanation for this fact. A clue to an understanding of our finding may be that in our environment the bottom and top of objects are often functionally different, the former being the portion on which the object rests on the ground. On the other hand, the sides of objects are not functionally differentiated in this manner although, to be sure, they may be different from one another. In fact the sides of an object are reversed when it is rotated 180 degrees about its vertical axis or when we come upon it in the opposite direction, thus pointing up the subjectivity of "left" and "right." There is nothing intrinsically "left" or "right" in external objects the way there is a bottom and top.[4] Symmetry about a vertical axis is widespread in the sphere of plant and animal life. It is also common in man-made objects. These facts about the environment are compatible with a theory that we learn to become sensitized to vertical symmetry or with a theory that such sensitization has come about through biological evolution.

Summary

Goldmeier's effect showing the greater saliency of vertical rather than horizontal symmetry was demonstrated with several new figures. The question of whether "vertical" here refers to the retinal image or to the direction perceived as phenomenally vertical was investigated by experimentally separating the two. This was accomplished either by tilting the subject's head or by inducing a set to see some other direction than that given by the environment as the upright of the figure. In two conditions where the phenomenal factor was present and the retinal factor was absent (exp. I, conditions 2 and 3) a strong effect was still obtained. In two conditions where neither axis was phenomenally vertical (exp. II, conditions 2 and 3) no effect was obtained despite the fact that one axis was retinally vertical. It is therefore clear that Goldmeier's effect depends exclusively on the phenomenal factor. Implications of these findings were discussed.

Notes

This study was completed when both authors were at the New School for Social Research. A paper based on these findings was read at the meeting of the Eastern Psychological Association in 1958.

1. It is possible, however, to show that under certain conditions, such as in viewing complex material with a tilt of 90 degrees or more, disorientation of the retinal image alone will also affect perception (See (3)).

2. This is one reason why Köhler failed to find evidence for the phenomenal factor. Since he used a picture of a face, the observer knew where its top was, regardless of its orientation.

3. In both exp. I and II, the first ten subjects were first shown six additional figures. Since these figures did not yield a clear cut Goldmeier effect in the control condition these results are not discussed further in this paper.

4. The sensitivity to symmetry in the vertical axis may be related to another finding that has recently been reported, namely the difficulty children and animals have in discriminating left-right (mirror-image) reversals of figures (4, 5). Since the sides of an object are not functionally differentiated, there is an equivalence in appearance in these two positions. Thus two apparently different facts—sensitivity to symmetry and insensitivity to left-right reversal of non-symmetrical figures—may have a common explanation. The functional

differentiation of top and bottom makes symmetry about a horizontal axis unnoticed and an up-down reversal of most figures a striking phenomenal change.

References

1. Goldmeier, E., Über Ähnlichkeit bei Gesehen Figuren, *Psychol. Forsch.* 1937, *21*, 146–208.
2. Rock, I., The orientation of forms on the retina and in the environment. *Amer. J. Psychol.* 1956, *69*, 513–528.
3. ——— and Heimer, W., The effect of retinal and phenomenal orientation on the perception of form. *Amer. J. Psychol.* 1957, *70*, 493–511.
4. Rudel, R., Discrimination of direction of line in children. Paper delivered at April 1959 meeting of the Eastern Psychological Association, Atlantic City.
5. Sutherland, N. S., Visual discrimination of orientation by octopus: mirror images. *Brit. J. Psychol.* 1960, *51*, 9–18.

Chapter 11
The Right Angle
Donatella Ferrante, Walter Gerbino, and Irvin Rock

Introduction

In his classical research on visual similarity, Goldmeier (1972) studied the
effect of orientation on the perception of the right angle. Observers were
shown a right angle and had to select the more similar out of three comparison angles, sized 87, 90 or 93 degrees. They were always correct
when the sides of standard and comparison angles were *normal* (i.e., vertical and horizontal), as in Fig. 11.1a, whereas they performed at chance
when the sides were oblique and the bisecting line vertical, as in Fig.
11.1b. The good discrimination of the normal right angle and the poor
discrimination of the oblique right angle will be referred to here as the
"Goldmeier effect." This effect was confirmed by Onley and Volkmann
(1958) using an entirely different method. Subjects were shown an angle
clearly different from a right angle, at various orientations, and asked
to adjust one side to achieve perpendicularity. Accuracy was always
very high (constant error less than ± 3 degrees) whereas precision was
strongly influenced by orientation: variability of the adjustment increased
abruptly as a function of deviation from the vertical/horizontal axes (up
to five times relative to the variability of adjustment for the normal
angle).

The Goldmeier effect shows that right angle discrimination is facilitated
by the reference to a privileged system of coordinates, but experimental
evidence does not tell us if this frame of reference is determined by
retinal, gravitational or visual information. Since it concerns the superior
performance with normal vs. oblique angles, such a superiority could be
considered as an example of the "oblique effect" (Appelle, 1972). If retinal
orientation is crucial, one might be inclined to regard it as a Class 1 oblique effect following the classification suggested by Essock (1980). Such
effects are thought to result from basic properties of the visual system,

Originally published in *Acta Psychologica* 88 (1995): 25–32, under the title "Retinal vs. Environmental Orientation in the Perception of the Right Angle." Reprinted with permission.

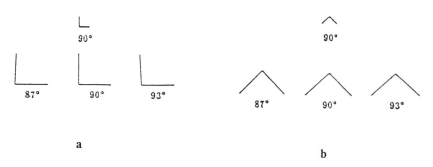

Figure 11.1
Orientation affects discrimination of the right angle. (a) The normal angle on the top is clearly more similar to the middle angle than to others (Goldmeier, 1972, Fig. 58). (b) The oblique angle on top is equally similar to all angles on bottom (Goldmeier, 1972, Fig. 57).

such as acuity, contrast threshold or other aspects of sensitivity, which seem to be fixed to retinal coordinates (Banks and Stolarz, 1975; Corwin et al., 1977; Lennie, 1974). The Goldmeier effect could be explained by higher selectivity of cell populations sensitive to vertical and horizontal orientations over those sensitive to oblique orientations.

However, this conclusion is not supported by an experiment by Rock and Leaman (reported in Rock, 1973, p. 16). When observers looked at Fig. 11.1a keeping their heads tilted 45 degrees, discrimination was still good, although the sides were retinally oblique. Analogously, when observers looked at Fig. 11.1b keeping their heads tilted 45 degrees, discrimination was still poor, although the sides were retinally normal. These results agree with the idea that perception of the right angle is connected to orientation constancy. In their experiment, Rock and Leaman put into conflict two types of information, retinal vs. environmental. Environmental information came from both gravitational and visual sources, because angles were displayed in an illuminated environment. This result suggests that the Goldmeier effect should be regarded as a Class 2 oblique effect (Essock, 1980). It would seem to have more to do with the perception of angle orientation than with an anisotropy of retinal sensitivity.

One might argue that in the experiment by Rock and Leaman visual information allowed good discrimination of the right angle because its sides were parallel to horizontal and vertical contours visually present in the scene. In order to clarify this matter we reproduced Rock and Leaman's experiment in *darkness*, so that no visual frame was present. Subjects were to judge angles that were either normal or 45 degrees oblique relative to gravity, labelling them as "right," "obtuse" or "acute"; subjects were either upright or tilted by 45 degrees. A strong Goldmeier effect was obtained when the subjects were upright despite the absence of visual contours to which the sides of the angle could be said to be either parallel or not. However, when subjects were tilted 45 degrees, the Goldmeier effect was weaker. Tilted subjects performed still better in judging gravitationally normal right angles than gravitationally oblique right angles, even though the latter now yielded retinally right-angle images. But, performance with gravitationally normal right angles was not as good as when subjects were upright.

The partial failure to obtain a full Goldmeier effect could be taken as a demonstration of the negative role of retinal misorientation: when the right angle was retinally oblique, performance was never as good as in the canonical situation (normal right angle and upright subject). However, we tend to consider this result not as a direct effect of retinal orientation, but as a consequence of environmental misorientation experienced by tilted subjects under dark-field conditions. Another possible criticism of this paradigm regards the task, which favoured an analytical attitude. When the tilted observer is asked to evaluate an angle which is environmentally vertical/horizontal but retinally oblique, the phenomenal singularity of the right angle can be overshadowed by observer's attempt to provide a precise measure of its size.

On the basis of previous studies, we concluded that the Goldmeier effect concerns the *perception* of the orientation of the sides of the angle as vertical and horizontal. Such a *perception* does not require that angle sides are retinally vertical and horizontal, nor their parallelism to visible contours in the environment. But it requires that the two sides are aligned with the axes of the subjective frame of reference. Alignment explains a basic phenomenological fact: normal right angles look singular; oblique ones do not. Since an oblique angle does not spontaneously look singular, one naturally has difficulty in the various tasks involving right angle perception: picking out the most similar among a set of comparison angles (Goldmeier's original task), adjusting one side to achieve perpendicularity (Onley and Volkmann's task), labelling angles appropriately (our variation of Rock and Leaman's experiment).

With the present experiment we suggest that a Goldmeier effect despite retinal misorientation can be obtained by using (a) an illuminated environment devoid of visible rectilinear contours and (b) a task based on the spontaneous phenomenological description. Subjects were shown a series of simple drawings, one of which was a right angle, and asked to provide a short verbal description of each. The issue was how the angle would be described as a function of its orientation and of the orientation of the subject.

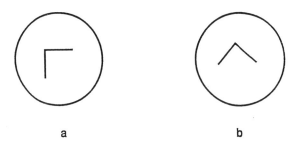

a   b

Figure 11.2
The angle figures used in the experiment seen within a circular homogenous white field without other visible contours. (a) The right angle in its normal orientation. (b) The right angle in its oblique orientation, rotated by 45 degrees clockwise.

Method

Observers
Four independent groups of 15 subjects each (undergraduates at the University of Trieste) were randomly assigned to each of the four conditions.

Conditions
There were four conditions obtained combining two orientations of the angle stimulus and two orientations of the observer's head. The two orientations were: vertical and 45 degrees oblique, relative to gravity. The vertical angle stimulus corresponded to the top and left sides of a square (Fig. 11.2a); the oblique angle was obtained by 45 degrees clockwise rotation, and therefore pointed upwards (Fig. 11.2b). In the two oblique-head conditions the subject tilted his/her head 45 degrees clockwise. The head was always locked into the required position by an apparatus that also limited the field of view to a circular aperture of about 30 degrees of visual angle. Thus the field of view did not contain any rectilinear contours other than the angle stimulus. It was thus equivalent to a dark room in that the angle sides were drawn not parallel to or oblique with respect to any reference lines. All stimuli were drawn at the center of a circular cardboard 20 cm in diameter and hung on a large white wall. Subjects sat at a distance of two meters from the wall.

Procedure
The angle was shown only once in the context of nine other "distractor" figures. The order of the ten figures was randomized from condition to condition and subject to subject. The experiment was designed to study the verbal descriptions of various patterns. Most of the distractors, being pictures of familiar objects, had a preferred interpretation in the vertical

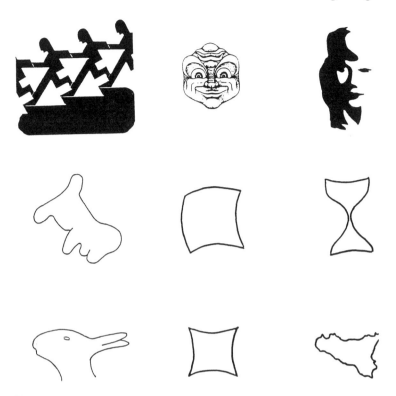

Figure 11.3
The nine distractor figures. They were always shown in the environmentally vertical orientation.

orientation (maps, faces, figure/ground patterns). The nine distractors were always shown in the environmentally vertical orientation, to reinforce the contrast between retinal misorientation and the environmental visual vertical. The 90 degree angle pattern was the only simple geometrical figure made of rectilinear segments. Other figures either contained curvilinear borders or were schematic pictures of well-known complex entities (see Fig. 11.3). Instructions did not refer in any way to angle size or to precise estimation. The observer were simply asked to "describe what each figure looked like, according to his/her immediate impression."

Results

Table 11.1 gives the number of subjects who spontaneously described the figure as a right angle or as something that can be unambiguously identified as rectangular, vs. those who did not, for the four conditions.

Table 11.1
Number of subjects who gave the specific *right-angle* response (or equivalent descriptions) or the generic *angle* response (or equivalent descriptions)

Condition	Angle orientation	Head orientation	*Right-angle* response	*Angle* response	N
A	Normal	Upright	10	5	15
B	Oblique	Upright	4	11	15
C	Normal	Tilted	10	5	15
D	Oblique	Tilted	2	13	15

Thus the following responses were scored as right-angle responses: "right angle," "90 degrees angle," "half square," "table corner," "L."

On the other hand, the following responses were *not* scored as right angle responses: "compass," "carpenter's zig-zag rule," "mountain," "roof," "pyramid," "uncollinear segments," "boomerang," "corner," "stair," "triangle without the base." Note the conservative choice of scoring only "table corner" as a right angle response and not "corner." As can be seen in the table, responses scored as "right angle" were far more frequent in the two conditions, A and C, in which the right angle was upright (vertical) in the environment regardless of the observer's orientation than in the two conditions in which the angle was oblique in the environment regardless of the observer's orientation. Conditions A and B more or less repeat the original conditions of the Goldmeier experiment in *that* they compare an upright and oblique angle viewed by an upright observer. The result shows a significantly greater number of right-angle descriptions when the angle is upright rather than tilted in the environment: $\chi^2 = 4.82$, $df = 1$, $p < 0.05$. Conditions C and D in which the subject's head was tilted, yield a similar outcome, in fact an even more significant difference, with $\chi^2 = 8.88$, $df = 1$, $p < 0.01$, despite the fact that in Condition D the angle's images become upright retinally and in Condition C it becomes oblique retinally. Yet it is Condition C that shows the significantly greater number of right-angle responses, not Condition D. Table 11.2 gives the results of the four conditions in terms of the environmental or retinal orientation of the angle figure.

Comparing the two environmental angle orientations across head orientation (A + C vs. B + D) yielded a highly significant difference, $\chi^2 = 13.4$, $df = 1$, $p < 0.001$. Conversely, comparing the two retinally-defined angle orientations across environmental orientation of the angle (A + D vs. B + C) yielded a non-significant difference, $\chi^2 = 0.28$, $df = 1$, $p > 0.1$. Moreover, as can be seen by inspection of the table, tilting the head did not diminish the number of right-angle descriptions of the upright right angle nor did tilting the head increase the number of right-

Table 11.2
Number of subjects (out of 15) describing the stimulus as a right-angle (or equivalent descriptions) as a function of its retinal vs. environmental orientation

| | Environmental orientation | | |
	Vertical	Oblique	Total
Retinal orientation			
Vertical	10 (A)	2 (D)	12 (A + D)
Oblique	10 (C)	4 (B)	14 (C + B)
Total	20 (A + C)	6 (D + B)	

angle descriptions of the oblique angle which then became retinally upright.

Discussion

In the present experiment subjects verbally described the stimulus as right-angle only when it was environmentally normal, independent of retinal orientation. If we extend the meaning of the "Goldmeier effect" to include such a labelling preference, then we can claim that the Goldmeier effect is a function of phenomenal orientation. It depends on the perception of the sides of a right angle as vertical and horizontal. Thus, it is a Class 2 oblique effect.

The effect of orientation on the perception of a right angle can be subsumed under the broader category of the effect of orientation on phenomenal shape. Indeed it provides at least a partial explanation of what was perhaps the first demonstration of this kind of effect, namely the example by Ernst Mach (1885) of the different appearance of a square when it is rotated 45 degrees; it then looks like a diamond. We can now say that, in the normal orientation, the four angles of a square look like right angles but in the tilted orientation they do not. This is undoubtedly only part of the explanation for the differing appearances of a square in these two orientations. Whether the sides or the diagonals of the figure appear to be vertical and horizontal probably also plays a role in its appearance. As with the experiments described here, it is also a fact that the phenomenal appearance of a square is not altered when it is viewed with the head tilted 45 degrees despite the fact that the retinal image is then that of a diamond (Rock, 1973).

There is an implication of our findings that we believe is of great importance. If right angles that appear to be in the oblique orientation, regardless of what source of information creates that appearance, do not spontaneously look like right angles, then perception of orthogonality cannot simply be a consequence of the geometry of the right angle. For if the geometry were all that mattered, orientation would be irrelevant. Rather it seems to be the perception of the vertical and horizontal orientation of the sides of the angle that matters. Therefore it follows that a phenomenally right angle is not an autonomous *Gestalt*, in the sense that it is not invariant under rotation, but is a derivative of the perception of the sides. One *might* define a *phenomenal* right angle as one whose sides appear to be vertical and horizontal.

Note

Part of this work has been supported by CNR grants to Walter Gerbino n. 90.00356.PF67 and n. 90.03517.CT08 and by Research Scientist Award KO5MH00707 from the National Institute of Mental Health to Irvin Rock.

References

Appelle, S., 1972. Perception and discrimination as a function of stimulus orientation: The oblique effect in man and animals. Psychological Bulletin 78, 266–278.
Banks, M. S. and S. S. Stolarz, 1975. The effect of head tilting on meridional differences in acuity: Implications for orientation constancy. Perception and Psychophysics 17, 17–22.
Corwin, T. R., A. Moskowitz-Cook and M. A. Green, 1977. The oblique effect in a vernier acuity situation. Perception and Psychophysics 21, 445–449.
Essock, E. A., 1980. The oblique effect of stimulus identification considered with respect to two classes of oblique effects. Perception 9, 37–46.
Goldmeier, E., 1972. Similarity in visually perceived forms. Psychological Issues 29. Original paper (1937) in German: Über Ähnlichkeit bei gesehenen Figuren. Psychologische Forschung 21, 146–208.
Lennie, P., 1974. Head orientation and meridional variations in acuity. Vision Research 14, 107–111.
Mach, E., 1885. Die Analyse der Empfindungen. Jena.
Onley, J. W. and J. Volkmann, 1958. The visual perception of perpendicularity. American Journal of Psychology 71, 504–516.
Rock, I., 1973. Orientation and form. New York: Academic Press.

Chapter 12
Masking
Charles W. White

Visual masking occurs whenever the presentation of one stimulus interferes with the perception of another stimulus. The general description has
been refined by many years of investigation of various types of visual
masking. Metacontrast, for example, is a special type of masking that
occurs whenever the target and the masking stimulus are flashed on adjacent, but nonoverlapping, parts of the retina. (See Lefton, 1973, for a
review of the metacontrast literature.)

Many theories of visual masking demand that the masking stimulus and
the target that is masked must stimulate the same or adjacent retinal areas
(Bridgeman, 1971, 1975; Matin, 1975; Weisstein, 1968, 1972; Weisstein,
Ozog, and Szoc, 1975). That assumption is not based on experimental
evidence, however, since most masking experiments have confounded the
retinal location of visual stimuli with their apparent location by anchor-
ing the observer's eye to a fixation point. If apparent location could be
separated from retinal location, then it would be possible to answer the
question: Which matters more for visual masking—that the target and
masking stimuli are flashed on the same part of the retina, or, that the
target and mask appear in the same place?

During pursuit eye movements, it is possible to separate apparent location from retinal location, since the apparent position of briefly flashed
targets depends on when and where they occur (Mack and Herman, 1973;
Matin, 1972; Stoper, 1973). Thus, stimuli that are separated by eye movements are presented when the relationship between retinal position and
spatial location is changing. Eye movements involve such a changing
relationship, since the observer must compensate for the motion of the
images of stationary objects across the retina by a relocalization process. Saccadic eye movements produce abrupt shifts in localization, but
smooth-tracking eye movements involve a fairly continuous localization
process (Matin, 1972).

Originally published in *Journal of Experimental Psychology: Human Perception and Performance*
2, 4 (1976): 469–478, under the title "Visual Masking during Pursuit Eye Movements."
Reprinted with permission.

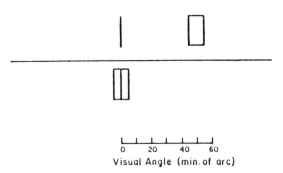

Figure 12.1
Stimuli for Experiment 1. (Vertical line targets and masking rectangles are shown in relation to the horizontal path of the tracking dot.)

Experiment 1

A demonstration experiment was designed to test the simple hypothesis that more masking would occur if the target and mask appeared in the same place than if they appeared in different places (White, Note 1).

Method

Observers. The observers were 12 volunteers recruited from graduate students and faculty. All had normal or corrected visual acuity.

Apparatus. A PDP-8/L computer with a KV graphic display system (Digital Equipment Corp.) was used in all three experiments. The oscilloscope display (Tektronix Type 611) was a 16 × 24 cm screen with a yellowish green phosphor similar to the standard P1 phosphor. The oscilloscope was modified to operate in a nonstorage mode; as a result, the luminance decayed to 10% within 24 msec after a point was displayed. Despite the persistence characteristic, the stimuli appeared well-defined without noticeable blur. The resolution on the screen was approximately 33 points per cm horizontally or vertically. The display was controlled by vector-drawing circuits that displayed a short straight line in .27 msec. The time required to display a figure made up of n straight lines was approximately $.34 (n + 1)$ msec. Thus a rectangle outline was drawn in 1.7 msec.

Stimuli. The computer was programmed to present a spot that moved across an oscilloscope screen while targets and masking stimuli were flashed at appropriate times. The stimuli for Experiment I as they appeared at different times on the screen are illustrated in Figure 12.1. The target lines were 20′ of arc in height, and the masking rectangle outlines were 10' wide and 20' high. The horizontal line represents the central 3° of the path of the tracking dot, which moved from left to right for 1.0 sec at .5 minutes/msec (approximately 8.3 degrees/sec). When the tracking dot reached the point midway between the two vertical line targets, the targets were briefly presented above and below the tracking path. When the tracking dot reached the point directly beneath the upper rectangle 100 msec later, the two masking rectangle outlines were flashed briefly. The lower mask was presented around the physical location of the lower target; the upper mask was presented directly above the tracking dot's position at the time. Thus, the upper rectangle was a retinal location mask, since it was flashed around the same part of the retina as the upper target. The observer's eye, of course, had moved from the target position to the upper mask position during the interstimulus interval. The lower rectangle was flashed around a different part of the retina, where it appeared to the observer in approximately the same spatial location as the lower target.

Viewing Conditions. The observers sat in an acoustically shielded room, which was dark except for a small desk lamp. The reflected light from the lamp made the oscilloscope screen and the black frame around the screen easily visible, even without dark adaptation. A chin rest was used to maintain the viewing distance at 103 cm.

Procedure. When the tracking dot appeared at the left edge of the screen, it remained in the same position for 500 msec before it began to move to the right. The observer fixated the point at the left edge of the screen and visually tracked the dot when it moved across the screen. After each presentation of the targets and masking stimuli, the observer reported which of the two vertical line targets appeared to be most clearly visible, that is, whether the upper target was more complete, had better defined edges, or appeared brighter than the lower target.

Results
Two observers reported that they could not see either target, but the other 10 observers, who could see at least one of the targets, reported that the upper target was clearly the most visible. The mask that appeared to be in approximately the same place, therefore, was much more effective in masking a target than the mask that stimulated the same part of the retina but appeared to be in a different place. Many subjective comments from the observers supported this conclusion. Several observers, who had no difficulty seeing the upper target, reported that they could not see the lower target and were surprised to see it when they viewed the stimulus display without tracking the moving dot.

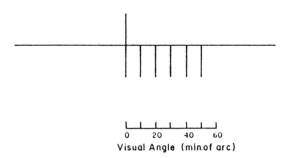

Figure 12.2
Mislocalization stimuli for Experiment 2. (Stimuli for determining the point of subjective equality [PSE] for two targets when one is presented 100 msec after the other. The tracking dot moves from left to right along the horizontal line. The upper vertical line is flashed when the tracking dot reaches it. One of the lower lines is flashed 100 msec later, when the tracking dot is at the end of the rightmost line. The observer's task is to decide whether the lower line appeared to the left or the right of the upper line.)

Experiment 2

Experiment 2 was designed to measure the magnitude of the masking differences that were reported in Experiment 1 and to use some masking stimuli that appeared in precisely the same place as the targets (White, 1974).

Mislocalization during Pursuit Eye Movements
The spatial position mask in Experiment 1 was only approximately an apparent position mask. Most of the observers reported that the lower target did not appear to be surrounded by the lower rectangle; rather, the rectangle appeared to the left of the target. Stoper (1973) had reported a similar displacement effect: Apparent motion occurred in a direction opposite the tracking dot's motion when a stimulus was flashed twice at the same place during pursuit eye movements.

In order to compare differences in masking between retinal and apparent locations, the mask and target in the apparent location condition were made to appear in the same place. That point on the screen, where a mask would appear to surround a target that preceded it by 100 msec, was called the point of subjective equality (PSE) for the apparent location of the target and the mask. During the first part of each experimental session, therefore, the method of constant stimuli was used to measure the PSE for each observer.

The stimuli that were presented during the PSE-measurement part of the session are depicted in Figure 12.2. The tracking dot moved from left to right along the horizontal path. The observer tracked the moving dot for 600 msec before it reached the position of the standard target, the vertical line above the path of the tracking dot. At that point, the standard target was flashed above the tracking path. The tracking continued to the position of the rightmost comparison target, where 100 msec later, a comparison stimulus was flashed at one of the locations indicated by the lower lines. There were six possible locations separated by 10' of arc. The observer's task on each trial was to judge whether the lower target appeared to the left or to the right of the upper target. After 30 practice trials, 120 data trials were run, and the proportion of trials that the observer called "right" was calculated for each position. The PSE was automatically calculated by a least squares regression technique as the 50% point of the ogive function (Guilford, 1954, p. 127). After a rest period of approximately 1 min., the observer continued with the main part of the experiment.

Method

Observers.   The observers were seven undergraduates and graduate students with normal or corrected visual acuity. Two observers did not perform at above-chance levels in the experiment; their masking effects were so large in all the experimental conditions that no differences between the conditions were indicated. The results from those two subjects were not included in the results presented here.

Apparatus and Stimuli.   The apparatus and viewing conditions were the same as in Experiment 1. Figure 12.3 illustrates the stimuli that were presented during the main part of Experiment 2. The three possible mask positions are represented from top to bottom in the figure; they defined three experimental conditions: (a) In the *spatial location* condition, shown in Figure 12.3A, the target and mask were centered on the same point on the screen, but the target usually appeared slightly outside the square to the right whenever it was visible. (b) In the *apparent location* condition, depicted in Figure 12.3B, the masking stimulus was flashed at the observer's PSE location, which had been determined in the first part of the experimental session. In this condition, the target usually appeared inside the masking rectangle whenever it was visible. (c) In the *retinal location* condition, shown in Figure 12.3C, the mask was flashed at the location of the tracking dot 100 msec after the target line was presented. The target line in the third condition appeared far to the left of the masking rectangle.

Procedure.   The amount of masking in each condition was measured by a tilt discrimination task. The targets in Figure 12.3 are shown tilted about 6° to the right, but on half the trials the line was tilted an equal amount to

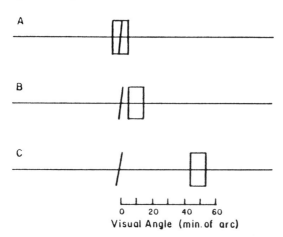

Visual Angle (min. of arc)

Figure 12.3
Stimuli for Experiment 2. (The horizontal line represents the path of the tracking dot. The near vertical line is the target, and the rectangle outline is the masking stimulus. A. The spatial location mask and the target are centered on the same point. B. The apparent location mask is displaced to the observer's point of subjective equality [PSE] location and appears to surround the target. C. The retinal location mask is displaced by 50' of arc to stimulate the same part of the retina as the target.)

the left. The amount of the tilt was chosen by pilot observations to produce an average accuracy of approximately 75% at identifying the tilt of a partially masked target. The observer's task on each trial was to press one of two keys to indicate whether the target appeared tilted to the left or to the right. Masking in this experiment was thus indicated by increased difficulty in identifying the slight tilt of the target. The tilt discrimination task was chosen in order to assess how clearly the partially masked targets were seen. Letter recognition and other traditional measures of masking were precluded by the relatively slow speed of the computer display system. A simple target detection procedure would have been inadequate for the task, since observers were able to detect the presence or absence of a masked target, often by changes in the appearance of the masking stimulus. As in the first part of the session, a short series of 30 practice trials were run before beginning to collect data. The practice trials were followed after a short break by a series of 180 masking trials.

Results
The percentage of correct target tilt judgments and the associated d' values were calculated for each mask position (Beck and Ambler, 1972). The d' value was an index of the discriminability of the target's orientation. More masking was indicated by lower d' values and less masking by higher d' values.

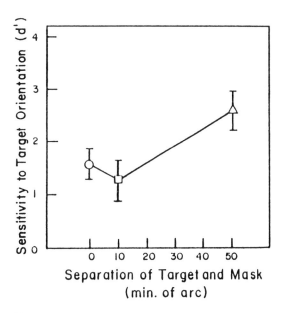

Separation of Target and Mask
(min. of arc)

Figure 12.4
Average results for Experiment 2. (More masking is shown by lower d' values. The circle indicates the mean d' value for the spatial location condition [the stimuli of Figure 3A]. The square marks the results for the apparent location condition [the stimuli of Figure 3B]. The triangle represents the retinal location condition [the stimuli of Figure 3C]. The separation of target and mask for the apparent location condition is the mean point of subjective equality [PSE] position for all five observers. Vertical bars indicate the mean values $\pm$ one standard error of the mean.)

The mean results for the five observers are shown in Figure 12.4. Each point represents the mean d' value for all five observers, and the vertical line segments mark one standard error above and below each mean value. As expected, the least sensitivity to the tilt of the target, and therefore the most masking, occurred in the apparent location condition. The spatial location mask produced slightly less masking, but the retinal location mask produced much less masking than either of the first two conditions. The mean d' value for apparent location is more than 1.3 d' units less than that for retinal location. The same differences hold for the percentages of correct responses in the different experimental conditions, of course, and fewer assumptions about signal and noise distributions are required. With the chance performance level at 50%, the mean percentages correct were 71% for the apparent location mask and 76% for the spatial location mask, but the accuracy rose to 88% for the retinal location mask.

The d' values were analyzed by a repeated measures analysis of variance, which revealed a highly significant main effect of the mask position,

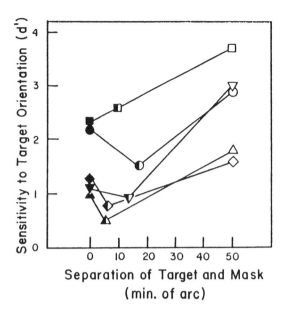

Figure 12.5
Results for individual observers in Experiment 2. (Each shape represents one observer. Filled symbols indicate targets and masks presented at the same spatial location. Half-filled symbols represent masks presented at the apparent locations of the targets, with the separation adjusted for each observer. Open symbols are used for masks presented at the same retinal location as the target.)

$F(2, 8) = 18.79$, $p < .001$. Paired comparisons of the means by Tukey's honestly significant difference method (Winer, 1971, p. 198) demonstrated that the retinal location mask produced significantly higher d' values than either of the other two conditions ($p < .01$), but the apparent location condition was not significantly different from the spatial location condition ($p > .10$).

The average results are reflected in the results for individual observers, which are shown in Figure 12.5. The mean d' value for each observer in the apparent location condition is plotted at that observer's mean PSE position. Four of the five observers have the most masking in the apparent location condition, the next most masking in the spatial location condition, and the least masking in the retinal location condition. The fifth observer, represented by squares in Figure 12.5, was highly sensitive to the target orientation in all the conditions. Perhaps a ceiling effect on that observer's performance obscured the difference that prevailed for other observers.

Experiment 3

To further investigate masking effects during pursuit eye movements and to compare the results with more traditional masking studies, a larger experiment was conducted with stimuli like those in Experiment 2, except that the interval between the time of presenting the target and the mask, the onset asynchrony, was varied from 0 to 150 msec in 50-msec steps (White, 1975).

Method

Observers. Four new observers, student volunteers with normal vision, were paid for participating in Experiment 3.

Apparatus and Stimuli. The stimuli and viewing conditions were the same as in Experiment 2, except that the actual displacements of the masking stimuli were adjusted to compensate for changes in the onset asynchrony, so that the retinal position mask was always presented at the position of the tracking dot. Since one of the onset asynchrony values was nominally zero (actually the time required to draw the target, approximately .7 msec), the actual displacement of the mask for zero onset asynchronies was zero in all three conditions. Since the tracking dot moved at .5 minutes/msec, the retinal location mask was displaced 25' to the right of the target for each 50 msec of onset asynchrony.

Procedure. The procedure was the same as in Experiment 2. Each experimental session began with practice on the PSE measurement task and was followed by trials to determine the observer's PSE location for the onset asynchrony in that session. The second part of each session was the main part, in which the tilt discrimination accuracy was measured for different positions of the masking stimuli. Each session lasted about 40 min. and was restricted to only one onset asynchrony value. Each observer completed two sessions for each of the four onset asynchronies, with no more than two sessions per day.

Results

The results confirmed Experiments 1 and 2. The mask was more effective if it appeared in the same place as the target, at least for those onset asynchronies that were expected to produce appreciable masking.

The average results are presented in Figure 12.6. The data are presented as percentages correct, rather than d' values, because tilt recognition performance for all observers was nearly perfect in several conditions, and false alarm rates are required to determine the value of d'.

With an onset asynchrony of 50 msec, the effects are stronger than the results of Experiment 2. For example, the mean tilt judgment accuracy was

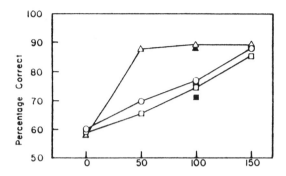

Figure 12.6
Results of Experiment 3: Mean percentage correct tilt discrimination versus onset asynchrony between target and mask for four observers. (Circles represent spatial location; squares, apparent location; triangles, retinal location; filled symbols at 100-msec asynchrony represent results for corresponding conditions in Experiment 2, with five different observers.)

88% for the retinal location condition but was only 66% for the apparent location condition. The spatial location condition produced an intermediate level of masking with 70% correct. The results of Experiment 2 are also shown for comparison in Figure 12.6 as filled symbols. The results were replicated remarkably well by the four observers in Experiment 3 for the 100-msec onset asynchrony.

The difference between mask positions was greatest for asynchronies of 50 and 100 msec and decreased for longer and shorter onset asynchronies. At zero asynchrony, of course, the masks were all presented at the same location on the screen. The near identity of the results for zero asynchrony provides a check on the reliability of the observations. The overall decrease in masking at 150-msec asynchrony was similar to previously reported masking functions (Lefton, 1973).

The results were analyzed by a repeated measures analysis of variance. The main effect of mask position was significant, $F(2, 6) = 10.49$, $p = .012$, as was the onset asynchrony main effect, $F(3, 9) = 7.25$, $p = .009$. The most critical test, the interaction effect of mask position and onset asynchrony, showed that the three masking functions in Figure 12.6 have significantly different shapes, $F(6, 18) = 7.14$, $p < .001$.

Discussion

The general conclusion from the three experiments is that, during pursuit eye movements, masking stimuli are more effective masks if they appear at the same place in the environment as the target rather than if they merely stimulate the same part of the retina.

Neurophysiological Theories of Masking
The results suggest that some of the neural interactions that underlie metacontrast occur at a level of visual processing so central that the visual representation does not change with eye movements. Experiments with dichoptic masking, in which the target is presented to one eye and the mask is presented to the other eye, have shown that both retinal and central interactions contribute to metacontrast phenomena (Lefton, 1973; Turvey, 1973). The present results suggest that at least some masking effects are more central than indicated by the dichoptic experiments.

The pursuit masking experiments pose serious problems for current neurophysiological models of visual masking that depend on interactions among topographically adjacent areas on the retina or in the visual cortex (Bridgeman, 1971, 1975; Matin, 1975; Purcell, Stewart, and Dember, 1968; Walley and Weiden, 1973; Weisstein, 1968, 1972; Weisstein et al., 1975). The present experiments suggest that metacontrast can be stronger for stimuli separated by almost one degree on the retina, and presumably also separated in the cortical projection, than for stimuli that are separated by only a few minutes of arc. Such a distance paradox is incompatible with current neural models of masking.

Perhaps the argument can be put more strongly. An additional degree of complexity would be introduced if the observers were lagging behind the tracking target. Electrooculograms from two observers in a pilot experiment suggested that eye movement velocities were slightly less than the velocity of the tracking target. Other evidence from a similar tracking task indicated that observers in the present experiments probably made smooth-tracking movements, but lagged behind the tracking dot by a few minutes of arc (Puckett and Steinman, 1969; Steinman, Skavenski, and Sansbury, 1969). If the lag were between 5' and 45' of arc, then both targets and the upper mask in Experiment 1 (see Figure 12.1) would stimulate parts of the retina that project to the left cerebral hemisphere, but the lower rectangle, which was the more effective mask, would stimulate the right hemisphere. Similar arguments could be made for the stimuli in Experiments 2 and 3. The masking that occurred in the same apparent location, therefore, must have been very central according to Turvey's (1973) analysis, since the interaction responsible for the masking effect probably required both hemispheres.

Eye Movements and Visual Masking
The theoretical significance of the present experiments lies in the relationship between eye movements and visual masking. The pursuit masking results appear to conflict with the saccadic results reported by Davidson, Fox, and Dick (1973). They measured masking effects during saccadic eye movements and found that, when several targets and a mask were

separated by a saccade, the target that stimulated the same retinal area as the masking stimulus was the target that was masked. They also reported that a masking stimulus often appeared superimposed on one letter, although it masked a different letter. The same effects were found with spatially overlapping pattern masks and metacontrast rings.

The saccadic masking results fit nicely with some other work that relates metacontrast to saccadic suppression. Matin, Clymer, and Matin (1972) suggested that the elevation of visual thresholds, which occurs prior to and during saccadic eye movements, is at least partially a result of backward masking by visual stimuli at the end of the eye movement. The action of the masking effect was to suppress the smear produced by bright stimuli that were presented during saccadic eye movements.

The apparent conflict between metacontrast results with saccadic and tracking eye movements can be resolved by considering the functional significance of visual masking associated with the two kinds of eye movements. Eye movement systems have evolved to see things in at least two different ways: (a) The saccadic eye movement system for inspecting visual scenes involves the integration of discrete time frames into a stable picture of the world. (b) The smooth-tracking system for pursuit eye movements has the function of locking onto a moving target and continuously relocalizing the background so that the background, and not the moving target appears relatively stationary.

From this point of view, visual masking may serve different functions for the two types of eye movements. After saccadic eye movements, visual masking by parts of the current retinal image may serve to erase the previous image and reduce the ambiguity that long-duration after-images of the previous scene would cause, as Matin et al. (1972) and Davidson et al. (1973) have suggested.

In the case of pursuit eye movements, the situation is entirely different. The function of tracking movements appears to be to maintain foveal fixation of a target. The present experiments have shown that backward masking during pursuit eye movements depends on the target and mask appearing in the same place. Something which appears to move across the scene, therefore, would not be masked. The background scene might be suppressed, however, since stationary objects could mask themselves. The result is functional, since either effect would enhance the relative visibility of the target that is pursued.

The differences between visual masking in saccadic and pursuit eye movements are summarized schematically in Figure 12.7. The left column represents various stimulus sequences. The Target Letters A and B are presented when the eye fixates Point A. The eye moves from A to B, and the circle mask is presented after the eye moves to B. Four different

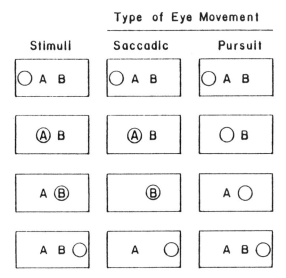

Figure 12.7
Schematic illustration of differences in visual masking during saccadic and pursuit eye movements. (Targets A and B are presented briefly when the eye is at A. The masking circle is
flashed after the eye moves to B. With pursuit eye movements, the ring always masks the
letter it surrounds, e.g., the missing B in the third row. With saccadic eye movements, the
ring masks the letter that had stimulated the same part of the retina as the ring, e.g., the
missing A in the third row.)

positions of the mask are illustrated. The masking effects depend on the
position of the mask and the type of eye movement.

The center and right columns depict what an observer might report
seeing with saccadic or pursuit eye movements, given an onset asynchrony that produced complete suppression of the target. The results of
the present experiments are shown in the right column of Figure 12.7 by
Target A, when the mask is in the second position, and by Target B, when
the mask is in the third position. The mask always surrounds the letter
that it masks during pursuit eye movements. The saccadic masking results
(Davidson et al., 1973) are illustrated in the center column by the disappearance of A when the mask surrounds B, and by the disappearance of
B when the mask is displaced to the right of B. The mask does not appear
to surround the figure that it masks; it always masks the stimulus to its
left, which has the same retinal location, for saccadic eye movements to
the right.

The differences between visual masking for saccadic and tracking eye
movements can be illustrated further by describing eye movements during reading. If the first fixation is on a word in the middle of a line of

Table 12.1
Effects of eye movements on masking and apparent motion

Type of eye movement	Positions of stimuli	
	Same spatial location (different retinal)	Same retinal location (different spatial)
Apparent motion		
Saccadic[a]	no	yes
Pursuit[b]	yes	no
Visual masking		
Saccadic[c]	no	yes
Pursuit[d]	yes	no

a. Rock & Ebenholtz (1962).
b. Stoper (1973).
c. Davidson, Fox, and Dick (1973).
d. White (Notes 1 and 2).

print, the fixated word and the adjacent words are clearly visible. During and after a saccadic eye movement to another word, the new phrase masks the old phrase. This is retinal position masking, and it is functional for saccadic eye movements. But suppose that a finger moves smoothly across the text and is visually pursued. Now the text continuously masks itself and the finger remains clear. This is spatial position masking, and it is functional for tracking movements.

Some support for the interpretation presented here lies in the relationship of the masking experiments to similar studies of apparent motion and eye movements. For example, Rock and Ebenholtz (1962) found apparent motion between stimuli that stimulated the same retinal location when the stimuli were made to appear in different places by saccadic eye movements. Stoper (1973) came to the opposite conclusion for apparent motion during pursuit eye movements; he obtained motion between stimuli that were presented in the same place but stimulated different parts of the retina. The pattern of effects for different types of eye movements on visual masking is the same as the pattern for apparent motion, as shown in Table 12.1, where *yes* or *no* indicates presence or absence of masking or apparent motion.

Kahneman (1967) has suggested that apparent motion in paradoxical directions might be responsible for metacontrast suppression. Although apparent motion and metacontrast have been shown to operate independently under some conditions (Weisstein and Growney, 1969), the pattern of effects with different types of eye movements implies that informa-

tion processing in visual masking and apparent motion have similar early stages of analysis, as Breitmeyer, Love, and Wepman (1974) suggested.
    In conclusion, it appears that the different outcomes of visual masking experiments with tracking and saccadic eye movements may be understood in terms of an approach that describes the functional role of masking in visual perception.

Notes

Portions of this article were presented at the meeting of the Association for Research in Vision and Ophthalmology, Sarasota, Florida, April 1974 (Experiments 1 and 2) and at the meeting of the American Psychological Association, Chicago, August 1975 (Experiment 3). The research was supported by a Biological Sciences Support Grant to the author through the Duke University Research Council (National Institutes of Health Grant 5505RR07070-09).
    I thank William St. Amant and Paul Gruenewald for their assistance in conducting the experiments and Deborah Solomon for a preliminary study. I also thank Gregory Lockhead for the use of the computer, which was supported by National Institute of Mental Health Grant MII-18617.

References

Beck, J., and Ambler, B. Discriminability of differences in line slope and in line arrangement as a function of mask delay. *Perception & Psychophysics*, 1972, *12*, 33−38.

Breitmeyer, B., Love, R., and Wepman, B. Contour suppression during stroboscopic motion and metacontrast. *Vision Research*, 1974, *14*, 1451−1456.

Bridgeman, B. Metacontrast and lateral inhibition. *Psychological Review*, 1971, *78*, 528−539.

Bridgeman, B. Correlates of metacontrast in single cells of the cat visual system. *Vision Research*, 1975, *15*, 91−99.

Davidson, M. L., Fox, M.-J., and Dick, A. O. Effect of eye movements on backward masking and perceived location. *Perception & Psychophysics*, 1973, *14*, 110−116.

Guilford, J. P. *Psychometric methods* (2nd ed.). New York: McGraw-Hill, 1954.

Kahneman, D. An onset-onset law for one case of apparent motion and metacontrast. *Perception & Psychophysics*, 1967, *2*, 577−584.

Lefton, L. A. Metacontrast: A review. *Perception & Psychophysics*, 1973, *13*, 161−171.

Mack, A., and Herman, E. Position constancy during pursuit eye movement: An investigation of the Filehne illusion. *Quarterly Journal of Experimental Psychology*, 1973, *25*, 71−84.

Matin, E. The two-transient (masking) paradigm. *Psychological Review*, 1975, *82*, 451−461.

Matin, E., Clymer, A. B., and Matin, L. Metacontrast and saccadic suppression. *Science*, 1972, *178*, 179−181.

Matin, L. Eye movements and perceived visual direction. In D. Jameson and L. M. Hurvich (Eds.), *Handbook of sensory physiology* (Vol. 7, Pt. 4). Berlin, West Germany: Springer-Verlag, 1972.

Puckett, J. D. W., and Steinman, R. M. Tracking eye movements with and without saccadic correction. *Vision Research*, 1969, *9*, 695−703.

Purcell, D. G., Stewart, A. L., and Dember, W. N. Spatial effectiveness of the mask: Lateral inhibition in visual backward masking. *Perception & Psychophysics*, 1968, *4*, 344−346.

Rock, I., and Ebenholtz, S. Stroboscopic movement based on change of phenomenal rather than retinal location. *American Journal of Psychology*, 1962, *75*, 193−207.

Steinman, R. M., Skavenski, A. A., and Sansbury, R. V. Voluntary control of smooth pursuit velocity. *Vision Research*, 1969, *9*, 1167–1171.

Stoper, A. E. Apparent motion of stimuli presented stroboscopically during pursuit movement of the eye. *Perception & Psychophysics*, 1973, *13*, 201–211.

Turvey, M. T. On peripheral and central processes in vision: Inferences from an information-processing analysis of masking with patterned stimuli. *Psychological Review*, 1973, *80*, 1–52.

Walley, R. E., and Weiden, T. D. Lateral inhibition and cognitive masking: A neuropsychological theory of attention. *Psychological Review*, 1973, *80*, 284–302.

Weisstein, N. A., Rashevsky-Landahl neural net: Stimulation of metacontrast. *Psychological Review*, 1968, *75*, 494–521.

Weisstein, N. Metacontrast. In D. Jameson and L. M. Hurvich (Eds.), *Handbook of sensory physiology* (Vol. 7, Pt. 4). Berlin, West Germany: Springer-Verlag, 1972.

Weisstein, N., and Growney, R. L. Apparent motion and metacontrast: A note on Kahneman's formulation. *Perception & Psychophysics*, 1969, *5*, 321–328.

Weisstein, N., Ozog, G., and Szoc, R. A comparison and elaboration of two models of metacontrast. *Psychological Review*, 1975, *82*, 325–343.

White, C. W. *Backward masking: Perceived location or retinal contiguity?* Paper presented at the Meeting of the Association for Research in Vision and Ophthalmology, Sarasota, Florida, April 1974.

White, C. W. *Visual masking during pursuit eye movements.* Paper presented at the Meeting of the American Psychological Association, Chicago, August 1975.

Winer, B. J. *Statistical principles in experimental design* (2nd ed.). New York: McGraw-Hill, 1971.

Chapter 13
Symmetry Based on Figure Halves
Janet P. Szlyk, Irvin Rock, and Celia B. Fisher

It is now a well-established fact that bilateral or mirror symmetry is spontaneously perceived when the axis of such symmetry is vertical (e.g., Mach, 1897/1959, 1898; Goldmeier, 1936, 1972; Attneave, 1955; Rock and Leaman, 1963; Arnheim, 1974; Garner and Sutliff, 1974). When the axis is in some other orientation, such as horizontal or oblique, we are not apt to perceive symmetry or, if we do, the impression of equality on two sides that is characteristic of such perception is not very striking.

A related aspect of the vertical symmetry effect that concerns us here bears on the equality of the two halves of the figure on either side of the axis of symmetry. Regardless of the figure's orientation in a frontal plane, these halves are equal in their retinal and thus in their cortical projection. But suppose the figure is slanted in the third dimension so it is no longer the case that the two halves will project equally because the image of the half on the far side of the axis will be foreshortened more than the half on the near side of the axis? If the symmetry effect is based on a low level of processing closely correlated with the proximal input, one might predict that it will be eliminated under these conditions. But if it is based on the perception of the equality of the two halves of the figure, then, given shape constancy operations, the two halves will appear to be equal and, if so, the impression of symmetry will be maintained. In that event, the effect would be based on a higher, post-constancy, level of processing.

If the perception of symmetry depends upon constancy operations that lead to the perception of an axis orientation as vertical or to the veridical perception of the width of the halves of a figure slanted in depth, then it can be regarded as an example of perceptual causality or perceptual interdependency, i.e., a state of affairs in which one perception depends upon or is linked to another (see Gogel, 1973; Hochberg, 1974; Epstein, 1982; Rock, 1983). The question we ask is this: does the spontaneous impression of symmetry about a vertical axis depend upon the perception of the slant

Originally published in *Spatial Vision* 9, 1 (1995): 139–150, under the title "Level of Processing in the Perception of Symmetrical Forms Viewed from Different Angles." Reprinted with permission.

of the figure and the achievement of veridical perception of the size of its two halves?

In a recent study, Locher and Smets (1992) compared symmetry detection in two- and three-dimensional volumetric dot patterns. The patterns were displayed orthogonally and non-orthogonally to the viewer's line-of-sight (in the investigation the forms were rotated) with full depth cues available. Because there were no differences in detection accuracy between the two- and three-dimensional patterns, they concluded that depth does not provide perceptually useful information about a pattern's symmetry. However, their subjects performed more poorly in the non-orthogonal condition.

In our present study, we assume that if shape constancy governs symmetry perception then the availability of depth cues should be critical. Therefore, a full depth-cue and a reduced depth-cue condition were included in this study, as was a measure of shape constancy. By manipulating these depth conditions, and having conditions where the subjects view the display screen at an angle, rather than the patterns being rotated, our intent was to determine the role of depth information in symmetry discrimination, and ultimately test the perceptual causality hypothesis.

Methods

Subjects
Sixty-four normally sighted subjects or subjects with corrected vision of at least 20/20 (Snellen visual acuity) between the ages of 18 and 27 yr were recruited.

Stimuli
There were 8 pairs of closed polygon holistic stimuli and 8 pairs of multi-element stimuli used for testing. Two additional sets of each pattern type were used to train subjects. Examples of these stimuli are illustrated in Fig. 13.1. By "pair" we only mean that for each particular pattern there was a version of it that was symmetrical and a version of it that was asymmetrical. However, the figures were seen one at a time and the symmetrical and asymmetrical versions of each pattern were randomly presented and, therefore, rarely shown one after the other but rather separated by many other figures. When viewed at a 65 deg angle, objectively symmetrical stimuli projected an asymmetrical retinal image and objectively asymmetrical stimuli projected a symmetrical retinal image. To maximize the retinal asymmetry while maintaining the slant within the range of shape constancy, we chose a slant angle of 65 deg, which has been found to be adequate for shape constancy under full cue conditions (King et al., 1976).

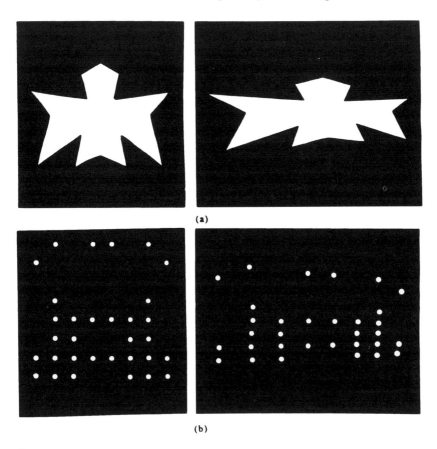

(a)

(b)

Figure 13.1
Examples of symmetrical and asymmetrical pairs of holistic (a), and multi-elemental stimuli (b).

The holistic figures were adapted from stimuli originally employed by Rock and Leaman (1963), Palmer and Hemenway (1978), and Fisher et al. (1981). The multi-elemental dot patterns were adapted from Royer (1981) and Fisher and Bornstein (1982). All figures were photographed with Kodalith film, and developed into slides. Two Kodak 4600 Carousel Slide Projectors back-projected slides of all stimuli onto a translucent screen. Both the projectors and the screen were hidden from the view of the observer behind a black partition. When projected onto the screen, the figures appeared white on an opaque black background. The figures subtended an average visual angle of approximately 4 deg. The average luminance of the figures was 6.1 cd m^{-2}. The projector luminance was increased by approximately 0.33 in the reduced-cue conditions to compensate for the decreased light entering the eye through the pinholes that were used in these conditions.

Design and Procedure
The 64 subjects, both men and women, were randomly assigned to one of four groups of 16 subjects each. The four groups included: the full-cue, 0 deg group; the full-cue, 65 deg group; the reduced-cue, 0 deg group; and the reduced-cue, 65 deg group.

Symmetry Identification. Prior to each experimental session, all subjects were instructed to label the figures presented to them as simply "symmetrical" or "asymmetrical." To insure that subjects understood the terms symmetrical and asymmetrical, two sets of asymmetrical and symmetrical forms (not used later in actual test trials) representing examples of the multi-element and closed polygonal patterns were shown in the vertical plane, outside the testing room prior to testing. All subjects identified all 4 training forms correctly.

In the full-cue conditions, the figures were viewed through either of two 15.3-cm apertures, both at 1.5 m from the screen. The screen was stationary and the depth tilt was produced by viewing the screen through the aperture straight ahead or the other one set at a 65 deg angle to the center of the screen. Through the apertures, subjects had full depth information concerning the orientation of the projector screen. In the reduced-cue conditions, both apertures were covered with black plastic and equipped with 1 mm pinholes. Subjects viewing the stimuli through the pinhole monocularly (with an eye patch over the non-dominant eye) saw only the white stimulus figure on a black background; they did not see the edges of the projector screen. Subjects in all conditions had their heads held in place by a chin-rest. To avoid dark adaptation, subjects were exposed to a low-luminance, diffuse light between trials that did not cause glare or localized light-adaptation effects.

Without binocular cues to depth or differential blur from far or near regions of the slide, reduced-cue subjects had only the retinal image on which to base their judgments of symmetry. By contrast, in the full-cue (binocular) condition, the subject had full view of the screen with both eyes and he or she could see its edges. Thus both binocular depth information and cues from the screen edge of the orientation of the screen were available to the full-cue subject.

Each subject saw 8 vertically symmetrical and 8 vertically asymmetrical holistic figures along with 8 vertically symmetrical and 8 vertically asymmetrical multi-element forms, presented in random order. All 32 stimuli were presented in blocks of two stimulus durations: 100 ms and 1 s. The order of the two exposure durations was counterbalanced across subjects, totaling 64 trials. A fixation point, projected from a third projector, appeared in the center of the screen immediately preceding each stimulus presentation so that the subject's gaze was localized.

Shape Constancy. Subjects from both the full-cue, 65 deg group and the reduced-cue, 65 deg group were tested for shape constancy following the standard 64 trial session. Subjects from these two groups received an additional 32 trials: eight trials (4 holistic and 4 multi-element figures) at each of two durations (1 s and 100 ms) in each of two viewing positions (0 deg and 65 deg) for a total of 32 trials. Only symmetrical slides were used. Each subject made 16 judgments of the extent of the figures viewing them in the 0 deg frontoparallel plane and 16 in the 65 deg plane. Shape constancy was defined by the comparison of height-to-width ratios between judgments made during frontoparallel (0 deg) viewing and judgments made during 65 deg viewing. An illuminated apparatus containing two glow-in-the-dark pegs was used to measure subjects' perceptions of vertical and horizontal figural extents in both frontoparallel and rotated presentations.

Results

Symmetry Detection
Subject performance is presented in Table 13.1 in terms of mean proportion of correct objective shape identifications (with their correspond-

Table 13.1
Mean proportions and standard deviations of correct objective shape identifications

	Holistic				Multi-elemental				
	100 ms		1 s		100 ms		1 s		
Overall	Sym	Asym	Sym	Asym	Sym	Asym	Sym	Asym	Means
Full-cue, 0 deg	0.89	0.81	0.89	0.93	0.82	0.66	0.91	0.79	0.84
	(0.08)	(0.19)	(0.13)	(0.13)	(0.19)	(0.19)	(0.14)	(0.20)	
Full-cue, 65 deg	0.76	0.66	0.82	0.79	0.75	0.50	0.77	0.56	0.70
	(0.16)	(0.21)	(0.15)	(0.21)	(0.18)	(0.21)	(0.20)	(0.20)	
Reduced-cue, 0 deg	0.87	0.66	0.90	0.79	0.72	0.49	0.83	0.55	0.73
	(0.14)	(0.30)	(0.14)	(0.23)	(0.15)	(0.19)	(0.23)	(0.24)	
Reduced-cue, 65 deg	0.58	0.29	0.47	0.31	0.44	0.34	0.41	0.27	0.39
65 deg	(0.25)	(0.19)	(0.21)	(0.19)	(0.19)	(0.20)	(0.19)	(0.16)	

Note: The maximum possible proportion correct for each condition was 1.00. The number of subjects in each cell was 16. Standard deviations for each cell appear in parentheses.

ing standard deviations). A five-way ANOVA was performed with the factors of viewing condition (full-cue, reduced-cue) × type of figure (symmetrical, asymmetrical) × viewing angle (0 deg, 65 deg) × pattern type (holistic, multi-element) × exposure duration (100 ms, 1 s). Viewing condition and viewing angle were between-subjects factors; the remaining were within-subjects factors. The proportion of judgments (out of eight) that were objectively correct was the dependent measure.

Main Effects. For the between-subjects factors, significant main effects were found for viewing condition [$F(1, 60) = 96.21$, $p < 0.001$] and viewing angle [$F(1, 60) = 117.58$, $p < 0.001$]. An advantage for symmetry emerged [$F(1, 60) = 44.85$, $p < 0.001$], with more correct judgments made for symmetrical patterns (mean proportion $M = 0.74$) than for asymmetrical patterns ($M = 0.59$). Consistent with expectations based on information processing models (Attneave, 1955; Chipman, 1977; Royer, 1981), the holistic patterns were judged correctly ($M = 0.71$) more often than multi-element patterns ($M = 0.61$), [$F(1, 60) = 44.73$, $p < 0.001$], and 1 s exposure durations resulted in more correct judgments ($M = 0.69$) than 100 ms exposures ($M = 0.64$), [$F(1, 60) = 10.29$, $p < 0.002$].

If perceptual equality is responsible for the perception of symmetry when shapes are viewed from a 65 deg angle, then the number of objective judgments of symmetry and asymmetry reported by subjects in the full-cue, 65 deg condition should not differ from responses of subjects in the full-cue, 0 deg condition, while objective judgments of reduced-cue, 65 deg subjects should drop significantly. Post-hoc analysis of the significant viewing condition by viewing angle interaction [$F(1, 60) = 21.48$, $p < 0.001$] yields such findings. Table 13.2 presents the means (combining correct reports of symmetry and asymmetry) involved in the interaction. Newman–Keuls tests ($p < 0.05$) on these means yielded significantly fewer objectively correct responses for the reduced-cue, 65 deg condition than for any of the other three conditions, which in turn did not differ from one another. Moreover, subjects in these three other groups identi-

Table 13.2
Mean proportions for between-subjects factors

	Angle	
Viewing condition	0 deg	65 deg
Full-cue	0.84a	0.70a
Reduced-cue	0.73a	0.39b

Note: Means with different subscripts are significantly different from each other at the 0.05 level (Newman–Keuls).

fied the objective shape of the stimuli above chance levels [$t(15) = 10.65$, $p < 0.01$; $t(15) = 6.39$, $p < 0.01$; $t(15) = 7.10$, $p < 0.01$; for the full-cue, 0 deg, the full-cue, 65 deg, and the reduced-cue, 0 deg conditions, respectively]. By contrast, the reduced-cue, 65 deg condition produced responding below chance level [$t(15) = -3.51$, $p < 0.01$], indicating judgments influenced by, but not exclusively dependent upon, the retinal projection of the stimuli (see below).

The focus of this investigation is on performance of the subjects when they view the figures at a slant but have full depth cues available, the full-cue, 65 deg condition. Do they respond in terms of the symmetry or asymmetry, as these properties may be perceived, or in terms of how they are given within the retinal image? The mean of 0.70 correct responses clearly is in the direction of the perceptual interpretation, since responding on the basis of retinal symmetry or asymmetry would lead to the expectation of a mean close to zero (because in the latter case the subjects would always be incorrect). Moreover, the mean of 0.70 should not be compared to the value of 1.00, the maximum proportion that could be correct, because in the full-cue, 0 deg condition the mean is only 0.84. For whatever reason, that value is the level of correct responses achieved when both perceptual and retinal symmetry is present.

Shape Constancy
The baseline ratio (of height in cm to width in cm) for the two frontoparallel plane conditions turned out to fall roughly between 0.94 and 1.14, depending upon whether full or reduced cues were available and upon the type of figure and duration of exposure. The means were 1.0 with full cues available and 1.07 in the reduced-cue condition. This result corresponds rather well with the objective height-to-width ratio, which approximates 1.0.

Were the subjects able to achieve full constancy for the shapes of the figures despite their rather extreme slant of 65 deg from the frontal plane? At the 65 deg angle in the full-cue condition, the mean ratio was 1.26 across exposure duration and type of figure, which significantly differed from the full-cue, 0 deg condition mean of 1.0 [$t(15) = 5.04$, $p < 0.01$]. This increase reflects the decrease in perceived width of the stimuli relative to the judgment of width in the frontoparallel position and represents a loss of constancy.

In the reduced-cue, 65 deg condition, where of course constancy is not expected to be obtained, the ratio rises sharply to a mean of 2.03 for the two kinds of figure and two exposure interval conditions combined. Using the full-cue, 0 deg mean height-to-width ratio of 1.0 as the value for complete constancy and the value of this ratio when the figures are viewed through the artificial pupil from an angle of 65 deg of 2.03 as the value for zero constancy, we can derive a measure for the degree of constancy obtained for the mean ratio in the full-cue, 65 deg condition of 1.26. Following the formula that is generally used, we have a Constancy Ratio = $(2.03 - 1.26)/(2.03 - 1.0) = 0.77$, which is, of course, an appreciable but not complete degree of constancy.

Furthermore, the mean value of the height-to-width ratio obtained in the reduced-cue, 65 deg condition, of 2.03, is lower than the value to be expected in this condition if the perceived width of the figure were a function of the compression of the projected figure images relative to the unchanged image of the height of the figures. We computed this value trigonometrically to be 2.35. The departure of 2.03 from 2.35 (which we take to be the objective value indicating zero constancy) is statistically significant $[t(15) = 5.99, p < 0.01]$. The Constancy Ratio $(2.35 - 2.03)/(2.35 - 1.0) = 0.24$. Thus, it can be concluded that the reduced-cue, 65 deg condition did not succeed in completely eliminating cues to depth. This in turn undoubtedly explains why symmetry and asymmetry responses in that condition were not what would have been expected if depth perception had been entirely eliminated. For, if it had, subjects should have responded incorrectly as often as they responded correctly in the 0 deg condition. That is because symmetrical figures yielded asymmetrical retinal images and asymmetrical figures yielded symmetrical retinal images in the reduced-cue, 65 deg condition and, without depth cues, these image relations should have determined responses. If so, the expected mean proportion correct should have been 1.0–0.73 (using the mean proportion correct in the reduced-cue, 0 deg condition as baseline) or 0.27. But the mean proportion of correct responses in the reduced-cue, 65 deg condition was 0.39.

The influence of exposure duration and pattern type on shape constancy was assessed by a two-way repeated measures ANOVA. Neither the main effects nor the interaction were significant $[F(1, 31) < 1.0]$. Thus, neither exposure duration, nor pattern type significantly affected shape constancy in our experiment.

Discussion

The results give a clear answer to the main question posed in this investigation. The perception and response to symmetry or the lack of it in patterns symmetrical about their vertical axis is determined by whether or not the two halves of the pattern appear to be equal. Thus, although a figure is rotated about its vertical axis quite appreciably away from the frontoparallel plane, it will generally continue to appear symmetrical if it is symmetrical and asymmetrical if it is not. This is so despite the fact that the symmetrical figures then project an image to the retina that is asymmetrical and the asymmetrical figures project an image that is symmetrical about the vertical axis.

The data that support this claim are the results of the condition in which the subject views the figures in a plane slanted away from him or her by 65 deg with full cues to depth available. In comparison to the results when the figures are seen in the frontoparallel plane, where the mean proportion of correct responses was 0.84, the mean proportion correct in the slanted-plane condition was 0.70. But, for responses based on the retinal state of affairs, the predicted mean ought to be close to 0, since responses based on retinal symmetry or asymmetry would always be incorrect. This prediction assumes that subjects would always be "correct." However, a more likely expectation would be the difference between the proportion correct in the frontoparallel plane condition and the perfectly correct performance of 1.00, namely 1.00 − 0.84, or 0.16. So the closeness of the obtained mean of 0.70 to 0.84 and its distance from 0.16 tells the story.

Moreover, the measure of shape constancy tells us that the perceived shape of the figures seen at a slant was not fully veridical. This is what might be expected for a slant as extreme as 65 deg. Thus a symmetrical figure might be expected to appear to be slightly less than perfectly symmetrical and an asymmetrical one to appear not quite as asymmetrical as it is. Given that expectation, the slight departure of the results in the slanted-plane condition from those in the frontal-plane condition become fully understandable.

The results in the condition in which subjects viewed the figures in the slanted plane, but presumably without any cues to depth, round out the picture. Here the mean proportion correct plummets to 0.39. Thus with the only difference between the two slanted-plane conditions being the presence or absence of depth information, the responses shift from those governed predominantly by the objective state of affairs to those governed predominantly by the retinal state of affairs. This is not to imply that subjects are perceiving their retinal images in the reduced-cue condition. A better formulation would be to say that in this condition subjects tend to perceive the figures as lying in a plane orthogonal to their line of sight and thus retinal symmetry or the lack of it would have to signify objective symmetry or the lack of it.

But the responses in these conditions are not fully in accord with a "retinal" prediction. The mean of 0.39 is significantly greater than the value suggested above of 0.16, which is what we should expect in this condition were retinal symmetry or asymmetry to govern the outcome. However, a further correction in this prediction is required. The use of the artificial pupil not only reduces depth information, but also appreciably lowers the luminance level of the figures. The greater intensity of light we introduced in the two reduced-cue conditions would not have totally compensated for the loss of luminance at the eye. Thus the results of the other reduced-cue condition, in which the figures were seen in a fronto-parallel plane, become relevant and useful. Here the mean proportion correct was 0.73. Therefore it is the difference between 1.00 and 0.73, or 0.27, that is the best prediction of what to expect in the reduced-cue slanted-plane condition if the retinal state of affairs governs the outcome. The obtained mean of 0.39 is still significantly greater than 0.27 [$t(15) = 3.60, p < 0.01$]. From this we can conclude that the artificial pupil did not succeed in completely eliminating cues to depth in this condition. This conclusion jibes with the fact that a slight tendency toward shape constancy was found to occur in this condition. It is possible that the asymmetrical retinal projection of the symmetrical slides served as a kind of perspective cue, suggesting a symmetrical pattern viewed at a slant.

Symmetry Bias
Subjects consistently did better with the symmetrical than with the asymmetrical patterns. They were more often correct on these trials. We believe that the finding reveals a bias. It must be borne in mind that our asymmetrical figures are deliberate distortions away from what is otherwise a symmetrical figure. Therefore, one might say that all the figures look somewhat symmetrical. The question the subject has to answer for him- or herself is rather whether a given figure looks *perfectly* symmetrical. Given some uncertainty, the subject is more likely to respond "symmetrical." A signal detection analysis supports this interpretation of a symmetrical bias. Across all conditions and stimuli, the average proportion of hits (symmetrical response when a symmetrical stimulus was presented) was 0.74, misses (asymmetrical response/symmetrical stimulus) 0.26, false alarms (symmetrical response/asymmetrical stimulus) 0.41, and correct rejections (asymmetrical response/asymmetrical stimulus) 0.59, yielding a d' of 0.87. Saying "symmetrical" when the stimulus was asymmetrical (false alarm) should have been as likely as saying "asymmetrical" when the stimulus was symmetrical (miss), if no bias were evident. However, false alarms were considerably more likely (0.41) than were misses (0.26), offering further support for a symmetrical bias, with beta = 0.82. This interpretation is supported by the further finding that the symmetrical bias increases with the difficulty of the condition.

Effects of Figure Type and Exposure Duration
We have already noted the expected finding that subjects do better with the holistic figures than with the multi-element figures. Similarly, it hardly

needs to be explained that subjects would do better with the longer 1 s exposure duration than the 100 ms one. The fact is that subjects do perform better in the slanted-plane full-cue condition with the holistic figures and with the longer exposure duration. However, such figural and duration differences occur for all the other conditions as well, so that, in the absence of a significant interaction effect, we cannot say that these factors specifically affect the constancy operation. Although it is known that constancy is achievable in brief durations, there is no evidence of which we are aware that shape constancy is a function of the particular shape or pattern investigated (except perhaps some bias that improves performance when the shape is a regular one such as a circle (King et al., 1976) or one with vertical symmetry as in our experiments here). Hence our failure to find specific effects of figural characteristics and duration of exposure do not violate existing knowledge on this subject.

A Test of Perceptual Causality
Some investigators might be inclined to regard our finding of the dependency of symmetry perception on constancy operations as surprising (Locher and Smets, 1992). That is because symmetry can be detected in exposure durations of as little as 50 ms followed by a mask. In fact, for this reason, the detection of symmetry has been thought to be preattentive as determined by studies using 2-D dot patterns rotated clockwise and counter clockwise in 2-D space (Wagemans et al., 1991, 1992), whereas it would seem unlikely to many that a constancy process of taking account of depth information would be preattentive. Some might even be inclined to reverse our claim about the direction of cause and effect of perception of the plane and perception of symmetry. The argument would be that the skewed symmetry projected to the retina in our slanted-plane conditions is preattentively interpreted as bilateral symmetry and this in turn allows the correct interpretation that the plane of the figure is slanted with respect to the viewer.

Our answer to this line of reasoning is as follows. First, none of all the preattentive research of which we are aware succeeds in testing perception without attention. Either a divided attention paradigm is employed or it is assumed that texture segregation or pop-out based on brief presentations of an array of multiple items must be preattentive because the outcome entails parallel processing (Treisman and Gelade, 1980; Julesz, 1981; Beck, 1982). But the fact remains that subjects in these paradigms are attending to the array. When this is prevented by a method in which the subject is not attending to the stimulus or stimulus array to be tested, then neither texture segregation, perceptual groupings, pop-out, nor shape is perceived (Mack et al., 1992; Rock et al., 1992). Therefore it is unlikely that any overall property of shape such as symmetry would be detected preattentively. Second, it does not at all follow that, *with* attention as in our experiments and others on symmetry, depth perception and shape constancy would not be achieved in brief durations. We are inclined to believe they would because there is evidence that processes such as depth from retinal disparity and constancy are indeed achieved in very brief durations (Dove, 1841; King et al., 1976). In our experiment, depth and constancy were achieved in 100 ms presentations although the figures were not masked.

Third, there is a test of the cause-effect reversal hypothesis contained in our experiment. We refer to the condition in which the pattern on the screen is viewed through a pinhole at a 65 deg slant thus reducing depth information. For in this case, the skewed symmetry image is available and should, according to the hypothesis, yield good symmetry perception of symmetrical figures. However, the other cues allowed in the 65 deg, full-cue condition are not available in this condition, but, according to the hypothesis, they are not relevant. The result in this condition is a marked decline in correct reports of symmetry and, going along with this, a marked decline in constancy. However, there still is a small residual tendency toward constancy and there are more correct symmetry responses than would be expected from the asymmetrical image of the symmetrical figures. Therefore, as we acknowledge above, it may well be that a skewed symmetrical image is one kind of cue that the object producing it is slanted away from the frontal plane.

There is another relevant fact to consider. It concerns the subjects' responses to asymmetrical figures presented in the 65 deg full depth-cue condition. These yield a symmetrical retinal image so that there is no skewed symmetry image present. If the outcome were not based on taking account of the slant of the screen, subjects should respond "symmetrical" given the symmetrical image. However, subjects tend to respond "asymmetrical" to these stimuli seen at a slant; whereas in the reduced-cue 65 deg condition subjects tend to respond "symmetrical" to these stimuli. This finding is no doubt the result of information from retinal disparity and the interaction of appropriate accommodation and convergence. The trapezoidal image of the slanted rectangular screen may also serve as a pictorial cue to the slant of the screen.

It can be argued that our findings are not exclusively concerned with symmetrical figures. While this is undoubtedly true, it does not imply that our findings have nothing to do with symmetry per se. One of the main purposes of this study was to demonstrate that there is nothing special about the perception of symmetry beyond the perception of the equality of the halves of a figure on each side of its vertical bisector. If such perception of equality is indeed crucial, as our data suggest, then we believe that the vertical-symmetry effect is one more example of perceptual causality.

References

Arnheim, R. (1974). *Art and Visual Perception*. University of California Press, Berkeley, CA.

Attneave, F. (1955). Symmetry, information, and memory for patterns. *Am. J. Psychol.* **68**, 209–222.

Beck, J. (1982). Textural segmentation. In: *Organization and Representation in Perception*. J. Beck (Ed.). Lawrence Erlbaum Assoc., Hillsdale, New Jersey, pp. 285–317.

Chipman, S. F. (1977). Complexity and structure in visual patterns. *J. Exp. Psychol.* **106**, 269–301.

Dove, H. W. (1841). Über stereoskopie. *Ann. Phys.*, *Series 2* **110**, 494–498.

Epstein, W. (1982). Percept-percept couplings. *Perception* **11**, 75–83.

Fisher, C. B. and Bornstein, M. H. (1982). Identification of symmetry: Effects of stimulus orientation and head position. *Percept. Psychophys.* **32**, 443–448.

Fisher, C. B., Ferdinandsen, K. and Bornstein, M. H. (1981). The role of symmetry in infant form discrimination. *Child Develop.* **52**, 457–462.

Garner, W. R. and Sutliff, D. (1974). The effect of goodness of encoding time in visual pattern discrimination. *Percept. Psychophys.* **16**, 426–430.

Gogel, W. (1973). The organization of perceived space: I. Perceptual interactions. *Psychologische Forschung* **36**, 195–221.

Goldmeier, E. (1936). Über Ahnlichkeit bei gesehen Figuren. *Psychologische Forschung* **21**, 146–208.

Goldmeier, E. (1972). Similarity in visually perceived forms. *Psycholog. Issues* **8**, 1–136.

Hochberg, J. (1974). Higher-order stimuli and inter-response coupling in the perception of the visual world. In: *Studies in Perception: Essays in Honor of JJ Gibson*. R. MacLeod and H. L. Pick, Jr (Eds). Cornell University Press, Ithaca, New York.

Julesz, B. (1981). Figure and ground perception in briefly presented isodipole textures. In: *Perceptual Organization*. M. Kubovy and J. Pomerantz (Eds). Lawrence Erlbaum Assoc., Hillsdale, New Jersey, pp. 27–54.

Locher, P. and Smets, G. (1992). The influence of stimulus dimensionality and viewing orientation on detection of symmetry in dot patterns. *Bull. Psychonom. Soc.* **30**, 43–46.

King, M., Meyer, G. E., Tangney, J. and Biederman, I. (1976). Shape constancy and a perceptual bias towards symmetry. *Percept. Psychophys.* **19**, 129–136.

Mach, E. (1898). *Popular Scientific Lectures*, 3rd edition. T. J. McCormack (translator). Open Court Publishing House, Chicago, Illinois.

Mach, E. (1899/1955). *The Analysis of Sensations*, Revised Edition. C. M. Williams (translator). Dover Publishing, New York, NY.

Mack, A., Tang, B., Tuma, R., Kahn, S. and Rock, I. (1992). Perceptual organization and attention. *Cognit. Psychol.* **24**, 475–501.

Palmer, S. E. and Hemenway, K. (1978). Orientation and symmetry: Effects of multiple, rotational, and near symmetries. *J. Exp. Psychol: Human Percept. Perform.* **4**, 691–702.

Rock, I. (1983). Perceptual interdependencies. In: *The Logic of Perception*. Bradford Books/MIT Press, Cambridge, Massachusetts, pp. 283–299.

Rock, I. and Leaman, R. (1963). An experimental analysis of visual symmetry. *Acta Psychol.* **21**, 171–183.

Rock, I., Linnett, C. M., Grant, P. and Mack, A. (1992). Perception without attention: Results of a new method. *Cognit. Psychol.* **24**, 502–534.

Royer, F. L. (1981). Detection of symmetry. *J. Exp. Psychol.* **7**, 1186–1210.

Treisman, A. and Gelade, G. (1980). A feature integration theory of attention. *Cognit. Psychol.* **12**, 97–136.

Wagemans, J., Van Gool, L. and d'Ydewalle, G. (1991). Detection of symmetry in tachisto-scopically presented dot patterns: effects of multiple axes and skewing. *Percept Psychophys.* **50**, 413–427.

Wagemans, J., Van Gool, L. and d'Ydewalle, G. (1992). Orientation effects and component processes in symmetry detection. *Q. J. Exp. Psychol.* **44A**, 475–508.

Part IV

Motion

Introduction

The message of this section is that the perception of motion is indirect in that it depends upon perceiving a change in the perceived direction of an object. It cannot be explained on the basis of either the direct stimulation of motion-detector cells or any other theory that seeks to reduce motion perception to the direct picking up of information concerning motion in the proximal stimulus.

The first chapter is a revised version of parts of chapter 5 of my 1975 textbook, *An Introduction to Perception*. It surveys the different kinds of perceived motion, namely, real motion, apparent motion, indirect motion, autokinetic motion and, in each case, from the standpoint of searching for a common basis of motion perception. That common basis is the following principle: *When an object is perceived to undergo a change in its location, it will be perceived to move, but if the change in the object's location is based on the observer's movement, it will be perceived as stationary.*

This analysis is supported by the evidence provided by the research described in the subsequent chapters. The first of these is a reprint of an article by myself and Sheldon Ebenholtz (see chapter 15). Apparent or stroboscopic motion depends upon conditions in which each stimulus in the alternating cycle of *a* and *b* is perceived as located in a different place in space, even when *that* perception entails stimulation of the *same* region of the retina by *a* and *b*. This state of affairs can be brought about by having subjects make eye movements so that both *a* and *b* fall on the fovea. The results bring into question theories that would explain apparent motion by the alternating stimulation of different neighboring retinal loci, as for example differing parts of a receptive field. Actually, the essential conditions for apparent motion include a change of perceived location, in which *a* and *b* alternately appear and disappear *inexplicably*— namely, no other stimulus information can account for why they suddenly appear and disappear. For example, occlusion of *a* and *b* at just the appropriate rate of alternation to yield apparent motion will *abolish* it if the observer can interpret the changing image as undergoing occlusion of *a* and disocclusion of *b* (see Sigman and Rock 1974).

In chapter 16 the investigators Ono and Gonda ingeniously create the perception of apparent motion by requiring subjects to alternatively view a stimulus with each eye, which the reader can see for him/herself by holding up a finger and alternately opening and closing each eye. When we alternately open and close each eye—namely, left open and right closed followed by right closed and left open—a point straight ahead will appear to move stroboscopically back and forth. This occurs even in an otherwise dark field, so that the effect cannot entirely be explained on the basis of the shifting parallax location of the point relative to background objects. What can one say about the perceived direction of a point that is straight ahead, but viewed with one eye closed? (See figure 16.1.) Suppose the closed eye, instead of maintaining its position symmetrical with the open eye, shifts somewhat based on heterophoria (a slight imbalance of the muscles of the two eyes). That combination of positions of the two eyes would no longer signify that the point was straight ahead but rather was shifted slightly in the direction of the deviated eye. When the closed eye then opens simultaneous with the closing of the other eye, the direction of the point is now seen incorrectly on the other side of straight ahead. Therefore, there is a change in the perceived direction of the point each time the alternation of eyes occurs. That this is the cause of the apparent motion effect was shown in experiments in which the observer's eyes were alternately occluded or disoccluded by opaque shields as they viewed a single point of light in the dark. A high correlation was obtained between the direction and magnitude of phoria for a given observer under either near or far viewing conditions and the direction and magnitude of apparent movement perception. This form of apparent motion shows that motion can result simply from perceiving changes in the phenomenal direction of the target object.

Chapter 17 reproduces an article by Attneave and Block published in 1973. It concerns a fact about apparent motion: namely, that the distance between a and b is a critical factor along with the temporal separation and brightness of the stimuli. If the temporal separation is increased then, according to one of Korte's Laws, the physical separation must be increased accordingly if apparent motion is to be optimally maintained (Korte 1915). The investigators ask the question: is it the retinal or the perceived separation between a and b that is relevant? If, for example, the separation is increased and it turned out that the *perceived* separation is crucial, then to perceive such an increased separation constancy operations are implicated. At any rate, this is what they found:

> The space-time relationships satisfying Korte's third law of apparent motion were studied in three experiments. The results generally confirm and extend Corbin's conclusion that apparent movement is not a projection-level phenomenon, but one involving spatial constancy, i.e., some representation of tridimensional space. Between situations in which the stimuli were retinally matched, the time interval necessary for apparent movement varied with their phenomenal separation, whether the latter was determined by the distance of stimuli from the O, deviation of stimuli from the frontal plane, or illusory slant of the stimulus plane produced by a perspective gradient. (P. 301)

The research described in chapter 18 by Arien Mack and her co-workers in 1989 is concerned with a phenomenon usually thought of as on a lower sensory level: namely, the motion aftereffect (or MAE). It refers to the fact that following prolonged viewing of a moving display (such as a set of parallel lines) stationary stimuli appear to move slightly. The MAE is in the opposite direction to that of the moving array. The traditional explanation has been the fatiguing of detector cells responsive to one direction of motion. Thus the cells' responses to the opposite direction of motion become ascendant.

In fact, elegant evidence for this theory came from a classic experiment (Anstis and Gregory 1965). In one condition, subjects tracked a dot moving back and forth over a stationary grid of parallel lines. Assuming constancy, one can describe this condition as the achieving of the displacement of the images of contours over the retina that nonetheless appear as stationary. In another condition, subjects tracked the moving grid. This resulted in no image motion of contours along with the perceived motion of the grid. So the experiments create a separation between the displacement of contours and the perception of moving contours. The claim was that it was the displacement of contours over the retina that mattered for the MAE. If so, the effect is misnamed. It is not an aftereffect of motion, but an aftereffect of image displacement.

However, the research of Mack, Hill, and Kahn calls this sensory-level account into question. In the experiment subjects were required to track a vertically oscillating dot while at the same time observing the lateral motion of a vertically oriented grating (or a random-dot pattern). Under these conditions, the motion of contours over the retina becomes oblique, but the perceived direction of contours remains horizontal. For this latter perception to be achieved, information about eye movement (corollary discharge) must be integrated with information about image motion, a constancy operation of a particular kind. The question concerned the perceived detection of the MAE, oblique if based on the retinal flow, but horizontal if based on the perceived direction of the moving contours. The answer by now will come as no surprise to the reader. Not only was the aftereffect in a horizontal direction, but it was no different from another condition in which the eyes fixated a stationary target. Clearly what matters in this case is the perceived direction in which the grid of lines appears to move.

The final chapter in this section is concerned not simply with motion but with the rate of motion: that is, perceived velocity. The constancy of perceived velocity of objects has always been listed among the other constancies. What is meant by constancy of perceived velocity is that the apparent speed of an object moving across the field does not change very much when that object is seen far or near. Yet such changes in distance affect the rate at which the object's image traverses the retina.

There are two theories of speed constancy, one of which might be thought of as direct and one of which is indirect. The direct view is based on the transposition velocity effect discovered by J. F. Brown in 1931, which says that objects that traverse a frame of reference in a certain period of time will be perceived as moving at a particular velocity, namely, that perceived speed is a function of rate of displacement *relative* to a frame of reference (see Brown 1931). Hans Wallach (1939) then was able to derive constancy from this principle by noting that the frames of reference being compared are often equal, but because they are seen at differing distances, the retinal images are transposed precisely as in situations studied by Brown.

The second theory maintains that speed constancy is a function of size constancy, the "size" being the separation (or distance) between the object's starting and ending position. Where objective velocity is defined as the change of distance per unit time, perceived velocity can be thought of as the perceived change of distance per unit of time. Therefore, as long as constancy holds for the size of the distance traversed, then speed constancy should also hold.

In the final chapter of this section, strong evidence for the second theory is provided. It is interesting to consider why this theory was only confirmed in 1968. An attempt had been made to test it earlier by requiring the same subjects to make both size and speed judgments of a moving target (Wallach 1939). The results showed that while size constancy held up with increasing distance, speed constancy declined. Therefore, it was concluded, speed constancy cannot derive from size constancy. However, to base such a far-reaching conclusion on this inference from a single experiment seems unwarranted. It is known that size judgments are, at least in some measure, a function of instructions to subjects, and thus the size judgments may be less affected by increasing distance than speed judgments. At any rate, the experiments in chapter 19 would seem to discredit that earlier attempt to test this theory.

If speed constancy is based on first achieving size constancy, then it is indirect. It is not determined by a relational transformation that would more directly yield the constancy outcome. The experiments described in the final chapter of the series deliberately ruled out any such relational change. The subjects viewed a single luminous circle moving vertically through an otherwise totally dark room. Therefore, only cues to the distance of the circle from the observer can yield constancy of distances or extents along the circle's pathway, orthogonal to the line of sight. That means that speed must be perceived indirectly by taking distance into account.

References

Anstis, S., and R. L. Gregory. 1965. The aftereffect of seen movement: The role of retinal stimulation and of eye movements. *Quarterly Journal of Experimental Psychology* 17:173–74.

Brown, J. F. 1931. The visual perception of velocity. *Psychologische Forschung* 14:199–232.

Korte, A. 1915. Kinematickoskopische Untersuchungen. *Zeitschrift fur Psychologie* 72:193–206.

Sigman, E., and I. Rock. 1974. Stroboscopic movement based on perceptual intelligence. *Perception* 3:9–28.

Wallach, H. 1939. On the constancy of visual speed. *Psychological Review* 46:541–552.

Chapter 14
The Perception of Movement
Irvin Rock

Why does the perception of movement present a problem? It would seem plausible to believe that when an object moves, its image will move on the retina and this image movement is interpreted by the perceptual system as movement of the object. If this were the case, movement perception would not present a problem. Indeed, insofar as lower animals are concerned, this account may be correct, but as an explanation of the perceptual experience of human observers, it is grossly inadequate.

The perceptual experience of movement is analogous to other qualities of sensory experience such as color or size—we perceive movement as a property of the object. The ability to perceive movement is clearly very fundamental in animals; it is necessary for survival. Various animals react to movement but not to stationary objects. In man, movement of an object in the periphery of the field can be detected before its exact form is apprehended.

Movement is an "either-or" experience. An object either appears to be moving or it appears to be stationary (although of course its perceived speed may vary). There is no middle ground. If an object is moving too slowly—as in the case of the minute hand of a watch—it will not appear to move at all, although after a while a change in position is detected. Thus, there is a threshold below which a given magnitude of objective displacement per unit time will not lead to perceived movement and above which it will. The task before us is to try to identify the conditions of stimulation or central processes that lead to the perception of movement.

Various kinds of conditions lead to movement perception. When we perceive movement where something actually is moving this is referred to as *real movement perception*. But often we perceive movement where nothing in the real world is in motion. There are several kinds of such illusory impressions of movement, each of which is considered in this

Originally published, in slightly different form, as chapter 5, "The Perception of Movement and Events," in *An Introduction to Perception*, by Irvin Rock (Macmillan 1975), 185–247. Reprinted with permission.

chapter: *stroboscopic movement, autokinetic movement,* and the *aftereffect of movement.* Then there is the situation that prevails when the *observer himself is moving,* which may or may not lead to the perception of the environment as moving.

The logical place to begin our inquiry would seem to be with real movement perception. When an object is actually moving, there are several possible explanations of why we see it moving: if the eyes are stationary its image will move over the retina; the eyes move if the observer tracks the object, thus keeping the retinal image stationary; or the image of the object changes its location with respect to that of other visible objects in the field, whether the eyes move or not. In order to separate these various factors and to develop a working hypothesis about the basis of movement perception, we begin with a discussion of the situation that exists when the observer is moving.

Movements of the Observer and Perceived Movement

Our perceptual experience during a period of movement in the stationary environment plainly contradicts the hypothesis that displacement of the retinal image leads to perceived movement of objects. When we move, or move only our eyes or head, the images of all stationary objects displace across the retina but things do not appear to move. This fact has been referred to as *position constancy.*

It would seem plausible to suppose that movement is not perceived under such circumstances because the perceptual system takes into account the fact that the displacement across the retina is simultaneous with and, therefore, caused by the observer's own movement. The image displacement is attributed to movements of the observer rather than to movement of the environment. Of course, for this process to operate, information that the observer has engaged in some movement must be available. Even though the hypothesis does not rest on any one characterization of the information, it is of interest to identify the nature of this information.

In any event, the fact is that displacement of the image does not lead to perceived movement if the perceptual system has information that the observer's own movement caused the image displacement. Therefore, movement across the retina clearly is not a condition that necessarily leads to perceived movement. There are also instances of the converse situation, namely, one in which the image does *not* move, but movement of objects *is* perceived. An example of this is the situation that arises during pursuit movements of the eye when an observer fixates an object and tracks it as it moves across his field. The image of the object will remain more or less fixed in position on the fovea of the retina. Nevertheless, the object will appear to move. Of course, in this situation the image of the stationary background will displace across the retina so someone might argue that the fixated object is seen to move because there is *some* image displacement on the retina. Or it may be argued that the displacement of the image of the object *relative* to that of the surrounding background is crucial here. However, the same observation can be made when the moving object is a single isolated spot in an otherwise homogeneous environment (such as a luminous point in a darkened room). An even clearer demonstration is based on first forming an afterimage and then noting how it behaves when viewed in a dark room (or with the eyes closed) when the eyes move. The afterimage is imprinted in one location on the retina and yet, when the eyes move, it appears to move [1].

Under certain conditions stationary objects appear to move slightly when the eyes move. When the eyes track a moving target, the stationary background appears to move in a direction opposite to that of the moving point, an effect known as the Filehne illusion. But the magnitude of such perceived movement is slight, and often observers do perceive the background as stationary. This finding perhaps can best be understood as a slight departure from complete constancy of position, analogous to similar findings with other of the perceptual constancies. As with such other constancies, there is reason for believing that the result is based on underregistration of the information that must be taken into account by the perceptual system, in this case of the rate at which the eyes are moving [2].

If displacement of the image is *not* the correlate of perceived movement, what is? From the examples considered thus far, the following principles can be formulated. *When an object is perceived to undergo a change in its location, it will be perceived to move. If the change in the object's location is based on the observer's movement, it will be perceived as stationary.* In the examples thus far considered, location can be defined as radial direction. The reason that stationary objects do not undergo a change in radial direction when the eyes are in different positions is that eye position is taken into account in interpreting the direction signified by particular retinal locations. Conversely, the reason why a fixated object that moves does undergo a change in its phenomenal location when the eyes change position should also be clear. In the case of movement of the observer, stationary objects do change their radial directions with respect to the observer, but this change is fully accounted for in terms of the observer's movement. Therefore, the objects appear stationary.

The Loss and Recovery of Position Constancy
When the observer moves—or just his head or eyes move—the retinal image displaces in a particular direction and at a particular rate. For example,

when the head turns 30 degrees to the right (and assuming the eyes remain fixed with respect to the head) the retinal image of the scene shifts 30 degrees to the right. This shifting of the image is discounted and no movement is perceived.[1] Therefore, we can ask the question, What will happen when the image behaves in a somewhat different fashion when the observer moves? It would seem to follow that if a 30 degree shift of the image to the right following a 30 degree head movement to the right *means* "world is stationary," any other direction or rate of image shifting must mean the world is not stationary. We have already encountered one such case, namely, the situation that exists when the image (or afterimage) is completely stationary and the observer—or just his eyes—moves. In keeping with the prediction, the afterimage appears to move.

It is possible to introduce a more drastic change in the behavior of the image. In a now classic experiment done at the turn of the century, the investigator, George Stratton, wore a lens system that had the effect of inverting the image and reversing it with respect to right and left [3]. He was interested in the question of whether the world would ultimately appear right side up again. However, the lens system changes the direction of movement of the retinal image based on observer movement. Stratton reported that whenever he moved his head or body, the entire scene appeared to move in the direction he was moving and twice as fast. He called this "swinging of the scene," an effect that follows from the account of movement perception presented here.

To make this clear, note that in Fig. 14.1*a* the observer fixates point 2. Because the image is not reversed as it normally is, he sees point 3 off to the left although actually it is to the right. Now if he moves his head to the right, *b*, point 3 stimulates the fovea. Hence point 3 traveled from the apparent left to straight ahead as the head moved to the right. A point changing its location in this manner when the head moves to the right would ordinarily be a moving point. Point 1 is about to move out of the field entirely, but since it has been displacing along the retina to the left, it will shortly be seen moving out of the field to the right, in the direction the head is turning. The observer, therefore, experiences a movement of the entire scene in the direction the head moves. As to the rate of perceived movement: if the image displaced normally, no movement would be experienced; if it were stationary, objects in the scene would seem to move as fast as the head, i.e., to keep pace with it. Because it displaces in the opposite direction by an amount equal to the amount of head displacement, objects in the scene must seem to move through twice the angle the head moves.[2]

A similar effect seems to occur in animals [4]. In one experiment the head of a fly was surgically rotated 180 degrees and kept in that position during the experiment. As a result, the left side of each eye was on the

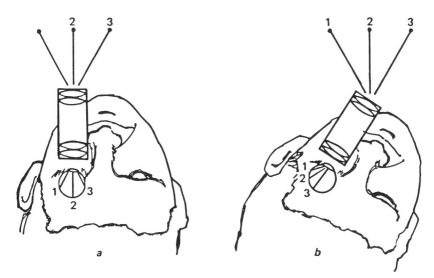

Figure 14.1

right side of the fly and vice versa. Consequently, when the fly moved, the images of external objects were displaced in a direction opposite to the customary one, just as in Stratton's experiment. Before examining the result of this experiment, it is necessary to consider how the fly behaves in the experimental situation under consideration when the head is *not* rotated. If a fly is placed in the center of a striped drum and the drum is rotated around the fly, then the fly typically begins to turn in the direction of the drum's movement (see Fig. 14.2). (This is a well-known, virtually universal, reflex referred to as the optokinetic or optomotor response. In many species, including man, the eyes will turn slowly with the drum until they have gone as far as they can, whereupon they snap back and the process repeats itself.) If the drum remains stationary and a fly is permitted to move freely around on the platform inside the drum, there is no indication of an optomotor response; yet the image of the drum is sweeping across the fly's retina precisely as in the first situation. We must, therefore, assume that the drum is not perceived as moving because the brain of the fly receives information that the fly's own movements are producing the displacement of the image. Discounting occurs.

When the fly's head is rotated and it is permitted to move freely around on the table, with the drum stationary, a curious thing happens. The fly begins to circle and continues to circle indefinitely. It would seem that the fly circles because the optomotor response has been triggered. This occurs because the direction in which the images of the stationary stripes displace is opposite to the one that would be discounted. Therefore, the

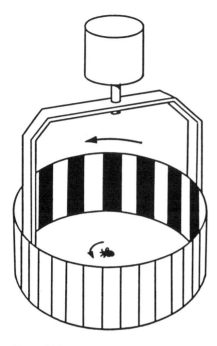

Figure 14.2

drum is "perceived" to turn—although it does not—and a drum "perceived" to be rotating induces the optomotor response.[3]

But now we must take a closer look at the problem of why the scene appears to move when the retinal image displaces abnormally during movements of an observer. It seems self-evident that if, normally, a certain direction or rate of displacement of the image for a given movement of the observer is discounted, i.e., it leads to perceiving the scene as stationary, then any other behavior of the image must lead to seeing the scene as moving. The question then is whether the normal movement of the image—for example from left to right with rightward head movement—is discounted by virtue of some innate linkage or whether it is perhaps learned.

It was noted earlier that the organism discounts the image displacement because information is available that its own movements have produced that displacement. How does the organism distinguish between instances where it has and instances where it has not produced the image displacement? A plausible answer is that self-produced displacement is perfectly correlated with bodily movement. It begins and ends concomitantly with the observer's movement and its rate is correlated with the observer's rate of movement. If this concomitance is indeed the crucial factor, then it would not seem to be necessary that the image displace in a particular direction or rate in order for the discounting process to take place. If the image were to shift from right to left instead of from left to right with rightward head movement, its displacement would still be perfectly correlated with the observer's movement.

Yet we have seen that under such abnormal conditions, discounting does not take place. The world does appear to move. May it not be the case, at least for human observers, that this effect is the result of a lifetime of experience in which the image always behaves in a particular way for any given movement of the observer? Based on such experience it is possible that we learn the rule that the retinal image moves in the same direction we move and at the same speed. Thus, only the normal displacement of the image comes to signify "world is stationary."

If this reasoning is correct, it should be possible to undo this learning by requiring an observer to view the world for some period of time through an optical device such as the one described earlier. The observer should adapt to the new state of affairs, and this is precisely what happened in the experiment by Stratton referred to previously. The "swinging of the scene" gradually decreased and, after 3 or 4 days, disappeared entirely. Upon removing the lenses Stratton reported that the scene again appeared to move when he moved, i.e., he experienced a negative aftereffect. This means that the abnormal, reversed direction of retinal displacement during observer movement had come to signify that the world was stationary; hence on removing the lenses, the reestablishment of the normal direction of displacement had to lead to an impression of object movement. Other investigators have confirmed Stratton's observations and recently short-range studies with large numbers of subjects and more objective methods of testing have been conducted [5]. On the basis of this work it is safe to conclude that in man there is no necessary, innately determined, linkage between the specific nature of self-produced image-displacement and constancy of position of objects in the world. Rather, it is clearly the case that position constancy is subject to learning.

Stroboscopic Movement

Everyone, it would seem, knows that moving pictures are made by projecting a series of stationary frames on a screen in rapid succession. Yet few people seem to be curious about the basis of this effect and those who are seem to be satisfied with an incorrect explanation. The incorrect explanation asserts that the effect is based on the fact that the cells of the retina continue to fire after a given frame is no longer present. Hence there is no experience of a gap or of a dark screen between successive frames. This is true and it explains why, at the optimum projection speed,

a   b

Figure 14.3

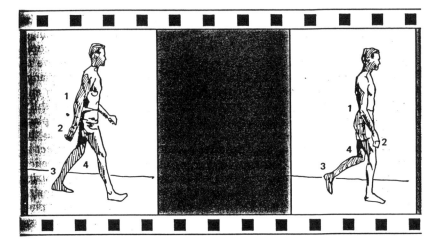

Figure 14.4

we do not experience a flicker (although in the early days of moving pictures flickering did occur). But this still leaves unexplained why we experience objects presented in these stationary pictures as *moving*.

The fact of the matter is that we do not know why movement is perceived, but psychologists have reduced the problem to its bare essentials in the laboratory. In a typical experiment, two points of light or two lines are projected alternately on the screen (see Fig. 14.3). First *a* is flashed briefly; then *a* goes off and there is a brief period when nothing is visible; finally *b* goes on for the same duration as *a*; followed by another brief interval; then *a* goes on again and so forth. At very slow speeds of alternation, the observer typically perceives two lines alternating, but no movement; at very fast speeds, he perceives two lines both of which seems to be present simultaneously; at some intermediate speed he sees movement, as if there were only one line moving back and forth.[4] The illusion of movement is so strong that it cannot be distinguished from real movement. This is clearly the case in modern motion pictures where the basic effect can be analyzed into several different components all of which are changing location simultaneously (see Fig. 14.4). In the figure several actions are depicted as occurring at the same time. The man's arm 1–2

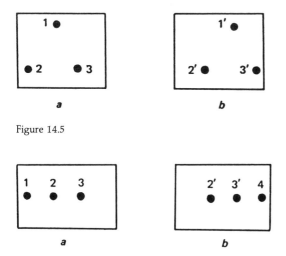

Figure 14.5

Figure 14.6

is moving forward and his leg 3–4 is moving upward. Needless to say, filmstrips can be either drawn to simulate such changes of position (animated cartoons) or achieved by moving picture photography. In the latter case, the camera records successive shots taken at brief intervals.

A further complication arises in the case of moving pictures that is based on the fact that objects rather than single points or lines are changing location. Suppose we consider a triangle and focus our attention on the three corners as illustrated in Fig. 14.5. If in one frame the triangle is in a given place, *a*, then in the next frame it may be somewhat to the right, *b*. If only point 1 were visible in *a* and only point 3' in *b*, then obviously point 1 would be seen to move to where point 3' is located. This is also true with respect to all other possible changes. But when the entire array 1, 2, 3 is shown in both *a* and *b*, 1 is seen to move to 1', 2 to 2', and 3 to 3'.

Therefore, it would seem that in addition to the basic stroboscopic illusion there is a further principle at work, a tendency to see objects move as-a-whole in such a way as to preserve their overall integrity. This fact has been demonstrated even more dramatically in the following type of experiment. In *a* in Fig. 14.6 three dots are exposed, 1, 2, and 3. In *b* three dots are again exposed, 2', 3', and 4. However, the leftmost two dots of *b*, 2' and 3', are in the identical place as the two rightmost dots of *a*, 2 and 3 (shown by locating the dots within the rectangular frame of the screen in *a* and *b*). Given these two arrangements, we should predict that only one dot will undergo a stroboscopic effect, namely the leftmost dot in *a*, dot 1, should appear to move to the location of the rightmost dot in *b*, dot 4.

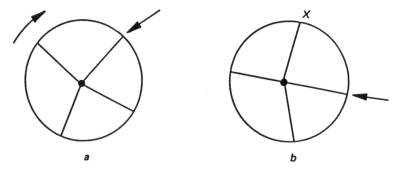

a   b

Figure 14.7

Since there is no change of location of the other two dots, they should appear to flash on and off in the same place. Instead, most observers perceive three dots shifting back and forth. The leftmost dot of *a* is seen to move to the place of the leftmost dot in *b*, the middle dot in *a* is seen to move to the middle dot in *b*, and so on. This effect, known as the *Ternus effect* in honor of the discoverer, illustrates the principle that there is a tendency to see an entire configuration move in such a way that each part maintains its role or function in the configuration (e.g., a center spot remains a center spot, and so on). Ternus referred to this tendency as "phenomenal identity" [6]. Were it not for this tendency, moving pictures would not be possible, the movement perceived would be utterly chaotic. If, however, the time interval (the ISI) is very brief, phenomenal identity does not occur, and the two overlapping dots do appear to flash on and off in place and only the remaining dot appears to move back and forth over the stationary dots [7].

An interesting effect that many people have noted in viewing moving pictures is that wheels often appear to be rotating backward, i.e., in a direction opposite to the forward motion of the vehicle. This "wagon-wheel effect" as it has been called, is easily explained. In Fig. 14.7*a*, a wheel is shown as it might appear in one frame of the filmstrip. Suppose the wheel turns approximately 50 degrees between successive frames. Then Fig. 14.7*b* shows how the wheel will look in the next frame. Thus, in actual fact, the spoke marked with an arrow in *a* will have advanced to the position that it is in in *b*. If that spoke in *a* were perceived to move to its position in *b* (and similarly for all other spokes), the wheel as a whole would appear to roll forward. But the spokes are all similar. The spoke marked *x* in *b* is nearer to the place of the spoke marked with an arrow in *a* than is the correct spoke in *b*. It is known that proximity governs stroboscopic movement, that is, other things being equal, movement will occur between objects that are nearest to one another in *a* and *b*. Therefore, under these conditions, movement will be perceived toward spokes in *b* that are actually counterclockwise with respect to those in *a*.

Psychologists have been intrigued with this illusion of movement—which has variously been called *stroboscopic movement, apparent movement, Beta movement,* or the *Phi phenomenon*—and the overwhelming bulk of research on movement perception has been concerned with this phenomenon. It is believed that a full explanation of this illusion would point the way to an overall theory of movement perception and, in general, would unlock some of the secrets of brain function. There is no movement whatsoever of the retinal image in this situation, thus constituting further evidence against the idea that the perception of movement is based on the movement of the image across the retina.

It was this illusion, among other facts, that led Wertheimer, one of the founders of Gestalt psychology, to conclude that perceptual experience could not be explained on the basis of a one-to-one correspondence between proximal stimulus and sensation [8]. Rather it would seem that the brain contributes something of its own to the raw sensory input. The component sensations are organized, and this organization then forms the basis or correlate of what we experience. In fact, Wertheimer went on to postulate a doctrine known as *isomorphism,* which holds that underlying every sensory experience is a brain event that, structurally considered, is similar to that experience. In the case of stroboscopic movement, since there is no movement in the proximal stimulation to account for the experienced movement, there must be some process taking place in the brain that has the necessary dynamic properties to give rise to such experience. He postulated that between regions of excitation corresponding to each image (such as *a* and *b* in Fig. 14.3), there is a flow of electrical energy that gives rise to the impression of movement.

This theory (or variations of it) has been widely respected, and a good deal of research has been directed at testing it. The feeling has been that the perception of movement under stroboscopic stimulus conditions reflects a fundamental fact of brain action on a primitive level. One reason for this belief is that lower animals and decorticated guinea pigs react as if they saw movement under these conditions [9]. This has been shown by training an animal to discriminate a moving target from a stationary one and then substituting a stroboscopically flashing stimulus for the moving one [10]. The animals tested continued to respond as if a moving stimulus were present. Another method involved the presentation of an array of vertical columns inside a drum (as in the situation employed to induce the optomotor response) [11]. When the columns were flashed in successive positions stroboscopically, the animals reacted precisely as they did when the drum actually rotated. In fact, using the technique that simulates movement in electric signs, it has been possible to show the presence of the illusion in newly born guppies, newly hatched insects, and human infants [12]. Another reason for the belief that the illusion of motion is based on some basic mode of brain function is the fact, already noted, that it requires rather specific stimulus conditions, such as a particular rate of stimulus alternation. Other factors known to be relevant are intensity of light and the distance between *a* and *b* [13].

Some evidence supports Wertheimer's theory or variations of it that holds that there is some interaction in the brain—or in the retina—between the excitations emanating from *a* and *b*. This might be called the *spread-of-excitation theory*. For example, it has been found that the illusion of motion occurs more readily if both *a* and *b* are placed so as to fall within one hemisphere of the brain rather than, as is more typically the case, when the observer is fixating a point midway between *a* and *b*, *a* is projected to one hemisphere and *b* to the other [14]. Also the effect is more readily obtained if both *a* and *b* fall in one eye as compared with *a* stimulating one eye and *b* the other [15].

One factor contributing to the plausibility of this theory is that some bridging process does seem necessary to explain an apparent motion between two discrete spatially separate retinal-cortical locations. But suppose stroboscopic movement does not require stimulation of separate retinal locations. Perhaps what is crucial is that *a* and *b* are perceptually localized in two separate places regardless of where their corresponding images fall on the retina. After all, as noted earlier in this chapter, we know that an object will be seen to move if the observer tracks it with his eyes as it displaces across his field of view despite the fact that the image then remains more or less fixed on the fovea. The experience of movement in this case is based on information from change of eye position that the object fixated is in varying phenomena locations.

May not the same be true for stroboscopic stimulus conditions? To test this, observers were required to move their eyes back and forth synchronizing their movements with the flashing of lines *a* and *b* [16]. In other words, as *a* flashed on, the observer's eyes were directed at *a*; as *b* flashed on, his eyes just reached the position where they were directed at *b*, and so forth. Under these conditions, *a* and *b* fell on the *same* retinal locus, not a different one as is usually the case. The majority of observers nevertheless experienced *a* and *b* moving back and forth.[5] In the converse experiment, it was shown that if only a single point *a* flashes intermittently and the observer is required to move his eyes rapidly back and forth, then no movement is perceived. Yet the eye movement guarantees that *a* falls on separate retinal loci in this procedure. The outcome is predictable in terms of position constancy. Apparently, therefore, spread of excitation is neither a necessary nor a sufficient determinant of stroboscopic movement perception.

From these experiments, one can conclude that what is crucial is the location of *a* and *b* in separate phenomenal places in space. Thus, the stroboscopic illusion fits with the principle suggested earlier, namely, movement will be experienced when an object appears to undergo a change in its location. The only difference between stroboscopic and "real" movement is the fact that in the former case the stimulus is not continuously present.

Why is movement seen in spite of the fact that the stimulus is intermittent? We cannot fully answer this question, but it is relevant to point out that the observer tends to identify *a* and *b* as the same object. If an object is now here and now there, it is "logical" to assume that it has moved from one place to the other particularly when the object *inexplicably* disappears from one place and *inexplicably* appears in another place. Experiments have shown that the illusion is facilitated if *a* and *b* are identical rather than different in shape or color. Movement can be perceived if *a* and *b* are different, but then one has the impression that *a* is changing into *b* during the movement.

Movement of a single object would not, however, be a valid "solution" of the problem of what was occurring in the world, if, when *b* appeared, *a* appeared with it. In other words, suppose the sequence were *a*; *a* and *b*; *a*; *a* and *b*; instead of *a*; *b*; *a*; *b*; and so on. Under such conditions it would not be plausible to suppose that *a* has moved to *b* for the simple reason that *a* is again present in the place where it had been a moment ago when *b* appears. If the procedure is varied slightly so that instead of *a* appearing with *b*, an object similar to *a* appears, *a'*, then it *is* an intelligent solution to perceive *a* as having moved to *b* and to perceive *a'* as some new object that appears and disappears in the place *a* had occupied. The two variations are illustrated in Fig. 14.8. The result of such an experiment is that it

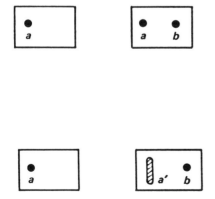

Figure 14.8

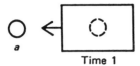

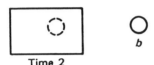

Figure 14.9

is difficult to perceive movement in the first condition but not in the second [18].

It would also follow from the hypothesis suggested here, namely, that the perception of movement under stroboscopic stimulus conditions is an intelligent solution of a problem, that information which suggests an alternative solution to the "problem" of the alternate appearance and disappearance of a and b, may eliminate the perception of movement. Suppose, for example, information is available that a and b have not actually disappeared but rather have been momentarily covered over. One way of achieving this is to move an opaque object back and forth, alternately covering and uncovering a and b, as shown in Fig. 14.9. Here a and b stimulate the retina alternately just as in ordinary stroboscopic movement conditions, but the observer does not typically perceive movement. Rather, he sees a and b as continuously present but as alternately covered and uncovered by the moving rectangle [19].

One might wish to argue that the introduction of the large moving rectangle interferes with the perceived movement of the dot, but the following variation proves this argument wrong. Let the rectangle move farther than it does in Fig. 14.9 as shown in Fig. 14.10. Now the rectangle is no longer covering the region where a or b had been seen a moment before (marked x and x' in the figure). The rectangle moves over that region and beyond it, so that it is evident that it is not covering a or b. Therefore, logically, the dot should be visible, but it is not (the technical method by which a and b are rendered invisible need not be discussed here). Consequently, the "solution" to the problem of the alternate appearance and disappearance of a and b can no longer be that they have been covered and uncovered. This leaves little alternative but to "solve the problem" by perceiving movement of a to b and this indeed is precisely what happens.

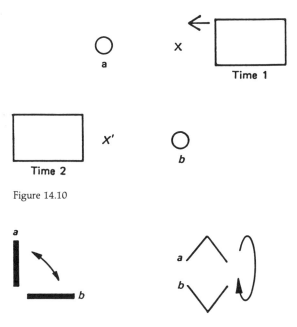

Figure 14.10

Figure 14.11

An additional fact that fits with the notion of stroboscopic movement perception as an intelligent solution to a problem is that the *kind* of movement perceived is tailored to the orientation of *a* and *b*, as shown in Fig. 14.11. Thus, the configuration seen in *a* will appear to rotate either in the frontal plane or in the third dimension as it moves to *b*. Such effects are not predictable in terms of a spread of excitation theory.

Ordinarily, when an object moves very rapidly, its image is little more than a blur across the retina. Perhaps, therefore, even in certain cases in which there is an actually moving object, the more important aspect of the stimulus information is the location of the object in its starting and terminal positions. The intervening stimulation characterized mostly by blur may not contribute much, if anything, to the impression of movement. Precisely this point has now been examined in an ingenious experiment in which the sight of the terminal locations of a moving object was blocked [20]. All the observer could see was the region between the terminal locations through which the object moved. As soon as the speed of the object was quite rapid, on the average beyond 8 degrees per second, it began to appear blurred. At the speed of around 17 degrees per second, a fused blinking line was perceived rather than a moving object. Yet when the terminal locations of the moving object *could* be seen, a sense of movement did occur at and even beyond these rapid speeds. Therefore, this perceived movement must be the result of the sight of the stationary positions of the object. In short, at these rapid speeds, real movement perception is based on the same stimulus information that gives rise to the perception of stroboscopic movement.

In fact, in the same experiment, it was shown that when the intervening space between the terminal locations was blocked from view—the conditions for generating stroboscopic movement—observers only began to perceive movement at a speed of the object, where, had the object been visible in the intervening space, it would have appeared blurred. At too great a speed, around 21 degrees per second, the observers no longer see the object as moving, but rather as simultaneously present in both terminal locations. From these findings the investigators concluded that stroboscopic movement perception has different time constants than real movement perception and that, therefore, the mechanism underlying *it* takes over, as soon as the speed of a moving object is too great for perception to be mediated by the mechanism underlying real movement perception.

The great merit of the notion that the perception of a very rapidly moving object is essentially stroboscopic, i.e., based primarily on the stationary stimulation from its terminal positions, is that it offers an explanation of why a mechanism for perceiving stroboscopic movement evolved. It is difficult to find instances in the natural environment where a moving object gives rise to stroboscopic stimulus conditions. Therefore, one might well ask why such perception evolved if it serves no adaptive purpose. The answer could be that it evolved to mediate the perception of rapid real movement.

Why though, does the perception of stroboscopic movement require just the rate of alternation that it does? One answer, implied by what was stated previously, is that it is based on a separate innate mechanism having its own time constants that is designed to take over when the perception of real movement fails because the movement is too fast. But, based on the hypothesis that stroboscopic movement perception occurs only when such perception is an intelligent solution to the problem presented by the stimulus input, one can argue that at slower rates of alternation, the perceptual system would "expect" to detect the motion from *a* to *b*. That is, a truly moving object whose speed was less than about 8 degrees per second would travel from *a* to *b* at a rate that should make it clearly visible in its intervening region. Therefore, when in stroboscopic stimulation, *a* and *b* flash at a rate compatible with such speed or lower, one ought to perceive the object in the intervening space. Since one does not, it constitutes a contradiction to the solution of movement. Thus, only when the rate of alternation is such that one would not expect to detect movement across this intervening space, is the "solution" of movement a truly good solution.

One can also say something sensible about the other end of the range of speeds at which stroboscopic movement ceases, namely, when the alternation is too rapid. At this rapid rate one perceives simultaneity, no doubt because of the persistence of neural discharge even after a is no longer physically present. The point is that it is not plausible to infer movement of a to b if a is still visible. The abolition of movement perception by the perceptual presence of a when b comes on has already been discussion (p. 200). This can also explain cases of failure to perceive the Ternus effect as discussed previously and illustrated in Fig. 14.6.

From this discussion we can readily see that two different theories of stroboscopic movement are possible. One theory claims that the impression of movement is based on an automatic tendency of the nervous system to react to discrete successive stimulation in the same way it would react to continuous movement stimulation because there is some form of spread-of-excitation or neural interaction between the successive stimuli or some other direct sensory mechanism. The other theory maintains that the discrete stimulation lends itself to the cognitive "solution" that movement has occurred and that movement perception occurs only if the stimulus events can best be interpreted in this way.

Although many of the findings seem either to contradict the spread-of-excitation theory or are not compatible with it, and many others support the cognitive theory, a number of other facts support the hypothesis that a direct sensory mechanism is responsible for the perception of movement under stroboscopic conditions. The perception of stroboscopic movement in newly born organisms, such as fish or insects or in decorticated guinea pigs, does not seem to jibe with the notion that a reasoning-like process is responsible for the movement perception although, admittedly, it is possible that the kind of nonconscious, nonverbal, problem-solving postulated could nevertheless occur in these cases.[6]

Also, as is made clear later in the chapter, there is direct evidence that units in the visual nervous system can "detect" stroboscopic movement because they respond uniquely to a given sequence of discrete stimulation. Therefore, one might conclude that there are two possible bases for the perception of stroboscopic movement, a direct sensory mechanism and a cognitive process of perceptual problem-solving.

The Autokinetic Effect

Another illusion that has intrigued psychologists is one in which a single stationary point of light appears to move. The point must be seen against a perfectly homogeneous background and the easiest way to achieve this is to view a luminous point in a completely darkened room. Under such conditions, and following some initial period of viewing, the observer typically experiences the point as drifting, either to one side or upward or downward. So real is the experience that the observer finds it hard to believe the experimenter when he is later told that the point has not moved at all.

This effect is considered to be as yet unexplained although many theories have been proposed to account for it. It has often been suggested that the illusion is based on movements of the observer's eyes. There are at least two things wrong with this notion. First, the observer is usually told to fixate the point and to the extent he succeeds in obeying instructions his eyes are, of course, stationary. Indeed it has been shown by photographing the observer's eyes under infrared illumination that they are in fact stationary at the very moment the point seems to be moving [23]. Second, as the reader should now understand, stationary things do not appear to move when the eyes move. The displacement of the image is discounted; position constancy obtains. Therefore, even if the eyes were in continuous motion there is no reason to consider this as an explanation of what is referred to as autokinetic movement.

However, it is possible to defend the eye movement theory if it is stated in a more sophisticated fashion. If, when the eyes moved, there were *no* centrally registered information to the effect that they had moved, then we would have to predict that the displacement of the image (of a stationary point) *would* give rise to an impression of movement. Ordinarily, the eyes either move in quick jumps from one location to another (saccadic movements) or slowly and smoothly as they track a slowly moving target (pursuit movements). Obviously, pursuit movements are not occurring in the case of a stationary target, and even if saccadic movements do occasionally occur, they would surely be discounted. But even when fixating, minute involuntary movements of the eyes do occur. They tend to drift slowly and to flick saccadically and in addition, to oscillate rapidly back and forth, a kind of continuous tremor. Collectively these involuntary eye movements are referred to as physiological nystagmus. The extent of these movements is extremely small. In all probability, this type of involuntary movement is *not* registered centrally and, therefore, would not lead to discounting of the displacing retinal image. Can eye movement of this kind explain the autokinetic effect?

To test this hypothesis, an experiment was performed that made use of a technique whereby an image on the retina is *prevented* from shifting at all. Various methods to achieve this stabilization of the image have been employed, such as projecting the image onto the retina from a device that is itself mounted on a contact lens placed on the eyeball [24]. Thus, when the eye moves the image moves with it. In the experiment under discussion the technique was modified in such a way that movement of the image was stopped in the horizontal direction only [25]. Therefore, no displacement of the image was caused by slight eye movements only in this direction. The observer, of course, knew nothing about this fact. There were few reports of movements of the target in that direction whereas there were many reports of movement in all other directions.

There is thus evidence to support this modified eye-movement theory.[7] One difficulty with it, however, is that the excursion of the eyes during these involuntary movements is very small (a few minutes of arc) in relation to the extent of autokinetic movement typically perceived (a few degrees or more). The theory would only be tenable if it were claimed that the cumulative effect of these eye movements over a period of time produced a sizable amount of displacement of the image. But there is a difficulty with this formulation because the target typically does not appear to erratically reverse direction (as do the eyes during nystagmus), but rather seems to drift continuously in one direction. Another difficulty for this theory is that nondiscounted image displacements based on such eye movements also occur under typical conditions in daily life whenever the observer fixates a point in the field. Therefore, the entire scene should appear to drift but, of course, it does not. An explanation is thus required of why such a mechanism only yields an autokinetic effect for a single isolated point in an otherwise homogeneous field.

The author would like to suggest a different approach to the problem of the autokinetic effect. As is brought out in the next section of this chapter, a very important source of information concerning movement is the change of location of one thing relative to other things. Therefore the opposite is also true, that when an object does *not* change its location relative to other objects this is information that the object is *not* moving. But it is precisely this kind of information which is lacking in the autokinetic situation because only a single point is visible. Therefore what one perceives in this situation depends entirely upon the accuracy of the following information: the displacement or nondisplacement of the retinal image and the movement or non-movement of the eyes. Let us assume for the moment that the eyes are stationary because the observer is fixating the point of light (and let us assume that the slight involuntary movement of the eyes is not relevant, contrary to the hypothesis explored in the preceding paragraphs). Then the retinal image does not move. Therefore it would seem that the only basis for perceiving the point moving rather than stationary is some failure of the perceptual system to appreciate that the eyes are indeed stationary. Perhaps, for reasons not yet clear this is the case, so that the system interprets the stationary eyes as slowly drifting. If they were really drifting slowly then a fixated point would have to be interpreted as moving, since the eyes would be tracking it.

There should be no record of eye movement if, with the eyes stationary, no "commands" are issued to the eye muscles to move.[8] But if for some reason an observer momentarily had the erroneous impression that he was viewing a moving point, then this impression would suffice to induce a feeling that his eyes were tracking it. It is known that effects of this kind occur, as, for example, when one has the illusory impression that an object that one is looking at is moving although it is actually its surroundings that are moving. (See the discussion of induced movement that follows.) False impressions of eye movement under such conditions can be thought of as instances of visual capture. Admittedly, it is not clear in the autokinetic situation what triggers the initial "belief" that the point was moving. But once that "belief" took hold it is understandable that the perceptual system could erroneously interpret the eyes as slowly tracking the point.[9] However, to repeat, this is only possible, because information concerning the point's fixed location with respect to other objects in the field is lacking.

The reader might object that to suffer the illusion that one was tracking a stationary point which was drifting by several degrees implies that the perceptual system would interpret a straight-ahead position of the eyes as turned to the side. Does this implication do violence to what is known about the precision with which the direction of the eyes is registered? Not necessarily. In studying the perception of radial direction, it was noted that observers are neither perfectly accurate nor consistent in setting a target to the straight-ahead position. They can perform this task only within a range of a few degrees of error. This suggests that at any given moment the eyes can deviate a few degrees from the true straight-ahead direction and still be interpreted as straight-ahead: conversely they may be straight ahead and still be interpreted as slightly off to the side. Therefore, if in the autokinetic situation the perceptual system were at a given moment to "interpret" the eyes as slightly turned (although they were not) the observer would have to see the fixated target off to the side.

Relative Displacement and Induced Movement

When an object moves across the field, it changes its location with respect to the observer but it also changes its location relative to all other visible things. What importance, if any, is this relative change? A simple experiment will make clear that relative change plays an important role in the perception of movement [28]. First, a single luminous point, a, is set to move at so slow a speed that it does not appear to be moving, i.e., it is below the threshold for the detection of movement (see Fig. 14.12). It is the only thing visible. Now a second stationary point b is introduced (see Fig. 14.13). Immediately the observer sees movement. The conclusion is

Figure 14.12

Figure 14.13

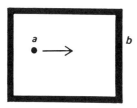

Figure 14.14

inescapable that the change in relative distance between points *a* and *b* leads to perceived movement. We refer to this as object-relative change in contrast to change of position in relation to the observer or subject-relative change. The threshold for object-relative change is lower than that for subject-relative change. Had point *a* been moving at a speed above the subject-relative threshold, the conclusion about the important role of object-relative change would not be warranted because the perceived movement could be a function either of *a*'s change of location with respect to the observer or with respect to point *b*. There are thus two separate and independent factors that can lead to the perception of movement: subject-relative change of location and object-relative change of location.

In fact, in the experiment described, it is not necessarily point *a* that is seen to move when stationary point *b* is introduced; *b* may be seen to move or both *a* and *b* may be seen as moving apart. This ambiguity is precisely what we should expect if the crucial information is relative, i.e., the increasing or decreasing separation between points *a* and *b*.[10] That information does not specify which point is moving.

Now let us change the experiment in one respect. Let the second object be a luminous rectangular perimeter, *b*, which surrounds *a* rather than a point (see Fig. 14.14). In this situation, all observers will see *a* as moving; the outcome is no longer ambiguous. Moreover the same is true if it is *b* that is made to move and not *a* (see Fig. 14.15). Whether *a* or *b* is actually moving, the observer will see *a* moving. If *b* is moved to the left, *a* will be seen moving to the right. When one objects moves and the observer sees

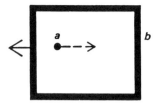

Figure 14.15

Figure 14.16

a stationary object near it as moving, the illusory effect is called *induced movement*.

Apparently a further principle is operating here in addition to the principle that change of relative position is a determinant of movement perception. That object that surrounds the other or otherwise dominates—such as by its greater size—tends to become a frame of reference and, as such, to be seen as stationary. The relative displacement is then interpreted as movement in relation to it. A good example of this effect in daily life occurs when the moon appears to be moving through the clouds (Fig. 14.16). The moon does change its location in the sky relative to us but at such a slow rate as to be far below our movement threshold. A cloud, however, is changing its position at a faster rate although this too may be below threshold. In any case, the relative change of position between cloud and moon provides the crucial information; the cloud serves as a frame of reference and it, therefore, induces movement in the moon. Induced movement is one more illustration of the fact that displacement of the image is not a necessary condition for perceiving movement. The image of the surrounded object is stationary and the object nevertheless appears to move.[11]

Induced movement can occur even when the object which is actually moving is displacing at a rate that is above threshold. In other words, a cloud that is moving so rapidly that when it is seen alone would clearly be perceived as moving, will nevertheless induce movement in the moon. This is surprising since the relative displacement between moon and cloud

Figure 14.17

is now fully accounted for by seeing the cloud move. Duncker suggested that the surrounded object is seen entirely in terms of its behavior in relation to its immediate frame of reference. What it does in relation to more remote reference systems is not relevant. Thus, although the moon is stationary with respect to a tree or with respect to the observer, this does not significantly interfere with the induced movement created by the immediately surrounding cloud. All that matters is that there is relative displacement between moon and cloud and that the cloud serves as frame of reference in the moon-cloud system.

The experience of the cloud on the other hand is a function of its behavior in relation to its immediate frame of reference, such as the buildings in Fig. 14.17. Or we may think of the frame of reference in terms of the subject-relative system of radial direction—straight ahead, left, above, and so on—which is present even when no objects other than the clouds are visible. Duncker, therefore, argued that there is a *separation of systems*: in our example the first is the moon-cloud system, the second is the cloud-building system or cloud-ego system. In this way one can explain why there is more movement perceived than is warranted on the basis of the relative displacement taking place. To repeat, when the cloud moves above threshold, its displacement relative to the moon is fully accounted for by the fact that it is seen to move; yet the moon is seen to move in the opposite direction by an equal amount. There is thus twice as much perceived movement as we might expect.

An interesting application of the concept of separation of system was made by Duncker in relation to the way we perceive movement of points on a wheel [28]. Consider a point *a* on a wheel rolling along the ground (Fig. 14.18). The dotted circles represent successive positions of the wheel

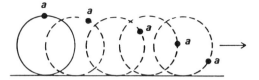

Figure 14.18

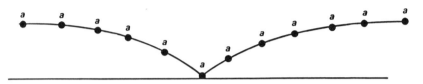

Figure 14.19

and in each the location of point *a* is shown. In Fig. 14.19 only the path taken by point *a* is shown. It can be seen that point *a* describes a path through space that is not circular; a path that mathematicians call a *cycloid*. If only point *a* were visible—made luminous in a dark room—and the wheel rolled forward the observer would then see this cycloid path.

The fact is, however, that ordinarily when we look at a rolling wheel, although every point on it (except the very center) describes a cycloid, we do not see this. We see points on the wheel turning in a circular path about the hub and we see the entire wheel moving forward along a straight path. Apparently, the hub of the wheel is the reference system for movements of points on the wheel; the background (or possibly the egocentric system of the observer) is the frame of reference for the wheel as a whole. Thus there is a separation of systems.

Returning to the phenomenon of induced movement, the question arises as to why the surrounding moving object is seen as stationary (at least when its movement is below the subject-relative threshold) and thereby serves as frame of reference for the surrounded object. Either could be seen as moving. Duncker attributed this fact to an innate selective principle of organization or preference of the perceptual system. It is also possible to argue that the principle is learned, since ordinarily it is the smaller object within the perceived environment that undergoes displacement.

The importance of object-relative displacement as a determinant of movement perception is made clear in the research of Johansson involving an array of separately moving elements [31]. In one experiment, two elements are moving at right angles to one another as shown in Fig. 14.20*a*. Since the elements both are moving well above the subject-relative threshold, and since there is no frame of reference present to

a   b

Figure 14.20

create a separate system, one would think that there is no good reason why the path of each element should not be veridically perceived. But, in fact, what one perceives is shown in Fig. 14.20b: the elements appear to be approaching and receding from one another along an oblique path. This is the dominant impression. In addition, however, the two elements, as a group, appear to be moving in the opposite oblique direction.

This outcome becomes understandable if one assumes that object-relative displacement exerts a stronger effect on perceived movement than does subject-relative displacement whenever a conflict between the two determinants exists. Ordinarily, the two are not in conflict but rather lead to the same perception, as when a single object moves in a stationary scene. But in the case of induced movement or the experiment illustrated in Fig. 14.20, a conflict exists. What the two elements are doing in relation to each other is not the same as what they are doing in relation to the observer. The former is apparently dominant, so that one primarily perceives the elements gliding toward and away from each other along the path of shortest distance between them, namely an oblique path. However, once that is perceived, there remains a component of the motion of the elements not accounted for [32]. If one analyzes the path of motion in terms of vectors, as Johansson does, then given the perception of motion along the common oblique path, the component not accounted for in this perception is indicated by a vector at right angles to this path (see Fig. 14.21). In other words, the true motion is dissociated by the perceptual system into two components.

Another example is shown in Fig. 14.22a where one element moves in a vertical path and a second element moves in a circular path. The motions are in phase in the sense that both dots reach the top and bottom of their paths simultaneously. What one typically perceives is shown in b: the dominant impression is of the element on the right approaching and receding from the one of the left along a horizontal path; secondarily one sees the two elements as a pair moving up and down. One does not perceive the element on the right traveling in a circular path although that in fact is what it is doing; a dissociation of motion occurs.[12]

The example of the perceived motion of elements on a wheel described earlier can be understood in terms of this analysis. The cycloid paths of the

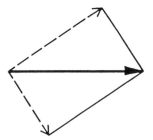

Figure 14.21

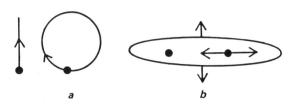

a   b

Figure 14.22

elements of a rolling wheel are perceptually dissociated into two components: an impression of their motions relative to one another, namely rotation about a center and an impression of the residual motion that all elements share, namely a rectilinear translation across the field.

What general conclusions can we reach from the work on relative displacement and induced movement? It would seem that the generalization made earlier remains valid, namely, that whenever an object seems to change its phenomenal location (at a rate above threshold) movement will be perceived. However, it is now necessary to add that phenomenal location may be defined not only egocentrically, in relation to the observer as origin of directions, but also *objectively*, in relation to other objects (which may or may not serve as frames of reference). We thus see that change of relative position is a potent source of formation in the perception of movement. This fact places the autokinetic effect in a context that makes it somewhat more intelligible: There are no reference objects for the single point of light. Ordinarily, the *absence* of change of relative position is information that objects are *not* moving. Such information is not available in the autokinetic situation.

Induced Movement of the Self
Among other objects in the visual field is the body of the observer. Parts of the body are, of course, often visible. But even when the body is not seen, it has an inferred location in relation to the scene, that is to say, we

Figure 14.23

are always aware of precisely where in the visual field we ourselves are located. Considering the self, therefore, as an object in the visual field, what should we predict if the observer is surrounded by a moving frame of reference? We should predict that the observer will perceive himself moving although he is stationary; induced movement of the self.

This is precisely what happens. A laboratory technique for studying this effect is shown in Fig. 14.23. The observer is seated on a stool in the center of a large drum (the drum can be a lightweight construction somewhat like a lamp shade). The drum is made to rotate around the observer. Ideally, the observer should not be able to see beyond the drum or above or below it. Within 10 or 15 seconds after the rotation begins, the observer typically experiences himself as rotating and the drum as stationary or as turning much slower than it actually is. This effect attests to the efficacy of the frame of reference in governing movement perception and also to the dominance of vision over proprioception. Cues concerning felt position such as the vertibular cues from the inner ear are informing the observer that he is stationary. Yet he feels himself turning (still another example of visual capture).

There are examples of this phenomenon in daily life, the best known being that of perceiving one's own train as moving when in fact it is not, as a result of the movement of a train on the adjacent track. This usually occurs when we are seated next to the window facing the other train. That train then fills most of the visual field. Induced movement of the self here includes one's own train. (If, however, we are looking through the window from across the aisle, our own train fills most of the field. In the latter case we might erroneously see a stationary train in the adjacent track as moving when our train is moving. This would be induced movement, but not of the self). Another example is that of experiencing one's own stationary automobile as rolling when we stop for a light as a result of viewing an adjacent car that in fact is rolling. When this happens one is inclined to jam on the brakes. Induced movement of the self also occurs in looking down at a moving current of water, either from a bridge or from a stationary boat.

It is probable, however, that induced movement of the self has applicability to a wider range of phenomena than these occasional instances in daily life would suggest. It is likely that in many situations where the observer is actually moving he would not experience himself as moving—and the environment as stationary—were it not for the induced movement effect. The reason for this deduction is as follows. In discussing position constancy earlier in this chapter, we noted that information to the effect that the observer is moving must be centrally registered before we can expect discounting of displacement of the retinal image to occur. One kind of information (relevant at least to active eye movements) is a record of outgoing signals to the musculature. Another is vestibular information that we can assume is present during acceleration and deceleration and in turning movements. Suppose, however, that neither of these is applicable as when the observer is a passenger in a vehicle moving at a constant speed along a straight path.

There would seem to be no information in the latter case. An experiment has confirmed this by showing that if an observer is moved in a wagon at uniform speed in a dark room, he will erroneously see a stationary spot of light on the wall as moving and experience himself as stationary. If, however, a pattern of luminous lines is displayed on the wall instead of the spot, the observer now veridically experiences the lines as stationary and himself as moving [33].[13] The only difference would seem to be that in the second situation the observer is surrounded by the displacing pattern, whereas in the first situation he is not. Therefore, the perception in the second situation would seem to be a manifestation of induced movement of the self. From this it follows that in many if not most instances of transportation in a vehicle, perception of one's self and vehicle as moving is a function of the inducing effect of the displacing field that surrounds the observer. This is a paradoxical conclusion—possibly confusing to the reader—because the observer is in fact moving. Yet, as the experiment cited shows, he would not perceive this were it not for the sight of the displacing environment. It is not beyond the realm of plausibility that even in the case where the observer is more actively moving, as in walking, or where he is passively moving but accelerating, the inducing effect of the displacing environment plays a contributory role in the perception of the self as moving and the environment as stationary.[14]

Can a Movement-Detector Mechanism Explain the Perception of Movement?

Units of the visual nervous system have been discovered in several species that respond to or "detect" movement of a contour over the appropriate region of the retina [34]. These units respond optimally to movement of a contour in a particular direction and not at all to movement in the opposite direction. Can such a detector mechanism explain the perception of movement?

One phenomenon of movement perception that has not yet been mentioned may be explained by this kind of sensory mechanism. If one observes a pattern, such as stripes, moving in a particular direction for a period of time, and then looks at a stationary pattern, for example the same stripes, the stationary pattern will now appear to move slowly in a direction opposite to the one in which it had previously moved. This effect is known variously as the *aftereffect of movement*, the *waterfall* or *spiral illusion* (because we can easily observe it after first viewing a waterfall or a rotating spiral). It is difficult to explain this kind of effect in terms of any of the principles considered in this chapter. In fact, in this aftereffect, stationary objects appear to be moving but do not seem to change their location, a paradoxical experience and contradictory to the main thesis developed in this chapter that movement perception results from a change in an object's perceived location.

However, it stands to reason that those neural units that are sensitive to a particular direction of movement would become fatigued by the continuous motion of the pattern in one direction. The possible consequences of this effect can best be elucidated by analogy to the negative afterimage that occurs when retinal cells sensitive to a given wavelength are fatigued. As a result, a subsequently viewed gray region takes on a color complementary to the one previously inspected. Hence, one might expect such an aftereffect of motion. In the example of the negative afterimage, the presumption is that cells sensitive to the opposite wavelength are now no longer balanced by equal activity of those sensitive to the color previously inspected. Therefore, they respond more than others and produce the impression of the complementary color. Thus, in the case of movement, it might be assumed that neural units sensitive to a direction opposite to the one just seen now respond more than any other directionally sensitive receptors. There is direct physiological evidence that this is the case. It was shown that the rate of discharge of ganglion cells of the retina of the rabbit decreases when the appropriate region of the retina is exposed to a pattern moving in a particular direction. When the pattern stops moving the rate of discharge from these cells falls below the so-called maintained or resting level of discharge that these cells typically display [35]. Consequently the negative aftereffect of movement may be based on the relatively greater frequency of maintained discharge of those cells that are sensitive to movement stimulation in a direction *opposite* to the one just encountered. There is now an imbalance between units that signal movement in opposite directions. In further support of this conclusion is the finding that after viewing a moving pattern, the threshold for detecting stripes moving in the opposite direction is lower than for stripes moving in the same direction as that of the just seen moving pattern [36].

In fact, it had been claimed in an early investigation that the aftereffect of motion depends on the displacement of the image of the moving pattern over the retina rather than on the perception of the motion per se [37]. If during the inspection phase one tracks the moving pattern, no aftereffect occurs, although the movement of the pattern was, of course, perceived. Here there is no image displacement during the inspection period. Conversely, if one moves one's eyes smoothly across a stationary pattern of stripes by tracking a moving fixation mark, the aftereffect *does* occur. Here there is image displacement during inspection phase, but no perceived movement of the stripes. Therefore, if these findings held up, the phenomenon can be said to be misnamed the aftereffect of movement; it would rather be an aftereffect of image displacement. However, later research failed to confirm these findings and, to the contrary, indicate that it is indeed the *perception* of motion of the pattern that matters in the aftereffect. In fact it was found that it is the *perceived* direction of the pattern, rather than the direction of motion of its image over the retina, that governs the perceived direction of the aftereffect (see chapter 18). Hence the neural units that are fatigued apparently are at a higher level than was originally thought to be the case. At any rate, the fact is that the perception of movement of contours in a specific direction fatigues the neural units that are sensitive to the direction of motion occurring, and that as a result units sensitive to movement in the opposite direction dominate for a short period thereafter and give rise to an impression that stationary contours are "sailing" in the opposite direction.[15]

However, the aftereffect of movement is clearly a very special case of movement perception. It is obviously caused by some changes of the neural medium and belongs in the category of other aftereffects of prior stimulation. The central question, therefore, is whether the perception of movement in general can be explained in terms of the activity of neural units that are fired by contours moving over the retina. It would seem that the answer to the question is negative. After all this kind of explanation may be reduced to one based on movement of the image, and virtually all of the evidence covered in this chapter contradicts that thesis. Movement of the image is neither necessary nor sufficient for the perception of movement.

We are left then with the puzzle of accounting for the purpose of these detector mechanisms if they cannot do justice to the perception of movement. Do they explain movement perception in animals lower in the phylogenetic scale, remaining as vestiges in higher animals? This argument presupposes a perfect correlation between image displacement and perceived movement in such species and it is doubtful this is the case. For example, all animals must discount image motion when they bring it about by their own movement and relevant experiments on the fly were discussed earlier in the chapter.

Perhaps the "detectors" are simply the mechanism which informs the perceptual system that a displacement of an image has occurred without any further implications about movement per se? Some of the investigators who have made these physiological discoveries favor this latter interpretation. According to this view, one could argue that displacement of the image is not necessary for the perception of movement but, if it occurs, it is detected by the neural units in the eye or brain. The information thereby obtained is then assessed by the perceptual system in terms of other information before a decision is reached as to whether or not motion in the environment is occurring. One might think of the discharging of these detector cells as primitive motion signals which then may be cancelled or "vetoed" on the basis of other information (for example if the observer's own movement occurs simultaneous with such signals).

But there are difficulties even with this interpretation. In the case of induced movement it would have to be argued that the motion signal emanating from the displacing image is transferred to the stationary image. Furthermore, the speed of the displacing object may be below threshold, in that with no other object visible no motion is perceived. Yet when the stationary object is introduced, induced movement occurs. Therefore here there is apparently no signal activating detector cells produced by the displacing image which can then be said to be transferred. Rather the information about the displacement is a function of the change of location of the objects relative to one another. Therefore activation of detector cells is apparently not the only source of information about image displacement. A related problem concerns the direction of perceived movement. As noted previously, a dissociation of perceived motion may occur, such that one perceives motion in directions which differ from those of the displacing retinal image.

Stroboscopic movement perception would seem to be another example which cannot be accounted for on the basis of detector units since there is no image displacement over the retina. However, it has been discovered that units of the visual nervous system will respond to discrete successive stimulation of the retina in addition to continuous displacement across it [38]. Can this mechanism then explain stroboscopic movement perception? It can not, for the following reasons:

1. Stroboscopic movement can be perceived across a very wide visual angle, 30 degrees or 40 degrees, and the mechanism discovered does not encompass separations of that magnitude.

2. Stroboscopic movement can be perceived when the identical region of the retina is stimulated successively, provided it "represents" two phenomenal locations in space (so here the activation of this mechanism is not necessary); conversely, when two regions of the retina are successively stimulated that represent only *one* region in space, no movement is perceived. (Here the activation of the mechanism is not sufficient.)

3. One can perceive movement when the image of the first stimulus falls in one eye and is projected to one hemisphere of the brain and the second falls in the other eye and is projected to the other hemisphere (hold up a finger so that it appears slightly left of a fixation spot on a far wall as seen with the right eye only; with the left eye only it then appears to the right of that spot: then open and close the eyes alternately at a rapid rate—the finger will appear to move back and forth. It is not likely that a mechanism of the kind described exists to cover this example). (See chapter 16 for a description of research using this method.)

4. Such a mechanism itself has little bearing on many of the factors that affect the perception of stroboscopic movement such as the similarity of *a* and *b*, the tendency to see the array moving as a whole (Ternus effect), the effect of presenting *a* and *b* by a covering and uncovering procedure, etc.

In conclusion then, the motion-detector mechanism may be sufficient to explain the aftereffect of movement illusion but not the other phenomena of movement perception. The purpose of such neural units, therefore, is not yet clear but perhaps it is to provide information that displacement or rapid change of location of an image is taking place. That information is then interpreted by the perceptual system as signifying movement or not depending upon a variety of other factors. But it does not necessarily follow that the activation of "motion detector" cells is the only source of information concerning image displacement.

Summary

What conditions of stimulation or what central events lead to the perception of movement? Many facts contradict the hypothesis that movement is perceived as the result of displacement of the image of the moving object over the retina.

When the observer moves, the images of stationary objects in the world shift across the retina, but these objects appear to be stationary (position constancy). Conversely, a stationary image on the retina will give rise to an impression of movement when the eyes move. Therefore, it would seem that the perceptual system takes eye or body movement into account when assessing the significance of the behavior of the retinal image. It was suggested that we perceive movement when an object appears to undergo change in its location in relation to ourselves.

Ordinarily, when the observer moves, the image of stationary objects displaces by an equal amount and in a particular direction. If conditions are such that this image displacement is of a different magnitude or in a different direction, then the world will seem to move when the observer moves. However, experiments have demonstrated that we can adapt to this new state of affairs, so that in time the world will appear stationary once again. Therefore, it would seem plausible to hypothesize that in principle any displacement of the image concomitant with observer movement will be discounted by the perceptual system, but that by virtue of past experience, only a particular displacement of the image during observer movement signifies a stationary world.

Stroboscopic movement perception is another fact which contradicts the hypothesis that image displacement underlies the perception of movement. The fact that it occurs only at certain rates of alternation, and that animals and infants perceive it, has suggested to many that it is based on a primitive tendency of the nervous system to react to a spread of excitation from one locus to another.

But a number of other facts seem to call for a different kind of explanation. For example, a necessary condition is that the first object suddenly disappear for no apparent reason and that the second object suddenly appear in a different phenomenal location. Thus the perception of stroboscopic movement can be thought of as a "plausible solution" to the "problem" of a sudden change in an object's location. Stroboscopic movement perception is similar to real movement perception when the object is moving rapidly. In fact, experimental work suggests that the perception of real movement at fast speeds is based on the same mechanism as stroboscopic movement since it depends only on sight of the object in the beginning and end positions.

A single stationary point of light in an otherwise homogeneous field such as a dark room will generally appear to drift. Various theories have been advanced to explain this autokinetic effect. There is some evidence to support the hypothesis that rapid fluttering of the eye that occurs even when the eye is felt to be at rest may be the cause. However, there are difficulties with this hypothesis. The central fact about the autokinetic stimulus situation is that there are no other visible objects present that ordinarily would clearly indicate that a change in position of the point has not occurred. Under these conditions, therefore, the perceptual system might easily be "deceived" into inferring that the point was drifting and that the eyes were slowly tracking it.

The change of location of an object relative to other objects in the field is an important determinant of movement perception. If the moving object surrounds the stationary one (so that it becomes the frame of reference), it will generally induce a sense of movement in the stationary object. Induced movement of the self also occurs when we misperceive our own bodies to be in motion as a result of movement of a surrounding reference system. The importance of change of location relative to other objects is also shown in situations where two or more objects are both moving in relation to one another. The actual path of movement is then often dissociated into two perceptual components, the more salient one being that based on the objects' approach to or separation from one another. Therefore, most of the facts about the perception of movement can be subsumed under the principle that movement is perceived when objects change their phenomenal location (above some threshold rate) where "location" is defined either subject-relatively or object-relatively.

Can the perception of movement be explained in terms of units in the visual nervous system that "detect" the displacement of the image over the retina? Such mechanisms have been discovered in various species. One phenomenon that may be explained along these lines is the aftereffect of movement. However, this phenomenon is a special case. Most of the other facts concerning the perception of movement such as are described in this chapter argue against an explanation along these lines since image displacement is neither a necessary nor a sufficient condition for seeing movement. Therefore, although the role of these so-called neural movement detector mechanisms is to detect the displacement of an image over the retina, information concerning image displacement may or may not lead to movement perception depending upon a variety of other factors.

The apparent velocity of a moving object cannot be a function of the rate at which its image displaces because perceived velocity is more or less constant despite the distance of the object from the observer. Two factors have been isolated. Perceived velocity is a function of the phenomenal extent traversed per unit time; in other words, it is based on size constancy. But perceived velocity is also a function of the rate of relative displacement per unit time. If a frame of reference is transposed in its linear dimensions, the velocity of the object must be transposed by a like amount in order that the phenomenal velocity in the two cases be identical. Constancy of speed in daily life is most likely a function of both factors.

Notes

1. The term *discounted* is used here to mean that no movement is perceived in the environment because the image displacement is fully accounted for by the movement of the observer. It has no other theoretical implications.

2. If the observer wearing lenses or prisms in goggles holds his head still and moves only his eyes, the scene does *not* appear to move. For example, if the observer desires to fixate an object that appears to be off to his left, he will turn his eyes to the left. The image of the object will then move toward the fovea just as it normally would. Of course, in doing so the observer will be turning his eyes away from where the object actually is, to his right. Only if prisms were attached directly to the eyes would the scene appear to move during eye movements.

3. It is possible that the optomotor response is based on the fact that the stationary animal perceives itself as turning in a direction opposite to that of the rotating drum. (See the discussion of induced movement of the self later in this chapter.) If so, the animal would try to "undo" this unwanted effect by rotating in the direction of the moving drum. However, it is unlikely that such an explanation could account for the forced circling of the *moving fly* when the head is rotated because here, to explain the result, it would have to be argued that based on induced movement of the self the fly perceives itself as turning in a direction opposite to the one in which it is actually turning. As noted previously, a human observer looking through reversing prisms or lenses perceives the scene as moving whenever he moves so that no induced movement of the self seems to occur.

    The complicating factor in the experiment with the fly is that the drum surrounds the fly, so that conditions exist to generate induced movement of the self. However, the same kinds of effects could in principle be obtained with only a single visual object: when the object moves, it will be perceived to do so; when the fly moves, the object will appear to be stationary; when the eyes are rotated and the fly moves, the object will appear to move and at a rate faster than the fly.

4. Since factors such as brightness and distance between *a* and *b* affect the outcome it is not possible to state what these rates are as a general rule. But typically, when *a* and *b* are a few degrees apart and are each on for around 50 milliseconds, the optimum interval or off-period, the later-stimulus interval (or ISI) when neither *a* nor *b* is on, is around 50 to 100 milliseconds. If this period is much greater, *a* and *b* will be seen to appear successively; if it is much less, they will appear to be simultaneously on; and in neither case will movement be perceived. However, the period between the onset of *a* and onset of *b* is now thought to be important. If *a* is on for 100 milliseconds or longer, optimum movement will be perceived when there is no off period at all between *a* and *b*.

5. It is important to make clear that eye movements per se cannot explain the stroboscopic illusion.

$a \quad\quad b$

$d \quad\quad c$

This was once a popular theory but was disproven by Wertheimer [8] who showed that observers could simultaneously see *a* moving to *b* and *c* moving to *d*, i.e., in opposite directions. The eyes cannot move in opposite directions at the same time. Also, Guilford and Helson [17] showed by photographing the eyes of their subjects that the eyes were often more or less stationary while they nevertheless experienced movement between the two stimuli. The experiment cited here is based on the argument that it is not eye movements that cause the impression of movement but that when the eyes happen to move in the manner indicated, so that only one region of the retina is stimulated, movement is nevertheless perceived.

6. It has been suggested that in fact there are two distinct kinds of stroboscopic movement perception [21] [22]. Short-range movement occurs with very brief ISIs and very slight changes in position of *a* and *b*, whereas long-range movement can occur with very appreciable change in position and greater ISIs. The claim that there are two such different kinds of stroboscopic motion is controversial but, if correct, could explain several of the different findings referred to here, some of which fit better into a lower-level sensory theory (short range) and some of which fit better into a higher-level cognitive theory (long range).]

7. In a subsequent study, an attempt was made to stabilize the retinal image in *all* directions by requiring the observer to view a small afterimage [26]. To prevent eye movements which would lead to an impression of motion of the afterimage for reasons unrelated to autokinetic movement, the observer fixated a small red dot and attempted to maintain the dot in the center of the circular afterimage. Apparently observers were able to do this while nevertheless frequently experiencing autokinetic movement of the afterimage.

8. One investigator has proposed that "commands" to move the eyes *are* issued in viewing the stationary point. This might result from a state of fatigue of the muscles on one side that would then require abnormal command signals to hold the eyes stationary. These signals are those that ordinarily would signify that the eyes are moving. It was demonstrated that following a period of straining the eye muscles in one direction for 30 seconds, the stationary point subsequently appeared to move in that (or the opposite) direction but not in any other direction [27].

9. It is interesting to note in this connection that the autokinetic effect is highly susceptible to suggestion, and therefore the phenomenon has been studied by social psychologists under conditions where planted "subjects" claim to see the point moving.

10. Change of an object's position relative to another can be thought of as a change in configuration or form. That there is merit in this way of looking at object-relative change is borne out by the demonstration that an object moving below the subject-relative threshold and rotating around a stationary point will also be seen to move (or the stationary point will). In other words, although there is no change in the relative distance between the two points in this case, there is a configurational change: the orientation of the imaginary line connecting the two is changing [29].

11. Other factors that determine which of two or more objects will tend to serve as frame of reference in addition to that of enclosure are relative size, intensity, orientation, and constancy. Other things being equal, the larger or more intense, or vertically oriented, or constant rather than changing object will tend to serve as frame of reference [30].

12. Johansson's theory about these effects is somewhat different from the one proposed here. He believes that the central factor is the tendency to group elements together and to perceive them as belonging together as a rigid entity on the basis of that vector component of their motion that they share in common. This reduces to the grouping principle of common fate, except that here the perceptual system must first "seek out" and "detect" the common vector and only then can a grouping occur on the basis of it. Once that grouping occurs (for example, two elements moving up and down together in Fig. 14.22) the residue of the motion of the elements is perceived in relation to that moving system as a frame of reference.

13. It was also shown, in a third situation, that the spot of light was seen as stationary and the self as moving, if the observer were continuously accelerated and decelerated.

14. When moving at high speed in a vehicle many observers report that objects such as trees, telephone poles, and the surrounding ground appear to be moving in the opposite

direction. This would imply a failure of position constancy. However, it is possible to argue that what one experiences here is the rapid displacement of objects out of the *visual field*, rather than a genuine movement of objects in the world. The term *pseudo-movement* has been used to describe this kind of experience. It may occur at slower speeds too and may even explain the Filehne illusion discussed earlier. This experience is analogous to other sensory impressions that are correlated with the proximal stimulus such as extensity in size perception.

15. The same reasoning can be applied to the perception of a rotating spiral. Depending on the direction of rotation, the spiral appears either to be moving radially outward from the center or inward toward the center. But no part of the spiral *is* moving in this direction, since it is rotation. Thus, the perception of the direction of movement during rotation is illusory and is an example of the barberpole illusion. In the aftereffect, the stationary spiral is perceived to be moving in the direction opposite to that experienced during its rotation. Observers often perceive the rotating spiral in depth, turning toward or away from them, and, in that case, the aftereffect also has a three-dimensional character.

References

[1] Mack, A., and J. Bachant. Perceived movement of the after-image during eye movement. *Perception & Psychophysics*, 1969, 6, 379–384.

[2] Mack, A., and E. Herman. Position constancy during pursuit eye movements: an investigation of the Filehne illusion. *Quarterly Journal of Experimental Psychology*, 1973, 25, 71–84. See also A. E. Stoper, Apparent motion of stimuli presented stroboscopically during pursuit movement of the eye. *Perception & Psychophysics*, 1973, 13, 210–211.

[3] Stratton, G. Some preliminary experiments on vision without inversion of the retinal image. *Psychological Review*, 1896, 3, 611–617; Upright vision and the retinal image. *Psychological Review*, 1897, 4, 182–187; Vision without inversion of the retinal image. *Psychological Review*, 1897, 4, 341–360, and 463–481.

[4] Mittelstaedt, H. Telotaxes und Optomotorik von Eristalis bei Augeninversion, *Naturwissen*, 1944, 36, 90–91; von Holst, E., and H. Mittelstaedt. Das Reafferenz-princip. *Die Naturwissenschaften*, 1950, 20, 464–476. See also R. W. Sperry, Neural basis of the spontaneous optokinetic response produced by visual inversion. *Journal of Comparative and Physiological Psychology*, 1950, 43, 482–489.

[5] Wallach, H., and J. H. Kravitz. The measurement of the constancy of visual direction and of its adaptation. *Psychonomic Science*, 1965, 2, 217–218; Rapid adaptation in the constancy of visual direction with active and passive rotation. *Psychonomic Science*, 1965, 3, 165–166; Posin, R. Perceptual adaptation to contingent visual-field movement; an experimental investigation of position constancy. Ph.D. dissertation, Yeshiva University, 1966 (described in I. Rock, *The Nature of Perceptual Adaptation*. Basic Books, Inc., Publishers, 1966, pp. 87–91).

[6] Ternus, J. Experimentelle Untersuchungen über phänomenale Identität. *Psychologische Forschung*, 1926, 7, 71–126 (Trans. and condensed in W. Ellis, *Source Book of Gestalt Psychology*, Selection 11. Humanities Press, Inc., 1950).

[7] Pantle, A. J., and L. Picciano, 1976. A multistable movement display: Evidence for two separate motion systems in human vision. *Science*, 1976, 193, 500–502.

[8] Wertheimer, M. Experimentelle Studien über das Sehen von Bewegung. *Zeitschrift für Psychologie*, 1912, 61, 161–266.

[9] Smith, K. U. The neural centers concerned in the mediation of apparent-movement vision. *Journal of Experimental Psychology*, 1940, 26, 443–466.

[10] Schiller, P. von. Kinematoskopisches Sehen der Fische. *Zeitschrift für vergl. Physiologie*, 1934, 20, 454.

[11] Gaffron, M. Untersuchungen über das Bewegungssehen bein Libellenlarven, Fliegen und Fischen. *Zeitschrift fur vergl. Physiologie,* 1934, 20, 299.

[12] Rock, I., E. S. Tauber, and D. Heller. Perception of stroboscopic movement: evidence for its innate basis. *Science,* 1965, 147, 1050–1052; Tauber, E. S., and S. Koffler. Optomotor responses in human infants to apparent motion: evidence of innateness. *Science,* 1966, 152, 382–383.

[13] Korte, A. Kinematoskopische Untersuchungen. *Zeitschrift für Psychologie,* 1915, 72, 193–206.

[14] Gengerelli, A. Apparent movement in relation to homogeneous and heterogeneous stimulations of the central hemispheres. *Journal of Experimental Psychology,* 1948, 38, 592–599.

[15] Ammons, C. H., and J. Weitz. Central and peripheral factors in the Phi phenomenon. *Journal of Experimental Psychology,* 1951, 42, 327–332.

[16] Rock, I., and S. Ebenholtz. Stroboscopic movement based on change of phenomenal rather than retinal location. *American Journal of Psychology,* 1962, 75, 193–207.

[17] Guilford, J. P., and H. Helson. Eye movements and the Phi Phenomenon. *American Journal of Psychology,* 1929, 41, 595–606.

[18] Sigman, E., and I. Rock. Unpublished experiment. However, the reader is referred to a recent book in which, contrary to what is claimed above, it is reported that a condition of presentation such as that shown in Fig. 14.8a *does* sometimes lead to an impression of movement. See P. Kolers, *Aspects of Motion Perception.* Pergamon Press, Inc., 1972. Perhaps the difference can be explained by noting that observers can perceive movement under certain conditions where *A* reappears with *B* but naive observers do not tend to do so very much of the time. Another relevant factor is the spatial separation between *A* and *B*.

[19] Sigman, E., and I. Rock. Stroboscopic movement based on perceptual intelligence. *Perception,* 1974, 3. Stoper, A. E. The effect of the structure of the phenomenal field on the occurrence of stroboscopic motion. Paper delivered at the 1964 meeting of the Eastern Psychological Association.

[20] Kaufman, L., I. Cyrulnik, J. Kaplowitz, G. Melnick, and D. Stoff. The complementarity of apparent and real motion. *Psychologische Forschung,* 1971, 34, 343–348.

[21] Braddick, O., 1973. The masking of apparent motion in random-dot patterns. *Vision Research,* 13, 355–369.

[22] Braddick, O., 1974. A short-range process in apparent motion. *Vision Research,* 14, 519–527.

[23] Guilford, J. P., and K. M. Dallenbach. A study of the autokinetic sensation. *American Journal of Psychology,* 1928, 40, 83–91.

[24] Riggs, L. A., F. Ratliff, J. C. Cornsweet, and T. N. Cornsweet. The disappearance of steadily fixated visual test objects. *Journal of the Optical Society of America,* 1953, 43, 495–501. Ditchburn, R. W., and B. L. Ginsborg. Vision with a stabilized retinal image. *Nature,* 1952, 170, 36–37; Pritchard, R. M. Stabilized images on the retina. *Scientific American,* 1961, 204, (6).

[25] Matin, L., and G. E. MacKinnon. Autokinetic movement: Selective manipulation of directional components by image stabilization. *Science,* 1964, 143, 147–148.

[26] Brosgole, L. The autokinesis of an after-image. *Psychonomic Science,* 1968, 12, 233–234.

[27] Gregory, R. L. *Eye and Brain.* World University Library, 1966, pp. 99–103.

[28] Duncker, K. Über induzierte Bewegung. *Psychologische Forschung,* 1929, 12, 180–259. (Trans. and condensed in W. Ellis, *Source Book of Gestalt Psychology.* Humanities Press, Inc. Selection 12, 1950).

[29] Wallach, H. The perception of motion. *Scientific American,* 1959, 201, 56–60.

[30] Oppenheimer, F. Optische Versuche über Ruhe und Bewegung. *Psychologische Forschung,* 1934, 20, 1–46.

[31] Johansson, G. *Configurations in Event Perception.* Almkvist and Wiksell, 1950.

[32] Wallach, H. Informational discrepancy as a basis of perceptual adaptation. Chap. 13 in *The Neuropsychology of Spatially Orientated Behavior* (edited by S. J. Freedman). Dorsey Press, 1968.

[33] Rock, I. The basis of position constancy during passive movement of the observer. *American Journal of Psychology,* 1968, 81, 262–265.

[34] See, for example, Lettvin, J. Y., H. R. Maturana, W. S. McCulloch, and W. H. Pitts. What the frog's eye tells the frog's brain. *Proceedings of the Institute of Radio Engineering,* 1959, 47, 1940–1951; Hubel, D. H., and T. N. Wiesel. Receptive fields, binocular interaction and functional architecture in the cat's visual cortex. *Journal of Physiology,* 1962, 160, 106–154. Barlow, H. B., R. M. Hill, and W. R. Levick. Retinal ganglion cells responding selectively to direction and speed of image motion in the rabbit. *Journal of Physiology,* 1964, 173, 377–407.

[35] Barlow, H. B., and R. M. Hill. Evidence for a physiological explanation of the waterfall phenomenon and figural after-effects. *Nature,* 1963, 200, 1345–1347.

[36] Sekuler, R. W., and L. Ganz. After-effect of seen motion with a stabilized retinal image. *Science,* 1963, 139, 419–420.

[37] Anstis, S. M., and R. L. Gregory. The after-effect of seen motion: The role of retinal stimulation and of eye movements. *Quarterly Journal of Experimental Psychology,* 1965, 17, 173–175.

[38] Grüsser-Cornehls, W., O. J. Grüsser, and T. H. Bullock. Unit responses in the frog's tectum to moving and nonmoving visual stimuli. *Science,* 1963, 141, 820–822; Barlow, H. B., and W. R. Levick. The mechanism of directionally sensitive units in rabbit's retina. *Journal of Physiology,* 1965, 178, 477–504.

Chapter 15

Apparent Motion Based on Phenomenal Location

Irvin Rock and Sheldon Ebenholtz

Although stroboscopic movement has been the subject of countless investigations over a period of many years, it remains to this day an unexplained phenomenon. For the most part, work on this problem during the last several decades has been directed at adducing evidence for or against two types of theories. The Gestaltists have hypothesized that the experience of movement is based on some central physiological interaction which takes place in the cortex between the loci of excitation yielded by the two light-sources.[1] Support for this position has been seen in the finding that the effect is superior or occurs more readily within one hemisphere than between the two,[2] in the finding that satiation of the cortical region between the loci of excitation will subsequently effect *phi*,[3] and conversely, in the finding that after-effects of stroboscopic movement can be predicted for objects which stimulate that cortical region or "field."[4]

Others have sought to show that the interaction is either retinal[5] or sub-cortical[6] and support for this view has been seen in the fact that the effect is more readily obtained when both sources stimulate the same eye than when each is located in a different eye,[7] and in the finding that decorticated guinea pigs apparently achieve stroboscopic movement.[8] Both theories share the common assumption that the effect depends upon a neural interaction between the excitations and that it is such interaction which creates the experience of movement.

The usual statement of the minimal conditions required to produce stroboscopic motion is that disparate retinal points must be exposed to alternate stimulation. Given the proper rate of such stimulation, the experience of motion will occur. While there can be doubt that the above statement represents a sufficient condition, one can by no means conclude on the same basis that it is also a necessary condition. The sources of stimulation—corresponding to the disparate retinal points—are typically

Originally published in *The American Journal of Psychology* 75, 2 (1962): 193–207, under the title "Stroboscopic Movement Based on Change of Phenomenal Rather than Retinal Location." Reprinted with permission.

localized phenomenally at distinct places in space. There are, therefore, two possible ways of stating the necessary conditions for movement, one in terms of anatomical locus of stimulation and the other in terms of experienced location of the sources of stimulation. It is to be noted that in the traditional statement of the minimal conditions required to produce stroboscopic motion these two possible alternatives are not distinguished, undoubtedly because change of retinal location is generally a concomitant of change of phenomenal location.

The possibility which was explored in the following experiments was that stroboscopic motion is primarily a function of change in *phenomenal location* of the source of stimulation and not at all a function of change in the anatomical locus of stimulation (neural interaction theories, as noted above, are based upon the assumption of change of anatomical locus).[9]

Experiment I

Part 1
The purpose of this experiment was to create conditions such that a single anatomical locus of stimulation be experienced at two different spatial locations. This was accomplished by having O so move his eye back and forth as to view each stimulus foveally. Thus, while O localized the distal object on his left and again on his right, the locus of retinal (and cortical) stimulation remained identical in both cases.

Procedure. O's head was held rigidly in a fixed position by a head-rest. He viewed the scene monocularly (generally with the right eye) and alternately through one of two artificial pupils. The artificial pupils were about 0.014-in. in diameter, about $\frac{5}{8}$-in. apart, punched in a circular piece of thin black paper surrounded by a shield which prevented O from seeing anything except through these openings. O could see through only one aperture at a time, in that light stimulated his retina only through the aperture his eye was facing at any moment.

The scene consisted of two vertical luminous lines on an otherwise dark homogeneous field. About 22 in. in front of the artificial pupils was the arrangement which produced the vertical lines. This consisted of a ground-glass screen upon which were mounted two pieces of black cardboard, each containing a vertical slit. (The slits were 3/16 in. in thickness and 3 in. in length.) The cardboard pieces, each containing a vertical slit, were mounted on a track over which they could be shifted horizontally behind the ground-glass screen so as to increase the distance between them when desired. Only one line was visible through each aperture and it was only visible when the eye was turned to fixate it through the aperture. Thus, when O viewed through the left aperture, only the left line was visible and when *O* viewed through the right aperture, only the right line was visible.

Extreme care was taken to insure that each line stimulated only the foveal portion of the retina. This was accomplished with each *O* in advance of the experiment by illuminating the aperture and the lines at the same time. *E* then moved the lines until their images were as close to the inner or nasal portion of each aperture as possible, while *O* fixated the lines. This insured that the lines would disappear from *O*'s view with the onset of the slightest lateral eye-movement in a nasal direction. With the eye so close to the aperture, any turning brings the pupillary opening out of alignment with the entire cone of light rays coming through the aperture from the line. It was not possible with the arrangement used here simultaneously to prevent *O* from seeing a given line peripherally through an aperture by turning his eye beyond the line. Under instructions to fixate, it is unlikely, however that this would occur. If it were to occur a theory based on neural interaction would have to predict movement in the opposite direction to that which was experienced based on an analysis of the proximal stimulus-situation. (See the discussion of this problem p. 203.) In other words, *O* could see each line by fixating it and nothing else was visible but the fixated line. As soon as the vertical lines were in place, the surrounding area was so darkened that the apertures were themselves no longer visible to *O*, but of course he could still see *through* them. By means of a dual projector and an episcotister, the two vertical lines were made to appear alternately, one through each aperture. *O* was then instructed to move his eyes from left to right, etc., so that the illuminated vertical lines would be in foveal view at each position of the eye. Fig. 15.1 illustrates the experimental arrangement. All *Os*, after a few trials, were able to synchronize their eye-movements to the alternating vertical lines.[10] *O* was then asked to report his spontaneous impression of the scene. The *Os* were students at the New School for Social Research; some of them probably had seen stroboscopic movement demonstrated in a class, but all of them were naïve about the hypothesis. Care was taken not to mention that the experiment had to do with stroboscopic movement.

The precise conditions of rate of alternation and distance between lines varied somewhat for each *O*, depending upon the rate of eye-movement he was able to attain. For one *O* believed to be representative, the rate of alternation was approximately 0.3 sec. with the lines set 7 in. apart. Each line remained exposed for approximately 0.13 sec.

In summary, the major point of the above procedure was to insure (1) that the proximal stimuli would fall in a single retinal region, and (2) that the corresponding distal stimuli would be experienced at different phenomenal locations, once to the left and once to the right. Such phenomenal localization is based on the change in eye-position.

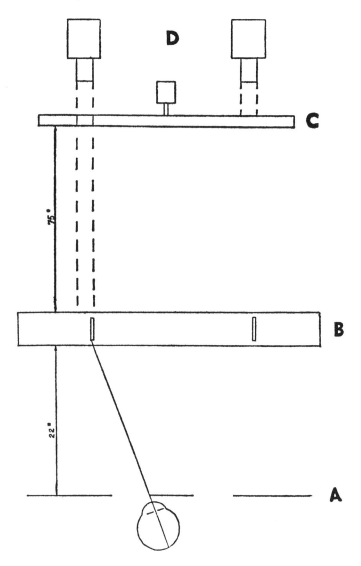

Figure 15.1
Schematic diagram of arrangement used in experiment I, part 1. A, artificial pupils; B, ground-glass screen, with vertical slits in cardboard; C, episcotister in position of transmitting light from left projector; D, dual 300-w. projector.

Results

Of 10 *Os* who succeeded in properly coordinating their eye-movements to the alternating stimulus, 6 reported seeing a single object in motion almost immediately following the onset of stimulation. The remaining 4 *Os* reported seeing 2 objects, both of which were flashing on and off in their respective positions. These same 4 *Os* were, however, unable to perceive apparent movement under normal viewing conditions.[11] These cases do not, therefore, represent negative instances of the hypothesis in question. The results thus far indicate that stroboscopic motion can be experienced in the absence of disparate retinal-cortical stimulation.

Part 2

In Part 2 of this experiment, the attempt was made to create a situation in which different regions of retinal stimulation were phenomenally localized in the *same* region in space. In this situation, one eye-position allowed for foveal stimulation of the object whereas the other eye-position allowed for peripheral stimulation by the same object while fixating a small stationary spot. In both cases, however, the stimulus-object was experienced at the same locus in space. This was accomplished by requiring *O* to move his eye back and forth so as to view a single stationary flashing line alternately foveally and peripherally.

Procedure.   As soon as Part 1 was completed, one of the vertical lines was removed and a hole $\frac{1}{2}$-in. in diameter was substituted for it. This hole was continuously illuminated and served as a fixation-point. The two projectors behind the episcotister were now both trained on the same vertical slit from behind the ground-glass screen. This arrangement was thus one which illuminated the vertical opening at a rate exactly twice that of Part 1. (The reason for the increased rate was that every other exposure was intended to correspond to the exposure of a second line. Thus, the rate between exposures of the line equalled that between exposures of the two lines in Part 1.) The scene, therefore, consisted of a line flashing on and off and a continuously illuminated fixation-point. *O* was then asked to view the scene monocularly through a circular hole cut in black cloth (placed about 3 in. above the artificial pupils used in Part 1). The opening was fitted with two polarizing filters at such an angle with respect to each other as to maintain a black homogeneous surround for the flashing line and the fixation-point. *O* was instructed so to adjust his gaze between the line and the point that the line would stimulate alternately the foveal and peripheral regions of the eye with each flash. This was accomplished by the following succession of eye-movements: *O* fixates point on right (line flashes in peripheral vision on left); *O* fixates line on left (line stimulates fovea); *O* fixates point on right (line flashes in peripheral vision on left) etc. Thus, as far as the retina or cortex is concerned, there is alternate stimulation of disparate points exactly as occurs in a more typical demonstration of apparent movement. The major difference, however, is that here the flashing source will be localized at one and the same place in space. After several trials, all Os were asked to report their spontaneous impressions of the scene.

Results
The six Os used in this part were the same Os who experienced movement in Part 1. Of the six, none reported the perception of movement under these conditions.

These results indicate that in the absence of divergent spatial locations of the distal stimuli, stroboscopic motion will *not* occur, even though disparate retinal points are being stimulated. Apparently the fact that the line is experienced in one and the same place in space eliminates the possibility of seeing movement.

Experiment II

Part 1
As in Experiment I, Part 1, the over-all intent of Experiment II was to create the conditions under which an object would stimulate a given (constant) portion of the retina, but be phenomenally localized at two different places in space. The two experiments differ, however, in the way in which the disparate object-localization was achieved. In Experiment I, change in eye-position may be assumed to have been the major determinant of change in phenomenal location. In Experiment II, it was decided to utilize as the determinant the change in relative position of one object with respect to another.

Procedure. The conditions employed are quite similar to those of Duncker's demonstration of induced motion.[12] In Duncker's demonstration, motion was attributed to an object that had no moving counterpart in the retinal pattern. He attributed this effect to what he termed object-relative displacement. In the case where one object may be said to surround another or to act as a frame of reference, when the latter (the frame of reference) is set in motion, the enclosed, surrounded object is characteristically perceived as moving in a direction opposite to its frame.

The present conditions differ from those of Duncker with respect to the fact that the object expected to be seen as moving is not continuously present but instead flashes on and off in the same physical locus. A luminous line was moved back and forth (frame of reference), while a shorter luminous line flashed on and off in a fixed position in space. The short line thus appeared now to the left of the larger moving line, now to the right. O was at a distance of about 4 ft. from a display which moved in a plane perpendicular to his line of sight. He viewed binocularly, in a completely darkened room, from a fixed head-position. The display consisted of the following: In the center of a black cardboard was a vertical luminous line of $\frac{1}{2}$-in. width and 8-in. length. In symmetrical positions, to the left and right of this line, were two slits, $\frac{1}{8}$ by 2 in. long. The slits were exactly $2\frac{5}{8}$ in. apart at their extreme edges.

The entire display was mounted on a wooden frame which moved in a track laterally, for a total distance of $2\frac{5}{8}$ in. Upon reaching the point of maximal displacement in any one direction, the display immediately changed its course and proceeded in the opposite direction. The speed of alternation could be varied by means of variable rheostat. The movement was accomplished by means of a reduction motor which drove a circular metal disk in a horizontal plane. A shaft mounted at a point on the perimeter of the disk was attached to the wooden frame. As the metal disk revolved, a force was applied to the frame via the shaft and the ensuing direction of movement was determined by the horizontal track. The total displacement of the display ($2\frac{5}{8}$ in.) was determined by the diameter of the metal disk (and angle of disk to track).

At a fixed point on a wall directly behind the display was a single luminous line of dimensions identical with one of the slits in the display. This line was so situated as to coincide with each slit at the two points of maximal displacement of the display. Thus, as the display reached its left terminal point, the right slit became coincident with the luminous line; as the display reached its right terminal point, the left slit coincided with the same luminous line. This situation provided, therefore, for the alternate illumination of the left and right slits, although the source of illumination was at a fixed point in space.

O was instructed to fixate a luminous spot fastened to a clear glass plate at a distance of about 2 in. in front of the display and placed directly in O's line of sight. Under these conditions, the stimulation (coming alternately from each slit and provided by the fixed luminous line behind the display) consistently fell on the same portion of the retina. Thus as in Experiment I, Part 1, the classical conditions for phi (viz. the alternate stimulation of disparate retinal points) were not present. The question was whether the possible shift in phenomenal location of the flashing line induced by the actual change in position of the larger line would yield the impression of movement.

When the apparatus was set in motion, O was required to report what appeared to be taking place in his field of view. Different Os participated in this variation.

Results

All of the Os (10) who took part reported viewing a single short luminous line describing a semicircular path about a taller luminous line in the third dimension. The center line was also seen to move back and forth. About as many Os reported the motion of the short line taking place behind the tall center line as did those reporting motion in front of the line. The results clearly support the hypothesis that change in phenomenal location without change of retinal location will yield the perception of stroboscopic motion.

This procedure on the surface is similar to one used by Duncker whereby stroboscopic motion can be used to illustrate induced movement. The relative position of an outer rectangle changes in two slides, alternately projected, while that of a central dot remains unchanged. The rectangle is seen to move but so is the dot, despite the fact that the dot's position is objectively unchanged. We would have cited this demonstration to support the proposition of the dependence of stroboscopic movement on change of phenomenal location rather than retinal location (instead of performing the above experiment) were it not for one flaw. The retinal position of the rectangle *does* change so that one might argue that the stroboscopic movement induced in the dot is transferred in some way from the stroboscopic movement of the rectangle and *that* movement *is* based on change of retinal location. In the present experiment, however, the central line is in *continuous* (real) movement and the short line merely flashes on and off in the same objective place. There is thus no stroboscopic motion to be transferred to the short line; nevertheless, a stroboscopic effect is achieved.

Part 2

The results of the previous experiment indicate that a discontinuous change in the relative position of the stimulus-object with respect to another object was sufficient to produce stroboscopic motion. This was the case despite the absence of disparate retinal stimulation.

If we consider this experiment from the perspective of Duncker's conceptual system, it is probable that the constantly illuminated center line served as a frame of reference, thereby 'inducing' stroboscopic motion in the alternately illuminated line. If Duncker's formulation can be applied to the present instance, then if the object, with respect to which a change in position takes place, were made relatively small as compared with the alternating stimuli, we should expect no induced movement because it would no longer have the character of frame of reference. The question remains, therefore, as to whether the experience of motion can be eliminated by changing the characteristic of the flashing stimulus to give *it* the property of frame of reference.

Procedure. The display of Experiment II, Part 1, was modified by making the slits 6 in. long. The luminous line, with respect to which the alternation occurred, was reduced to a tiny luminous spot ($\frac{1}{4}$ in. square). The same apparatus and method of illumination was used as in the first part of Experiment II. Thus, the left and right slits were alternately illuminated from a fixed source behind the display.

Five naïve *O*s and five *O*s who were sophisticated about stroboscopic movement, but not the hypothesis under investigation, were used. They were given the instructions of Experiment II, Part 1.

Results
None of the 10 *O*s reported any motion of the vertical line. All indicated that the same line was going on and off at the same point in space. Of course, the small spot actually moving back and forth was seen to do so.

Part 3
In Part 3 an attempt was made to utilize Duncker's principles to interfere with stroboscopic movement under conditions where it might be expected to occur. It was required that the object, which now appeared in a constant position relative to another object, stimulate disparate portions of the retina. Thus, although the relative position of the stimulus-object remained constant, the corresponding retinal stimulation alternated between two points. Here, as in Experiment I, Part 2, we have represented, therefore, the classical conditions for stroboscopic motion.

Whereas in that experiment a change in retinal location was accompanied by a constant phenomenal location, in the present experiment it might be thought that the change in retinal location is accompanied by a change in phenomenal location. Insofar, however, as relative position is also a determinant of phenomenal location, and insofar as the latter does *not* change, this experiment is, in essence, putting in conflict two systems of cues to phenomenal location.

Procedure. In this part the apparatus remained the same as in Part 1 of Experiment II. The display, however, was modified in two ways. First, the left slit was covered over to block out any illumination from behind. Secondly, a second luminous strip of the same dimensions as the one used in Part 1 was mounted on the wall behind the display. This was positioned in such a manner as to correspond with the right slit at the extreme point of its left movement; and, as in Part 1, the right slit was illuminated at the extreme point of its right movement. Thus, the same slit was illuminated alternately at the two extreme points of its lateral displacement. The long center line remained continuously in view as it moved, as in Part 1. The outcome of this arrangement was that an 8-in. line moved back and forth and a 2-in. line flashed on $2\frac{5}{8}$ in. to the right of the longer line at each of the terminal positions of the longer line. *O* was instructed to fixate a luminous point in front of the display as in Part 1 and to describe the visual scene.

Results

The *O*s of Part 1 were also used for Part 3. All *O*s found great difficulty in describing their experience. A typical report was as follows: "The small line seems to be moving and at the same time standing still." It will be recalled that in this condition, two systems of cues which normally act jointly to determine the spatial location of objects, are here opposed. That is, normally a change in retinal location with eye- and head-movement eliminated, will indicate a change in phenomenal location. On the other hand, the maintenance of a constant position relative to some external frame of reference serves to indicate a constant phenomenal location within that system. In light of this analysis the ambiguity expressed in the *O*'s reports is readily understandable.

On the whole, the results of this experiment seem to imply that to obtain the unequivocal experience of stroboscopic motion, change in phenomenal location must itself be unequivocally given. That is, when stimulus-conditions are such that phenomenal location is ambiguous, so too is the resultant stroboscopic movement experience.

Discussion

One criticism that at an earlier time might have been made against Experiment I, Part 1 (undoubtedly our most important experiment) is that the cause of the experienced motion can be attributed to the eye-movements. By now, of course, it is clearly established that eye-movement is not a necessary condition for stroboscopic movement[13] and no one has ever demonstrated that it is a sufficient condition. We believe, therefore, that we are free to use change of eye-position as a technique for bringing about change of phenomenal location. In Experiment I, Part 2, the same eye movements do not yield any experience of motion. Also it may be noted that Experiment II, Part 1 does not entail change of eye-position as an independent variable.

There are several facts about stroboscopic movement that support our over-all conclusions.

(1) A theory of stroboscopic motion based on neural interaction could never, in itself, be a complete theory for the following reason: Logically it is possible that the interaction could explain why an experience of movement occurs but it does not adequately deal with the problem of the experienced directions in space of the starting and ending positions of that movement or, in short, its path. If location were purely a matter of the

locus of the proximal stimulus (as is no doubt the case in species whose eyes do not move), then the "path" of the neural interaction would correspond with the path of the seen movement in space. Where, however, eye-position plays a central role in the location of objects with respect to the perceiver, certain logical difficulties arise. Suppose O does move his eyes somewhat while viewing the flashing points. Suppose, for example, he fixates one stimulus and fixates only slightly to the side of the other. If he sees movement, as we have every reason to assume he will, it will not merely be a slight movement, as might be predicted from the slight retinal shift involved in our example. Rather he will see the movement between the two points as veridically localized in phenomenal space, each on the basis of eye-position together with retinal position. Hence, the interaction between the anatomical loci of the stimuli per se does not tell us anything about the path of motion. That path corresponds with the phenomenal location of the terminal positions and not necessarily with the retinal (or cortical) terminal positions. From this analysis, our experiments, in which no shift in the retinal stimulus occurs at all, represent the extreme case and show in addition that no interaction is necessary for the movement experience.

A related fact is that stroboscopic motion occurs in the third dimension of space under conditions where the source is phenomenally located at different distances from O. This illustrates the point made above; namely, the path of the movement does not correspond in any direct way with the path one would predict based on retinal stimulation—i.e., the "path" of the alleged interaction between the anatomical loci of excitation.

(2) After these experiments were completed, a paper by Verhoeff which reports on certain clinical observations bearing on the present problem came to our attention.[14] Verhoeff demonstrated that stroboscopic movement can be elicited by alternate stimulation of the two foveas of squinters with anomalous projection. In such patients the image on one fovea is generally localized separately from that on the other. Thus, here, too, we see that the movement experience occurs so long as the light-sources are localized separately in space, despite the fact that only one retinal (and cortical) region is stimulated.

(3) The effect has been obtained with interocular stimulation, where the two excitations emanate from different eyes and end in different hemispheres of the brain.[15] This condition would seem to preclude peripheral interaction and to make unlikely central neural interaction. The effect has also been obtained across acquired scotomata of cerebral or retinal origin.[16]

(4) It has long been known, as one of Korte's Laws,[17] that as the distance between sources is increased, the time-interval between exposures must also be increased if an effect of movement is to continue to occur. The

question arises, however, whether distance here is to be conceived of in retinal or in phenomenal terms. Corbin showed that Korte's effect occurs when the distance is so increased along a plane inclined to O as to hold constant the retinal distance.[18] If stroboscopic movement does depend on stimulus-conditions which yield change of phenomenal location as we have argued, then, insofar as distance enters into the process, we would expect it to be phenomenal distance, which apparently is the case.

(5) There is considerable evidence that set, experience with the effect, and extent of training influence the perception of stroboscopic motion.[19] Such facts do not seem to follow from neural interaction theories which must necessarily regard the effect as autochthonously determined.

There are both negative and positive implications of our finding. On the negative side, it seems to follow that all theories which seek to explain the experience of stroboscopic movement in terms of some neural interaction between the loci of excitation are in error. A theory of interaction is only appropriate if it is correct that a necessary condition is stimulation of anatomically separate regions, and we have shown that this is not a necessary condition. In Gestalt thinking such a theory exemplified the postulate of isomorphism—viz. if motion is seen between two points in space, then some neural correlate of motion must exist between the cortical excitations representing those points in space. Without necessarily challenging isomorphism as such, our findings do challenge the way isomorphism has been applied in perception; namely, the seeking of correlates of various aspects of phenomenal space in terms of interactions within the cortical space. In other words, facts of space-perception cannot be accounted for purely in terms of a theory tailored to the *spatial* dimensions of the visual cortex. If, for example, only a single cortical region is excited, it can nevertheless represent various points in phenomenal space, depending on eye-position. In principle, all of space could be represented by a single retinal (and cortical) point, thus showing that perceived spatiality does not necessarily correspond with cortical spatiality in any simple or direct fashion.[20] This is not to deny, of course, that perceived spatiality corresponds with some cortical events which represent space. In the long run, an appropriate neural explanation for the experience of stroboscopic movement will be found—which may or may not be compatible with the doctrine of isomorphism—but it will undoubtedly be quite different from present theories. We suspect, in line with the discussion below, that such an explanation will be similar to that which will be found to explain all perceived movement.

Somewhat similar reasoning applies to the peripheral theories of interaction. Only if it were the case that phenomenal space corresponds in a direct fashion with retinal "space," could such theories logically be considered tenable. Whatever, therefore, may be the evidence for neural interaction in the retina, our evidence shows that it cannot be considered a necessary condition for stroboscopic movement.

On the positive side, our finding that stroboscopic movement will only be experienced when change of phenomenal location is involved dovetails nicely with certain facts about the perception of movement in general. In the case of fixating a moving object, it is also clear that it will be perceived as moving, if its displacement is above threshold, despite the fact that here, too, there is no retinal (or cortical) displacement. (Cf. the analogous Experiment I, Part 1.) Of course, the converse, sweeping the eyes past a stationary object, does not yield an impression of movement despite the displacement of the image. (Cf. the analogous Experiment I, Part 2.)[21]

In the case of induced motion, the stationary object is seen as moving and, if below threshold, the moving object as stationary. Here, again, it would seem that change of phenomenal location occurs. The induced object is seen as changing its location with respect to the inducing one which acts as a frame of reference. (Cf. the analogous Experiment II, Part 1.)

Our findings also fit in with what is now known about phenomenal velocity, which is the quantitative aspect of phenomenal movement. Brown showed that perceived speed is a function not of the absolute rate at which an object's image traverses the retina but rather of the rate at which it displaces relative to its frame of reference.[22] In other words, we may say that phenomenal velocity is a function of rate of change of phenomenal location, not of retinal location. The fact of speed-constancy also supports this conclusion.[23]

It therefore seems correct to generalize that the perception of movement depends on those stimulus-conditions which can yield an experience of change of an object's phenomenal location, providing, of course, that the change is above some threshold-value.[24] There is a certain logic to this, since, in reality, if an object changes its location, it does so by moving. (The focus of interest, therefore, shifts to the problem of uncovering the precise determinants of phenomenal location and to the problem of threshold.) Ultimately, an explanation in terms of brain-process will be one tailored to deal with this central fact.

From this point of view, there is only one remaining problem about stroboscopic movement that in any way makes it a special case. That is the fact of discontinuous rather than continuous stimulation. Some authors have tried to argue that this is not a crucial distinction, since the retina consists of cells which, even if adjacent, also are discontinuous. Hence, even real movement involves discontinuous stimulation, only less so. But as shown by the results reported in this paper, the discontinuity should not be thought of in retinal terms at all but rather in spatial terms. Even a flashing on and off in the *same* retinal location will, under the proper conditions, yield an impression of movement across space. In these terms, the problem *does* remain of why movement is perceived across a rather substantial stretch of space when there is no stimulation corresponding to continuous displacement.

Once it is realized, however, that stroboscopic movement can be subsumed under the general principle of change of phenomenal location, this phenomenon is perhaps no longer so puzzling. In line with the "logic" that perception often manifests, if the identical thing is now "here" and now "there," then it can only have changed position by moving. (The notion of identity has been stressed by many investigators of stroboscopic movement and the similarity of the two exposed objects is now known to be important.) Furthermore the stimulus-conditions are quite similar to those which obtain during real movement. The terminal positions of a really moving object perhaps form the more important component of the stimulus-conditions, particularly if the object moves rapidly, since the intervening positions are often blurred out or not noticeable as such. From this point of view, one might predict the phenomenon of stroboscopic movement even if it were not known, based on similarity—a kind of stimulus-generalization.[25] It, therefore, becomes at least plausible that the effect is a function of past experience with real movement.

Summary

The question was raised whether stroboscopic movement depends upon successive stimulation of separate retinal (and therefore cortical) points or of points located separately in phenomenal space. Ordinarily the latter requires the former, but it is possible to create conditions where phenomenal separateness is experienced even when only one region of the retina is stimulated. With the use of two different techniques, it was shown that under such conditions stroboscopic movement is experienced. Conversely, it is possible to stimulate separate retinal points in such a manner that the source will not be experienced in two localities but, rather, in only one. It was shown that under such conditions movement will not be experienced. These findings were taken to imply that neural interaction between two loci of excitation (on any level) cannot be a general explanation of stroboscopic movement. It was pointed out that the findings are consistent with certain facts concerning movement-perception in general; namely, that motion is experienced whenever above-threshold change in the phenomenal location of the source occurs.

Notes

This study was supported by Research Grant M-2082, National Institute of Mental Health, Public Health Service.

1. Max Wertheimer, Experimentelle Studien über das Sehen von Bewegung, *Z. Psychol.*, 61, 1912, 161–278.
2. A. Gengerelli, Apparent movement in relation to homonymous and heteronymous stimulation of the cerebral hemispheres, *J. exp. Psychol.*, 38, 1948, 592–599.
3. B. H. Deatherage and M. E. Bitterman, The effect of satiation on stroboscopic movement, *Amer. J. Psychol.*, 65, 1952, 108–109.
4. N. H. Livson, After-effects of prolonged inspection of apparent movement, *Amer. J. Psychol.*, 66, 1953, 365–376.
5. C. T. Morgan, *Physiological Psychology*, 1943, 203–206; Koiti Motokawa, Retinal traces and visual perception of movement, *J. exp. Psychol.*, 45, 1953, 369–377; The physiological mechanism of apparent movement, *idem*, 378–386.
6. K. U. Smith, The neural centers concerned in the mediation of apparent movement vision, *J. exp. Psychol.*, 26, 1940, 443–466; K. U. Smith and W. E. Kappauf, A neurological study of apparent movement, *J. gen. Psychol.*, 23, 1940, 315–327.
7. C. H. Ammons and Joseph Weitz, Central and peripheral factors in the phi phenomenon, *J. exp. Psychol.*, 42, 1951, 327–332.
8. Smith, *op. cit.*, 1940, 443–466; Smith and Kappauf, *op. cit.*, 315–327.
9. Of course, phenomenal location depends upon certain underlying neural events, but not necessarily upon a particular location of the excitation in either the retina or in area 17 of the visual cortex. Throughout this chapter "phenomenal location" (in contradistinction to "anatomical location") will be used in this sense.
10. The main purpose of using the alternating projection of the vertical slits was to force *O* to achieve a particular speed of alternation of eye-movement. No doubt a stroboscopic effect would have been achieved even with both slits continuously illuminated because only one is visible at a time, but then there would be no control over rate of eye-movement and, hence, over rate of alternation. It is, however, possible that our arrangement did also contribute to a flashing on-and-off effect. Without it, *O* might have in some way sensed that it was his own eye-movement which "turned off" a line and, if so, the lines may have been seen as permanently on but not always visible, which probably is not an ideal condition for producing a movement-effect.
11. They were given the opportunity to view the alternating stimuli monocularly and without an artificial pupil. The rate of alternation was kept identical with the highest rate of eye-movement attained in the experiment proper. The reason these *O*s did not experience movement may be that their threshold for stroboscopic motion required a rate of alternation well above that at which they were capable of maintaining lateral eye-movements.
12. Karl Duncker, Über induzierte Bewegung, *Psychol. Forsch.*, 12, 1929, 180–259.
13. Wertheimer, *op. cit.*, 161–278; J. P. Guilford and Harry Helson, Eye-movements and the phi-phenomenon, *Amer. J. Psychol.*, 41, 1929, 595–606.
14. F. H. Verhoeff, Phi phenomenon and anomalous projection, *Arch. Opthal.*, 24, 1940, 247–251.
15. K. R. Smith, Visual apparent movement in the absence of neural interaction, *Amer. J. Psychol.*, 51, 1948, 73–78.
16. H. L. Teuber and M. B. Bender, Perception of apparent movement across acquired scotomata in the visual field, *Amer. Psychologist*, 5, 1950, 271 (abstract).
17. Adolf Korte, Kinematoskopische Untersuchungen, *Z. Psychol.*, 72, 1915, 193–206.
18. H. H. Corbin, The perception of grouping and apparent movement in visual depth, *Arch. Psychol.*, 38, 1942, (No. 273), 1–50.

19. C. I. Hovland, Apparent movement, *Psychol. Bull.*, 32, 1935, 755–778; W. S. Neff, A critical investigation of the visual apprehension of movement, *Amer. J. Psychol.*, 48, 1936, 1–42; E. E. Jones and J. S. Bruner, Expectancy in apparent visual movement, *Brit. J. Psychol.*, 45, 1954, 157–165; H. E. Toch and W. H. Ittelson, The role of past experience in apparent movement: re-evaluation, *ibid.*, 47, 1956, 195–207; William Epstein and Irvin Rock, Perceptual set as an artifact of recency, *Amer. J. Psychol.*, 73, 1960, 214–228.

20. We do believe that the spatial dimensions of the cortex correspond with the experienced (two dimensional) topological relations of the momentary visual field. Perhaps all original experiences of extensity, shape, relative position, and the like depend upon the spatiality of the visual cortex. Nevertheless the stable visual world involving the location of things with respect to the observer is also very much a function of eye-position, i.e., of where the momentary field is "aimed." Thus objects stimulating, say, the fovea, although always located in the center of the momentary field, are located in space with respect to the self in whatever direction the eye is turned. (Cf. J. J. Gibson, *The perception of the visual world*, 1950, 26–43.) The integration of retinal position with eye-position in determining phenomenally perceived direction may be a matter of development and learning, at least in humans.

21. In the case of real movement, Gestalt psychologists, as for example Duncker or Koffka, have been well aware of these facts, but curiously they failed to see that they might equally be true of stroboscopic movement, and that, if so, it would contradict Wertheimer's type of theory.

22. J. F. Brown, The visual perception of velocity, *Psychol. Forsch.*, 14, 1931, 199–232.

23. Hans Wallach, On constancy of visual speed, *Psychol. Rev.*, 46, 1939, 541–552.

24. Below threshold, a change in position will be noted but it will not be accompanied by the equality of movement, as for example the minute hand of a watch.

25. Cf. R. S. Woodworth and Harold Schlosberg, *Experimental Psychology*, 1954, 515.

Chapter 16
Apparent Motion Based on Changing Phoria
Hiroshi Ono and Gail Gonda

Introduction

When an observer alternately opens and closes each eye, there is an apparent movement of visual objects toward left or right. The apparent movement can be explained by the difference in the relative locations of retinal images of a given object in the two eyes with respect to those of other objects located at different distances. However, this cannot be the sole explanation because apparent movement is seen when an observer's eyes are alternately occluded while he is viewing a single light source presented in the dark. The aim of the experiments reported in this paper was to test the hypothesis that the apparent movement of a stimulus is due to a deviation of the occluded eye, i.e., phoria. In experiments 1 and 2, the direction of the apparent movement, eye position, and eye movements were measured when occlusion for the two eyes alternated in time. Experiments 1 and 2 differed in that eye movements were expected to occur in experiment 1 but not in experiment 2. In experiment 3, the magnitude of the apparent movement and the extent of phoria were measured to determine the extent of the association between the two.

Experiment 1

Hering's principles of visual direction state that an object stimulating the fovea is seen on a line passing through the cyclopean eye and the intersection of the two lines of sight (Fry 1950; Hering 1942; Ono 1975). Thus, if the line of sight of the occluded eye is not directed toward the object and if that of the nonoccluded eye is, the apparent direction of the object should be nonveridical. If the right eye is occluded and it deviates outward (exophoria), the apparent direction of the stimulus should be displaced to the right; if it deviates inward (esophoria), the apparent direction should be displaced to the left. Figure 16.1 illustrates what the

Originally published in *Perception* 7 (1978): 75–83, under the title "Apparent Movement, Eye Movements and Phoria When Two Eyes Alternate in Viewing a Stimulus." Reprinted with permission.

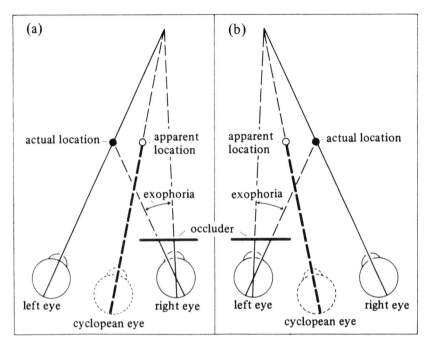

Figure 16.1
Apparent locations of a stimulus as a result of exophoria of the occluded right eye (a) and occluded left eye (b). The figure is drawn with the assumption that the line of sight of the nonoccluded eye is on the stimulus and the distance of the stimulus is correctly perceived.

apparent direction should be when there is exophoria of the occluded right eye (figure 16.1a) and when there is an exophoria of the occluded left eye (figure 16.1b). With exophoria, there should be apparent movement toward the right when occlusion shifts from the left eye to the right eye, and toward the left when the shift is reversed. With esophoria, the apparent movement should be in the opposite direction.

Experiment 1 tested the above predictions. The placement of the two occluders, one for each eye, alternated every 5 s. While eye position and eye movements were being recorded, the subject was asked to report the direction of the apparent movement of a visual stimulus. The stimulus was placed near the subject in one condition and farther away in another condition, since there is a tendency for exophoria to occur for near stimuli and for esophoria to occur for distant stimuli (Morgan 1968; Ogle 1964).

Method

Apparatus.   A single light-emitting diode (LED, Texas Instrument TIL 109 TI) in otherwise dark surroundings served as the stimulus in the experimental session. It was situated at eye level in the median plane 25 cm from the front surface of the eyes in the near-viewing condition and at a distance of 2.5 m in the far-viewing condition. Alternate occlusion was achieved by a device consisting of a tubular solenoid (Guardian, T4X16 INT 24 DC). The occluders were attached to the shaft of the solenoid such that each of the eyes was alternately occluded and nonoccluded at 5 s intervals by means of a continuous cycling timer (Lafayette Instrument, Model 52021). The occluders were designed so that the subject never viewed the stimulus binocularly. Eye movements were recorded by a photoelectric technique (Biometrics SGH/V-Z) and a Beckman Type R Dynograph which was run at a paper speed of 10 mm s^{-1}. This system is capable of measuring horizontal eye movements linearly up to approximately ±20 deg with a resolution of 0.25 deg. The instrument was calibrated by asking the subject to fixate binocularly each of a row of five LEDs arranged at eye level, 57 cm from the eyes: a central one, two 3 deg on either side of the center, and two 5 deg on either side of the center. The subject's head was kept fixed by means of a biteboard. The Maddox rod test for phoria was also applied at both viewing distances.

Procedure. Five measures of phoria for each eve were taken for both experimental distances with the use of the Maddox rod. The recorder pens of the dynograph were initially set in the central position of each channel while the subject binocularly viewed the single LED. The occluding device was then placed in front of the subject's eyes. Eye positions were recorded during ten complete cycles of alternate occlusion. The direction of apparent movement was recorded on the dynograph when the subject moved a switch to left or right. Four subjects were run in the near-viewing condition first and three in the far-viewing condition first.

Subjects. Three male and four female graduate and undergraduate students with normal vision participated in the experiment.

Results and Discussion
For each subject and under all conditions, the direction of apparent movement of the stimulus agreed with the direction predicted from the sign of the phoria. Results are summarized in table 16.1.

Figure 16.2 is a partial record from one subject taken during the near-viewing condition. It shows (a) the time course of phoria before occlusion shifted, (b) when occlusion shifted, (c) binocular eye movements that occurred, and (d) the subject's report of the direction of apparent movement. The records from other subjects contained more "noise" than the one shown, but the directions of the phoria were clearly indicated. Figure 16.2 and the records from other subjects showed that (a) after the occluding device was placed in front of the eyes, the occluded eye began to

Table 16.1
Direction of phoria and predicted and obtained directions of apparent movement in two conditions.

Viewing condition	Direction of phoria[a]	Direction of apparent movement	
		Predicted	Obtained
Near	exophoric (all subjects)	right (when right eye occluded)	right
		left (when left eye occluded)	left
Far	esophoric (four subjects)	left (when right eye occluded)	left
		right (when left eye occluded)	right
	exophoric (two subjects)	right (when right eye occluded)	right
		left (when left eye occluded)	left
	no measurable phoria (one subject)	none	small apparent movement and nonsystematic direction

a. For six subjects the directions of phoria obtained by means of the Maddox rod and eye movement monitor were in agreement. For one subject, use of the Maddox rod to measure phoria was not possible since he "fused" the "line" with the "dot," i.e., he reported that the line and the dot automatically superimposed for various settings of the variable prism. His eye position records, however, indicated clearly that he was exophoric in both conditions. Figure 16.2 is a partial record from this subject taken during the near-viewing condition.

deviate and the deviation reached an asymptote before occlusion shifted, (b) the magnitude of the saccade that occurred when occlusion shifted was approximately equal to the extent of phoria, and (c) because of the saccade, the line of sight of the newly occluded eye deviated from the stimulus by an amount equal to that of the phoria of the previously occluded eye, i.e., the extent of the phoria was equal for both eyes.

Although the results agree with our predictions, the process upon which the predictions were based does not completely account for the results. The predictions for experiment 1 are based on the apparent direction of the stimulus after the saccade; they do not deal with the apparent direction of the stimulus before the eye movement. We became aware of the incompleteness of our initial thinking because one subject often reported the apparent movement before the saccade took place. At first we thought that this subject was anticipating the percept, but we realized that another principle of visual direction predicts the apparent movement before the eye movement. Experiment 2 was conducted to test the prediction based on this other principle.

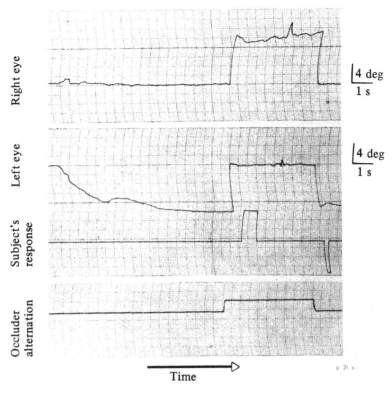

Right eye

4 deg
1 s

Left eye

4 deg
1 s

Subject's response

Occluder alternation

Time

Figure 16.2
Records of eye positions, eye movements, and direction of apparent movement of a stimulus during alternate occlusion. An upper deflection in the tracing indicates movement to the right or occlusion of the right eye; a downward deflection indicates movement to the left or occlusion of the left eye. The occluder was placed prior to the onset of phoria and is not indicated in the record.

Experiment 2

Although some textbooks (e.g., Howard and Templeton 1966; Ogle 1962) only discuss Hering's principles of visual direction for an object stimulating the fovea, the principles account for the apparent direction of other stimuli. Another of Hering's principles states that an angular direction of an object to each eye with respect to the line of sight is projected to the cyclopean eye. If the deviation due to phoria does not change immediately after occlusion is shifted, the line of sight of the previously occluded eye is not directed to the stimulus, i.e., the retinal image of the stimulus will not be on the center of the fovea. The apparent direction will be nonveridical as predicted from two of Hering's

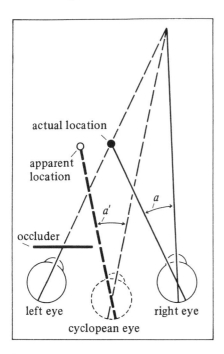

Figure 16.3
Apparent location of a stimulus as a result of exophoria of the right eye immediately after occlusion has been shifted and before eye movements have occurred.

principles taken together, the principle above and the principle invoked for experiment 1.[1]

Figure 16.3 illustrates the expected apparent direction of the stimulus just after occlusion has been shifted. The two eye positions depicted in the figure correspond to the positions of the two eyes before the eye movements observed in the near-viewing condition in experiment 1 have occurred. Before the eye movements are made, the extent of non-veridicality is the same as that after the eye movement. (Compare figure 16.3 to figure 16.1b.) When the occluder is moved from the right eye to the left eye, an apparent leftward movement should occur (this sequence is depicted by figure 16.1a and figure 16.3). The direction of the apparent movement should be opposite when the occluder is moved the other way. Experiment 2 tested the above prediction. The stimulus and experimental setup were the same as those of the near-viewing condition in experiment 1, but occlusion was shifted for only a brief time period such that eye movements would be unlikely to occur. The expectation was that the direction of apparent movement would be the same as that of the near-viewing condition in experiment 1.

Method
The procedure differed from that of experiment 1 in the following way. The direction of apparent movement and eye positions were measured for the near-viewing distance only. No Maddox rod measures of phoria were taken. The rate of occlusion was manually controlled and the duration of shifting the occluder was set for 100 ms on the timer, which was found to produce an actual time of 113 ms. One half of the experimental session entailed five occlusion cycles: during each cycle the occluder was in front of the left eye for 2 s and in front of the right eye for 113 ms.[2] For the other half, the occlusion periods were reversed for the eyes. The subject was told that he might initially see an apparent movement toward one direction then soon after a movement in the opposite direction. He was instructed to indicate the direction of the first movement.

Subjects.   The subjects for experiment 2 were six of the seven who had participated in experiment 1.

Results and Discussion
The direction of the reported apparent movement as a function of phoria when occlusion was shifted was the same as that for the near-viewing condition in experiment 1 for all subjects. Two subjects showed almost no change in eye position for the briefly nonoccluded eye during the experimental session. Figure 16.4 is a partial record typical of one of these two subjects. The records for the remaining four subjects indicated occasional small saccades but all of their records showed instances of no eye movement when occlusion was briefly shifted. All subjects reported directions of apparent movement that agreed with the prediction when there was no eye movement associated with the shifting of occlusion. Thus, the results confirmed the prediction concerning the direction of apparent movement based on Hering's principles of visual direction invoked for experiment 2 together with that invoked for experiment 1.

Considering the results of experiments 1 and 2 together, we can now give a more complete account of the direction of apparent movement found in experiment 1. Before occlusion shifts from one eye to the other, the stimulus is seen in a nonveridical direction owing to phoria. The extent and direction of nonveridicality can be specified by the principle of visual direction invoked for experiment 1, which states that an object stimulating the fovea is seen on a line passing through the cyclopean eye and the intersection of the two lines of sight. When occlusion shifts there is a displacement of the apparent direction of the stimulus according to the account given above for the results of experiment 2. If the time duration between the shift of occlusion is longer than that of experiment 2, a saccade equal in magnitude to the extent of phoria occurs, and this

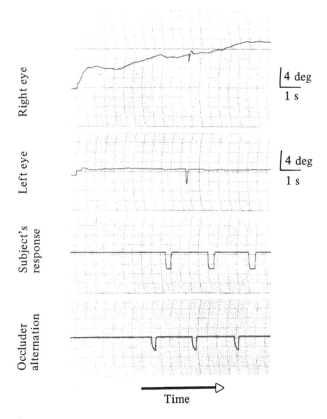

Figure 16.4
Records of eye positions and direction of apparent movement of a stimulus during brief periods of nonocclusion of the right eye and occlusion of the left eye.

saccade moves the image of the stimulus onto the fovea of the non-occluded eye. The magnitude of the saccade corresponds to the magnitude of the image displacement on the retina; thus the apparent direction of the stimulus remains the same, i.e., "compensation" for a retinal image movement occurred.

Experiment 3

Although experiments 1 and 2 dealt only with the direction of the apparent movement, the principles of visual direction considered for those experiments can predict the magnitude of the apparent movement as well. For our experimental situation, the magnitude should be larger when phoria is greater. Experiment 3 tested this prediction.

Method

Apparatus. The experimental stimulus, occluders, and viewing distance were the same as those used in experiment 2. The extent and direction of phoria were measured by means of the Maddox rod. We used a Maddox rod to measure phoria instead of the eye movement monitor because the latter would have involved considerably more time.

Two additional pieces of apparatus were required to record the subject's judgments of the magnitude of apparent movement. One was a 30 cm metal rod to which a fixed and a variable collar were attached. The variable collar could be moved to some distance from the fixed collar to indicate the magnitude of apparent movement. The other was a pair of LEDs symmetrically placed 1 cm on either side of the median plane, 25 cm from the front surface of the eyes. A timer switched on each LED alternately for periods of 5 s. This stimulus arrangement simulated the apparent movement that occurs in the experimental situation. It was used to familiarize subjects with the use of the metal rod for reporting the magnitude of apparent movement. A chinrest replaced the biteboard used in experiments 1 and 2.

Procedure. Before the experimental session, the subject observed monocularly the pair of LEDs as they were alternately illuminated five times each. The subject then indicated his estimate of the average magnitude of apparent movement by moving the variable collar along the rod away from the fixed collar. This procedure was repeated four times. The experimental session consisting of eight trials followed immediately. Each trial involved a measure of phoria for each eye and a period of five complete cycles of alternate occlusion. One cycle consisted of each eye being occluded for 5 s. The subject was instructed to report the direction of movement of the stimulus when it first occurred for each cycle. After each trial the subject reported his estimate of the average magnitude of apparent movement for the five cycles, using the collar of the metal rod. In four trials the right eye was initially occluded; in the other four trials the left eye was initially occluded.

Subjects. Six male and six female undergraduates with normal vision were paid to participate in the experiment. None of these subjects had participated in experiments 1 and 2.

Results and Discussion

For the experimental situation used in experiment 3, the principles of visual direction predict that the magnitude of apparent movement should be directly proportional to the extent of the phoria. This prediction was confirmed by the results of experiment 3.

According to their Maddox rod settings, seven subjects were consistently exophoric on all trials, three were consistently esophoric on all trials and two were exophoric on some trials but esophoric on others. Nine subjects' reports of the direction of apparent movement agreed in all cases with the predicted direction, but those of the three remaining subjects did not always agree. (The results from these subjects are discussed in more detail shortly.) To determine the degree of association between the predicted magnitude (or the extent of phoria) and the actual magnitude of apparent movement, the mean values of these variables were computed for each subject. The mean extent of phoria was computed, positive values were assigned to exophoria and negative values to esophoria. The predicted magnitude of apparent movement for each subject was computed by using the mean extent of phoria given the assumption that the perceived distance of the stimulus coincided with the actual distance. Also, the mean value of the magnitude of the apparent movement was computed, assigning a sign to each report of magnitude depending on which eye was occluded at the beginning of a trial. A positive sign was assigned to the magnitude when the direction reported was that predicted by exophoria and a negative sign when it was that predicted by esophoria. The Pearson r between the extents of phoria and the reported magnitude of apparent movement or that between the predicted and observed magnitude of apparent movement was 0.95 (d.f. $= 10$; $p < 0.001$) across subjects. The slope and intercept of the regression line for the extent of apparent movement on the predicted extent were 1.09 and -0.48, respectively.

As noted earlier, for three subjects the direction of apparent movement did not always agree with that predicted. A possible explanation for the disagreement is that the direction of phoria might have changed between the time the Maddox rod was used and when the occluder was shifted for the first time, i.e., these subjects' direction of phoria may have been unstable. To check the correctness of this explanation, these three subjects participated in a further experiment which involved monitoring eye position with a procedure almost identical to that used for the near-viewing condition in experiment 1. It differed from the general procedure of experiment 3 in that the direction of apparent movement was obtained throughout a trial. The results indicated that, when the direction of phoria was obvious, the reported directions of apparent movement were consistent with those predicted. Thus the results of these subjects support the predictions of experiment 3, and what appeared as a contradiction in their earlier data can be dismissed.

General Discussion

Phoria, in conjunction with Hering's principles of visual direction, predicts the direction and magnitude of apparent movement of a single stimulus seen when the two eyes alternate in viewing it. When a subject is exophoric, the apparent movement is in the same direction as that of the shifting of the occluder, for instance, when the occluder shifts to the right eye, the apparent movement is toward the right. When a subject is esophoric, the direction is reversed. Furthermore, the magnitude of apparent movement covaries with the extent of phoria. The apparent movement occurs as soon as the occluder shifts from one eye to the other. If the shift of occlusion is not too brief, saccades equal in magnitude to that of the phoria occur to bring the retinal image of the stimulus onto the fovea of the now nonoccluded eye. The apparent direction of the stimulus remains the same before and after the saccade because of the visual compensation mechanism in which eye position is taken into account.

The results of the three experiments provided strong confirmation for the predictions based on Hering's principles of visual direction. A counterintuitive aspect of the predictions is that the direction and magnitude of apparent movement are a function of the position of the nonseeing eye. The results, however, clearly indicated that the position of the occluded eye as well as that of the nonoccluded eye determined the two nonveridical visual directions which led to the apparent movement. The process which gives rise to apparent movement reported in our study is based upon a change in egocentric perceived direction.

In the present study, the direction and magnitude of apparent movement were measured but not visual direction per se, since our primary concern was to explain the apparent movement that occurs in our stimulus situation. If one were concerned with agreement between visual direction and predicted visual direction based on Hering's principles, a more appropriate measurement would involve pointing responses or a more direct directional judgment. For an example of such studies, see Ono et al. (1972) or Ono and Nakamizo (1977).

Notes

This research was supported by Grant A0296 from the National Research Council of Canada. The impetus for these experiments was provided by a communication with Irvin Rock concerning visual direction. The authors wish to thank their many colleagues in Perception at York University for their helpful comments on an earlier version of this paper. We would also like to thank C. Reid for her help in conducting the experiments.

1. Given the principle stated for experiment 2, the egocentric direction of the stimulus would be indeterminate, i.e., the projection of angle a (figure 16.3) to the cyclopean eye would be indeterminate without use being made of the principle invoked for experiment 1. This principle establishes the line from the cyclopean eye to the intersect of the two lines of sight. Angle a' is formed with respect to this line and the other line which specifies the extent of a' is the predicted, apparent direction.

2. For one subject the duration was set for 200 ms because he reported two stimuli with 113 ms. The reason for this is not clear, but with a setting of 200 ms he saw one stimulus. His record is shown in figure 16.4.

References

Fry G. A., 1950. "Visual perception of space" *American Journal of Optometry and Archives of American Academy of Optometry* **27** (11) 531–553.

Hering F., 1942. *Spatial Sense and Movements of the Eye* translated by A. Radde (Baltimore, Md.: American Academy of Optometry).

Howard I. P., Templeton W. B., 1966. *Human Spatial Orientation* (New York: John Wiley).

Morgan M. W., 1968. "Accommodation and vergence" *American Journal of Optometry and Archives of American Academy of Optometry* **45** 417–454.

Ogle K. N., 1962. "Spatial localization according to direction" in *The Eye* Ed. H. Davson (New York: Academic Press) pp. 219–245.

Ogle K. N., 1964. *Researches in Binocular Vision* (New York: Hafner).

Ono H., 1975. "Directions of objects seen from the cyclopean eye" *Saensu* (Japanese edition of *Scientific American*) **5** (4) 88–99; the English translation appeared as Department of Psychology Reports, number 29, York University, Toronto, 1976.

Ono H., Nakamizo S., 1977. "Saccadic eye movements during changes in fixation to stimuli at different distances" *Vision Research* **17** 233–238.

Ono H., Wilkinson D., Muter P., Mitson L., 1972. "Apparent movement and change in perceived location of a stimulus produced by a change in accommodative vergence" *Perception and Psychophysics* **12** 187–192.

Chapter 17

Apparent Movement in Tridimensional Space

Fred Attneave and Gene Block

According to Korte's (1915) third law of apparent movement, an increase in the spatial separation between two successive stimuli must be accompanied by an increase in their temporal separation for an optimal appearance of movement to occur. This principle has been repeatedly verified, usually for stimuli in the frontal plane. Some years ago, however, Corbin (1942) raised an interesting question: Is the spatial separation to which Korte's law applies a matter of retinal distance or of distance in perceived space? He dissociated proximal from distal separation by varying the slant at which his Ss viewed the screen on which stimuli appeared. Shrinking retinal separation in this manner, while holding physical separation constant, seemed to have no effect whatever on the temporal threshold for optimal movement, whereas variation in physical separation (either in the frontal plane or in depth) yielded a typical Korte's law relationship.

If Corbin's results can be taken at face value, they strongly support the view that an approximately isotropic tridimensional model of physical space is constructed internally (see Attneave, 1972), and that apparent movement is based on events within this analog model. We have repeatedly encountered psychologists who are reluctant to accept this conclusion, and who suppose that Corbin's experiment must have contained some catch or loophole that would allow a peripheral explanation of the results. It may be noted, for example, that Corbin's stimuli appeared on a well-defined rectangular screen which was horizontally contracted on the retina when viewed at a slant; therefore, the important variable might have been retinal separation relative to retinal frame width [cf. the experiments of J. F. Brown (1931) on frame of reference and perceived velocity]. If this were the case, the results would still be interesting, but would not necessarily require the assumption that perceived objects are mapped into a tridimensional analog space. A similar and perhaps more serious criticism is that the stimuli themselves (bright horizontal lines) were likewise contracted retinally under the slant conditions, and it is known otherwise

Originally published in *Perception & Psychophysics* 13, 2 (1973): 301–307. Reprinted with permission.

that decreasing stimulus size in a constant frontal plane, like decreasing brightness, increases the time interval required for apparent movement (see Koffka, 1935, pp. 289–298).

Considering that the issue here is of basic importance for a theory of spatial representation, we were led to do the following studies. They are essentially similar to Corbin's, but also entail our best efforts to eliminate possibilities for attributing positive results to peripheral mechanisms.

Experiment I

Method

Subjects. Six paid student volunteers from the University of Oregon served as Ss. In both this and the subsequent experiments, a preliminary screening session was held for each prospective S. About half of those screened were rejected, either because their judgments were excessively variable or (what was usually the same thing) because their time thresholds for apparent movement showed no clear separation between different distances in the frontal plane. Screening sessions never included any of the critical conditions involving depth manipulations.

Apparatus and Experimental Conditions. The two stimulus lights were mounted at eye level, 6 ft (1.82 m) in front of the seated S on separate movable posts which stood on a table. Each consisted of a neon bulb enclosed in a small black pillbox lined with reflective foil. In the front cover of the box, a .2 × 1 cm horizontal slit was cut; behind this was a diffusing surface of tracing paper.

The luminance of these stimulus lines was about 5.5 cd/m^2. The experimental room was illuminated by a single $7\frac{1}{2}$-W red-coated incandescent bulb behind the S and outside his field of view, which produced an average luminance of the order of .015 cd/m^2 in the S's field. This level of illumination was not great enough to suppress apparent movement between the stimuli, but was sufficient to allow their spatial locations to be clearly perceived.

The stimuli were positioned at either a 4-in. (10.16-cm) or an 8-in. (20.32-cm) separation in the frontal plane or, in the critical condition, at an 8-in. separation on a diagonal such that the visual angle between them was equated to that of the 4-in. separation in the frontal plane (3 deg 11 min). The three conditions are shown superimposed in Fig. 17.1. Although the plane of movement was rotated by about 60 deg in the diagonal condition, the light boxes were not themselves rotated; thus the S still viewed the stimulus apertures orthogonally. In the diagonal condition, different box covers were used, with apertures altered slightly in size to

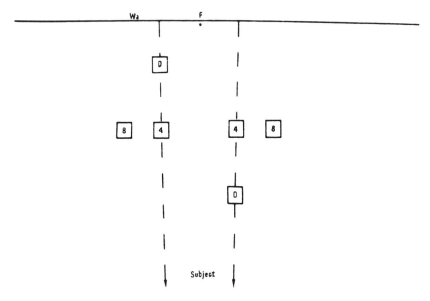

Figure 17.1
The three stimulus arrangements of Experiment I are superimposed in this diagram to show
how the 8-in. separation of the diagonal stimuli subtended the same visual angle as the 4-in.
frontal separation. The S is located outside the drawing, at the intersection of the dashed
lines.

compensate for the changes in distance from the O; however, these cor-
rections were so minute that they could hardly have made any difference.
Six inches behind the (frontal plane) stimuli was the black wall of the
experimental room, on which a small luminous fixation point was located
2 in. below the bisector of the angle formed by the stimuli.

Stimulus durations and intervals were controlled by Hunter decade
timers.

Procedure.   On each presentation, the two stimuli, of 50 msec duration,
were separated by an interval that varied from trial to trial. Three such
presentations, 2 sec apart, made up a trial; thus, the S saw a light line that
moved three times in a particular direction, provided the variable interval
was great enough to permit apparent movement. The use of several presentations per trial seemed to contribute to the stability of results.

The interval or asynchrony between stimuli, which will be described
throughout this article in onset-to-onset terms, was varied by an ascending method of limits. On the first trial of an ascending series, the interval
was set 10, 20, or 30 msec (randomly decided) below the value at which
the S had reported movement on the immediately preceding series

(except at the beginning of a block, in which case a safely low starting point was used); from this level, the interval was increased by either 5- or 10-msec steps (randomly decided) until movement was again reported.

The first day was a screening session for all prospective Ss and served further as a practice session for those who were continued. The S was first reminded of the commonly seen signs and advertising displays in which discrete lights produce apparent movement, and was told in general terms that our object was to study the conditions under which such movement occurs. He was shown examples of movement at optimal time intervals in the experimental situation and was told to adopt as stable a criterion as he could for what constituted "good" or "believable" movement. It was explained that he might see movement on the first trial of a series, but that more typically he would have to wait for some irregular number of trials before movement appeared. Thereafter, he was run for as many threshold determinations in the 4- and 8-in. frontal plane conditions as the hour session permitted.

In each of the two subsequent experimental sessions, the S was initially adapted for 10 min to the room illumination. Thresholds for movement were then obtained under all three conditions—4-in. frontal, 8-in. frontal, and 8-in. diagonal—which were counterbalanced over 12 blocks per session. Since 5 thresholds were determined in each block, a total of 40 thresholds per condition per S were obtained in all.

The spatial locations of the stimuli were reasonably obvious under the experimental conditions. All the Ss reported that they saw the movement in depth in the diagonal condition.

Results

If the threshold for the 8-in. diagonal condition were equal to that for the 4-in. frontal condition, we would conclude that it depended entirely on proximal separation, whereas if it were equal to that for the 8-in. frontal condition, we would conclude that it depended entirely on distal separation. If values of zero and unity, respectively, are assigned to these unequivocal extremes, any result obtained can be expressed in comparable terms, i.e., as a Brunswik ratio with an immediately obvious interpretation.

Results are shown for individual Ss in Table 17.1. With one exception (a case of "over-constancy"), the Brunswik ratios have values between zero and one, their mean being .77 with a standard error of .12. This differs from zero (no constancy) by a $t(5) = 6.50$, $p < .005$, and from unity (perfect constancy) by a $t(5) = 1.97$, which is not significant at the .05 level but is large enough to make us doubt the null hypothesis. On the latter point, our results are not quite as unequivocal as Corbin's, which showed practically no deviation from perfect constancy. On the major issue, however, the conclusion is clear enough: apparent movement de-

Table 17.1
Stimulus onset asynchrony (in milliseconds) at threshold for apparent movement: Experiment I

	Stimulus arrangement		
S	4-in. Frontal	8-in. Diagonal	8-in. Frontal
1	95	102 (.76)*	104
2	113	119 (1.24)	117
3	154	172 (.78)	177
4	173	195 (.64)	207
5	123	128 (.82)	130
6	106	112 (.35)	122
Means	128	138 (.77)	143

$$* \text{Each parenthetical value is a "Brunswik Ratio"} = \frac{t(8\text{-in. diagonal}) - t(4\text{-in. frontal})}{t(8\text{-in. frontal}) - t(4\text{-in. frontal})}$$

pends on perceived separation, even with retinal separation, retinal size, and retinal frame of reference held constant.

Experiment II

This experiment was designed to determine whether the manipulation of apparent separation by purely pictorial means could likewise affect the time interval required for apparent movement. Since the preceding experiment (like Corbin's) was carried out with binocular viewing, in the diagonal condition the two stimuli differed in retinal disparity. It might be argued that the increase in temporal threshold was *directly* due to this disparity difference and had nothing to do with phenomenal separation, particularly in view of the Barlow, Blakemore, and Pettigrew (1967) finding that there are disparity-specific units in the primary visual cortex. On the other hand, if phenomenal separation is the important variable, it should not matter how the separation came to be so represented.

Method

Subjects. Six new Ss were employed; they were screened as in Experiment I.

Apparatus. The stimuli were viewed monocularly in an enclosed display box. Under *all* conditions, they were located in the frontal plane, 47 cm from S's eye, but in the critical conditions, a perspective drawing was used to make them appear to lie in an oblique plane. This is shown, together

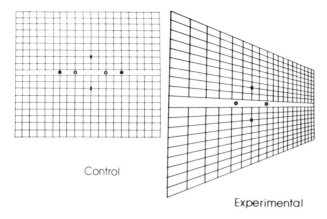

Control

Experimental

Figure 17.2
The two pictorial displays used in Experiment II. The 4-cm separation is shown by open circles; the 8-cm separation is shown by closed circles.

with the control drawing which did not produce an appearance of depth, in Fig. 17.2. These two patterns were equal in length (19 cm), in average width (15.8 cm), and in number of lines or textural elements on each dimension, as well as in the number of textural elements separating lights 4 cm apart. They were drawn, on a black ground, with fluorescent threads which glowed red (approximately the same hue as the neon stimulus lights) under ultraviolet illumination. The stimuli between which movement appeared were 2-mm apertures illuminated by neon lamps at an intensity of about 225 cd/m², located either 4 or 8 cm apart in a central alley unobstructed by lines, as shown in Fig. 17.2.

Procedure. Preliminaries of screening, instruction, adaptation, and practice were essentially as in Experiment I.

Each trial consisted of a 2-sec period during which the two stimulus lights regularly alternated. Stimulus duration was always 50 msec; inter-stimulus intervals, which were the same in both directions, varied from trial to trial. When this interval was adequate, the light appeared to oscillate rapidly back and forth (rather than to move repeatedly in the same direction as in Experiment I). At shorter intervals, both lights appeared to stay on, with some flicker, throughout the trial. Thresholds for movement were found by the ascending method of limits used in Experiment I, with this minor modification: the starting point of each ascending series was tied to the lower of the two preceding threshold determinations, not always to the one immediately preceding as before.

Again, there were two control conditions and one experimental condition: the stimuli were separated by either 4 or 8 cm in the control display, or by 4 cm in the experimental display. The parallel between this and the design of Experiment I is not as exact as it may appear at first glance. Whereas the S could be expected to perceive depth relationships more or less veridically before, in Experiment II depth was entirely illusory and the magnitude of the illusion was not known in advance. In theory, the experimental display was a projection of a rectangular grid rotated approximately 70 deg from the frontal plane. If the plane had been perceived at this angle, extents along the central alley would presumably have appeared about three times as great as retinally equivalent extents in the control display. It was evident from the beginning that the perceived depth effect would really be much weaker than the hypothetical; hence, the two control separations were varied by a factor of two instead of three. Note that the separation of 8 cm was chosen quite arbitrarily to provide a second anchor point for the Korte's law relationship in the apparent frontal plane and was not supposed to be equated on any basis to the experimental condition.

The major question asked by the experiment was simply whether the 4-cm experimental condition would require significantly longer time intervals for apparent movement than the 4-cm control condition. However, to have any expectations about the magnitude of such a difference, we needed to know, at least roughly, how much the phenomenal separation between the lights was increased by the perspective gradient. Therefore, we spent a few minutes at the end of each session having the S make judgments of the depth effect. He judged the separation between the lights (simultaneously on) in both the 4-cm conditions by (a) drawing lines of appropriate length on paper, in the first two sessions, and subsequently (b) marking off the perceived distance with a slider on a dowel. He also (c) judged the slant of the apparent plane in the experimental display by setting a binocularly viewed stick orthogonal to it; see Attneave and Frost (1969) and Attneave (1972) for details of this method.

The three conditions were counterbalanced over 12 blocks within each of four sessions, essentially as in Experiment I except that each block included six instead of five threshold determinations. In the first and third sessions, the displays were oriented horizontally, as in Fig. 17.2, whereas in the second and fourth they were oriented vertically, so that the experimental display looked somewhat like a floor or ground surface. Two fixation regions were provided, equidistant from the two lights and 2 cm to either side of the path between them. The S alternated between these two fixation regions from one ascending series to the next, to minimize local adaptation effects. (This was also the reason for using fixation regions, bounded by four points, rather than single fixation points.) These procedural variables were of some incidental interest in their own right, since the horizontal movement was presumably interhemispheric, whereas the

Table 17.2
Thresholds for apparent movement compared with apparent stimulus separations: Experiment II

	Threshold for Apparent Movement (Onset Asynchrony in Msec) by Condition				Judged Separation (Cm)			Judged Slant (Deg)	
S	C4	E4	C8	β^*	C4	E4	γ^{**}	E4	$\lambda^\dagger$
1	174	193	220	.41	3.3	3.7	.12	49	.52
2	97	110	146	.25	3.3	3.8	.15	36	.24
3	86	95	130	.22	2.9	3.9	.35	31	.17
4	115	136	206	.23	3.5	4.5	.29	33	.19
5	146	170	213	.37	3.6	5.7	.31	41	.33
6	131	144	221	.14	3.3	3.7	.12	34	.21
Mean	125	141	189.3	.27	3.32	4.05	.22	37	.28

$$^*\beta = \frac{t(E4) - t(C4)}{t(C8) - t(C4)}$$

$$^{**}\gamma = \frac{\text{Judged Separation (E4)}}{\text{Judged Separation (C4)}} - 1$$

$^\dagger\lambda = \text{Secant Judged Slant (E4)} - 1$

vertical movement was presumably represented in either the left or the right hemisphere, depending on the fixation region. However, a careful inspection of the data yielded no hint that either of these variables (inter- vs intrahemisphere or left vs right hemisphere) make any difference; therefore, they will not be considered further.

Results
In the data summarized in Table 17.2, it may first be noted that every one of the Ss required longer intervals to see movement in the 4-cm experimental condition (E4) than in the 4-cm control condition (C4). To make Ss more comparable, we calculated for each a pseudo-Brunswik ratio, β, which tells where the experimental threshold fell as a proportion of the way between the thresholds for the two control conditions. It is not a real Brunswik ratio, since a hypothetical value of unity would in no way signify veridical perception. However, a hypothetical value of zero would mean that thresholds were identical for the C4 and E4 conditions. The obtained distribution of β values differs from zero by a t(5) of 6.97, p < .001. This comparison establishes firmly the major point that when *phenomenal* separation is varied by pictorial context, the time interval required for apparent movement varies with it, even though *physical* separation and *retinal* separation are both held constant.

Let us now look at the magnitude of the effect. The average value of β is .27, which means that the experimental threshold is 27% of the way between the 4- and 8-cm control thresholds, about what we would expect (by linear interpolation) from a separation of slightly more than 5 cm in the apparent frontal plane, or (incidentally, owing to the particular separations used) from a 4-cm separation that was overestimated by 27% because of the depth illusion. According to the somewhat crude judgments of separation in the C4 and E4 conditions, the latter was overestimated (relative to the former, which showed a strong constant error that is of no great interest to us) by about 22% on the average; this proportional overestimation is called "γ" in Table 17.2. The mean β value of .27, then, is just a little greater than we would expect from the judged separations. An additional, indirect measure of overestimation in the experimental display is given by the slant judgments. The stimulus plane was judged to deviate from the frontal plane by an average of 37 deg—considerably less than the 70 deg or so that the perspective gradient was drawn to depict. A small extent on such an apparently slanting plane (taken in a direction orthogonal to the apparent axis of rotation) should appear greater than a frontal plane extent subtending the same visual angle by a factor approximately equal to the secant of the slant. The proportional overestimation of the experimental separation inferred on this basis, designated "λ" in Table 17.2, has a mean value of .28, which is almost exactly equal to the mean value of .27 for β.

These correspondences between means are as close as anyone could reasonably expect, but we can further ask whether those Ss whose thresholds for apparent movement were most modified by the perspective display were the ones who got the strongest illusions of depth from it. Individual values of β do not covary with the obtained judgments of separation: $r_{\gamma\beta} = -.04$. Judged slant, however, is a remarkably good predictor: $r_{\lambda\beta} = .89$. Even with the very small N of 6 (df = 4), this relationship is significant at the .02 level. It appears that the slant judgments were simply a great deal more reliable than the separation judgments.

Experiment III

For the sake of generality, we wished to untie retinal from phenomenal separation by another, quite obvious operation, i.e., by varying the viewing distance of stimuli in the frontal plane. This was done under conditions roughly similar to those of Experiment I.

Method

Subjects.   Six new Ss were selected as before.

Apparatus. The stimuli were viewed binocularly in a room illuminated dimly with red light, as in Experiment I. Again, the stimulus lights were mounted in pillboxes on posts above a table. They were circular apertures of either $\frac{1}{4}$ in. (.64 cm) or $\frac{1}{2}$ in. (1.27 cm) illuminated at an intensity of about 5.5 cd/m². These were located at eye level, always in the frontal plane, and were horizontally separated by either 4 in. (10.16 cm) or 8 in. (20.32 cm). A small luminous fixation point was located in the same plane, either 1 in. (2.54 cm) or 2 in. (3.08 cm) below the midpoint of the two lights. The S viewed the stimuli from a distance of either 4 ft (1.22 m) or 8 ft (2.44 m).

Procedure. Screening, practice, etc., were essentially as in the two previous experiments. Only the two control conditions were employed in the preliminary session.

Each trial consisted of a 4-sec period during which the two stimuli, each of 50 msec duration, were regularly alternated (as in Experiment II, except for the length of the period). An ascending method of limits was used as before, except that interstimulus interval was increased always in 10-msec steps and that each ascending series was started 10, 20, 30, or 40 msec (randomly decided) below the lower of the last two thresholds determined under the same conditions.

At the closer (4-ft) viewing distance, the smaller stimuli ($\frac{1}{4}$-in. diam) were separated by either 4 or 8 in., with fixation 1 in. below their midpoint. These two conditions, designated C4S and C8S, may conveniently be thought of 25 control conditions, establishing the frame of reference for the others. In Condition F8L, the S sat at the farther viewing distance (8 ft) and was shown the larger stimuli ($\frac{1}{2}$-in. diam) at a separation of 8 in., fixating 2 in. below their midpoint. Thus, F8L was equivalent, in terms of the *proximal* configuration provided by the stimulus lights, to C4S, since in both conditions the two stimuli were separated by the same visual angle (4 deg 56 min) and individually subtended the same visual angle (18 min); in other words, extents in C4S were doubled in F8L to compensate for the doubling of viewing distance. Condition F8L was physically equivalent to C8S in stimulus separation, but not in stimulus size; note that the size variable prevents us from setting up two control conditions of which one is retinally identical and the other physically identical to an experimental condition at a different viewing distance. Therefore, a fourth condition, F8S, was added; this was the same as F8L except that it used the smaller ($\frac{1}{4}$-in.) stimuli. It was, therefore, *physically* identical, in both size and separation of stimuli, to C8S. Comparing results from F8S and F8L will show the effect of doubling stimulus diameter (i.e., quadrupling area) with separation and viewing distance constant.

These four conditions were counterbalanced over 16 blocks (a block being five threshold determinations) in each of four sessions.

Table 17.3
Stimulus onset asynchrony (in milliseconds) at threshold for apparent movement: Experiment III

S	C4S	F8L		F8S		C8S
		Condition				
1	90	96	(.27)*	103	(.54)	115
2	119	135	(.27)	161	(.68)	181
3	120	132	(.33)	139	(.52)	156
4	98	107	(.27)	115	(.53)	131
5	110	123	(.39)	132	(.63)	144
6	116	133	(.34)	148	(.64)	166
Mean	109	121	(.31)	133	(.59)	149

*Parenthetical values are Brunswik ratios; cf. Table 17.1.

Results

Doubling the separation of the lights at the closer viewing distance caused the mean threshold for movement to increase from 109 to 149 msec, as Table 17.3 shows. These values (or, rather, their counterparts for individual Ss) provide the zero and unity points, respectively, for "Brunswik ratios" describing the results of the other two conditions. For F8L, the condition of retinal equivalence at the farther distance, the mean ratio is .31. Though rather small, this is quite significantly different from zero [t(5) = 15.7, p < .001]; therefore, we can again conclude that Korte's third law involves some degree of extent constancy, in this case over variation in viewing distance. For Condition F8S, in which proximal stimulus size was allowed to vary normally with viewing distance, the mean ratio increases significantly [t(4) = 9.4, p < .001] to .59; this difference between F8S and F8L shows the effect of doubling stimulus diameter with separation and viewing distance constant. Condition F8S also differs quite significantly from C8S (i.e., the mean ratio of .59 is reliably different from unity: t(5) = 15.2, p < .001). This difference, with *physical* size and separation equated, shows that constancy was considerably less than perfect for the extents pertaining to Korte's third law.

General Discussion

These three experiments unequivocally support Corbin's major thesis: apparent movement occurs at a postconstancy level of the perceptual system. The only discrepancies between our results and Corbin's, or between the results of one and another of our own studies, have to do with the amount or degree of constancy that is involved.

Corbin found essentially perfect constancy for the separations pertaining to Korte's law. So did Kahneman, in an ingenious study that has not been published in detail.[1] He displayed stimuli for apparent movement at the front of a large room, and Ss seated at various distances and viewing angles rated the goodness of the movement. Ratings varied systematically with the physical spacing and timing of the stimuli, but *not* with the S's location in the room. Since neither Corbin nor Kahneman compared conditions that were strictly matched with respect to proximal stimulation, they left open the possibility (never a very plausible one) that peripheral factors of some sort might account for the effects. The present studies rather thoroughly rule out this possibility and show that the representation of distances in tridimensional space is antecedent to the occurrence of apparent movement. Once having firmly established this conclusion, however, we may admit and even emphasize that the manipulations to which we resorted were not as natural, or as representative of real-life situations, as those of Corbin or Kahneman: e.g., outside the laboratory retinal size does *not* stay constant as distance changes.

We cannot be sure that perfect constancy (with respect to the Korte's law relationship) did or did not obtain in Experiment I, since the mean Brunswik ratio was less than unity, but not significantly so. In Experiment III, however, the results were clear: with retinal stimulus size controlled, the degree of constancy (.31), though highly significant, was very far from perfect. When retinal size varied "naturally" with distance, constancy was considerably greater (.59), but still by no means perfect.

The concept of constancy does not apply literally to Experiment II, in which the true physical separations were beside the point. However, that experiment showed an exceedingly close agreement between the temporal thresholds for movement and the picture-based *phenomenal* separations between stimuli in space, particularly when the latter were inferred from slant judgments. This suggests that we were remiss in not likewise obtaining judgments of spatial separation in Experiments I and III. We did not do so because it seemed clear, from casual observation, that any such judgments would have been practically veridical. However, phenomenal extent can be quite an elusive variable to pin down experimentally—as many investigators of the size-distance invariance hypothesis, for example, have discovered. It is entirely possible for an O to judge, correctly, that a pair of large circles and a pair of small circles are each separated by about 8 in., and nevertheless to perceive the larger ones as closer together. Likewise, large objects appear to move more slowly than small ones. It seems likely (since peripheral explanations of apparent movement have been otherwise disconfirmed) that the effect of stimulus size on apparent movement, as between Conditions F8L and F8S of Experiment III, is not a direct effect, but one mediated by phenomenal separation; cf.

Koffka's (1935, pp. 286–298) discussion of Korte's laws in relationship to the work of J. F. Brown and others. Why constancy was at best so imperfect in Experiment III remains somewhat puzzling. It is possible that in the course of a long session during which the S's attention is restricted to a relatively small segment of his surroundings, the phenomenal distance that he assigns to the focal objects may regress toward some preferred or normal value, like the "specific distance" at which the Ss of Gogel (1969) locate objects under conditions of reduction.

Although it is not essential to the purpose of these studies, we should like to understand more clearly than we do the mechanism that underlies Korte's third law in any case. Why, in either a tridimensional medium or otherwise, do greater spatial separations require greater time intervals for apparent movement? The superficially obvious answer is that the velocity of movement through the representational space is limited, so that an object needs more time to traverse a long distance than a short one. This explanation has serious difficulties, however. It assumes (or seems to assume) that the movement starts at the time of the first stimulus and ends at the time of the second. But how is the perceptual system to "know" in what direction (or at what velocity) to move the object until *after* the second stimulus has occurred? It might be supposed that anticipation, based on repeated trials, enables the system to get the movement under way at once; in that case, Korte's third law would depend upon the predictability of the events. In fact, it does not: our colleague, Professor Jacob Beck, has unpublished data that show clearly the Korte's law relationship under conditions in which the S could anticipate neither the direction nor the distance of the second stimulus from the first. The only remaining possibility that we can see for explaining Korte's law in terms of a moving process (such as an image of the object that moves continuously through the representational space from the initial to the terminal locus) would involve the postulation of a peripheral memory store in which both temporal and spatial information are accumulated over a brief time-span before being mapped (matched?) in the representational system.

The study of Shepard and Metzler (1971) on mental rotation and subsequent unpublished studies by Shepard and his collaborators show beyond any reasonable doubt that when a mental image is rotated, either in the frontal plane or tridimensionally, it *moves continuously* through intermediate positions in going from one aspect to another. Our results, along with those of Corbin and Kahneman, show clearly that apparent movement occurs between loci in a tridimensional phenomenal space. This may very well be the same medium as that in which mental images are rotated. We cannot be at all certain, however, that the apparent movement itself is represented in an analog manner, by a process that moves through the medium. One of several alternatives is that there are higher-level "movement detectors" that are stimulated by changes of locus in the representational medium; some velocity-tuning of such detectors might account for Korte's third law. Whether apparent movement is *modeled* or *described* (or modeled before it is described) is an interesting issue, which we hope to clarify in further investigation.

Notes

This research was supported by NIMH Grant MH 20 449-01 for "Studies on Spatial Representation."
1. Personal communication from Daniel Kahneman. The study is described briefly in a paper, "On Masking and Motion," that Kahneman presented at the International Psychological Conference, London, 1969.

References

Attneave, F. The representation of physical space. In A. W. Melton (Ed.), *Coding processes in human memory*. Washington, D.C.: Winston, 1972.

Attneave, F., and Frost, R. The determination of perceived tridimensional orientation by minimum criteria. Perception & Psychophysics, 1969, 6, 391–396.

Barlow, H. B., Blakemore, C., and Pettigrew, J. D. The neural mechanism of binocular depth discrimination. Journal of Physiology, 1967, 193, 327–342.

Brown, J. F. The visual perception of velocity. Psychologische Forschung, 1931, 14, 199–232.

Corbin, H. H. The perception of grouping and apparent movement in visual depth. Archives of Psychology, 1942, No. 273.

Gogel, W. C. The sensing of retinal size. Vision Research, 1969, 9, 1079–1094.

Gogel, W. C. Perception of off-sized objects. Perception & Psychophysics, 1969, 5, 7–9.

Koffka, K. *Principles of Gestalt psychology*. New York: Harcourt Brace, 1935.

Korte, A. Kinematoskopische Untersuchungen. Zeitschrift für Psychologie, 1915, 194–296.

Shepard, R. N., and Metzler, J. Mental rotation of three-dimensional objects. Science, 1971, 171, 701–703.

Chapter 18
Motion Aftereffects and Retinal Motion
Arien Mack, James Hill, and Steven Kahn

Introduction

Observation of a pattern moving in one direction will, after a period of time, cause a subsequently viewed stationary pattern to appear to move in the opposite direction. This motion aftereffect (MAE) has been intensively studied. Nevertheless, there remains a question about the nature of the adaptation process which underlies the effect. Is the adaptation a response to retinal motion or is it rather a response to motion processes which occur at later stages in the processing of visual information? An answer to this question may be of importance because the motion signal which accounts for the aftereffect is likely to be the basic signal to which the visual system responds.

The evidence is conflicting. Data reported by Anstis and Gregory (1965) and Tolhurst and Hart (1972) are consistent with a strictly retinal motion account of the aftereffect. Both sets of investigators found that retinal motion produced by the tracking of a moving point over a stationary grating caused an MAE that was indistinguishable from that which followed fixation of a stationary point while a moving grating drifted across the visual field. Furthermore, Anstis and Gregory found no MAE in subjects after a period in which the moving grating itself was tracked, apparently ruling out the possibility that perceived motion or the motion signal issued from the compensation process believed to match eye movement information (corollary discharge) against the image motion signal is the cause of the aftereffect (Holst and Mittelstadt 1950). This signal is frequently, but not invariably, the basis of perceived motion. For example, it is the basis for the perceived motion of a smoothly tracked target but cannot account for the perception of induced motion.[1]

In contrast, results reported by Morgan et al. (1976), Weisstein et al. (1977), and Mack et al. (1987) are incompatible with a retinal motion account of MAEs but are consistent with the view that the aftereffect entails adaptation to a motion signal which occurs at a later stage in the

Originally published in *Perception* 18, 5 (1989): 649–655. Reprinted with permission.

information processing chain. Weisstein et al. found MAEs in subjects who had observed drifting phantom contours. Since these cannot be based on adaptation to retinal motion the involvement of some higher level process is implicated. Morgan et al. (1976) and Mack et al. (1987) have also reported results which are incompatible with a retinal motion account of MAEs. Unlike Anstis and Gregory (1965), both groups of investigators failed to find normal MAEs from the retinal motion of a physically stationary grating caused by the tracking of a moving point across it. In one experiment (Mack et al. 1987), observers tracked a moving grating which displaced between flanking stationary gratings. The MAE produced by this condition was compared with the effect obtained after steady fixation of a point centered on the stationary middle grating while the flanking bars moved together across the field. The retinal motion in the two conditions was virtually identical. Nevertheless, during testing when all three sets of bars were stationary, the MAE associated with tracking appeared in the middle set of bars that fell on an area of the retina not previously exposed to motion. Moreover, it was in the *same* rather than the opposite direction to the adapting retinal motion and was apparently induced by a very weak below-threshold MAE in the flanking gratings which had displaced over the retina by virtue of the pursuit eye movements. (A similar induced MAE obtained under similar conditions was reported earlier by Morgan et al. 1976.) In contrast, observation of the moving flanking gratings during steady fixation of the middle stationary grating led to a normal MAE in the flanking gratings.[2]

The principal question posed by the Mack et al. (1987) and the Morgan et al. (1976) results is why retinal motion caused by tracking yields an aftereffect that is so much weaker than that produced by the equivalent retinal motion caused by actual pattern motion. Why is the tracking MAE below threshold and therefore only evident by virtue of the aftereffect it induces in a surrounded pattern?[3] Mack et al. (1987) proposed the tentative answer that MAEs may be based on the motion signal issued from the comparator which sums eye movement and image motion information (Holst and Mittelstadt 1950). It is this mechanism which is believed to account for position constancy and, under the tracking conditions of the Mack et al. (1987) experiment, would have signalled that the retinally moving, physically stationary flanking gratings were either not moving or moving only slightly (Mack and Herman 1978). Moreover, since there is sometimes a small loss of position constancy during tracking which is associated with a signal indicating some stimulus motion, this could account for the slight below-threshold aftereffect which did occur. It is also possible that at least some of the difference between MAEs that occur after tracking and fixation might be due to a difference in *perceived* motion. During tracking, the retinal motion of physically stationary elements causes little or no perception of motion. In contrast, the retinal motion caused by actual stimulus motion normally produces a clear perception of motion. Therefore this difference must be considered a potential source of the difference in the strengths of the MAEs.

The present research was designed to provide independent evidence for these speculations. The principal question is whether retinal motion alone or the motion signal derived from the compensation process is the basis of the MAE. We did not attempt to evaluate independently the role of perceived motion in these experiments, and the predictions from the two hypotheses were the same.

The stimulus conditions permitted a direct comparison of the efficacy of the retinal motion signal and that of the signal issuing from the compensation process in generating MAEs. The stimulus conditions were such that if the MAE were a direct function of retinal motion, its direction would differ from an MAE based on the comparator motion signal. Each observer tracked a vertically moving point while an adapting pattern drifted horizontally across the field. The vertical motion of the eye caused the adapting pattern to drift obliquely over the retina so that if the MAE were based on retinal motion, a subsequently viewed stationary pattern should appear to move obliquely in the opposite direction. However, if the aftereffect were based on the comparator motion signal, then the subsequently viewed stationary pattern should appear to move horizontally in the opposite direction to the adapting motion, because during adaptation the comparator which matches the vertical eye motion signal against the oblique image motion should signal horizontal pattern motion (see figure 18.1).

Experiment 1

Method

Subjects.   Ten observers with normal or corrected-to-normal vision were paid for their participation.

Apparatus and Stimuli.   The adapting display consisted of a tripartite square-wave grating and a fixation point (see figure 18.1a). The display was the same as one that has been used previously (see Mack et al. 1987, for a complete description). It was presented on a fast phosphor (P15) cathode ray tube. The three square-wave gratings and fixation point could be swept independently across the screen. The display appeared as three rows of light grey vertical bars (with contrast levels approaching 1) vertically separated by 1.06 deg, and a horizontally centered fixation point. The background was black. The alternating light and dark bars each subtended a horizontal extent of 2.12 deg. The outer flanking bars subtended

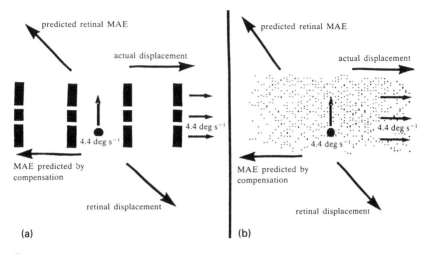

Figure 18.1
The adapting displays used in (a) experiment 1 (grating) and (b) experiment 2 (random-dot pattern) to induce motion aftereffects (MAEs).

a vertical extent of 5.30 deg, and the center row of bars subtended a vertical extent of 3.18 deg. The bars in each row formed a square-wave grating with a spatial frequency of 0.236 cycle deg^{-1}. When they moved, they covered a distance of 21.18 deg. Their motion was rightward at 4.4 $deg\ s^{-1}$. On trials in which the fixation point also moved, it travelled vertically upward at the same rate as the bars, starting from a position at the bottom of the screen. When it reached the upper edge of the screen the entire display vanished for 700 ms. It then reappeared, with the fixation point again centered at the bottom of the screen, drifting upwards while the bars drifted rightward. (This blank interval allowed the observer more than enough time to saccade back to the bottom of the screen and refixate the moving point when it appeared, without the possibility of undesirable retinal stimulation.)

Procedure.   There were two adaptation conditions: one involved tracking the vertically moving fixation point while the bars drifted rightward (tracking condition); the other involved fixation of the stationary point centered in the display as the bars drifted rightward (fixation condition). The tracking condition always preceded the fixation condition. The display was viewed from a distance of 34.5 cm and an adaptation trial lasted 90 s, during which time the fixation point and/or the bars swept across the screen eighteen times. In the fixation condition the display blanked every 4.42 s during adaptation (the fixation point remained visible), simulating the blanking that was necessary in the tracking condition. In both conditions, after the eighteenth sweep the display blanked for 700 ms and

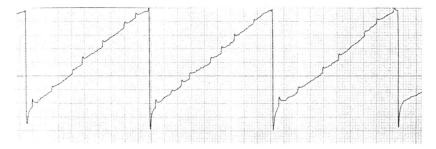

Figure 18.2
A sample segment of an eye movement record.

reappeared centered and stationary. This marked the start of the test period.

During the test period, the observer fixated the stationary centered point and reported any apparent motion (and its direction) of the now stationary bars. The observer then reported when the test pattern no longer appeared to drift. The interval between the appearance of the stationary test pattern and the observer's verbal statement served as the index of MAE duration. The observer indicated the direction of the aftereffect by noting the number towards which the pattern appeared to drift on a circular clocklike figure. If an observer failed to report an MAE after the first adaptation period, a second trial was provided. Prior to actual testing observers were given practice in repetitively tracking the vertically moving fixation point. During this training period, the vertical bars were absent.

Eye movements were monitored in three randomly selected observers to rule out the possibility that results in the tracking condition might reasonably be attributed to the failure to track vertical motion adequately. An SRI Purkinje Image tracker was used as the monitoring device (Crane and Steele 1978) and yielded an analogue eye movement record.

Results
The eye movement records indicated that the three observers whose eye movements were monitored tracked the vertical motion adequately, thus ruling out the likelihood that the tracking results were caused by faulty pursuit motions. A sample segment of an eye movement record appears in figure 18.2. All observers perceived the horizontal adapting motion as horizontal, although the point which was tracked appeared to move obliquely. The perceived oblique motion was, of course, due to the motion induced by the horizontally drifting adapting pattern. In the tracking condition, eight of the ten observers reported a leftward horizontal MAE (mean duration 11.1 s, standard deviation 3.8) after the first adaptation

trial. The remaining two observers reported a leftward horizontal MAE after the second adaptation trial. No observer reported an oblique MAE. In the fixation control condition all ten observers reported an MAE after the first adaptation trial (mean duration 12.8 s, standard deviation 2.12). It was, of course, leftward.

The absence of any directional difference between the MAEs reported in the fixation and tracking conditions seems strong evidence for the hypothesis that the adaptation on which MAEs are based is a response to the motion signal derived from the compensation process (bearing in mind a possible role for perceived motion). There was, however, another possible explanation of these results which we examined.

It was possible that the horizontal MAE in the tracking condition was an instance of the operation of a rule, first stated by Wallach (1976, page 203), that "a line in a homogeneous field is always seen to move in a direction perpendicular to the line itself." Since the test pattern consisted of vertical bars, this rule predicts a horizontal MAE. Although there appeared to be good and sufficient reasons for thinking this rule was not operative, e.g. the ends of the bars were visible, as were the edges of the screen, and therefore the field was not homogeneous, it, nevertheless, seemed advisable to be certain that this was so.

To this end, we used adapting and test patterns which comprised a field of random dots which, in the adaptation period, drifted rightward across the field. Since there were no visible lines, there could be no line effect. Everything else remained the same, so if tracking of the vertically moving point again produced a horizontal MAE, it could not be attributed to the line effect.

Experiment 2

Method

Subjects. Ten new observers were tested in both the tracking and the fixation conditions. The tracking condition again preceded the fixation condition.

Apparatus, stimuli, and procedure. The adapting and test patterns comprised a field of random dots which, in the adaptation period, drifted rightward across the display at 4.4 deg s^{-1} (see figure 18.1b). Position and movement of the fixation point were as in experiment 1. All other details and procedures were also as in experiment 1.

Results

All ten observers reported a horizontal leftward MAE after the first tracking trial (mean duration 11.03 s, standard deviation 2.82). Identical results were obtained in the fixation condition, where the mean duration of the MAE was 12.14 s (standard deviation 3.19).

Discussion

The results of experiment 2 eliminated the possibility that the direction of the MAE could be explained in terms of the Wallach line effect, therefore increasing the likelihood that MAEs are based on the signal derived from the compensation process rather than on the retinal motion signal alone. These results are consistent with those reported earlier (Mack et al. 1987). Together they make a case for the critical role in the adaptation of the motion signal derived from the compensation process. Since in animals with moving eyes it is this signal which disambiguates image motion due to object motion from image motion due to eye motion, it is not surprising that it may be this signal, rather than "raw" retinal motion, to which the visual system is primarily attuned. Distinguishing between these two sources of retinal motion is frequently critical to an organism's survival.

There is at least one other possible explanation for these results which was suggested to us after these experiments had been completed.[4] It is based on the fact that relative motion is more effective in generating MAEs than is absolute motion (Day and Strelow 1974). This explanation accounts for the failure to obtain an oblique MAE by assuming that the vertical motion vector of the adapting motion is only weakly relational. The reasoning is as follows. When the observer is tracking the vertically moving point, the oblique retinal motion of the adapting pattern is a conjoint function of the actual horizontal motion of the pattern and the vertical motion caused by the tracking. The horizontal vector of this motion is relative with respect to all the visible stationary references in the field, such as the screen frame. The vertical vector, however, is relative with respect to the tracking point only, which is assumed to mean that its relative aspect is minimal. Given the established importance of relative motion for MAEs, a paucity of relative motion associated with the vertical motion vector might account for the fact that the subsequent MAE is horizontal rather than oblique. Were this correct, it would not be necessary to invoke the compensation process to account for the results. Although a direct test of this alternative explanation is in order, there are reasons for doubting its applicability. In earlier work (Mack et al. 1987), where the subject tracked a moving grating centered between two flanking stationary gratings, the relative displacement of the retinal motion of the flanking gratings caused by the eye movements was completely equivalent to that in the fixation control condition.[5] Nevertheless, the tracking condition produced an MAE that was below threshold whereas the fixation condition produced a normal MAE. Since in those experiments

the tracking condition produced a very weak MAE despite ample availability of relative motion, it seems unlikely that the paucity of relative
vertical motion in the present experiments accounts for the failure to find
an oblique MAE. Moreover, it might be noted that there is no published
evidence suggesting that relative motion with respect to one point is
weaker than relative motion with respect to many contours. Only if this
were true, would the alternative ingenious explanation offered by Anstis
be tenable.

Notes

This research was supported by an NIH research grant (5 RO1 MH42573).

1. For example, in the classic case of induced motion the observer fixates a stationary point
   while a surrounding frame moves, inducing the opposite motion in the enclosed point.
   Only if the eye movement command to fixate were captured by the perceived induced
   motion, or if the oculomotor command to fixate entailed countering a tendency to track
   the moving frame, would it be possible to consider the signal from the eye movement
   compensation process the basis of the induced motion. There is evidence that no such
   oculomotor visual capture occurs (Mack et al. 1985).
2. Anstis and Reinhardt-Rutland (1976) reported that an MAE can induce motion. However,
   the conditions in which this was demonstrated were quite different from those used by
   Mack et al. (1987) and Morgan et al. (1976).
3. Duncker (1929) established that a motion which is below threshold can induce motion in a
   neighboring stationary stimulus.
4. This alternative explanation of our data was suggested by Stuart Anstis in a personal
   communication.
5. This is why observers tracked a moving grating flanked by stationary gratings rather than
   simply a moving point over a stationary grating as in Anstis and Gregory (1965).

References

Anstis S. M., Gregory R. L., 1965. "The aftereffect of seen motion: the role of retinal stim-
    ulation and of eye movement" *Quarterly Journal of Experimental Psychology* **17** 173–
    174.
Anstis S. M., Reinhardt-Rutland A. H., 1976. "Interactions between motion aftereffects and
    induced motion" *Vision Research* **16** 1391–1394.
Crane H., Steele C. H., 1978. "Accurate three dimensional eye tracker" *Applied Ophthalmol-
    ogy* **17** 691–704.
Duncker K., 1929. "Uber induzierte Bewegung" *Psychologische Forschung* **12** 180–259.
Day R. H., Strelow C. H., 1974. "Reduction or disappearance of visual aftereffect of move-
    ment in the absence of patterned surround" *Nature (London)* **230** 55–56.
Holst E. von, Mittelstadt H., 1950. "Das Reafferenz-prinzip" *Die Naturwissenschaften* **20** 464–
    467.
Mack A., Goodwin J. H., Thordarsen H., Palumbo D., Hill J., 1987. "Motion aftereffects with
    pursuit eye movements" *Vision Research* **27** 529–536.
Mack A., Herman E., 1978. "The loss of position constancy during pursuit eye movements"
    Vision Research **18** 55–62.
Mack A., Heuer F., Fendrich R., Vilardi K., Chambers D., 1985. "Induced motion and oculo-
    motor capture" *Journal of Experimental Psychology: Human Perception and Performance*
    11 329–345.

Morgan M., Ward R., Brussell E., 1976. "The aftereffect of tracking eye movements" *Perception* **5** 307–317.

Tolhurst D. J., Hart G., 1972. "A psychophysical investigation of the effects of controlled eye movements on the movement detectors of the human visual system" *Vision Research* **12** 1441–1446.

Wallach H., 1976. "The direction of motion of straight lines" in *On Perception* Ed. H. Wallach (New York: Quadrangle Press) pp 201–216.

Weisstein N., Maguire W., Berbaum K., 1977. "A phantom motion aftereffect" *Science* **198** 955–958.

Chapter 19
Speed Constancy and Size Constancy
Irvin Rock, A. Lewis Hill, and Mark Fineman

The rate at which an image moves across the retina is a function of the rate at which the object moves across the O's field *and* the distance of the object from the O. If the speed of the moving object is constant, then the farther away it is, the slower is the rate of displacement of its image. Therefore, if perceived speed were solely a function of speed of image displacement, the farther away the object, the slower should it appear to move. But it would seem to be the case in daily life that perceived speed does not change very much as a function of the distance of the moving object so that it is appropriate to consider this fact as another perceptual constancy. Laboratory experiments confirm the fact of speed constancy (Wallach, 1939).

If perceived velocity were to be a function of phenomenal extent traversed by the object per unit time, then speed constancy is derivable from size constancy. If, for example, an object moves at a speed of 1 ft per sec, then as long as the O veridically perceives the extent of 1 ft as 1 ft and not a lesser extent, despite the smaller visual angle subtended by that extent at greater distances, he should continue to experience the object as traversing 1 ft per sec. This obvious solution to the problem of speed constancy was entertained some years ago, but not pursued, for certain reasons. One reason was that it had been found that when Os were given tests of both size and speed constancy in the same situation, speed constancy fell off while size constancy remained more or less complete (Wallach, 1939). In the light of present-day knowledge about the suceptibility of size judgments to instructional sets and the like, however, it is questionable if this finding should carry much weight. It may even prove not to be a reliable fact. In any case, based on a discovery by Brown (1931), Wallach (1939) was ultimately able to derive speed constancy from the transposition principle. Brown's transposition principle states that perceived speed is a function of rate of displacement of an object *relative* to a frame of reference. If point A moves from top to bottom of a

Originally published in *Perception & Psychophysics* 4, 1 (1968): 37–40, under the title "Speed Constancy as a Function of Size Constancy." Reprinted with permission.

rectangle in a given time, then in order to be seen as moving at the same speed, point B in a rectangle of a different size must move not the same physical distance point A moves in that same time, but rather from top to bottom of its rectangle. This is the case even when A and B are equidistant from the O. Wallach then pointed out that in the constancy situation, the frames of reference of the objects being compared are equal— for example the cross-section of a corridor—but because one is further away than the other, the retinal images are transposed precisely as in the situation studies by Brown. Therefore speed constancy is predictable from the transposition principle, and there is no need to invoke theories about taking distance into account as in the derivation based on size constancy stated above.

However, the two explanations are not necessarily mutually exclusive. In fact, the speed transposition effect may itself be based in part on a size transposition effect such as has recently been demonstrated by Rock and Ebenholtz (1959). It remains eminently plausible that perceived speed is a function of phenomenal extent traversed per unit time. In the light of Wallach's deduction, however, it becomes difficult to test this hypothesis. In the typical environment—such as in the case of an indoor corridor— the frame of reference is of constant size at various distances from the O so that the transposition principle can be invoked to explain whatever speed constancy may be obtained. The critical test of the size constancy hypothesis, therefore, is one in which speed perception is studied under conditions where no frame of reference exists, such as in a totally dark room.

Experiment 1

Method
The basic idea of the experiment was to require O to compare the speeds of two vertically moving luminous circles in an otherwise dark room. The standard circle, to the O's right, was 18 in. from his eyes. The variable circle, to his left, was 72 in. from his eyes. If distance is to be taken into account in assessing the extent traversed by the far circle, it is necessary for at least some information about distance to be registered. We assumed that the combination of accommodation and convergence would prove adequate provided we did not work at very great distances. However, it was by no means certain that size constancy would be complete under these circumstances and, if not, there would be no reason to expect speed constancy to be complete. In fact the degree of speed constancy should be a function of the degree of size constancy. Therefore each O was also required to compare the sizes of triangles at the 18 in. and 72 in. positions. We will refer to this situation as the binocular condition.

If all information concerning distance were to be eliminated, then it must be predicted that speed and size would be judged on the basis of visual angle. Therefore both the speed and size comparisons were also obtained under conditions of monocular vision through an artificial pupil (artificial pupil condition). Separate Os were employed in this condition because it was thought that otherwise there would be a carry-over from one condition to the other, thus affecting the purity of either the binocular data or the artificial pupil data, depending upon which was tested second.

Apparatus
For the speed comparison, two vertically moving endless belts running over moving cylinders were used, the speed being adjustable by means of a variac control. The height of the exposed portion of each belt was $9\frac{1}{2}$ in. For the binocular condition, two luminous circles 5/8 in. in diameter were painted on each belt but only one was visible at a time. The standard was set at a speed of approximately 3 in. per sec. When the circle reached the bottom of the belt it disappeared from view until it reappeared once more at the top. In the case of the artificial pupil condition, it was expected that the distant circle would appear to be moving through a much shorter phenomenal extent than the standard circle, so in order to correct for this, a mask was placed over the nearby standard with an opening which was 1/4 of the height of the belt aperture or about $2\frac{1}{4}$ in. It was also expected that the distant circle would appear much smaller than the standard circle and since size is known to affect speed (Brown, 1931), the distant circle was made four times larger than the standard. Thus the size of the dots and the distance traversed were phenomenally equal. One other factor that had to be considered in the case of the artificial pupil condition was the *number* of circles that would move across the field per unit time. If the distant belt were to be adjusted by O to move at a much faster rate in order to match the apparent speed of the standard circle, more circles would be seen per unit time. Phenomenal speed might be affected by number of circles. To offset any possible effect of this kind one circle rather than two was exposed on the distant belt in this condition.

For the size comparison, a standard luminous triangle 2 in. in height was placed 18 in. from O's eyes. A larger luminous triangle of the same shape was placed 72 in. from O's eyes. By means of a string the O could raise it or lower it behind the top of the table, thereby varying its visible size.

In the binocular condition, the circles or triangles were made visible by luminous paint which was exposed to bright light prior to darkening the room and, periodically as needed, during the trials. For the artificial pupil condition, however, this technique proved inadequate because the luminous objects were invisible by virtue of the loss of light through the artificial pupil. Therefore ultraviolet lamps were used and remained on during the trials. The circles and triangles were made of white paper. Although other background surfaces were illuminated by this light and were visible to the E, only the circles or triangles were visible to the O.

A chin-rest bar was used to stabilize the position of O's head in relation to the objects being compared. O was told to place his chin at the left side of the bar in looking at the comparison object and at the right side of the bar in looking at the standard object. The comparison and standard objects were separated by 90 deg and a shield was afixed to the bar between the two chin positions to prevent simultaneous vision of both objects.

To prevent O from judging speed on the basis of the sound of the motor which drove the belts, since the sound tended to reflect the speed, O was required to wear earphones during the speed comparison task which transmitted from a tape recorder the sound of a single motor at a constant speed. This effectively masked the sounds of the two motors.

Procedure

To prevent O from seeing the distances of the moving belts and triangles in advance, he was led in blindfolded and seated in front of the table. E helped O locate the bar on which his chin was to rest and explained the two positions of the head to be used. The speed comparison came first. O was told that a moving circle would appear on his right and that he was to turn his head to the left side of the bar once the circle disappeared from view at the bottom. There he would see another circle moving downward. He was to adjust the speed of this circle by means of a knob until it appeared to be identical with that of the other circle. He was permitted to look back and forth as often as he wished, but in any single view of the standard he was only permitted to see the circle *once* as it moved downward along the belt. Since only one circle at a time was visible on each belt and the standard circle could not be viewed for more than one cycle at a time, it was thought that this precaution would prevent O from matching the speeds by a process of counting number of circles per unit time (see Smith and Sherlock, 1957).

In the size comparison, which always followed the speed comparison, the standard triangle was displayed to O's right, and he was told to adjust the comparison triangle to his left by means of the string until it appeared equal in size.

The procedure was identical for the artificial-pupil condition except that O wore a patch over both eyes. The patch over the right eye had a pin hole in the center approximately 1 mm in diameter. It required a bit of practice before O was able to locate the circles or triangles through the artificial pupil.

Table 19.1
Experiment 1: Binocular condition: Mean speed and size settings

0	Speed of standard circle (inches per sec)	Speed of variable circle (inches per sec)	Size of variable triangle (inches)
1	3.3	5.2	2.3
2	3.3	3.7	2.5
3	3.2	4.0	3.0
4	3.2	3.7	1.5
5	3.4	3.6	2.4
6	2.6	3.1	1.2
7	2.3	5.3	3.5
8	2.3	4.7	2.8
$\overline{X}$	3.0	4.2	2.4

In both conditions and for both speed and size comparisons, four set-tings were made by each O, two ascending and two descending in a ADDA or DAAD order. The speed of each of O's settings was deter-mined by timing the duration of three cycles, computing the average, and converting this to inches per sec. The speed of the standard for each O was based on timing the duration of three cycles both before and after O made his variable settings and averaging these values.

Subjects
Sixteen Os were employed, eight in each of the two conditions. They were students at Mills College of Education or Yeshiva University and were naive as to the purpose of the experiment. They were paid for participating.

Results
We will consider first the results of the binocular condition. Despite the intention to set the speed of the standard circle precisely at 3 in. per sec, it turned out that its speed varied somewhat from O to O. Therefore, in Table 19.1 the first column gives the exact speed of the standard for each O and the second column gives the mean speed of the variable setting for each O. To interpret the speed settings it must be borne in mind that complete constancy would require setting the distant circle at the speed of the standard, whereas if speed were judged on the basis of rate of dis-placement of the retinal image, the distant circle would have to move at four times this speed, or around 12 in. per sec, since it was four times as far away. Therefore it is clear from the overall average of 4.2 in. per sec

Table 19.2
Experiment 1: Artificial pupil condition: Mean speed and size settings

0	Speed of standard circle (inches per sec)	Speed of variable circle (inches per sec)	Size of variable triangle (inches)
1	3.2	12.8	7.7
2	3.3	12.5	8.3
3	3.4	11.4	8.1
4	3.4	13.2	7.5
5	3.1	12.2	7.9
6	2.8	10.7	8.0
7	2.7	9.1	8.9
8	2.7	11.0	8.9
$\overline{X}$	3.1	11.6	8.2

that by and large constancy prevailed. This value is, however, greater than the average speed of the standard, which was 3.0 in. per sec, and for each O the average variable setting was somewhat higher than the corresponding speed of the standard. Hence it is also clear that constancy was not complete.

The third column gives the mean size setting of the variable triangle for each O. Since the standard was 2 in. high, it is clear that, by and large, constancy of size prevailed, but it also appears to be the case that there was some departure from complete constancy. The average variable setting was 2.4 in. Therefore it would seem reasonable to conclude that because information about distance was not completely accurate, a given extent at 72 in. appeared slightly smaller than an objectively equal extent at 18 in. Consequently if the far circle moved at objectively the same speed as the nearby standard it would appear to be moving somewhat slower and, therefore, the O typically adjusted the far circle to move slightly faster than the standard.

When information concerning distance is eliminated, the settings are very much in accord with what one would predict on the basis of visual angle matching, as is indicated in Table 19.2. By and large, the variable circle is now set at about four times the speed of the standard for each O. Similarly, the variable triangle is set at about four times the height of the standard.

Experiment 2

In the binocular condition of Experiment 1 the O was instructed to turn his head away from the standard after he saw the circle move downward

Table 19.3
Experiment 2: Binocular viewing limited to a single exposure of both circles

0	Speed of standard circle (inches per sec)	Speed of variable circle (inches per sec)
1	1.9	2.5
2	2.7	3.8
3	3.4	5.3
4	2.0	5.1
5	2.0	2.2
6	3.1	5.3
7	3.3	4.8
8	4.0	4.3
9	2.8	3.6
10	2.7	4.0
11	2.0	2.1
12	3.2	4.3
$\overline{X}$	2.8	3.9

for one cycle. However he could view the variable over a longer time span and therefore typically did see a succession of circles in any given trial. Thus, to some extent, number of circles appearing per unit time, a numerical impression, may have had some effect on the outcome. In the present experiment, this possibility was eliminated by using shutters which were manipulated by E. As soon as the standard circle had moved across the opening a shutter between O and the standard was closed. The same was done for the variable circle. Repeated comparisons were permitted, but in each only one exposure of circles was given. The procedure was otherwise identical with the binocular condition of Experiment 1 except that size judgments were not obtained.

The results are given in Table 19.3. They are quite comparable with those of Experiment 1.

Experiment 3

It may be objected that the artificial pupil condition is not a perfect control for the binocular condition because several changes were made in addition to the elimination of distance cues, namely in the size of the variable circle, the number of circles, and the size of the opening in front of the standard. We made these changes because we sought to avoid a

Table 19.4
Experiment 3: Revised artificial pupil condition: Mean speed settings

0	Speed of standard circle (inches per sec)	Speed of variable circle (inches per sec)
1	2.1	5.3
2	1.9	4.1
3	1.4	2.8
4	1.5	3.0
5	1.3	2.4
6	1.6	3.4
7	2.1	6.5
8	2.5	4.0
9	2.7	6.9
10	2.7	5.9
11	2.1	5.7
$\overline{X}$	2.0	4.5

contaminating effect of other determinants of perceived speed. We did, however, also run the "perfect control," i.e., the procedure was identical with that of the binocular condition except that an artificial pupil was employed. The results for 11 new Os are shown in Table 19.4. On the average, the variable speed was now set at 2.25 times the speed of the standard. The difference between this result and that of the artificial pupil condition of Experiment 1 is largely attributable to the effect of size and number of circles seen per unit time. Five additional Os who viewed a single large circle on the comparison side through the artificial pupil set it at an average speed of 7.3 in. per sec. The standard for these Os averaged 2.2 in. per sec.

Discussion and Conclusions

It would seem that the result of the binocular viewing conditions in Experiments 1 and 2, indicating a strong tendency toward constancy of speed, are based on the presence of cues to distance. When these cues are eliminated, the variable circle is set on the average at a much higher speed than that of the standard.

There is, however, still one possibly uncontrolled factor to consider, namely the duration of time a circle is visible. At a given speed, a circle may be visible for varying durations, depending upon its distance and the size of opening. It is possible that this affects phenomenal speed or that the O confuses duration with speed. Suppose O were to count to himself at a steady rhythm while viewing each circle. Then in the binocular condition, if he set the variable at a speed such that the circle was visible for the same "count" as the standard circle, this would result in a match that approached objective equality of speed, or constancy. That there is something to this argument is borne out by the following finding. The Os of Experiment 2 were also required to match speeds (under binocular conditions of viewing) when a mask was placed in front of the standard belt. The mask reduced the visible path of the circle to 1/4 of its length as was the case in the artificial pupil condition of Experiment 1. The average setting for the 12 Os was now 5.8 in. per sec (in view of a quite deviant average setting by one O, the median for the group of 5.2 is perhaps more representative).

Thus, the duration of time in which a circle is visible does seem to affect the O's matches, although it is certainly not the case that they match primarily on the basis of this factor. For that to be true the variable circle would have to be set at an average speed of 11.2 in. per sec (four times the average speed of the standard of 2.8 in. per sec). Thus even with the mask present, matches were closer to constancy than to equality of time visible or to rate of displacement of the retinal image.

One can also consider the results of artificial viewing conditions to assess the probable role of duration of time visible on O's judgments. Based on this factor, one must predict a marked tendency toward objective equality of speeds whether O views through an artificial pupil or with normal binocular vision, provided a mask is not used in front of the standard belt. Only when the speeds are objectively equal will circles then be visible for the same duration. The results of Experiment 3 are therefore relevant because here a mask was not used. The average setting of the variable is 2.25 times the average speed of the standard. However even more to the point is the result for the five O's who viewed a *single large* circle through an artificial pupil since here the contaminating factor of size and number were eliminated, leaving duration of time visible as the only possible determinant other than rate of speed of the retinal image. For these O's, the variable is set on the average at a speed 3.3 times that of the standard (7.3 and 2.2 in. per sec, respectively). Therefore the marked tendency toward constancy under binocular viewing cannot be explained in terms of the period during which circles are visible.

By way of conclusion, it would appear that a sufficient condition for speed constancy is information about the distance of the moving object such that perceived speed becomes a function of phenomenal extent traversed per unit time. Thus wherever size constancy prevails and to whatever degree, speed constancy should also prevail to the same degree.

Since speed constancy can also be explained in terms of the transposition principle—an explanation which requires no assumption about taking distance into account—it appears to be the case that there are two bases for speed constancy in daily life.

Notes

This research was supported in part by the National Science Foundation under Grant No. GB-3410 and in part by a Public Health Service Research Scientist Award, K3-MH-31, 361-02, from the National Institute of Mental Health to the senior author. The authors are indebted to Larry Fisher and Barbara Chang for their participation in this project during its early stages and to Joel Goldberg for his help with apparatus.

References

Brown, J. H. The visual perception of velocity. *Psychol. Forsch.*, 1931, 14, 199–232.

Rock, I., and Ebenholtz, S. The relational determination of perceived size. *Psychol. Rev.*, 1959, 66, 387–401.

Smith, O., and Sherlock, L. A new explanation of the velocity-transposition phenomenon. *Amer. J. Psychol.*, 1957, 70, 102–105.

Wallach, H. On constancy of visual speed. *Psychol. Rev.*, 1939, 46, 541–552.

Part V
Illusions

Introduction

Romi Nijhawan raises the retinal/phenomenal question about the well-known Müller-Lyer illusion: namely, is it based on the retinal orientation of the arrowlike fins or on their perceived orientation in three-dimensional space? To be more specific, he asks whether the illusion is based on the retinal image of the illusion figure in which the outward-going extension of the fins of one shaft vies with the inward-directed placement of the fins of the other shaft; or is the illusion based on *perceiving* the fins in these locations even if it can be so contrived that the retinal images of the fins do not correspond with these directions.

Chapter 20 describes Nijhawan's ingenious solution to separating what would seem to be inseparable factors; namely, how the fins point in a three-dimensional version of the illusion from how the images of the fins point. In fact a direct conflict between these two determinants was created so that the image-based theory makes one prediction and the perceived object-based theory makes the opposite prediction. (See Figure 20.7.)

The reader may object to a formulation in which the retinal image is pitted against any other determinant. The retinal image is the starting point for all perception, not a factor that can be said to be present or absent as the case may be. That is true. The retinal image is the starting point, but the shape it signifies is another matter. A given image is infinitely ambiguous as to what shape in three-dimensional space it signifies. While the traditional Müller-Lyer illusion figure drawn on a flat surface will always be perceived in direct accord with the retinal image, no such constraint exists for a three-dimensional Müller-Lyer *object*.

One can think of Nijhawan's experiment as a conflict between lower and higher levels of determination. The illusion *could* be based on the particular configuration of the retinal image because its registration occurs at an earlier stage of processing and it remains present even after it becomes a perceptual object. As Nijhawan points out, given his results showing the causal role of the *perceived* three-dimensional configuration, that would seem to rule out many theories of the illusion that have been advanced over the years because they are predicated on mechanisms that would have to be based on the retinal image, for example, its spatial frequency spectrum.

On the other hand, the results strongly favor another theory of the illusion, namely, the incorrect-comparison theory, in which despite instructions, the observer is unable to exclude a given region. So in the case of the Müller-Lyer illusion, if the observer includes the outward-going fins in the judgment of the shaft's length, that length will appear much longer than the other shaft. If this theory is correct—and I always felt that the weight of all the evidence supported it—it tells us something interesting about the limitations of conscious intention: it sometimes cannot overcome stimulus factors in arriving at a perception or perceptual judgment. At any rate, Nijhawan's findings offer additional support for the incorrect comparison theory. It boils down to the conclusion that "this region of space (where the fins are) is an extension of (belongs to) this region of space (where the shaft is)." Hence this object is longer than that one. Moreover, the experiments indicate that only the component of the fin's extension outward that projects to the plane of the shaft creates the illusion.

As to our central issue, one can hardly find a better example of the indirectness of a perceptual phenomenon. If and only if one first perceives the structure of a three-dimensional configuration does it even make sense to ask about the illusion. The illusion is caused by the *perception* of the illusion pattern as a three-dimensional structure. That structure is a percept and not just a copy of the retinal image.

The second chapter in this section, by myself and Gilchrist, describes another kind of illusion that I include in this section, faute de mieux: It is hardly a well-known geometrical illusion. It concerns the perception of lines that increase and decrease slowly in length and whether they appear to be doing so or appear differently. What is crucial is whether viable alternatives to the shortening-lengthening "solution" are available. These alternatives, such as occlusion, govern how the line will be perceived. If it can be seen as undergoing occlusion-disocclusion behind an opaque surface, then that solution is preferred.

Here is where this research has engendered a clear disagreement between a direct and an indirect interpretation of the line-length outcome. In research on the role of occlusion and disocclusion, Gibson and his associates have argued that the alternating accretion and deletion of the elements of texture at a border is the direct stimulus basis for the appearance of depth (Gibson, Kaplan, Reynolds, and Wheeler 1969). However in our experiments, Gilchrist and I show that a region must be *figural* before perception of the accretion and deletion of texture elements adjacent to it will give rise to the perception of depth, with the textured region moving under the figural region.

Therefore, before depth perception from occlusion and disocclusion of texture can occur, a particular figure-ground organization must first be perceived. That certainly might dot occur when the stimulus is ambiguous. Once it does occur, however, and only then, will the occlusion-disocclusion paradigm reliably lead to perceived depth.

References

Gibson, J. J., G. A. Kaplan, H. N. Reynolds, and K. Wheeler. 1969. The change from visible to invisible: A study in optical transformations. *Perception & Psychophysics* 5:113–16.

Chapter 20
The Müller-Lyer Illusion Reexamined
Romi Nijhawan

Geometrical illusions, which usually involve judgments of size, curvature, angular extent, and so forth, were among the first topics addressed by experimental psychologists. However, despite the fact that the experimental procedures for investigating geometrical illusions are rather straightforward, a rigorous theory that adequately explains even one of the illusions has yet to be proposed. Consequently, interest in the study of geometrical illusions has waxed and waned. The Müller-Lyer is the most extensively investigated geometrical illusion for which a satisfactory theory still eludes psychologists.

The pattern originally presented by Müller-Lyer (1889) himself consists of a "longer half" (in which the horizontal line appears longer) and a "shorter half" (in which the horizontal line appears shorter) (Figure 20.1). Each half of the illusion pattern consists of two parts: the inducing elements (IEs) and the test element (shaft). The shafts extending between the IEs, although they have the same physical length, appear to the average observer to be unequal by more than 20%.

Numerous variations of the original pattern have been created for the study of the phenomenon in its full generality, the simplest of which was the removal of the shafts (see Figure 20.2a, after Brentano, 1892). In other important variations, the IEs have been presented in the shape of semi-circles (Figure 20.2b, after Delboeuf, 1892) and brackets (Figure 20.2c, after Brentano, 1892). All of these patterns yield the illusion originally observed, although its strength is reduced. A rigorous theory must be general enough to explain the illusion found in all these variations, as well as the others that exist too. Unfortunately, in most of the explanations forwarded (see, e.g., Ginsburg, 1984, 1986; Gregory, 1963, 1966, 1968), researchers have sought primarily to explain the illusion in the classical figure and have generally not given the variants due consideration.

The Müller-Lyer illusion is usually presented as a line drawing on a two-dimensional (2-D) surface in the frontal plane. Therefore, the shape of

Originally published in *Perception & Psychophysics* 49, 4 (1991): 333–341, under the title "Three-Dimensional Müller-Lyer Illusion." Reprinted with permission.

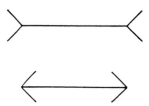

Figure 20.1
The original Müller-Lyer pattern (Müller-Lyer, 1889).

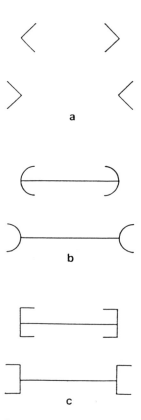

Figure 20.2
Some of the variants of the original Müller-Lyer illusion pattern: (a) without the shafts; (b) the inducing elements shaped as curves instead of angles; (c) the inducing elements shaped as brackets.

the pattern and the shape of the projected retinal image are more or less identical. A major consequence has been that most of the proposed explanations hinge on the shape of the retinal image of the figure (see, e.g., Ginsburg, 1984, 1986; Gregory, 1963, 1966, 1968). The present study was designed to show that the illusion occurs readily with 3-D patterns. This not only challenges the traditional method of presentation of the figure, but also shows that the shape of the retinal image may not be critical to the understanding of the illusion, as has also been suggested by previous researchers who used binocular presentation (Coren and Girgus, 1978; Julesz, 1971; Papert, 1961).

Two theories, both of which hinge on the 2-D shape of the retinal image, will be discussed in this chapter. Gregory (1963) proposed that the illusion is caused by the depth features contained in the retinal image of the pattern. It is generally believed that depth features present in the retinal image give information regarding an object's distance, which is then used in the computation of the object's size. Gregory (1963) suggested that the Müller-Lyer figure contains perspective depth features, which for the longer half indicate a larger distance for the shaft than for the shorter half. Thus, given their identical retinal image size, the shaft that is cued as being farther is perceived to be longer. In Gregory's view, the illusion occurs via the process of primary constancy scaling in which the *perception* of depth is not necessary in scaling size.

Ginsburg (1984, 1986) proposed that the selective spatial frequency filtering, a general physiological property of the visual system, could account for the Müller-Lyer illusion. The visual system acts as a low band-pass filter, selectively filtering out the higher spatial frequencies from the retinal image. When such a filter function is mathematically applied to the Müller-Lyer pattern, the output (peak) shows that the arrowheads for the longer half have shifted away from the shaft and those for the shorter half have shifted toward the shaft, producing the typical "illusion." These distortions account for as much as 80% of the illusion reported by human observers, thus supporting the view that a substantial part of the illusion is due to the selective filtering process of the human visual system.

Other investigators have relegated the Müller-Lyer illusion to a class of 2-D phenomena by resorting to general theoretical arguments. For example, Gibson (1966) suggested that the rich 3-D geometry of the world is necessary for accurate perception, and that illusions occur because 2-D drawings do not contain the invariant information necessary for accurate perception.

The assumptions mentioned above, which imply that the Müller-Lyer illusion should not occur with 3-D patterns, are questioned in the present study through the use of new 3-D variants. One general consequence of studying 3-D patterns in place of 2-D line drawings is that the retinal image shape of the pattern can be manipulated more or less independently of its 3-D shape. Thus, the question of the specific contribution of the shape of the retinal image to the phenomenon under investigation can be addressed directly. In other words, if the effect is not correlated with the shape of the retinal image, it would imply that the specific shape of the retinal image is not *necessary* for producing the illusion (Experiments 1 and 2). Also, if the effect is *not* produced, even though the typical retinal image shape is obtained, it would imply that the specific image shape is not *sufficient* (Experiment 3).

Papert (1961) reported an ingenious technique for addressing this issue. The observers viewed, either monocularly or binocularly, dot patterns that were located in two different planes, one behind the other. On one plane, the dots formed the shape of, say, the Müller-Lyer pattern, while the other plane consisted of random dots. When the display was viewed monocularly, only a flat pattern of random dots was seen, whereas with binocular (or cyclopean) viewing, the planes were separated, and the illusion pattern was seen in the field of random dots. The observers reported a strong illusion in the latter condition, implying that processing beyond the retina must be involved in producing the Müller-Lyer.

Other techniques have also been used to study the level-of-processing issue. For example, Goldstein and Weintraub (1972) and Kanizsa (1974) used subjective contours to study the Poggendorff and Ponzo illusions. The removal of contours (generated by brightness difference) from the image automatically excludes the processing due to retinal neurons. Similarly, Schiller and Weiner (1962) presented the IEs of the illusion pattern to the one eye and the shafts to the other. In all cases, the magnitude of the illusion was diminished. The illusion reduction led these and other investigators (e.g., Coren and Girgus, 1978) to conclude that both retinal and central processes are involved in producing the illusions.

These techniques are, however, not without difficulties; for the subjective contours, the patterns contained new stimulus properties not present in the original stimulus, and the technique of presenting a pan of the pattern to each eye led to binocular rivalry, so that the resulting percepts were unstable. It is possible that the illusion decrement might be due to these factors rather than to the elimination of retinal neural interaction.

Julesz's (1971) technique was similar to Papert's. Julesz generated a cyclopean random-dot version of the Müller-Lyer illusion, but found that the resulting illusion did not differ in strength from the classical version. He concluded that peripheral neural interactions, prior to the lateral geniculate body (LGN), could not explain the illusion, and that more central processes must be involved. However, in spite of Julesz's claim, Coren and Girgus (1978) found that the cyclopean version of the Müller-Lyer illusion was greatly reduced.

In the present study, the potential contribution made by the shape of the retinal image to the illusion was tested in several new ways. A 3-D structure that projected the same retinal image as that of the classical pattern was used, with the following considerations in mind. First, the involvement of the peripheral (before LGN) processes remained unresolved and thus required further study. Second, the techniques of Papert (1961) and Julesz (1971) were specifically aimed at ascertaining the role of peripheral processes in causing the illusion, but they were not designed to address general neural processes, such as selective filtering, which *do* occur both before and after the LGN (see, e.g., DeValois and DeValois, 1988). The new method was intended to assess the role of such processes in addition to the peripheral processes.

Other 3-D patterns used in the study to produce an illusion projected images that were drastically different from those of the classical pattern. Nonetheless, an illusion produced by these patterns might be attributed either to image processing of the new retinal image (of the 3-D shape) or to the *represented* 3-D shape. The magnitude of the illusion obtained in the monocular view, with other depth cues removed, was compared with that of the binocular view, in which the subjects achieved a 3-D perception of the pattern. This issue of image processing versus 3-D representation was addressed in Experiments 1 and 2.

Experiment 1

The 3-D Müller-Lyer pattern used in Experiment 1 generates a retinal image whose shape is drastically different from that of the classical pattern. Any image-processing theory (e.g., the theory based on retinal neural interactions) should either be general enough to accommodate these differences in the retinal images or be held untenable. In the 3-D pattern, dihedral angles were substituted for the arrowheads of the classical figure (see Figures 20.3 and 20.4). DeLucia and Hochberg (1985, 1986) have reported on a 3-D illusion pattern similar to that shown in Figure 20.3. The present models, however, which the author created independently in 1985, differ from their model in several important ways. The DeLucia and Hochberg model was made out of plywood and was presented under normal room lighting. In contrast, the present models were made out of transparent Plexiglas, to which fluorescent material was attached. The reflection of black light, which was the source of illumination, from most surfaces is invisible, whereas that from fluorescent material is visible in bright color. The fluorescent material was attached to the dihedral angles so that the planes appeared either as outline rectangles or as dotted "solid" rectangles with no visible perimeter.

The dihedral angles were positioned relative to the shafts so that in one half of the pattern, the concave sides faced away from the shaft (longer

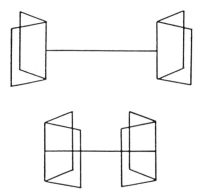

Figure 20.3
A picture of the dihedral-angles (outlines) Müller-Lyer pattern used in Experiment 1. The dihedral angles were made out of Plexiglas.

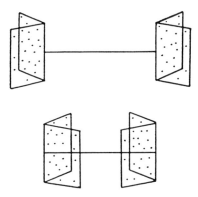

Figure 20.4
A picture of the dihedral-angles (dotted planes) Müller-Lyer pattern used in Experiment 1. The appearance of the dihedral angles was contingent on binocular viewing, without which each dihedral angle appeared as a single cluster of random dots instead of two distinct planes intersecting. The outlines present in the figure above are included only for the purpose of illustration.

half), and in the other half, the concave sides faced toward the shaft (shorter half).

Method

Subjects.   Thirty subjects from the Rutgers University subject pool took part in the experiment for course credit. All were naive with respect to the purpose of the experiment.

Apparatus.   The apparatus consisted of a rectangular frame that held the 3-D Müller-Lyer pattern. The longer half of the pattern was placed on top of the frame and the shorter half on the bottom. A track was constructed on the bottom part of the frame; on it, a cart could be moved smoothly to the left or the right, with the pull of one of two strings. The cart carried one of the four dihedral angles, while the other three dihedral angles were fixed. The displacement of the cart caused the distance between the bottom pair of angles to increase or decrease and also caused the covering/ uncovering of a line, so that its length varied. All four dihedral angles were constructed from transparent Plexiglas.

Stimuli.   Two illusion patterns were created. The planes of each dihedral angle intersected at 90°. For one of the patterns, thin strips of fluorescent material were used to outline each rectangular plane (Figure 20.3); for the other, random dots were placed on the interior of the planes, thus removing all contours from the dihedral angles (Figure 20.4). The outlines shown in Figure 20.4 are meant only for the purpose of illustration. A string covered with fluorescent material extending between the midpoints of the "spines" of dihedral angles represented the shaft. With the exception of the four dihedral angles (visible as outlines for one pattern and as random dots for the other) and two horizontal lines (shafts), the room was completely dark. Black lights were used as illumination. The length of the top shaft was fixed at 45.7 cm. Each rectangle of the dihedral angles measured 15.2 × 11.4 cm. For the random-dot pattern, the radius of each dot was .3 cm and 25 dots were used to define each rectangle. The left dihedral angles of the top and bottom pairs were offset so that the subjects could not simply use imaginary vertical lines to make the judgments. The distance between the subject's eyes and the middle of the display was 152.4 cm.

Procedure.   There were two groups of subjects. The first group consisted of 16 subjects who were shown the outline version of the pattern. The second group consisted of 14 subjects who were shown the random-dot version of the pattern. Each subject was given six trials, three ascending and three descending. The ascending and descending trials were given alternately, with half the subjects beginning with ascending trials and the

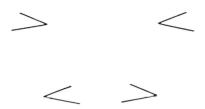

Figure 20.5
The top portion of the 3-D pattern (outlines) used in Experiment 1. This resembles the 2-D
pattern shown in Figure 20.2a.

other half with descending. The ascending trial began with the length of
the comparison line set at 25.4 cm; the descending trial, with the length
set at 66 cm. The subjects were asked to equate the lengths of the two
lines by pulling on the appropriate string. On any given trial, the subject
was asked to move the variable dihedral angle in only one direction, left
or right. The settings were recorded from a scale fixed alongside the track,
out of the subject's view. The subjects held their heads stationary while
viewing the display binocularly.

Results and Discussion

Outline Version Group. For this group, the mean setting of the line length
for the shorter half was 54 cm. Since the top shaft (longer half) was
45.7 cm in length, the magnitude of the illusion was 8.3 cm or 18.2%
[$t(15) = 12.11$, $p < .001$].

The 3-D image shown in Figure 20.3 contains both 2-D and 3-D information. Is it possible that certain 2-D (e.g., see Figure 20.5) properties of
the outline version of the pattern might have caused the illusion? The part
of Figure 20.3 shown in Figure 20.5, which resembles the classical figure,
might have been responsible for the illusion while the 3-D shape of the
pattern had no effect. The outcome with the random-dot version, which
does not contain the stimulus property shown in Figure 20.5, resolves this
issue.

Random-Dot Version Group. For this group, the mean setting of the shaft
length for the longer half was 55 cm which is 9.3 cm longer than that of
the shorter half. Thus, the shaft of the longer half appeared to be 20.4%
longer than that of the shorter half [$t(13) = 10.79$, $p < .001$]. A significant
illusion was thus observed with the randomdot version, even though the
lines that could have produced a 2-D illusion were removed.

Two main questions remained unaddressed following Experiment 1.
Was it possible that in the random-dot version of the pattern, the illusion,
even though not caused by the stimulus property shown in Figure 20.5,

might have been caused by some other information present in the retinal image that had nothing to do with the 3-D *representation* of the pattern? The image of the IE of the random-dot pattern, which is shaped like a "blob," contains information similar to that contained in the variant shown in Figure 20.2c, where the "blob" has the shape of a bracket. Could the mere placing of dot clusters at the shaft ends have produced the illusion?

The second question concerned whether it was appropriate to group the new 3-D illusion with the classical illusion. Might the 3-D illusion belong to a different category of phenomena? If the present illusion is indeed homologous with the Müller-Lyer illusion, then there ought to be some characteristics common to the two. Both these issues were addressed in Experiment 2.

Experiment 2

Experiment 2 was designed for the purpose of studying the variation in the illusion magnitude as a function of the angle between the planes of the dihedral angles. One characteristic of the classical pattern is that smaller angles tend to yield a stronger illusion than larger angles do (Lewis, 1909). (The angles referred to here are those between the two line segments of the IEs.) Lewis (1909), who used angles between 20° and 180°, found that the maximum illusion occurred with a 20° angle and that the illusion decreased as the angle was increased. If such a variation in magnitude were to be found with the 3-D pattern as well, then we could conclude that a common causal mechanism underlies the classical and the 3-D Müller-Lyer illusions.

Experiment 2 consisted of five conditions, four of which involved binocular viewing of the pattern, with angles between the planes of the dihedral angles set at 30°, 60°, 90°, and 120°. The fifth condition consisted of monocular viewing of the 30° display. It was reasoned that monocular viewing would not yield the 3-D shape of the random-dot pattern, whereas binocular viewing would. A comparison of the two conditions of viewing would the allow an assessment of the role of the 3-D shape of the pattern in causing the illusion. In fact, one could conceive of the monocular condition as a 0° condition. In this condition, motion parallax was eliminated by having the subject look through a small aperture, so that when the subject's head moved, the pattern would go out of view, thus ensuring head-stationary viewing. If the 3-D shape of the dihedral angles plays an important role in producing the illusion, the magnitude of the illusion found with binocular viewing should be greater than the magnitude found with monocular viewing.

Method

Subjects. Fifty subjects from the subject pool at the University of California at Berkeley participated in Experiment 2 for course credit. All subjects were naive with respect to the purpose of the experiment.

Apparatus. A new apparatus was constructed for Experiment 2. The planes of the dihedral angles were connected with hinges so that the angle between the planes could be varied. Moreover, instead of the two halves of the display being separated vertically, they were placed laterally to minimize the possibility that the subjects might use a strategy such as drawing imaginary lines to make their length judgments. Both the track for the motion of the can and the covering/uncovering mechanism were similar to those used in Experiment 1.

Stimuli. So that the generality of the results could be studied, the stimuli were very different in size from the stimuli in the previous experiments. The shaft length of the standard display was 20.32 cm. The lower and upper limits of length of the variable shaft were 11.43 and 29.21 cm, respectively. Each rectangular plane of the dihedral angles was 5.08 × 6.60 cm. As in the second condition of Experiment 1, fluorescent random dots were placed on the interior of the planes, and the perimeter of the planes was invisible. The radius of each dot was .1 cm, and 20 dots were used to define each rectangle. In order to ensure that the 3-D nature of the display was not perceived with monocular viewing, the dots were placed so that a texture density gradient ought not to have been present in the retinal image.

Procedure. With the exception of variation of the angles, the binocular conditions were identical to those in Experiment 1. In the monocular condition, the subject wore plain glasses with one side occluded and looked with one eye through an opening that was 1 × 1 cm. When the subjects had finished making the length judgments, they were asked to give an estimate of the angle between the planes that they perceived by manually adjusting two planes under normal room lighting conditions.

Results and Discussion

Binocular Viewing. As with the classical pattern, the illusion was strongest with the smallest angle and weakest with the largest angle. The magnitudes of the illusion at 30°, 60°, 90°, and 120° were 22.23%, 21.49%, 17.78%, and 13.69%, respectively. An analysis of variance for independent samples yielded an $F(3, 36) = 7.41$, $p < .01$. In Figure 20.6, the magnitude of the illusion is plotted as a function of the angle between the planes.

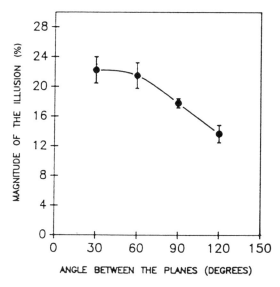

Figure 20.6
The graph in which the magnitude of the illusion experienced by the subjects is plotted as a function of the angles between the planes of the dihedral angles (dotted planes). Each point represents a mean based on 10 scores. Error bars represent the standard error of the mean.

The main outcome of the binocular conditions supports the view that the 3-D Müller-Lyer illusion being studied is indeed *homologous* with, rather than merely analogous to, the classical illusion.

Monocular Viewing. In the monocular condition (using the 30° pattern), the magnitude of the illusion was 8.82%, which is two fifths of the magnitude obtained in the binocular condition. A *t* test for independent samples comparing the 30° monocular and binocular conditions yielded a $t(18) = 25.71, p < .001$.

In the monocular condition, the two planes of the dihedral angles were collapsed into one, and the subjects perceived single 2-D surfaces on which the dots were located. This was evident when, following this condition, the subjects were asked to adjust the planes in accordance with the way in which they perceived the dotted planes; all the subjects collapsed the two planes into one. The difference between the magnitudes of the illusion in the monocular and the binocular conditions indicates that the 3-D representation of the pattern plays an important role in the production of the illusion.

As noted before, the illusion with the random-dot version (binocular viewing) might have been caused by the mere presence of dots at the shaft ends, which are shaped like "blobs." This illusion is similar to the

Figure 20.7
The cube figures show the 3-D shape of the stimuli used in Experiment 3. The actual stimuli with this 3-D structure, however, were made from thin fluorescent material.

bracket version shown in Figure 20.2c. The illusion magnitude of 8.82%, in the monocular condition, may indeed have been due to this factor.

Another observation from Experiment 2 is that in the angle adjustment task, following the binocular conditions, there was a consistent underestimation of the angle between the planes of the dihedral angles. Thus, the depth perception was not perfect, and the 3-D shape of the dihedral angles was not perceived veridically (see also the Results and Discussion section of Experiment 3).

Experiment 3

Experiment 3 also addressed the question of the level of processing that underlies the Müller-Lyer illusion, but with a rather different technique. When the figure is studied, the shaft and the IEs typically lie in the same plane—the plane of the surface on which the figure is drawn. In Experiment 3, this coplanarity was removed by arranging the IEs in a plane that was at right angles to the shaft (as is depicted schematically in Figure 20.7). Nonetheless, the projection of this 3-D structure in the plane of the retina was identical to that of the classical 2-D figure (see Figure 20.7). The 3-D objects composed of cubes shown in Figure 20.7 are, however, *not* the stimuli used in the experiment, their purpose being only to illustrate the 3-D structure. The actual stimuli were constructed from thin fluorescent material.

The 3-D shapes were designed to address the following question: Is the shape of the 3-D display (as it is represented after 3-D shape processing), or the shape of the retinal image (projected by the display), more critical in causing the illusion? If what matter for the illusion are processes such as retinal neural interactions or selective spatial filtering, the illusion should be unaffected by the orthogonal orientation of the IEs relative to the shaft, because what is crucial for these processes is the information that they receive from the retinal image. On the other hand, if what matters is how the resulting structure is *represented* in 3-D space, the illusion might disappear. This is perhaps because in the 3-D display the concave (or convex) side of the IEs lies orthogonal to the shaft, whereas in the 2-D figure the concave side of the IEs faces either toward the shaft (for the shorter half) or away from the shaft (for the longer half). Another reason for why the illusion might disappear will be discussed in the General Discussion section. It was hypothesized that the illusion found with the present 3-D display would either be reduced in strength or disappear entirely.

Method

Subjects.   Sixteen subjects from the Rutgers University community volunteered to take part in Experiment 3. All subjects were naive with respect to the purpose of the experiment.

Apparatus.   A system of pulleys allowed a rectangular block of wood to slide vertically on a surface in the frontal plane. As before, the subject varied the length of one shaft to equate it to the other. For varying the length of the comparison shaft, a metallic object (counterweight), attached to the block of wood by two strings, could be moved up or down on another vertical surface near the subject. Thus, the variable part of the apparatus consisted of the following: a block of wood that could slide smoothly on a surface; a system of pulleys and two strings, with one end of each string connected to the block of wood; and a counterweight attached to the other ends of the strings.

When suspended freely, this system was in balance, owing to friction between the counterweight and its surface and between the wood block and its surface. A slight force upward or downward allowed the wood block to move smoothly. The wood block carried one IE and a mechanism, similar to the one used for the previous experiments, to cover or uncover the comparison line. The subject could move the counterweight up or down, and by doing so decrease or increase the length of the shaft extending between one pair of IEs. For measurements, a scale that was out of the subject's view was fixed next to the counterweight.

Stimuli.   Two vertical lines made of fluorescent material were placed side by side. On the ends of each line, a pair of IEs, made of strips of fluorescent material, was attached. The IEs were all 90° angles and the length of each angle arm was 3.2 cm. The IEs were oriented so that an IE pair lay either in the same plane as the shaft (control) or in planes orthogonal to the plane of the shaft. The former will be referred to as the *planes-parallel* display and the latter as the *planes-perpendicular* display.

Traditionally, when the Müller-Lyer illusion is studied, the observer's line of sight meets the midpoint of the shafts at right angles. As can be seen from Figure 20.7, if this condition were met for the planes-perpendicular display, the angles would project straight lines on the retina. To allow the projected shape of the IEs to be identical to that of the classical pattern, the shafts of the planes-perpendicular stimulus were placed below the observer's eye level. To match the viewing conditions, the classical (planes-parallel) display was also placed below the observer's eye level. For both displays, the observer's line of sight made an angle of 25° at the midpoint of the shafts. The longer half, located toward the subject's left, contained the standard shaft (31.1 cm). The top IE of the right pair (shorter half) could be moved up or down with the mechanism described earlier, which also made the comparison shaft longer or shorter. All stimuli were viewed binocularly while the subjects held their heads still. The distance between the subject's eyes and the midpoint of the test lines was 101 cm (approximately).

Procedure. Experiment 3 consisted of two conditions: planes-perpendicular and planes-parallel. Eight of the 16 subjects participated in the planes-parallel condition, which essentially involved the classical illusion, the only difference being that the subject's line of sight did not meet the midpoints of the shafts at right angles. This served as a control for the planes-perpendicular condition, in which the other 8 subjects participated.

Each subject was given three ascending and three descending trials, alternately. Half the subjects began with an ascending trial and the other half with a descending trial. For the ascending trial, the length of the comparison shaft was set at 18.4 cm; for the descending trial, it was set at 43.8 cm. For a given trial, the subject was instructed to move the counterweight only in one direction, up or down, to equate the shaft lengths.

Results and Discussion
The mean setting for the shaft of the shorter half for the planes-parallel group was 36.1 cm. Thus, on the average this shaft was set 5.0 cm longer than the shaft of the longer half (an illusion of magnitude of 16.07%). This illusion is somewhat weaker than the illusion typically observed, which may be due to the observer's line of sight not meeting the midpoint of the shaft at right angles.

The mean setting of the shaft for the shorter half (retinally defined) of the planes-perpendicular group was 33.6 cm. Thus, for this display, the mean setting for this shaft was 2.5 cm longer than the shaft of the longer half (retinally defined). The parenthetic qualifiers used above are necessary, because the given descriptions for the planes-perpendicular display may not be valid if we consider the 3-D shape of the pattern. The above setting amounts to an illusion magnitude of 8.04%. In short, as we go from the planes-parallel display to the planes-perpendicular display, the magnitude of the illusion is halved. The two groups differ significantly in the magnitude of illusion perceived. A t test for independent samples yielded a $t(14) = 6.78, p < .001$.

The retinal images of the two halves of the planes-perpendicular display are identical to those of the planes-parallel display. If all that mattered in the production of the illusion was a peripheral process associated with the retinal neural interaction or 2-D selective spatial filtering, then the illusion should be unaffected by a change in the orientation of the IEs relative to the shafts. Thus, the outcome of Experiment 3 is inconsistent with the retinal neural interaction and selective filtering theories of the Müller-Lyer illusion. The outcome of Experiment 3 supports the hypothesis that the illusion is affected by the representation of the extent between the IEs in 3-D space.

The observation that the illusion did not totally vanish may at first seem surprising. However, it was observed during the experiment that subjects never perceived the IEs to be oriented at right angles to the shaft. This observation is quite similar to the underestimation of the dihedral angles obtained in Experiment 2 (see the Results and Discussion section of Experiment 2). The perceived angle was somewhere between the objective angle (90°) and the angle in the 2-D image (0°). Observations that the computation of depth of a 3-D shape is influenced by the retinal image features abound in the literature (see, e.g., Gogel, 1977; Ono and Comerford, 1977). If one conceives that the IEs influence the shaft such that any *component* of the "bend" in the angles is perceived to lie toward the shaft, then an illusion, intermediate in magnitude, corresponding to that component will be observed. A slight tilt toward the shaft would cause the concave side of the IEs to face toward the shaft, whereas a slight tilt away from the shaft would cause the concave side of the IEs to face away from the shaft. The reader can get a sense of this from reviewing Figure 20.7, in which, despite the pictorial depth, the IEs of the right half appear to be bent toward the shaft and those of the left half bent away from the shaft.

General Discussion

It has been demonstrated in Experiments 1 and 2 that the Müller-Lyer illusion occurs easily with 3-D figures. Also, it has been shown in Experiments 2 and 3 that the 3-D *representation* of the patterns may be critical to the understanding of the illusion.

In light of these findings, let us examine the two theories discussed earlier: the constancy scaling theory (Gregory, 1963, 1966, 1968) and the selective spatial frequency filtering theory (Ginsburg, 1984, 1986). Numerous experimenters have already shown that certain predictions that ought to follow from the constancy scaling hypothesis do not hold. For example, Waite and Massaro (1970) reasoned that if a constancy operation were at the root of the illusion, then a rectangle, substituted for the shaft, ought also to show a width distortion in addition to the length distortion. Their studies, however, revealed no such effect. It is possible, however, that constancy scaling occurs only along one dimension and not the other. Some authors (e.g., Day, 1972) have argued that the constancy scaling theory is too specific to be regarded as a general explanation. For example, the variants shown in Figures 20.2b and 20.2c both yield the illusion, with some reduction in magnitude, and yet neither of them contains any of the known depth features necessary for the constancy scaling mechanism. The illusion found in these variants shows that the constancy scaling theory is limited in scope because of its intimate link to the perspective depth features. One could, however, argue that the illusion obtained with, for example, the "curves" version of the Müller-Lyer is due to mechanisms unrelated to constancy because, after all, the properties of this stimulus are quite different from those of the classical pattern. Furthermore, the reduction in the magnitude of the illusion might also reflect involvement of new mechanisms. What this amounts to is the claim that these variants represent a more or less different illusion.

Such arguments, however, do not hold for the 3-D Müller-Lyer figures studied in Experiments 1 and 2. In terms of the illusion strength, these figures match the classical illusion. Furthermore, in Experiment 2 these figures were shown to be *homologous* with the classical figure, which suggests the involvement of a common causal mechanism underlying the two types of figures.

Is it possible that constancy scaling might produce the illusion found in the 3-D pattern? Obviously, the dihedral angles of the 3-D figures do not contain perspective information that could trigger primary scaling that in turn would compute a distance for the shaft of the longer half greater than the distance for the shaft of the shorter half. Furthermore, the IEs of the "dotted-planes" figure of Experiments 1 and 2 contained no lines that would be considered an important stimulus property for size scaling due to perspective. The presence of the illusion in other figures that do not contain lines was also found by Coren (1970), who used the classical figure made out of dots. In summary, an illusion *was* observed in the 3-D figure, which was shown to be homologous with the classical figure. Since this 3-D illusion does not lend itself to the constancy scaling interpretation, it is unlikely that constancy scaling is an important contributor to the production of the classical illusion as well.

The three techniques discussed earlier (subjective contours, binocular presentation, and cyclopean presentation) represented attempts to isolate the location along the information-processing pathway at which the Müller-Lyer illusion might occur. In all these studies, the following question was addressed: Is the neural processing at the retina and/or peripheral processes (prior to LGN) caused by a pattern such as the Müller-Lyer *necessary* for producing the illusion?

The 3-D illusion patterns in Experiments 1 and 2 directly address the involvement of retinal processes. First, it is clear that the retinal neural interactions due to the 3-D patterns are very different from the interactions due to the classical illusion, simply because their 3-D shapes create a very different distribution of stimulation of neural units across the retina. The resulting alteration in the neural interactions ought to have affected the illusion, but an illusion of magnitude comparable to that of the classical pattern was obtained. Furthermore, retinal processes should not be affected by monocular or binocular viewing of the dotted-planes pattern of Experiment 2, yet enormously different illusion magnitudes were obtained in these two conditions. These observations support the view that a retinal image in the shape of the Müller-Lyer figure is *not necessary* for producing the illusion.

The issue of whether the retinal image of the classical pattern is *sufficient* for producing the illusion seems to have been neglected. In the cyclopean presentation, for example, once the shape of the illusion pattern is recovered by the comparison of the two images, processes such as selective filtering could become operative and, in principle, cause the illusion. The question of the sufficiency of the retinal image (addressed in Experiment 3) allows the assessment of peripheral processes in addition to processes such as selective spatial filtering. In both conditions of Experiment 3 (planes-parallel/perpendicular), the shape of the retinal image is the same. The selective filtering process, like that proposed by Ginsburg (1984, 1986), should produce identical distortions for the two conditions. The observed illusion for the planes-perpendicular condition was, however, half the magnitude of that of the planes-parallel condition. The crucial role played by the orientation of the IEs relative to the shaft in 3-D space suggests that the Müller-Lyer illusion occurs after the 3-D processing.

There are, however, other possibilities that might explain the reduction in the illusion. For example, it is possible that the main illusion occurs primarily due to spatial filtering applied to the image, but that some later 3-D process weakens the effect. This could be a cognitive or judgmental process, or a neural mechanism that alters the output of selective filtering.

This of course is speculative, but the plausibility and/or evidence for such a mechanism will determine whether or not selective filtering is indeed a significant factor.

Briefly, the results of Experiment 3 suggest the following. If a selective filtering function were applied to the planes-perpendicular display, the resulting distortions would be identical to the distortion that results when the same function is applied to the planes-parallel display. And yet the magnitude of the illusion obtained by human observers is enormously different for the two displays. Thus, the selective filtering function is "blind" to the 3-D properties of the pattern. The filtering hypothesis may possibly be extended to explain the diminution of the illusion found with the planes-perpendicular display, but only if plausible 3-D processes are discovered.

There is a somewhat different interpretation of the results of the planes-perpendicular condition that may be of interest. If the objects shown in Figure 20.7 are mentally rotated, we find that they are identical (in 3-D shape), except for a 180° rotation around the vertical axis (see Shepard and Metzler, 1971). It is clear, however, that the shapes of the retinal images and the ensuing processes *prior* to the computation of depth that are yielded by these figures are not identical. The *difference* between the two projected shapes yielding two different distributions of processes on the surface of the retina might, in principle, produce an illusion, but their *identity* in 3-D space should oppose any illusion, simply because identical figures should yield processes that are at least in part identical. The finding that the illusion was *not* produced (assuming for the sake of the argument that the illusion actually observed was entirely due to inaccurate depth perception) suggests that the processes that establish the identity of the two figures in 3-D space are crucial. It would be interesting to find out whether or not performing an explicit mental rotation prior to length judgments would further reduce the illusion, as well as whether or not the illusion is affected when the two objects are used in an apparent motion display in which the "same" object rotates in depth. In another terminology, the findings above mean that the illusion occurs beyond the stage of viewer-centered processing and may fall in the category of object-centered perception (Marr, 1982). Again, the fact that some illusion *is* produced with the planes-perpendicular display is to be expected, since the subjects did not perceive the correct perpendicular orientation of the IEs relative to the shaft.

Some authors, most notably Coren and Girgus (1973), have favored a multimechanism approach. There is general agreement regarding the visual information processed at various levels. Is it not then likely that several different levels may simultaneously contribute to the Müller-Lyer illusion? The finding of Coren and Girgus (1978) that a greatly reduced illusion was obtained with the cyclopean version might suggest that peripheral processing is an important contributor in the formation of the illusion. In light of Experiment 3, such a view might imply that the 8.04% illusion obtained with the planes-perpendicular display is caused by mechanisms that are unaffected by the perpendicular orientation of the IEs relative to the shaft (e.g., retinal interaction and optical blur). On the other hand, the *reduction* in the illusion magnitude from 16.07% may be due to the elimination of some of the other cortical mechanisms that *are* sensitive to orientation. However, as was discussed above, the results of Experiments 1 and 2 cast a further doubt on the strength of the peripheral factors. Moreover, such a view would account for the results fairly well, were it not for the observation that the subjects misperceived the orientation of the IEs. Since it is being argued here that the depth processing mechanism may be located *before* the illusion-causing mechanism, it follows that any error in the output of the former mechanism will be transmitted to the latter. Presently, experiments in which the orientation of the IEs is veridically perceived are being undertaken to address this issue.

Note

This chapter is based in part on a dissertation submitted by the author to Rutgers University, New Brunswick. The author wishes to acknowledge the contribution of Shinsuke Shimojo, who provided ideas for new experiments. The author also wishes to thank Irvin Rock and Beena Khurana for many helpful suggestions, and to thank an anonymous reviewer for comments on an earlier draft.

References

Brentano, F. (1892). Über ein optisches Paradoxen. *Journal of Psychology, 3*, 349–358.

Coren, S. (1970). Lateral inhibition and geometric illusion. *Quarterly Journal of Experimental Psychology, 22*, 274–278.

Coren, S., and Girgus, J. S. (1973). Visual spatial illusions: Many explanations. *Science, 179*, 503–504.

Coren, S., and Girgus, J. S. (1978). *Seeing is deceiving: The psychology of visual illusions*. Hillsdale, NJ: Erlbaum.

Day, R. H. (1972). Visual spatial illusions: A general explanation. *Science, 175*, 1335–1340.

Delboeuf, J. L. R. (1892). Sur une nouvelle illusion d'optique. *Academie Royale des Sciences, de Lettres et des Beaux Arts de Belgique Bulletins, 24*, 545–558.

DeLucia, P., and Hochberg, J. (1985). Illusions in the real world and in the mind's eye. *Proceedings of the Eastern Psychological Association, 56*, 38. (Abstract)

DeLucia, P., and Hochberg, J. (1986). Real-world geometrical illusions: Theoretical and practical implications. *Proceedings of the Eastern Psychological Association, 57*, 62. (Abstract)

DeValois, R. L., and DeValois, K. K. (1988). *Spatial vision*. New York: Oxford University Press.

Gibson, J. J. (1966). *The senses considered as perceptual systems*. Boston: Houghton Mifflin.

Ginsburg, A. P. (1984). Visual form perception based on biological filtering. In L. Spillman and B. R. Wooten (Eds.), *Sensory experience, adaptation and perception* (pp. 53–72). Hillsdale, NJ: Erlbaum.

Ginsburg, A. P. (1986). Spatial filtering and visual form perception. In K. R. Boff, L. Kaufman, and J. P. Thomas (Eds.), *Handbook of perception and human performance* (Vol. 2, pp. 34-1–34-41). New York: Wiley.

Gogel, W. (1977). The metric of visual space. In W. Epstein (Ed.), *Stability and constancy in visual perception: Mechanisms and processes* (pp. 129–181). New York: Wiley.

Goldstein, M. B., and Weintraub, D. I. (1972). The parallel-less Poggendorff: Virtual contours put the illusion down but not out. *Perception & Psychophysics*, **11**, 353–355.

Gregory, R. L. (1963). Distortion of visual space as inappropriate constancy scaling. *Nature*, **199**, 678–680.

Gregory, R. L. (1966). *Eye and brain.* New York: World University Library.

Gregory, R. L. (1968). Visual illusions. *Scientific American*, **219**, 66–76.

Julesz, B. (1971). *Foundations of cyclopean perception.* Chicago: University of Chicago Press.

Kanizsa, G. (1974). Contours with gradients or cognitive contours? *Italian Journal of Psychology*, **1**, 93–112.

Lewis, E. O. (1909). Confluxion and contrast effects in the Müller-Lyer illusion. *British Journal of Psychology*, **3**, 21–41.

Marr, D. (1982). *Vision.* San Francisco: W. H. Freeman.

Müller-Lyer, F. C. (1889). Optische Urteilstäuschungen. *Dubois-Reymonds Archive für Anatomie und Physiologie* (Suppl.), 263–270.

Ono, H., and Comerford, J. (1977). Stereoscopic depth constancy. In W. Epstein (Ed.). *Stability and constancy in visual perception: Mechanisms and processes* (pp. 91–128). New York: Wiley.

Papert, S. (1961). Centrally produced geometrical illusions. *Nature*, **191**, 733.

Schiller, P., and Weiner, M. (1962). Binocular and stereoscopic viewing of geometric illusions. *Perceptual & Motor Skills*, **13**, 739–747.

Shepard, R. N., and Metzler, J. (1971). Mental rotation of three-dimensional objects. *Science*, **171**, 701–703.

Waite, H., and Massaro, D. W. (1970). A test of Gregory's constancy-scaling explanation of the Müller-Lyer illusion. *Nature*, **227**, 733–734.

Chapter 21

The Conditions for Perceiving Dynamic Occlusion of a Line

Irvin Rock and Alan L. Gilchrist

There are several possible perceptions that can result from a change in the length of the retinal image of a line. One can perceive a line of changing length; one can perceive a line of constant length changing its orientation in depth; one can perceive a line-as-a-whole changing its distance; or one can perceive a line of constant length undergoing covering or uncovering by another object.

In this chapter we are concerned with the conditions that lead either to the first or to the last of these perceptual outcomes. The second outcome, the perception of a line changing its orientation in depth, tends not to occur spontaneously if the line does not simultaneously change its orientation in a frontal plane (Wallach and O'Connell, 1953). Furthermore, if the line has any perceptible thickness, the absence of any perspective gradient of thickness as it changes in length will serve as a cue that no change in depth is occurring. The absence of *any* change in thickness would also tend to oppose the perception of a line approaching or receding from the observer, the third outcome. Otherwise, the change in overall size of the image would surely lead to an impression of an object of constant size moving back and forth in the third dimension. In the research to be described, these factors—plus the possible additional one that the image of the line was displaced only at one end—effectively eliminated either of these kinds of perceptual impressions of change in the third dimension.

Concerning the other two possibilities, perceived change of length and perceived constancy based on covering and uncovering, one might predict that the latter would be dominant because the progressive change in length constitutes information that the end of the line is undergoing occlusion or disocclusion (Gibson, Kaplan, Reynolds, and Wheeler, 1969; Kaplan, 1969). The hypothesis guiding our research, however, was that

Originally published in *American Journal of Psychology* 88, 4 (1975): 571–582, under the title "The Conditions for the Perception of the Covering and Uncovering of a Line." Reprinted with permission.

no such objectively specifiable change in the proximal stimulus determines the perceptual outcome; rather, that which is perceived is the result of an inferencelike process and depends upon the most plausible "solution" to the "problem" posed by the changing proximal stimulus.

If, for example, nothing is visible except a line whose length is changing, the only supportable inference is that the line is undergoing a change of length. For if the line is being occluded or revealed by an opaque object, why is no such object visible? (Whereas an observer might still make a *non*perceptual inference that the line is being covered and uncovered, it is our contention that perceptual inference must be rooted in stimulus information.) But if, on the other hand, a large rectangle remains adjacent to the end of the changing line, then an alternate inference is possible, the inference that a line of constant length is being alternately covered and uncovered by the rectangle. However, it should be added that the change-of-length solution remains possible here: the line with a rectangle at one end could be undergoing a change of length.

Experiment I

Experiment I compared three main conditions. In *condition A*, the observer viewed an isolated line that was changing in length, alternately elongating and shrinking. In *condition B*, the observer viewed a line that was changing in length as in condition A, but a large outline rectangle moved in such a way that one of its ends was always in contact with the displacing end of the line. The rectangle here was large enough to cover the segment of the line that was eliminated by its shrinkage. In *condition C*, the observer viewed the line with a rectangle at one end as in condition B, but the rectangle was too narrow to cover the eliminated segment of the line. Consequently, it was predicted that the observers in this condition would tend to perceive a line that was changing rather than constant in length. Figure 21.1 illustrates these displays.

As a supplementary experiment, an additional condition was included, *condition D*, to determine whether the narrow rectangle used in condition C would lead to different results if the display changed in such a way as to be compatible with the "solution" of a line of constant length undergoing occlusion and disocclusion. To that end, the line was now visible on both sides of the rectangle. Under this condition, some portion of the segment of the line that is eliminated on one side of the rectangle can be interpreted as constituting the now-enlarged segment of the line on the other side of the rectangle. This interpretation is not possible in condition C. As a control for condition D, an additional group of observers, *condition E*, was shown a display in which there was a gap in the line; the gap was of the same width as the rectangle, but no rectangle was visible.

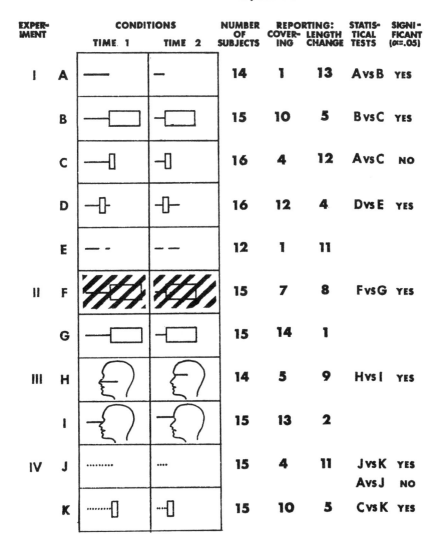

EXPER- IMENT	CONDITIONS		NUMBER OF SUBJECTS	REPORTING: COVER- ING	LENGTH CHANGE	STATIS- TICAL TESTS	SIGNI- FICANT (α=.05)
	TIME 1	TIME 2					
I A			14	1	13	A vs B	YES
B			15	10	5	B vs C	YES
C			16	4	12	A vs C	NO
D			16	12	4	D vs E	YES
E			12	1	11		
II F			15	7	8	F vs G	YES
G			15	14	1		
III H			14	5	9	H vs I	YES
I			15	13	2		
IV J			15	4	11	J vs K A vs J	YES NO
K			15	10	5	C vs K	YES

Figure 21.1
The experimental conditions and outcomes.

Thus, there were two lines here, one of which was undergoing elongation as the other was shrinking, and vice versa. Therefore, it was predicted that observers would tend to perceive this display as two line segments one of which is elongating and the other of which is shrinking. However, we did consider the possibility that this display might lend itself to an impression of some not fully visible structure with subjective contours covering a moving gap.

Method

Animated photography was used to create video tape recordings of each of the displays. Referring to the display as seen by the observer on the television screen, for all conditions the displacing end of the line moved back and forth a distance of $5\frac{1}{8}$ in. at a rate of 2 in. per sec. The line was $\frac{1}{4}$ in. thick and changed its length from $\frac{1}{2}$ to $5\frac{5}{8}$ in. In condition B, the rectangle was $3\frac{5}{8}$ in. high and $8\frac{1}{2}$ in. wide; in condition C it was $3\frac{5}{8}$ in. high and $1\frac{1}{8}$ in. wide. The line and the outlines of both rectangles were black.

The display was visible for 10 sec, which in most conditions was equivalent to about two complete cycles of increasing and decreasing line length. The observer sat 6 ft from the television screen. He was told simply to look at the picture, and as soon as it was turned off, he was asked to describe what he had seen. Approximately 90% of the descriptions were unambiguous, but when they were not, the observer was questioned carefully until it could be established whether he had perceived a line of changing length or a line of constant length being covered and uncovered. In order to avoid "leading" questions, care was taken that no question implied that the line either changed length or was covered. "How long was the line?" is an example of such a neutral question. The only nonneutral terms used in the questioning were those the observer had already introduced into the dialogue. In all experiments combined, less than 3% of the observers claimed to have perceived the line both as changing in length and as remaining constant while being covered and uncovered, and these observers are not included in the results given below.

College students naive about the purpose of the experiment were randomly assigned to the different conditions, a given observer participating in only one condition. There were 14, 15, and 16 observers in conditions A, B, and C respectively, and 16 and 12 in conditions D and E.

Results

All but one observer in condition A perceived a line changing its length. By contrast, only 5 of the 15 observers perceived the line in this way in condition B, 10 perceiving a line of constant length being alternately covered and uncovered. In condition C, 12 observers perceived the line changing its length and 4 perceived it as constant in length. The distribution of responses for condition B differs significantly from that of condition A and condition C, but the latter two distributions do not differ significantly from one another.

In condition D, 12 observers perceived one line of constant length with a rectangle moving over it; 4 perceived two line segments undergoing elongation and shrinkage. In condition E, 11 observers perceived two line segments undergoing enlargement and shrinkage; 1 perceived one line of constant length. The difference is, of course, statistically significant.

Experiment II

In condition B of the previous experiment, the rectangle was large enough to support the "solution" of a line of constant length undergoing covering and uncovering. The majority of observers did perceive the line in this way. However, this solution presumably requires that the rectangle be perceived as opaque. If it were instead perceived as hollow, as a mere line perimeter, this solution is no longer plausible. Experiment II, therefore, compared a display intended to create the impression of a hollow rectangle moving back and forth, *condition F*, with a display like that in condition B of the previous experiment, *condition G*.

Method

The method followed that of Experiment I except that in condition F the line and large rectangle were seen on a field of oblique lines. The oblique lines were $\frac{1}{2}$ in. wide, light gray, stationary, and $\frac{3}{4}$ in. apart. Therefore, the display created the impression of a hollow rectangular perimeter moving back and forth. For purposes of comparison, condition B of the previous experiment was repeated. In this condition, condition G, the oblique lines were not present. There were 15 naive observers in condition F and 15 in condition G.

Results

In condition F, 8 observers perceived the line as changing its length and 7 perceived it as of constant length being alternately covered and uncovered. In condition G the corresponding distribution was 1 and 14. The difference is statistically significant.

Experiment III

In this experiment, the entire line, one end of which remained contiguous with the outline contour of a human head, displaced upward and downward. Thus, the change in length of the line was given solely by the fact that one end maintained contact with the contour. The opposite end of the line did not displace horizontally. In *condition H*, the line was on the inside or "figural" side of the contour. Consequently there would be no basis for perceiving it as undergoing covering and uncovering if the outside of the contour is seen as ground. In *condition I*, the line was on the outside or "ground" side of the contour, allowing the perception of the line as moving behind the figure.

Method

The line, which was $\frac{1}{8}$ in. thick, varied in length from $3\frac{3}{4}$ to 5 in. and displaced $5\frac{3}{4}$ in. vertically at a rate of $2\frac{1}{2}$ in. per sec. The head contour was $8\frac{1}{2}$ in. high by $6\frac{1}{2}$ in. wide.

There were 14 naive undergraduate observers in condition H and 15 in condition I.

Results

Nine of the 14 observers in condition H perceived the line as changing in length as it moved vertically; 5 perceived it as of constant length and undergoing covering and uncovering. Thirteen of the 15 observers in condition I perceived the line as constant in length and going behind a figure; 2 perceived it as changing in length. The two distributions differ significantly.

Experiment IV

All of the experiments above used a solid line as the figure to be described. There are reasons for believing that a dotted line might yield a different result. One might argue that there are no textural elements visible in a solid line, elements whose successive accretion or deletion is the stimulus information that leads to the perception of occlusion or disocclusion. Against this, however, is the fact that the line visibly changes its length so that the "elements" can be thought of as hypothetical subparts of the line—as well as the fact that the line *is* perceived as undergoing occlusion and disocclusion by a majority of observers in some conditions and by some observers in all conditions.

Another reason for believing a dotted line might yield a different result concerns the question of phenomenal identity. When the line is perceived as constant in length and being covered and uncovered by another figure, each point of the line retains its identity. But when the line is perceived as enlarging or shrinking, the situation is ambiguous. Such changes could occur if new parts of the line were suddenly appearing or old parts disappearing, but they could also occur if the visible portion of the line was undergoing elastic stretching or compression. In the former case, the identity of points is maintained, but in the latter case, it is not. If instead of a solid line a dotted line is used, the identity of each point is unambiguously given and, therefore, the possibility of elastic deformation is excluded. With this alternative essentially ruled out, more observers might perceive a line of constant length undergoing occlusion and disocclusion. Accordingly, two of the conditions tested in Experiment I, conditions A and C, were repeated here as conditions J and K with a dotted line instead of a solid line. In *condition J*, the dotted line alone was visible, and in *condition K*, a narrow solid-outline rectangle remained next to the displacing end of the dotted line.

Method
Except for the displays, the method and procedure were identical with those of Experiment I. A condition analogous to that of condition B in Experiment I, that using a large rectangle, was not included because the change to a dotted line was, if anything, expected to lead to *more* observers perceiving a line of constant length being occluded. In condition B of Experiment I, a majority had perceived the line in this way.

There were 15 naive undergraduates in condition J and 15 in condition K.

Results
Eleven observers perceived the dotted line elongating and shrinking in condition J, but only 5 did so in condition K. Conversely, 4 observers perceived a line of constant length undergoing occlusion in condition J, and 10 did so in condition K. The difference in the distribution of results for the two conditions is statistically significant. The difference between the results of condition K and the results of the corresponding condition, condition C, in Experiment I is also significant.

Discussion

We believe there is a strong preference to perceive a line whose retinal image changes its length as a line of constant length undergoing occlusion and disocclusion, a preference strong enough that wherever this solution is supported by the stimulus information or can be rationalized, it will occur. That is why the line was generally perceived in this way in conditions B, D, G, and I. Conditions such as A, E, and J offer no such support and, therefore, this solution rarely occurred. That it occurred at all in these latter conditions is surprising, but it is possible that it is rationalized by the perception of a subjective contour of a covering surface.

All the remaining conditions are somewhat more equivocal insofar as the stimulus information is concerned. Condition C of Experiment I provides an outline of a rectangle that tends to yield an impression of being a solid rectangle and can therefore be perceived as covering and uncovering the solid line. However, it is not large enough for this solution to make complete "sense." Therefore, a majority of the observers perceived the line as changing in length, but a few nonetheless perceived it as being covered and uncovered. But when the line is dotted rather than solid, as it was in condition K of Experiment IV, the majority then perceived it as being covered and uncovered. We suspect that this shift occurs because with the dots unambiguously establishing the identity of points on the line, it is no longer possible to perceive the line as elastically stretching and compressing. Therefore, one must either perceive the dotted line as inexplicably increasing and decreasing in length as the rectangle moves back and forth, or as undergoing covering and uncovering. (In passing it is interesting to note that several more observers saw the line being covered and uncovered in condition J of Experiment IV than in the corresponding condition, condition A, of Experiment I). How the perceptual system tolerates the contradiction implied by the small width of the rectangle (or absence of the rectangle in condition J) in favoring the covering/uncovering solution is not clear.

Condition F of Experiment II is also equivocal. Here the rectangle is large enough to support the covering/uncovering solution, but it ought to be perceived as hollow rather than opaque. The presence of the oblique lines that presumably lead to this perception clearly has a powerful impact, because eight times as many observers perceived the line as changing in length than did so in condition G. Yet 7 of the 15 observers perceived the line as undergoing covering and uncovering. Again, the question arises as to how the perceptual system rationalizes the contradiction. It is, of course, possible to perceive the rectangle as opaque in spite of the oblique lines. One can somehow ignore the oblique lines. In this connection, it is interesting that of 6 observers in this condition whom we questioned directly afterward, the 4 who had reported a line being covered and uncovered did not recall seeing oblique lines within the rectangle; the 2 who had reported a line changing in length did recall the oblique lines.

It is perhaps also worth noting that in conditions such as C, K, or F (and, of course, in other conditions where a line is contiguous with a rectangle), the stimulus conditions for interposition obtain. Therefore, even in a stationary display of this kind, there would be a predisposition to perceive a line that is partly covered by a rectangle. Therefore, the stage is set for the observer to perceive covering and uncovering even before any motion is introduced.

It should not be possible to solve the problem posed by condition H of Experiment III by perceiving the line as being covered and uncovered because there is no figure under which the end can be perceived to be moving. Yet 5 observers did perceive the line in this way. What we believe happened is that the region intended to be perceived as ground was in fact perceived as figure by these observers. Some of them reported this fact in the interview after the period of observation, and the authors and several other observers in our laboratory have experienced the same effect. In principle, of course, the figure is reversible, but ordinarily the combined factors of closure and familiarity strongly favor perceiving the region of the face as figure. Without the moving line it is doubtful any naive observer would experience a reversal of this figure during the brief period of observation. But the presence of the moving line changes the equation, so to speak. The preference to perceive the line as undergoing covering and uncovering leads to a figure/ground reversal which then fully rationalizes that perception.

The basis for the preference to perceive an object as of constant size and undergoing occlusion or disocclusion is not known, although it is consistent with the general tendency to perceive objects as constant rather than as distorting wherever possible. It is certainly rare in either the natural or man-made environment that objects increase or decrease in size in a brief period of time, whereas it is quite common that objects become occluded by other objects. Therefore, the preference could be based *either* on an innate selective principle that emerged because of its adaptive value *or* on past experience. However, from the view of perception presented here—namely, the view of perception as the end result of problem solving—one might say that the perception of an object as changing its length under certain conditions is not an elegant solution. If, as in several conditions of our experiment, a second object is contiguous with the object undergoing change (the line), then the presence of that second object and its continued contiguity with the line must be a matter of pure coincidence *if* the line is perceived as changing in length. In other words, by this solution the moving object plays no role at all, and yet its motion is perfectly correlated with the change in the length of the line. But *all* aspects of the proximal stimulus are accounted for by the solution that the line is undergoing covering and uncovering by the second object. What we are suggesting, then, is that the preference is based on a more general tendency of the perceptual system to seek the most elegant solution and to reject coincidence.

The experiments reported here are relevant to the claim of Gibson and his associates that the perception of the covering of one surface by another—with the consequent phenomenal impression of permanence of the object covered—is based on the stimulus information of accretion or deletion of textural elements. Typically, units of one region progressively are deleted when it moves behind another region or that region moves in front of it; and units of a region are accreted when it moves *out* from behind another region or that region moves away from it. It is not clear from this statement whether it is believed that the second, unchanging, region must be a "figure." In describing an experiment on the progressive disappearance of a disk where nothing but the disk is visible (Michotte, Thinès, and Crabbé, 1964), Gibson (1966) implies that the progressive deletion of parts of the object is what is crucial, since no other figure is visible. (Interestingly enough, in this demonstration the disk is perceived to be undergoing occlusion by passing under a slit although no slit is physically present.) In subsequent reports, all examples refer to two surfaces or regions, the units of one of which are undergoing accretion and deletion and the units of the other of which are unchanging (Gibson et al., 1969) or the units of both of which are undergoing accretion and deletion (Kaplan, 1969). But the question nevertheless arises whether it is a necessary condition of Gibson's hypothesis that a second surface be present and, if so, how its presence is defined. One might argue that this question is meaningless because the changing surface is necessarily adjacent to *some* other surface whether that be perceived as belonging to a bounded figure or to unformed ground. If so, one wonders why our observers generally did not perceive the changing line as an object undergoing occlusion and disocclusion in those conditions where no figure other than the line itself was visible.

Therefore, for the accretion/deletion hypothesis to be viable, it seems necessary to assume that the region perceived as occluding the other surface be perceived as a figure rather than as ground. This in itself would seem to be a very serious challenge to the view that one can state the conditions for phenomenal covering and uncovering purely in terms of proximal stimulus features. Figure/ground organization is a perceptual outcome, not something given by the proximal stimulus. But passing over this question, the further fact remains that for the covering/uncovering effect to predominate, other properties of the "covering" object are important. Ideally, it should be phenomenally opaque and sufficiently large. We do not see how Gibson and his associates can account for findings such as those of conditions C and F.

The outcome of the experiment on the progressively disappearing disk cited above (Michotte et al., 1964) constitutes a problem for the theory we are defending. The disk is perceived as undergoing occlusion despite the absence of a visible object that can be interpreted as the covering object. On the face of it, the result is a direct contradiction of what we found to occur with an isolated line. There seem to be two differences between the disk experiment and our isolated-line conditions: the first is that the disk is two-dimensional, so that occlusion affects its width as well as its height (and thereby alters its shape); the second is that the disk as a whole moves until one edge reaches the (invisible) occluding edge. Either of these factors or both together may explain why in this case as compared to our one-dimensional line, observers have the impression that a constant object is progressively disappearing from view, *provided that* the observer "perceives" ("imagines"?) that an invisible object is covering the disk. The two-dimensional character of the disk produces a phenomenal "edge" behind which the disk can be seen to go. In other words, the strong preference for the constancy outcome that we found to obtain in most of our conditions in this case leads to the subjective construction of an opaque surface with only a minimum of supporting "evidence."

There is one feature of our findings that we believe has important theoretical significance. Perception can often only be understood as resulting from or dependent upon certain other, temporally prior, perceptions. Thus, for example, we can understand the main trend of the results of Experiment III only if we assume that the line is perceived in terms of the figure/ground organization of the display. Therefore, the information used by the perceptual system in arriving at "solutions" is often given in the form of already achieved perceptions, although admittedly such a two-stage process is very rapid and we are not phenomenally aware of separate stages. There are many examples in the field of perception where one can argue that such a process occurs, and recently additional evidence of this kind has been reported for the perception of a figure through a moving aperture (Rock and Sigman, 1973) and the perception of stroboscopic movement (Sigman and Rock, 1974).

Intuitively, most of our results are not particularly surprising. One might even ask how the outcome could be other than what it was. For example, would anyone expect an isolated line that changes its length to be perceived as a line of constant length being covered and uncovered? On an intuitive level the answer is no, but why does this answer cause so much difficulty on a theoretical level? The intuitive answer is based on the certainty we feel that to perceive one thing going behind another, that other thing must itself be perceived. This means that intuitively we grasp the fundamental fact that perception is rational, but there is nothing in current psychological theory to require that it be.

References

Gibson, J. J. 1966. *Senses considered as perceptual systems.* Boston: Houghton Mifflin.

Gibson, J. J., Kaplan, G. A., Reynolds, H. N., and Wheeler, K. 1969. The change from visible to invisible: A study of optical transitions. *Perception and Psychophysics* 5:113–116.

Kaplan, G. A. 1969. Kinetic disruption of optical texture: The perception of depth at an edge. *Perception and Psychophysics* 6:193–198.

Michotte, A., Thinès, G., and Crabbé, G. 1964. *Les compléments amodaux des structures perceptives*. Louvain, Belgium: Publications de l'Université de Louvain.

Rock, I., and Sigman, E. 1973. Intelligence factors in the perception of form through a moving slit. *Perception* 2:357–369.

Sigman, E., and Rock, I. 1974. Stroboscopic movement based on perceptual intelligence. *Perception* 3(1):9–28.

Wallach, H., and O'Connell, D. N. 1953. The kinetic depth effect. *Journal of Experimental Psychology* 45:205–217.

Part VI
Lightness

Introduction

In the introductory chapter, the ambiguity of "adjacency" was discussed in relation to the problem of lightness perception. When Wallach (1948) demonstrated that the perceived lightness of a region was based on the ratio of its luminance to that of an adjacent region, it was implicit that "adjacent region" referred to the retinal projection.

Only thirty years later was it shown definitively by Alan Gilchrist (chapter 22; 1980) that the adjacent regions whose ratios determine phenomenal lightness must be regions perceived to be in the same plane. To be sure, there had been some precursors leading to this conclusion, or if not to the conclusion as just stated, then to the realization of the problem that arises with complex, three-dimensional spatial arrangements (see Hochberg and Beck 1954; Gogel and Mershon 1969). However, no previous investigator had obtained the almost total determination of phenomenal lightness by coplanar ratio as Gilchrist did, nor had anyone clarified why some experiments lead to different results.

In any event, the reader will see in chapter 22 not only that perceived lightness is governed by luminance relationships among regions in the same perceived plane, but also how the standard concept of lateral inhibition, long held to be the mechanism underlying perceived lightness, contrast, and constancy, cannot account for these perceptions.

As to *why* it is adjacent ratios within a plane rather than within the retina that governs perceived lightness, a plausible answer is that the perceived edges of regions within a plane can generally be assumed (by the perceptual system) to have arisen because of a difference in reflectances. When retinally adjacent regions lie in different planes, other interpretations are possible, such as that the luminance difference derives from differences in illumination. Therefore, to "get at" the correct lightness, one should deal only with luminance ratios within a plane. To "get at" the correct illumination, one should compare adjacent luminances *across* planes.

At any rate, to the extent that perceived lightness is based on perceived spatial arrangement, the achievement of the outcome (perceived lightness) is quite indirect. It is based first on perceiving the spatial arrangement. It therefore seems to implicate cognitive processes in first achieving that prior spatial perception and then assigning lightness values to luminance values as "required" by their spatial position. It cannot be dealt with adequately in terms of the higher-order stimulus of ratios, although in some respects ratios are ideal exemplars of a higher-order stimulus.

References

Gilchrist, A. 1980. When does perceived lightness depend on perceived spatial arrangement? *Perception & Psychophysics* 28:527—38.

Gogel, W. C., and D. H. Mershon 1969. Depth adjacency in simultaneous contrast. *Perception & Psychophysics* 5:13—17.

Hochberg, J., and J. Beck. 1954. Apparent spatial arrangement and perceived brightness. *Journal of Experimental Psychology* 47:263—66.

Wallach, H. 1948. Brightness constancy and the nature of achromatic colors. *Journal of Experimental Psychology* 38:310—24.

Chapter 22
Perceived Lightness Depends on Perceived Spatial Arrangement
Alan L. Gilchrist

A change in the perceived spatial position of a surface can change its perceived color from black to white or from white to black. This finding challenges the widespread view that denies any substantial role of depth perception in the perception of surface lightness (the shade of gray between white and black).

Since 1948, when Hans Wallach published his classic experiments in lightness constancy (1), a consensus in this field has held that perceived lightness is a function of luminance ratios between adjacent parts of the retinal image, regardless of where those parts are perceived to lie in three-dimensional space. Moreover, because of Wallach's emphasis on retinal adjacency, many researchers (2) have concluded that lateral inhibitory connections among retinal cells provide the neural mechanism underlying the ratio principle.

A number of investigators (3–7) have sought to show that retinal ratios do not tell the whole story. Essentially the approach has been to change the apparent spatial position of a target surface so that it either appears to lie in the same plane as that of its surrounding surface or in a different plane in order to determine whether the apparent spatial separation between the surfaces reduces their interaction and thus produces a different perceived color in the target even though the two-dimensional retinal pattern remains unchanged. Two studies (3, 4) reported changes as great as one and a quarter steps on the Munsell scale (8), or 17 percent of the difference between black and white. Most (5–7) have reported little or no change.

With a few exceptions (9), it is now generally agreed (10) that perceived lightness is essentially determined by the relative intensities of adjacent parts of the retinal array. The experiments that I report here grew out of a seeming inconsistency between the retinal ratio theory and everyday experience. Rarely are black, white, and gray surfaces grossly misperceived. Yet the retinal ratio theory would predict consistently

Originally published in *Science* 195 (14 January 1977): 185–187. Reprinted with permission.

accurate lightness perception only when the difference in luminance at the retina is produced by a difference in the reflectance of the external surfaces. When the difference occurs because external surfaces that receive unequal amounts of illumination are imaged on adjacent parts of the retina, sizable lightness illusions should be expected. This difficulty is mitigated by the fact that the boundary between different levels of illumination is frequently gradual. However, illumination boundaries are by no means always gradual. For example, the retinal image can contain adjacent, sharp-edged patches of radically different luminances when two walls of equal color but unequal illumination meet at a corner, or when a near surface partially occludes an unequally illuminated far surface. Yet no one has suggested that lightness constancy is poorer near such corners.

Perceived lightness might be determined primarily by ratios within perceived planes rather than by all retinal ratios regardless of perceived depth. This "coplanar ratio hypothesis" is illustrated by the following experiment, in which a depth illusion is created in order to determine whether perceived lightness is affected. Observers looked through a pinhole in a screen (Fig. 22.1) through which they saw a dimly illuminated near wall. Through an opening in this wall, a brightly illuminated far wall could be seen. A piece of white paper (the target surface) and a piece of black paper were attached to the near wall so that they extended into the opening. Another piece of white paper (the same white as the target) was attached to the far wall and was partly overlapped by a gray strip, the purpose of which was simply to prevent the white piece from appearing to float in midair. Interposition cues were used to create two variations of the display. The unaltered square target (Fig. 22.1B) appeared to lie in the plane of the near wall. The target could also be made to appear on the distant wall by means of two notches, cut out of the corners of the target so as to coincide with edges of both the near black and the far white paper (Fig. 22.1C). A separate group of eight observers viewed each array and indicated the apparent lightness of the target by selecting a matching sample from a 16-step Munsell scale on which black was 2 and white was 9.5.

Changing the perceived location of the target in this way caused its perceived color to vary from white (near condition) to almost black (far condition) (Fig. 22.1C). Note that this difference was obtained without any significant change in the retinal pattern (11) nor any change in retinal intensities.

Theories that emphasize retinal interactions would have predicted no differences in the study just described. On the other hand, the results follow from the coplanar ratio hypothesis. That is, the perceived lightness of the target is governed by the luminance relationships between the target and whatever regions are seen as coplanar. The luminance relationship

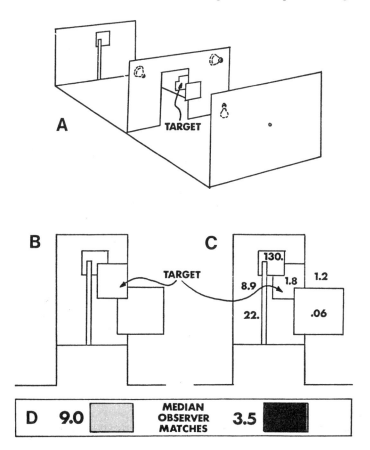

Figure 22.1
(A) Perspective view of the apparatus showing hidden light bulbs. The displays (as seen through the pinhole) in which the target appeared to be located either (B) in the near plane or (C) in the far plane. (D) The average match from a Munsell chart for the two displays. Luminances (C) are in foot-lamberts.

between the target and noncoplanar regions (despite retinal adjacency) is substantially irrelevant to the lightness of the target.

It is possible to construct a critical test in which the coplanar ratio hypothesis would make opposite predictions to those of a retinal theory. In the stimulus display shown in Fig. 22.2, the horizontal plane contained a large white square with a black trapezoidal tab that extended outward toward the observer. The vertical plane contained a large black square and a small white tab that extended upward. The tabs were trapezoidal in order to permit a spatial position illusion (4, 5). Seen with one eye through a carefully positioned hole, each tab appeared to be a square

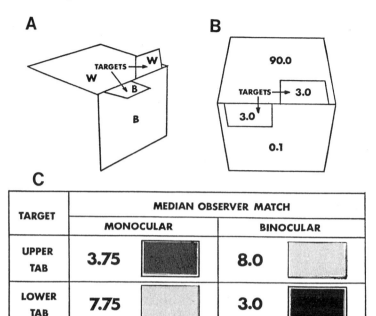

Figure 22.2
(A) Perspective view of the stimulus display showing color (B, black; W, white) of each part. (B) Monocular retinal pattern showing luminances in foot-lamberts. (C) Average Munsell matches for monocular and binocular viewing conditions.

lying in the same plane as the larger square that surrounded it on three sides. Seen with both eyes the tabs were seen to be trapezoids lying in their actual planes. A light bulb, unseen by the observer, was located above the display so that the horizontal surfaces received 30 times as much illumination as the vertical surfaces. Therefore the tabs were equal in luminance.

A retinal ratio theory would predict that, as the upper tab is surrounded on three sides by a very intense region, it should appear darker than the lower tab, which is mostly surrounded by a very dark region.

The results were the opposite of this prediction (Fig. 22.2C). When viewed binocularly and the actual spatial layout was correctly perceived, the upper tab was seen as near white, the lower tab as black. When viewed monocularly so that each tab appeared to lie in the plane of its principal background, the perceived colors reversed, the upper appearing black, the lower, white.

The central conclusion of this research is that perceived surface lightness depends on ratios between regions perceived to lie next to one another in the same plane. Kardos (12) proposed the similar idea that relative luminance within coplanar spatial regions determines perceived lightness, because illumination tends to be uniform within planes but separate planes tend to be unequally illuminated. This view, however, reflected the general opinion of that period that the perception of lightness depends on the prior registration of the level of illumination.

Koffka (13) argued that perceived lightness depends on gradients of light intensity (at the retina) but added the important qualification that some gradients are more effective than others with regard to lightness. Gradients of intensity between coplanar surfaces, he said, are more effective than those between noncoplanar regions.

Gogel and Mershon (6) interpreted their results in terms of simultaneous lightness contrast governed by the adjacency principle. Their view is that the degree of simultaneous lightness contrast is inversely related to the separation of the target and "induction" surfaces, both in depth (as they showed) and laterally [as others have shown (14)]. Thus the present results would have been predicted, at least qualitatively, by their adjacency principle (15).

We can now understand why previous studies (4–7) have shown such a small effect of depth on perceived lightness. If lightness is a frame of reference phenomenon, as the coplanar ratio principle implies, then it is not sufficient to merely remove the target surface from the plane of its retinally neighboring surface. The array must be such that the target will be seen as a member of one coplanar ratio when it appears in one spatial position, but a member of quite a different ratio when seen in the alternative plane (16).

These experiments show that the perceived lightness of a surface can vary from white to black depending merely on its perceived spatial position, without any significant change in the retinal array. This result implies that lateral inhibition at the retina has little to do with everyday perception of lightness. Certainly the available theories that reduce lightness perception to lateral inhibition are in error.

Another important implication also follows. If the perceived lightnesses of surfaces depend on their perceived location in space, depth processing must occur first and be followed by the determination of surface lightness. That is, processing is initiated by a pattern of intensity differences on the retina; then the nervous system uses various depth cues to construct a spatial model to fit the retinal pattern. As this spatial model is completed, lightnesses are assigned to the various surfaces in accord with the coplanar ratio principle.

References and Notes

1. H. Wallach, *J. Exp. Psychol.* **38**, 310 (1948).
2. T. Cornsweet, *Visual Perception* (Academic Press, New York, 1970).
3. D. H. Mershon, *Vision Res.* **12**, 969 (1972).

4. J. Beck, *J. Exp. Psychol.* **69**, 170 (1965).
5. J. E. Hochberg and J. Beck, *ibid.* **47**, 263 (1954).
6. W. C. Gogel and D. H. Mershon, *Percept. Psychophys.* **5**, 13 (1969).
7. H. R. Flock and E. Freedberg, *Percept. Psychophys.* **8**, 251 (1970); W. Epstein, *J. Psychol.* **52**, 51 (1961); T. Gibbs and R. B. Lawson, *Vision Res.* **14**, 983 (1974); B. Julesz, *Foundations of Cyclopean Perception* (Univ. of Chicago Press, Chicago, 1971).
8. D. B. Judd, in *Handbook of Experimental Psychology*, S. S. Stevens, Ed. (Wiley, New York, 1966), p. 847.
9. J. Beck, *Surface Color Perception* (Cornell Univ. Press, Ithaca, N.Y., 1972); I. Rock, *An Introduction to Perception* (Macmillan, New York, 1975).
10. L. Kaufman, *Sight and Mind: An Introduction to Visual Perception* (Oxford Univ. Press, Oxford, 1974); G. M. Murch, *Visual and Auditory Perception* (Bobbs-Merrill, Indianapolis, 1973); R. N. Haber and M. Hershenson, *Psychology of Visual Perception* (Holt, Rinehart & Winston, New York, 1973).
11. Although the area of each square changed somewhat as a result of the notches, the length of contour shared by the target and each retinally neighboring square did not.
12. L. Kardos, *Z. Psychol.* (No. 23) (Erg.-Bd., 1934).
13. K. Koffka, *Principles of Gestalt Psychology* (Harcourt, Brace & World, New York, 1963).
14. B. Dunn and H. Leibowitz, *J. Exp. Psychol.* **61**, 505 (1961); H. Leibowitz, F. A. Mote, W. R. Thurlow, *ibid.* **46**, 453 (1953); E. C. Stewart, *ibid.* **57**, 235 (1959).
15. Two features of the adjacency principle suggest ways in which it could be tested against the coplanar ratio principle. (i) According to the adjacency principle, the perceived lightness of a target should move continuously through the gray scale as its apparent position between two inducing fields is varied continuously. The coplanar ratio principle would predict a sharp break in perceived lightness at whatever point in space the target changes its plane of reference. (ii) Gogel and Mershon use adjacency to describe the workings of contrast. The coplanar ratio principle need imply no contrast process. Indeed, a subsequent article will provide further evidence that lightness perception does not involve contrast in any important way (A. L. Gilchrist, in preparation).
16. Mershon (3) did provide separate inducing fields for two of the depth planes in which the target appeared. Presumably his results involved less change in lightness than those reported here, because even when his target and inducing fields were coplanar, they were still somewhat separated retinally. In addition, both of his inducing fields had luminances greater than that of the target whereas, in the present studies, the luminance relationship of the target and the surrounding coplanar surfaces reversed for the two different conditions of each experiment.
17. Partially supported by Bell Laboratories, Murray Hill, N.J. 07974. I thank J. Johnston and C. Harris for advice on the writing, D. Dinnerstein for introducing me to lightness perception, H. Wallach for his inspiring example, and especially I. Rock for his formulation of the original problem and for his continued interest in this research.

Part VII
Final Considerations

Introduction

The final chapter by Walter Gogel discusses a number of ideas not yet covered elsewhere in this book that are nevertheless quite germane to the overall thesis of indirect perception. Because Gogel's chapter contains a vocabulary somewhat idiosyncratic to his own research, the brief review that follows may help to make it more intelligible to readers not yet familiar with his work.

The basic idea in Gogel's article, as I see it, is that there is an interaction between two or more perceptions. In this respect, it is quite similar to the idea of percept–percept couplings discussed by me and by Epstein in the first two chapters of this volume. A good example of such interaction would be that of constancy (which Gogel and others call the "invariance hypothesis"): namely, that a given stimulus on the retina determines a unique relation between the perception of one aspect of that stimulus (e.g., its perceived distance) and other aspects of it (e.g., its perceived size or perceived speed of motion). He argues that the interaction or coupling hypothesis of constancy requires a predictable perception even when no cues to distance are available. Other theories might maintain that the interaction hypothesis simply breaks down under such conditions, but Gogel shows that it is *not* the case when there are no cues to distance. Rather, the observer "supplies" information about distance in the form of what would nowadays be called "heuristic assumptions" or "default values." For example, Gogel argues persuasively that there is a strong tendency for observers to perceive two objects as being at the *same* distance in the absence of distance cues. He refers to this as an example of "observer tendencies," more specifically as the "equidistance tendency." That is, the perceptual system "assumes" equidistance in the absence of information to the contrary.

Another observer tendency Gogel documents is the "specific distance tendency." This says that, all else being equal, when there are no external cues to absolute distance, the observer localizes objects at a specific distance: namely, 4 to 8 feet. This perception of localization would of course affect many other perceptions, of which perceived size would be one clear example.

One new idea here is that the coupling between two perceptions may entail one factor that is not "given" in the stimulus, but must be supplied by the observer. Gogel, whose thinking about coupling anticipated or paralleled that of other theorists (e.g., Hochberg 1968; Attneave 1972; Epstein, chapter 2), supplies us with different evidence than that summarized by Epstein or elsewhere in this volume. I will not bother to repeat it here, for the reader will encounter it soon enough in reading his chapter.

In my opinion, the most interesting formulation of Gogel's, to use his own term, concerns what he calls *perceptual equations*. This is elaborated in a second article by Gogel on this topic (Gogel 1973) as follows:

> An expression of a perceptual interaction in equation form is termed a perceptual equation, in contrast to a psychophysical equation. In order to validly test perceptual equations, the response being measured must reflect perceptual, not cognitive, factors.... Such expressions which contain terms for at least two different perceptions [e.g., perceived size and perceived distance] as well as a term for the proximal stimulus, can be called perceptual equations.

The independent perceptual dimension is often perceived distance with the dependent perceptions being of some other phenomenal characteristic, such as perceived size, shape, orientation, lightness, or motion. In short, the perceived characteristics of objects are affected by their perceived location in three-dimensional space. Note that Gogel is going beyond the notion of coupling in his idea of perceptual equations by asserting that the independent perceptual dimension governs the dependent one. The very use of the terms "independent" and "dependent" suggests the existence of *causal* relations between events. This harks back to my discussion in chapter 1 where I raised this issue. There I argued that, for the most part, when perceptual coupling occurs, it implies a one-way causal relation of dependence in which one factor determines another, even though some might maintain that the notion of coupling does not require that one percept precede and cause another. However, the notion of perceptual equations, for which Gogel supplies much evidence, does imply such a one-way sequence, as is the case for equations in general. The temporally directed, causal sequence of perceptions implied by perceptual equations thus provides a very strong argument for the existence of indirect perception.

References

Attneave, F. 1972. Representations of physical space. In *Coding processes in human memory*, ed. A. W. Melton and E. Martin. New York: Winston.
Hochberg, J. 1968. In the mind's eye. In *Contemporary theory and research in visual perception*, ed. R. N. Haber. New York: Holt, Rinehart and Winston.

Chapter 23
The Organization of Perceived Space
Walter C. Gogel

Perceptual Constancy and the Invariance Hypotheses

One of the basic problems in the study of perception is the problem of understanding the processes that determine the relation between perception and stimulation at the receptors. Stimulation defined at the level of the receptors is called proximal stimulation. Stimulation defined at the level of the physical objects outside O is called distal stimulation. Although it is clear that the adequate stimulus must be defined at the proximal rather than the distal level, it is often found that perceptions are more proportional to distal than to proximal stimulation. A proportionality between perceptions and distal rather than proximal stimulation is termed "the constancy phenomena." Consider, for example, the perception of size. An object of constant physical size will subtend a decreasing size on the eye with increasing distance from O. But, in a situation containing many cues to distance (a full cue situation) it is found that the perceived size of the object remains more constant than would be expected from the decreasing size on the eye. The result in which perceived size is proportional to object size despite changes in retinal size is called size constancy. Similarly, for a constant velocity of an object moving in a frontoparallel plane the velocity on the eye of O will decrease as the distance of the frontoparallel plane from O increases. But, if adequate cues to distance are available, the perceived velocity of the object will remain more constant than would be expected from the decreasing velocity on the eye. The result in which perceived velocity is proportional to object velocity despite changes in the velocity on the eye is known as velocity constancy. As another example, the shape of an object on the eye will change as the object is rotated in depth from a frontoparallel plane. But, if adequate depth cues are available, the perception of the shape of the object will remain more constant than would be expected from the changing shape

Originally published in *Psychologische Forschung* 36 (1973): 195–221. Reprinted with permission.

on the eye. The result in which perceived shape is proportional to object shape despite changes in the shape on the eye is termed shape constancy.

The usual interpretation of size, velocity, and shape constancy is that the correct perception of the distance of the object in the case of size and velocity constancy or the correct perception of the slant of the object in depth in the case of shape constancy for a given size, velocity, or shape on the eye is essential for the correct perception of size, velocity, or shape. In other examples of constancy perceived distance does not play so obvious a role. For example, in visual fields containing many objects the perceived brightness of an object tends to be relatively independent of the general level of illumination. The result that the perception of brightness is proportional to the albedo (reflectance) of the object despite changes in the intensity of the light on the eye is called brightness constancy.

If perceptions were always proportional to distal, not proximal, stimuli, the lack of proportionality between proximal stimulation and perception would present an explanatory problem, but at least the perceptions always would be readily predictable. But this is not the case. There are conditions under which perceptions tend to be more proportional to proximal than to distal stimuli. One of the most important of these conditions involves the reduction or removal of distance cues (reduced conditions of observation). An instance of the effect of the systematic reduction of distance cues is found in a study of perceived size by Holway and Boring (1941). In this study discs subtending a constant visual angle were placed at different distances from O. It was found that, when a variety of distance cues were present, perceived size was proportional to physical size. But, as distance cues were progressively reduced, perceived size tended to be increasingly proportional to retinal size. Similarly, it is found that as cues to perceived slant in depth are reduced perceived shape tends to resemble retinal shape (Epstein and Park, 1963). Or, when a reduction screen is used to eliminate the view of surrounding stimuli, the perceived color of an object tends to vary with the luminance, not the albedo, of the object (Katz, 1935).

In the ease of size, shape, and velocity perception the presence of cues of perceived distance seems to be the significant factor that determines whether the perceptions will more nearly resemble the proximal or distal stimulus. Two interpretations of this phenomenon are possible. One will be called the core-context hypothesis (see Boring, 1946). This hypothesis states that O has available two sources of information for the perception of object characteristics such as size, shape, or velocity. One of these, the core stimulus, is the size, shape, or velocity of the object on the eye. The other, the context stimuli, are the cues of distance that determine perceived distance. In the Holway-Boring experiment, it is assumed that a reduction in the amount of distance cues resulted in a greater weight given to the core as contrasted with the context stimuli with the result that the perception of size became increasingly proportional to the core stimulus. According to this hypothesis, the complete reduction of distance cues eliminates the role of perceived distance in the perception of size, shape, and motion and, as a result, the perception resembles the core stimulus. A different interpretation is implied in a formulation called the invariance hypotheses (Koffka, 1935). One of these, the size-distance invariance hypothesis (Kilpatrick and Ittelson, 1953), states that for all conditions of observation (whether full or reduced), a given retinal size determines a unique relation between perceived size and perceived distance. The shape-slant invariance hypothesis (Epstein and Park, 1963) states that a given shape on the eye for all conditions of observation determines a unique relation of perceived shape to perceived slant in depth. Similarly, the movement-distance invariance hypothesis would specify that a given movement on the eye determines a unique relation of perceived movement to the perceived distance of the plane of the moving object. The aspect of these invariance hypotheses of importance for the present discussion is that for a given stimulus on the eye, the perception of distance or slant in depth is necessarily a part of the perception of size, shape, and motion, etc. In other words, one perception (perceived distance) is essential for transforming a proximal stimulus (of size, shape, or motion) into another perception (perceived size, shape, or motion). In order to emphasize the essential interrelations of perceptions involved in this transformation of retinal to perceived events, this point of view will be called the hypothesis of perceptual interactions.

According to the invariance hypotheses, the interaction of perceived distance with perceived size or motion is such that a change in perceived distance for a constant retinal size or motion will result in a predictable change in perceived size or motion. For example, for a constant retinal size or velocity, perceived size or perceived velocity is expected to increase with an increase in perceived distance. An expression for the more general concept of perceptual interactions, of which the invariance hypotheses are perhaps the best known examples is that

$$\psi_2 = f(R, \psi_1) \tag{1}$$

where ψ_2 is the perceived size or perceived velocity, R is the retinal size or velocity and ψ_1 is perceived distance. The best known instance of Equation 1 is the size-distance invariance hypothesis which expressed in simplest form is that

$$S' = K\Theta D' \tag{2}$$

where S' is perceived size, Θ is retinal size, K is an observer constant, and D' is perceived distance. The shape-slant invariance hypothesis can be regarded as an instance of the size-distance invariance hypothesis. For example, if the object is slanted in depth by rotation around a horizontal axis, its perceived shape can be defined as the integration of the perceived width of successive horizontal segments of the object. But each horizontal segment of perceived width is determined according to the size-distance invariance hypothesis by the size of the horizontal segment on the retina and by the perceived distance of this horizontal segment from O. According to the statements of the invariance hypotheses given above, a particular value of R specifies a unique (invariant) relation between ψ_2, and ψ_2. Invariance hypotheses stated in this stringent manner have not always been verified (see Epstein, Park and Casey, 1961; Epstein and Park, 1963). For the present discussion a less stringent statement will suffice. It will be required only that, for a given value of R, all other factors equal, ψ_2 will be a monotonic increasing function of ψ_1 without requiring that this function necessarily be invariant for different conditions of observation. Also, in most of the discussion that follows, perceived distance will be the independent perception with the perception of shape, or velocity etc. the dependent perception.

The hypothesis of perceptual interactions, unlike the core-context hypothesis, does not regard the core and context stimuli as opposing factors that are given different weights in determining perceptions as a function of the amount of distance information (context) available. Instead, the hypothesis of perceptual interactions assumes that perceptual interactions occur and involve the same processes for all conditions of observation, i.e., regardless of whether many or no cues of distance are available. The experimental result that perceptions tend to resemble the distal more than the proximal stimuli under full cue conditions of observation is explained by the hypothesis of perceptual interactions in that, under these conditions, perceived distances often approximate physical distances. But, a problem is posed for the hypothesis of perceptual interactions by the perceptions of size, shape, and velocity, etc. that occur under reduced conditions of observation. Under these conditions it might be expected from the hypothesis of perceptual interactions and, contrary to the obtained results (see the above study by Holway and Boring), that perceived size, shape, or velocity would disappear or become indefinite because perceived distance disappeared or became indefinite. But, there is reason to question the conclusion that perceived distance disappears or becomes indefinite even with total cue reduction. As will be discussed, it has been found that under conditions of total cue reduction observer processes supply a perceived distance, with this perceived distance consistent with the finding that under reduced conditions of observation perceived size, shape and velocity tend to be proportional to the size, shape, and velocity of the object on the eye.

Observer Tendencies in the Perception of Distance

The Equidistance Tendency
Two factors (tendencies), supplied by *O* rather than determined by stimuli, that can influence a perception of depth or distance have been identified. These are called the equidistance tendency and the specific distance tendency. Their effect is most evident when all of the usual cues to distance are removed and least evident when effective distance cues are present. As distance cues are increasingly removed or weakened, the contribution of the equidistance tendency and specific distance tendency to the perception of distance is increasingly obvious. They are termed tendencies not only because they are supplied by *O* but, more importantly, because they are at least potentially available to determine perceptions of distance in all situations as is indicated by their increased effectiveness with increased reduction of stimulus cues of distance [Gogel, 1965, 1969 (1)].

There are two types of perceived distance to consider. The perception of absolute or egocentric distance is the perception of the distance of an object or a part of an object from *O*. The perception of relative or exocentric distance is the perception of the depth between objects or between parts of objects without regard to the perceived distance of these objects or parts from *O*. The equidistance tendency is involved in the perception of relative or exocentric distance and is the tendency for objects or parts of objects to appear at the same distance from *O* with the strength of this tendency inversely related to the directional separation of the objects or parts. The evidence for the equidistance tendency is clear (Gogel, 1956; Lodge and Wist, 1968; Roelofs and Zeeman, 1957). If two objects, for example a disc and rectangle, are placed at different distances from *O* with no stimulus cues as to the distance of the objects, these objects will usually appear to be at the same distance. Since the objects appear at the same distance their perceived sizes, in agreement with the size-distance invariance hypothesis, will be proportional to their retinal sizes. Thus, if the diameter of the disc is physically the same as the width of the rectangle, but the rectangle is at twice the physical distance of the disc, the perceived width (diameter) of the disc will be twice the perceived width of the rectangle. Since the ratio of the widths of the disc and rectangle on the eye are also 2 to 1, the perception of size under these reduced conditions will be proportional to retinal size. It will be noted that the perception of distance (in this case, perceived equidistance) is as necessary for the perceptions of size as it would be in more full cue conditions in which the disc and rectangle were perceived as being at different distances. Also, some effect attributable to the equidistance tendency usually will be present if, instead of totally reduced conditions of observation, a limited amount of distance information is introduced by providing, for example, the cue of accommodation between the disc and rectangle. In this latter case, it is likely that the perceived depth between the disc and rectangle, expected from the accommodative difference, would be reduced but not eliminated by the equidistance tendency. It is very likely that the equidistance tendency can reduce the perceived exocentric depth expected from the relative size cue (Gogel, 1971), and under some circumstances can reduce even the perceived depth expected from the normally very effective cue of binocular disparity (Gogel, Brune and Inaba, 1954).

The reader can demonstrate for himself the effectiveness of the equidistance tendency and its inverse relation to directional separation. All that is required is a sheet of glass oriented at about 45° to the line of sight so that a lighted room viewed directly through the glass and a disc of light in a dark surround (located to the left or right of the observation position) and viewed by reflection from the glass can be seen simultaneously. The observation should be monocular, and preferably the scene should be viewed through a small restrictive aperture to eliminate the accommodative cue between the disc and objects in the lighted room. By turning the sheet of glass, the disc will appear to be projected to different parts of the room. As the disc is made to appear in the directional vicinity of a particular object in the room the disc will appear to move toward that object in depth. The more adjacent the disc is directionally to a particular object (relative to that of other objects) the more adjacent it will appear in depth to that object. This situation also can be used to demonstrate the size-distance invariance hypothesis. Since the disc is of a constant physical size at a constant physical distance, its retinal size (visual angle) is constant and, in agreement with Eq. 2, its perceived size will vary directly with its perceived distance.

The equidistance tendency applies to the perceived depth between parts of objects as well as between objects. A luminous irregularly shaped surface, slanted in depth with respect to the frontoparallel plane of O, when viewed in the dark without cues to exocentric distance (viewed monocularly through a small aperture), will appear in the fronto-parallel plane as a result of the tendency of all parts of the surface to appear equidistant. Also, consistent with the size-slant invariance hypothesis the perceived shape of the surface will be proportional to its retinal shape, not its physical shape. But again, the perception of exocentric depth, in this case the perception that all parts of the surface are at the same distance, is as essential to the perception of shape under these conditions as it is in other situations in which the surface is perceived as slanted and hence perceived as similar to its physical shape.

In summary, the perception of relative size or shape that occurs under reduced conditions of observation and tends to be proportional to retinal size and shape cannot be considered to be independent of the perception of exocentric distance occurring between the objects or between the parts of the object. In these cases, the equidistance tendency is available to produce a particular perception of distance, i.e., a perception of the objects as equidistant or of the slant as frontoparallel, with the perceived size and shape in agreement with the invariance hypotheses. Also, since the effect of the equidistance tendency does not entirely disappear when some but not totally effective cues to exocentric distance are present, it is expected from the equidistance tendency and Eq. 2 that the increasing reduction of exocentric cues will result in perceived size and perceived shape becoming increasingly proportional to retinal size and shape. The data obtained under conditions of cue reduction do not support the notion that the importance or role of perceived distance in determining the perception of size, shape, or motion etc. has either decreased or changed as a function of the amount of distance information available.

The Specific Distance Tendency
As is indicated by the phenomenon of size constancy, if an object is presented in a frontoparallel plane with veridical cues to egocentric distance, perceived size, in agreement with Eq. 2, will be proportional to physical, not retinal, size. This proportionality between perceived and physical size can be demonstrated, for example, by presenting the same object at different distances to different groups of Os under full cue conditions of observation and obtaining verbal reports of size from both groups. But, if instead of using full cue conditions of observation, the reports of perceived size are obtained under conditions of total cue reduction, it will be found that the ratio of the perceived sizes of the object at the two different distances obtained from the two groups will tend to be proportional to the ratio of the retinal sizes of the object at the two distances [Gogel, 1969 (2)]. The equidistance tendency occurring between objects presented either simultaneously or successively cannot explain this result since each presentation contained only one object and the objects at different distances were presented to different groups of Os. If Eq. 1 and 2 are to apply under these circumstances it must be postulated that a tendency occurs for an object to appear at a particular constant distance whenever cues to distance are eliminated. The occurrence of such a tendency, called the specific distance tendency, has been demonstrated. The specific distance tendency is the tendency for objects to appear at a near distance from O (about 4 to 8 ft.) in the absence of egocentric cues. Direct evidence for the specific distance tendency is found in two experiments [Gogel, 1969 (2), Exper. 3 and 4] in which a monocularly observed luminous rectangle was presented above the floor of a long visual alley. As a consequence of the more distant portions of the alley being directionally

closer to the rectangle than the nearer portions, the equidistance tendency resulted in the rectangle appearing toward the back of the alley [see Gogel, 1969 (2)]. Following the simultaneous presentation of the alley and rectangle, the lights in the alley were turned off eliminating the equidistance tendency, with the rectangle the only object visible. When presented to the same Os who had previously seen the rectangle and alley together, the rectangle appeared at a nearer distance than it had previously. Also, the change in the apparent distance of the rectangle, from its distant position in the alley to a nearer position when presented in the dark, usually resulted in a decrease in its perceived size in agreement with Eq. 2 but in disagreement with common sense (see Carlson, 1960, 1962). It follows that the tendency for the rectangle to appear at a near distance with the alley absent was a perceptual effect and not merely a "best bet" response to inadequate distance information. Indirect evidence for the specific distance tendency is available from egocentric judgments of distance obtained under reduced or relatively reduced conditions of observation. It is often found that when convergence or accommodation are the only distance cues available, objects physically distant appear relatively close to O [Foley, 1968; Biersdorf, 1966; Gogel, 1972 (1)]. As will be discussed in a following article (Gogel, 1973), there is also evidence to indicate that with only familiar size as a possible cue to distance, familiar objects, consistent with appearing at a near distance and Eq. 2, tend to have a perceived size proportional to their retinal size. It seems that not only is there a tendency for objects in the absence of distance information to appear at a near distance but also that this tendency can modify perceived distance in the presence of weak cues to egocentric distance. Thus, with increasing cue reduction an object will increasingly appear at a near distance and, in agreement with this near distance and the size-distance invariance hypothesis, the object will have a perceived size proportional to its retinal size. Again, it is suggested that perceived distance is as much involved in the perception of size under conditions of cue reduction as in the situation in which adequate cues to distance are available. If all cues of egocentric distance are eliminated, perceived distance does not disappear but instead is determined by an observer process indicated by the specific distance tendency.

In summary, the tendency for a number of perceptions such as perceptions of size, shape, and motion to be increasingly proportional to core retinal stimuli with increasing cue reduction does not indicate that the role of perceived distance in determining these perceptions is changed or reduced as compared to situations in which adequate cues to object distance are available. In agreement with the hypothesis of perceptual interactions, perceived distance is equally involved under all conditions of observation in specifying the perceptual response of size, shape and motion from a proximal stimulus.

Additional Evidence for Perceptual Interactions

There are experimental results in addition to those directly concerned with the invariance hypotheses to support the hypothesis that one perception can affect another. Some of this evidence is found in additional studies of motion perception. If two points of light are presented sequentially at different positions in the visual field, and are separated by the appropriate interval of time, O will perceive the first light as moving to the position of the second. This apparent motion is called stroboscopic motion. In a study of stroboscopic motion by Rock and Ebenholtz (1962) it was found that retinal displacement in the absence of phenomenal (perceived) displacement did not produce stroboscopic motion. On the other hand, phenomenal displacement in the absence of retinal displacement was adequate for the perception of motion.

The apparent motion between successively presented lights at different positions depends upon the separation of the lights as well as the time interval. Corbin (1942) investigated whether the objective or retinal separation of objects was the important factor in stroboscopic motion. The differentiation between these two factors was accomplished by physically slanting in depth the plane on which the objects (lines) were presented. Cues to the orientation of this surface were sometimes present. It was found that the threshold between apparent simultaneity and apparent motion differed depending upon whether cues to slant were present or absent. It can be concluded that phenomenal as contrasted with retinal separation is the effective separation of the apparent motion. This conclusion is supported by the results from a recent study by Attneave and Block (1973) in which several alternative explanations of this phenomenon were eliminated. Another kind of apparent motion is called induced motion. This occurs when a stationary object, a disc for example, is presented within a frame moving right and left in a frontoparallel plane with no other objects visible except the frame and disc. In this case, the frame often appears to have a smaller movement than would be expected and, as a result of this perception, the object within the frame appears to move in a direction (phase) opposite to that of the frame. A situation involving a different type of motion is a rotation of the object in depth. If an object is rotating in depth with few cues to its depth orientation it will sometimes appear to reverse its direction of rotation, even though the direction of its physical rotation is constant. It has been found that the direction of apparent rotation of the object depends upon the apparent depth orientation of the object (Day, 1969). Brown [1931 (2)] has summarized a number of factors that determine apparent velocity in a frontoparallel plane under a concept termed the transposition principle. It was found that the ratio of perceived velocities of objects moving within frames of different physical sizes at the same distance from the observer were proportional to the ratio of the frame sizes and not proportional to the ratio of the physical velocities. It has been suggested (Gogel, 1970) that this result can be attributed to the relative size cue between the frames resulting in the two displays appearing at different distances. This is equivalent to suggesting that perceived velocity depends upon the perceived, not the physical or retinal, distance through which the object moves (see Rock, Hill and Fineman, 1968). Also of importance for the present discussion, Brown [1931 (1)] found that the phenomenal rather than the physical velocity was correlated with other perceptual qualities, i.e., with the difference threshold for perceived movement, the threshold for an increase in the apparent number of the successively presented moving objects, and the threshold for the perception of the fusion into a line of moving objects presented sequentially. If O fixates his gaze for a period of time on a spiral painted on a rotating disc, it will be found upon stopping the disc that an apparent rotation will occur that is opposite in direction to the previous physical rotation. This is called the spiral aftereffect. In several experiments on the spiral aftereffect (Mehling, Collins and Schroeder, 1972; Williams and Collins, 1970), it has been found that the duration and magnitude of the aftereffect is influenced by the apparent size (S') per unit of retinal size (θ) or, since $S'/\theta = KD'$ in Eq. 2, by the apparent distance of the spiral. Neither the retinal nor the physical characteristics of the spiral per se were able to account completely for the aftereffect. Also in a study by Bonnet and Pouthas (1972), it was found that the duration of the spiral aftereffect increased with the apparent distance of the test surface on which the aftereffect was projected. That this result was not due to the physical distance of the test surface is indicated by the elimination of this increase when cues to the distance of the test surface were reduced. Also in agreement with the occurrence of perceptual interactions Rock and Halper (1970) in a study of form perception generated by a moving stimulus found that phenomenal rather than retinal displacement was the essential factor for perceived form.

Another example of a perceptual interaction is the dependence of perceptual grouping upon perceived separation. If a display consisting of points of light is arranged in rows and columns, the lights will be perceived as organized into rows or columns depending upon whether the separations of the lights is less in the rows or the columns. If the display is slanted in depth around a vertical axis, the slant will produce a decrease on the retina in the separation of the lights in the rows relative to their retinal separation in the columns. If adequate cues to the perception of depth slant are available in the display, the perceived separation of the lights in the rows will tend to remain constant despite the change in retinal separation. Using such a display, Rock and Brosgole (1964), consistent with a previous experiment by Corbin (1942), found that the reorganization from columns to rows occurred at a greater slant when cues to the physical slant of the display were available. Measures of the perceived separations of the lights supported the interpretation that the perceived rather than the retinal separation was the significant factor in determining this result. Consistent with the results obtained by Corbin it would be expected from the equidistance tendency that, when cues to perceived slant in depth are absent, the display would appear frontoparallel and, since under these conditions perceived separation and retinal separations are proportional, the erroneous interpretation might be made that under reduced conditions perceptual grouping is determined by retinal separation. It seems from these examples that variations in one perception can affect another perception despite constant values of the relevant proximal stimulation.

Also, in support of the hypothesis of perceptual interactions, there is evidence that perceived egocentric distance is important in the perception of an exocentric distance resulting from the cue of binocular disparity. An illustration of the binocular disparity cue is shown in Fig. 23.1. Fig. 23.1 is a top view schematic drawing of two luminous points of light, n and f located in the median plane of O and viewed binocularly in an otherwise dark visual field. The physical egocentric distances of the points from O are labeled D_n and D_f, with d_{nf} the physical depth between the points of

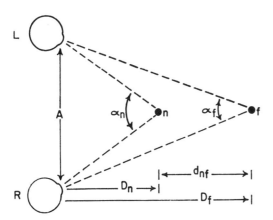

Figure 23.1
A top view schematic diagram illustrating the relation between the proximal stimulus measured by $\alpha_n - \alpha_f$ and the distal stimulus d_{nf} for a number of exocentric cues to distance.

light. The dashed lines indicate the lines of direction from each of the points to each of the eyes of O shown at the left of the figure. These lines also indicate the orientation of the visual axis of the eyes when the eyes converge to fixate the particular point. Thus, α_n and α_f represents the convergence of the axes of the eyes when O fixates points n and f. The binocular disparity γ between points n and f is defined at the proximal level as the difference in horizontal separation of n and f in the two eyes. This difference for points not too close to O is proportional to the difference between the α values for the two points. The equation relating binocular disparity to the physical exocentric distance is

$$\gamma_{nf} = \frac{Ad_{nf}}{D_n D_f} \tag{3}$$

where A is the interpupillary distance of O. If D_n and D_f are not too different, Eq. 3 becomes

$$\gamma_{nf} = \frac{Ad_{nf}}{D^2} \tag{4}$$

where D is the average of D_n and D_f. It is clear from Eq. 4 that, although a binocular disparity γ defined on the eye will specify that one point f is more distant than another n, is binocular disparity is ambiguous with respect to the distal stimulus d_{nf}, since different values of d_{nf} can produce the same γ_{nf} depending upon the distance of the configuration of points from O. It seems reasonable to expect, therefore, that the perceived exocentric distance d' associated with a particular binocular disparity γ will depend upon the perceived egocentric distance D' of the configuration. Since a number of experiments support this expectation [see Wallach and Zuckerman, 1963; Foley, 1968; Gogel 1972 (2)] it can be concluded that the perception of an exocentric distance d' from a binocular disparity γ is an increasing function of the magnitude of the average perceived egocentric distance D' of the configuration from O. In many experiments in which the perception of d' resulting from γ has been investigated, the only available cues to egocentric distance were the oculomotor cues of accommodation and convergence. But it should not be concluded that oculomotor cues of egocentric distance must be present in order to transform a binocular disparity to a perception of exocentric distance. In an experiment by Gogel [1964 (1)] the effect of perceived egocentric distance D', independent of oculomotor cues, upon the perceived depth d' from binocular disparity was studied by using a mirror to reflect a constant binocular configuration into a monocularly observed visual alley. The visual alley was varied so as to modify the perceived egocentric distance of the binocular configuration by means of the equidistance tendency. It was found that d' increased with increases in D' despite the unchanging accommodative and convergence values of the binocular configuration.

Fig. 23.1 can be used to describe other distance cues. Another exocentric cue of distance is that of relative motion parallax. Relative motion parallax can be represented by Fig. 23.1 if the L and R positions of the eyes are considered to represent two successive positions of a single eye (monocular observation) as the head of O is moved horizontally. Moving the head from L to R will change the direction of a point (n or f) with respect to the eye. This change in angular direction will be larger for n than for f since f is the more distant of the two points from O. In particular if Point n is fixated while moving from L to R, Point n will remain constant on the retina whereas Point f will move retinally from a position to the left of Point n to a position to the right of Point n. This differential movement of objects at different distances, as a function of head movement, is the cue of relative motion parallax. It is obvious that the geometry of relative motion parallax is identical to that of binocular disparity and, if the psychophysics of binocular disparity is any indication, it is likely that perceived egocentric distance is necessary in order to translate a relative motion parallax to a d'.

Fig. 23.1 can also be used to discuss the exocentric distance cue of relative size. In this case instead of the width A representing inter-pupillary distance or a movement of the eye, A is the width of an object (for instance, a rectangle) presented at the physical distance D_n or D_f from O. If two identical rectangles of width A are presented simultaneously, one at the distance D_n and the other at the distance D_f from O, or, if one rectangle is presented successively at these two distances, the difference in retinal size between the simultaneous or successive presentations will produce a perception of exocentric distance d' (Gogel and Sturm, 1971). It will be noted that the difference in retinal size (width) is proportional to $\alpha_n - \alpha_f$, with the geometry of the relative size cue to exocentric distance identical to that of the binocular disparity cue. For the relative size cue to distance, as for the cue of binocular disparity or relative motion parallax, it is likely that a perception of egocentric distance is necessary in order for these exocentric distance cues to mediate a perception of exocentric distance.

In summary, the cue of binocular disparity, relative retinal size, and relative movement parallax all involve differential displacements (differential directions or extents) either between the two eyes or on a single eye. Since these differential displacements are indeterminant with respect to an exocentric distance without specifying an egocentric distance, a *perception* of egocentric distance is required to translate these cues to a *perception* of exocentric distance. Also, it is possible that perceptual events in addition to a perception of egocentric distance are sometimes involved in transforming the proximal stimuli to a perception of exocentric distance. For example, the usual description of the process involving the relative size cue to distance is that O assumes that the two objects (rectangles) are of the same physical size and interprets the difference between their retinal sizes as a difference in distance. There are two kinds of evidence that suggest some limitation on this description of the relative size cue to distance. Although two objects of the same shape and different retinal sizes presented under reduced conditions of observation usually appear more similar in size than would be expected from their retinal sizes, they often do not appear to be identical in size. This probably is a consequence of a reduction in perceived distance between the two objects resulting from the equidistance tendency. Also, as is indicated by a study by Epstein and Franklin (1965) some difference in perceived distance will occur with this cue even though the objects are clearly different in shape. Despite these limitations, however, it is likely that an equality in the shape of the two objects increases the effectiveness of the relative size cue to distance (Hochberg and McAlister, 1955). It should be noted parenthetically that the tendency for objects of the same shape but different retinal size to appear to be more similar in size than is indicated by their retinal size, under otherwise reduced conditions of observation, argues against the validity of the core-context hypothesis. If the core-context hypothesis were valid, relative retinal size would not be a determiner of perceived exocentric distance. A perception of object identity may also be involved in the perceived exocentric distance associated with relative movement parallax in that a necessary condition for the operation of this cue may be that Objects n and f (Fig. 23.1) are assumed to be the same two objects despite their differential displacements on the eye. A tendency to perceive object identity whenever possible can be considered as part of the minimum principle (Hochberg, 1957) in which, all other conditions being equal, perceptions tend to be as simple as the changing stimulus conditions permit. Unfortunately such a principle of perceptual organization is often more successful as an *ad hoc* hypothesis than in supplying predictions. Nevertheless, it does suggest that, in the achievement of perceptual invariance despite changing proximal conditions of stimulation, more perceptual interactions may be involved than are usually realized.

The motion parallax associated with a single object is also a possible cue to egocentric distance. Consider the situation represented in Fig. 23.1 but with only one point (n) present and with head motion from L to R. If the gaze is fixed on Point n, the direction of the gaze will change when the eye is moved from L to R. The geometry of this cue is identical to that of the convergence cue to egocentric distance except that, in the motion parallax cue to egocentric distance, the change in eye direction is successive over time. Or, if the gaze is always straight ahead, moving the eye from L to R will change the position of Point n on the retina (Fig. 23.1). A particular change in the direction of an object with respect to the eye, or a particular change in the position of the object on the eye can be produced either by moving the head with the object at a constant position, or by moving the object laterally with the position of the head constant. Usually with head movement Point n is seen as stationary (constancy of visual direction) whereas with the physical movement of Point n and a stationary head, Point n is seen to move. The difference in the perceptions from these two cases is often explained by the reafference principle (Teuber, 1960). Voluntary movement of the head is produced by efference signals to the neck muscles. The change in the proprioceptive impulses from the muscles of the eye if the eye is fixated on Point n, or the change in the afferent impulses from the retina associated with the changed retinal position of Point n if the fixation is unchanged when *voluntarily* moving the eye from L to R in Fig. 23.1, is a reafference. According to the reafference principle, the comparison between the efference and reafference signals determines whether Point n is perceived as stationary or as moving. There is evidence, however, that the perception of Point n as stationary despite head movement (the perception of the constancy of visual direction) depends upon the perception of the egocentric distance of Point n. Hay and Sawyer (1969) examined the constancy of visual direction using a nodding motion of the head with binocular observation. The nodding motion produced a vertical displacement of the eyes with respect to the direction of a point of light. To test the effect of perceived distance upon the constancy of visual direction, the binocular convergence to the point of light was changed independently of the change in visual direction caused by the nodding motion. It was found that changing the convergence cue to distance modified to some extent the relation between the perception of visual direction and the perceived motion resulting from the nodding. A study by Wallach, Yablick and Smith (1972) in which both accommodation and convergence were discrepant with respect to the directional changes produced by the nodding showed still larger effects upon the constancy of visual direction. Also, Wallach and Frey (1972) had found that the perceived egocentric distance associated with accommodation and binocular convergence could be modified by having O move about in normal visual environments while wearing glasses that changed the accommodation and convergence of objects. This recalibration presumably was achieved by the conflict between the modified oculomotor cues and the unmodified distance cues in the normal environment. Applying these results to the modification of the constancy of visual direction, Wallach, Yablick, and Smith found that the recalibration of the perceived distance associated with accommodation and convergence produced a modification in the perception of visual direction with head nodding, when binocularly viewing a point of light under otherwise reduced conditions of observation with the glasses removed. The effect of apparent distance upon the perceived motion associated with head motion was studied further by Gogel and Tietz (1973) by viewing a stationary point of light in a dark surround at different physical distances while moving the head, using either monocular or binocular observation. The direction and magnitude of errors in perceived distance were determined by the position of the light relative to the distance defined by the specific distance tendency. It was hypothesized that the direction of perceived motion of the point from head motion would differ depending upon whether the point was physically closer to or more distant from the observer than the specific distance tendency. The results of this study provide support both for the validity of the specific distance tendency and for the effect of perceived distance on the direction of perceived motion resulting from head motion. It seems that the perception of egocentric distance determines the relation between efference and reafference that will produce directional constancy despite movement of the head. These results suggest that the *perception* of egocentric distance is essential both to the *perception* of motion with head motion and to explanations of perceptual stability described in terms of the reafference principle.

Evidence for the importance of perceptual interactions also is found in research concerning the "adjacency principle." The adjacency principle states that the effectiveness of cues between objects or parts of objects in determining perceived characteristics is inversely related to the relative separations of the objects or parts (Gogel, 1970). The relative separation can be either frontoparallel (directional) separation or separation in depth. Of importance for the present discussion, some of this research indicates that perceived separation as contrasted with retinal separation is the significant factor in the adjacency principle. An illustration of the application of the adjacency principle to the cue of binocular disparity can be discussed with the aid of the top view schematic drawing Fig. 23.2. The line LR in Fig 23.2 represents an Ames trapezoidal window (Ames, 1961). The physically smaller left end of the window (labeled L) is physically closer to O than the physically larger right end (labeled R), and also is the smaller of the two ends of the window on the eye. The decrease in the retinal size of the window from the right end to the left end (the relative size cue to distance) will result in the left end of the window appearing to be more distant than the right end, as indicated by L'R' in Fig. 23.2. Two points of light labeled A and B located directionally to the left and right of the window, respectively, are physically equidistant from O and are at the physical distance of the middle of the window. The observation of all objects is binocular with the position of O shown at the bottom of the figure. The binocular disparity produced by the window normally would

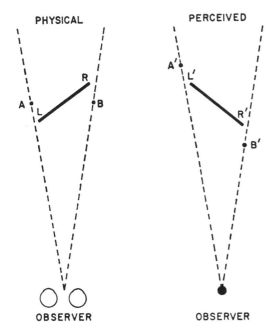

Figure 23.2
A top view schematic diagram illustrating the effect of an error in the perceived orientation of a binocularly observed trapezoidal window (L, R) upon the perceived orientation of two binocularly observed points of light (A, B).

result in End L of the window appearing closer than End R. But, despite this disparity, the relative size cue from the trapezoidal shape results in the perception of the illusory depth orientation shown as L'R'. When this occurs it is found that Points A and B will be perceived approximately at A' and B'. As a consequence of the error in the perceived orientation of the window an error will occur in the perceived exocentric depth between Points A and B. It will be noted that the perception of the depth between a point of light and the end of the window most adjacent to this point of light is in agreement with the binocular disparity between this point and the end of the window. But the disparity cue between a point of light and the end of the window displaced from this point or between the two points of light is ineffective in determining apparent depth positions. As expected from the adjacency principle, the binocular disparity between adjacent objects or contours is dominant over that between directionally displaced objects or contours in the perception of exocentric distance. It has recently been found that if the pair of lights A and B are both placed increasingly behind or in front of the window while remaining physically equidistant from O, the effect of the window in inducing an error in the

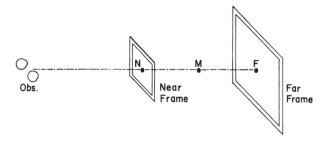

Figure 23.3
A perspective diagram illustrating the apparatus used to investigate the motion induced in a stationary point of light by moving frames as a function of the stereoscopic location of the point of light with respect to each of the frames.

apparent positions of the lights decreases [Gogel, 1972 (2)]. In other words, a perception of an illusory orientation of the window induces a perception of an illusory depth orientation of the points of light with respect to each other, with this induced effect decreasing with increased apparent separation of the points from the distance of the window. Clearly, interactions are involved here between different perceptions of depth.

An application of the adjacency principle to the perception of induced motion is indicated by the perspective drawing of Fig. 23.3. As mentioned, induced movement can be illustrated by observing a stationary point of light in a luminous frame with the frame moving right and left (oscillating) in an otherwise dark surround. The moving frame will tend to appear stationary and the stationary point of light will appear to move in a direction (phase) opposite to the physical movement of the frame. Fig. 23.3 illustrates one condition of an experiment by Gogel and Koslow (1972). Two frames were located at different physical and perceived distances from O. A point of light was located at either the distance of the near frame (N), a distance midway between the frames (M), or at the distance of the far frame (F). The viewing of all objects was binocular so that stereoscopic cues were available to determine that physical depth relations between the frames or between the point of light and each frame were correctly perceived. The point of light was always physically stationary whereas the simultaneously presented frames physically moved right and left. When the near frame was moving to the left, the far frame was moving to the right, i.e., the two frames moved in opposite phase, with the movement of the point of light induced by a particular frame opposite in phase to the physical movement of that frame. From the results of the experiment, the direction of the induced movement of the point of light was usually determined by the near frame for Position N, by the far frame for Position F, and often by neither frame at Position M. In other words, the induced motion of the point of light was mostly determined by the frame located at the same perceived distance as the point of light. One perception, the perception of the depth relation between the frame and point of light affected another perception, the perception of the motion of the point of light. In the situations illustrated by both Figs. 23.2 and 23.3 the magnitude of the induction effects decreased as a function of the increased perceived separation between the test and induction objects even though the directional (retinal) separations of the several objects were essentially unchanged. These experiments not only demonstrate perceptual interactions, but also indicate that the perception of equidistance between the test and induction object is essential for the large induction effects obtained when the test and induction objects are presented in the same frontoparallel plane with adequate cues to perceived equidistance. As was suggested by the discussion contrasting the hypothesis of perceptual interactions and the core-context hypothesis, whenever the test and induction object are at the same perceived distance, the induction effects seem to be determined by retinal relations. It is clear, however, that the particular value of perceived exocentric distance specified as perceived equidistance is essential for this result.

The importance of perceived separation in determining induction effects has also been demonstrated in the perception of whiteness resulting from simultaneous whiteness contrast in which, for example, the apparent whiteness of a test object is reduced by the presence of an adjacent surface of greater luminance. Simultaneous whiteness contrast can be reduced by increasing the separation of the test and induction object in a frontoparallel plane (Freeman, 1967). But this induction effect can also be reduced, it seems, by stereoscopically separating the test and induction object in apparent depth (Gogel and Mershon, 1969; Mershon and Gogel, 1970; Mershon, 1972). In agreement with the effect of perceived depth relations on whiteness contrast, Wist and Susen (1973) have found that the magnitude of simultaneous contrast in a Koffka ring is lessened as a perceived difference in depth is introduced stereoscopically between the bisecting line and the Koffka figure. Also, Flock (1972) has shown that whiteness contrast is reduced somewhat as a result of a difference in the apparent orientation of the test and induction object. It seems that a number of induction effects are reduced by either frontoparallel or depth separation between the test and induction objects. It is as though many of the perceptual characteristics of objects are affected by the perceived three-dimensional structure of the visual field in which they appear (also see Attneave, 1972). If the visual field appears two dimensional the perceptions tend to be proportional to stimuli or to ratios of stimuli defined at the retinal level. But, as discussed above, it is suggested that this is merely a happenstance of the objects appearing at the same frontoparallel plane and that the processes involved in the perception of object characteristics under the circumstance of perceived equidistance are identical to those occurring with objects distributed in apparent depth.

Perceptual interactions may be involved in some perceptual phenomena that are often considered as reflecting simpler processes than those presumably underlying perceptual interactions. There are some indications that accommodation or convergence in addition to determining perceived distance can also be influenced by perceived distance (Hennessy and Leibowitz, 1971; Ittelson and Ames, 1950). Also, there is some evidence to suggest that threshold measures can be influenced by the phenomenal aspects of the stimuli. Two studies (Ross and Gregory, 1964; Seashore, 1896) have indicated that the difference threshold for lifted weight is affected by the perceived as contrasted with the physical weights of the stimuli. Visual acuity (Luckiesh and Moss, 1933, 1941), the contrast threshold for the detection of a small stimulus (Richards, 1967), and the critical flicker frequency (Harvey, 1970) have been shown to vary as a function of the distance of the stimuli from O. It has been suggested that the latter two changes in threshold are the result of changes in perceived size resulting from the oculomotor cues with the perceived size modifying the retinal receptive fields (Harvey, 1970; Richards, 1967). Although it has not been tested, it is possible that a similar effect would occur for other distance cues than those of accommodation and convergence. If so, it would follow that perceived distance, not a particular distance cue per se, is the significant factor. A different effect upon perceived thresholds as a result of perceptual interactions can occur for differential thresholds associated with perceived size or perceived motion or in general with any perception dependent upon perceived distance. If the perceived size or perceived movement associated with a given retinal (or physical) size or movement is determined by perceived distance, the variability associated with the perceived distance will contribute to the variability (threshold) of the judgment of whether one size or motion is greater or less than another. Also, since the lesser of two sizes or velocities can be perceived as the greater by the appropriate manipulation of perceived distance, it would seem that the Weber fraction as well as the psychophysics of the perception of size or motion can be modified by perceived distance.

There is evidence that under some conditions the perception of contour can occur despite the absence of an abrupt change in the gradient of light falling on the eye (Schumann, 1904). Lawson and Gulick (1967) using matrix stereograms have demonstrated that subjective contours (anomalous contours) can result from a binocular disparity. To produce this contour a stimulus situation analogous to an invisible but obscuring surface located between O and a matrix of black dots on a white surface can be used. Despite the absence of a physical contour for the simulated near surface, the perception is that of a contoured surface interposed between *O* and the matrix background, with the perceived distance between this surface and the background varying with the magnitude of the binocular disparity. Also, anomalous contours can be generated by distance cues in addition to stereoscopic cues [Coren, 1971 (1)] although in some cases it is difficult to decide whether the perceived depth is contingent upon the anomalous contour or the anomalous contour is determined by the perceived depth. But regardless of the direction of the relation, the occurrence of anomalous contour and its relation to apparent depth provides another example of a perceptual interaction.

There is also some evidence that is equivocal or in opposition to the occurrence of some perceptual interactions. For example, it has been shown by Kolehmainen and Tuomisaari (1969) that the perceived sizes of afterimages are independent of the perceived sizes of the stimuli producing the afterimages. On the other hand it is clear that the perceived size of an afterimage, in agreement with the size-distance invariance hypothesis, will increase with an increase in the perceived distance of the afterimage (Price, 1961). The perceptual displacement of contours as a function of prior stimulation is known as a figural aftereffect. For example, stimulating a particular part of the retina by a disc of light (the inspection object) for several minutes can modify the perceived size of a retinally smaller disc of light (the test object) presented subsequently and centered on the same retinal area. A considerable amount of research had been addressed to the problem of whether the ratio of the perceived or retinal sizes of the inspection and test disc is the important variable without arriving at a clear decision (see Sutherland, 1961). From several more recent studies by Kolehmainen [1968 (1), 1968 (2), 1969] it seems that either the ratio of the perceived size, slant, or distance of the inspection and test figure is a significant factor in the aftereffect. In addition, it has been found by Kolehmainen and Cronhjort (1970) that aftereffects can be produced by geometrical illusions or components of geometrical illusions with these aftereffects in general consistent with the illusory, not the retinal, shapes expected from the displays. Stadler and Crabus (1972) have indicated that figural aftereffects can be produced by anomalous contours, amodal perceptions, and imagined inspection figures. Amodal perceptions involve the perceptual completion of lines between parts of a figure despite the lack of a corresponding stimulus. Also, Stadler and Crabus have found from varying the fixation between the inspection and test figure that both the apparent and the retinal position of the test figure with respect to the inspection figure will influence the magnitude of the aftereffect. In agreement with the role of central (perceptual) processes in figural aftereffects Weitzman [1963 (1)] has found that the figural aftereffects were greater for a portion of the inspection object seen as figure than for the portion seen as ground. It seems also that the figure-ground relation is an important perceptual differentiation for the perception of whiteness resulting from whiteness contrast (Coren, 1969) and for the magnitude of discrimination threshold [Weitzman, 1963 (2)].

Although as indicated by Kolehmainen (1969) two-dimensional geometrical illusions can produce aftereffects, Horrell (1971) has found that the change in the magnitude of a form of the Zöllner illusion as a result of a change in the distance or slant of the display was consistent with retinal, not the phenomenal, characteristics of the illusion. On the other hand, a study by Coren [1971 (2)] indicates that a size-contrast illusion can result from a difference in the perceived size of surrounding discs produced by a change in their perceived distance, even though the retinal size of the surrounding discs remains constant. Also it has been demonstrated that the magnitude of the Ponzo illusion can be modified by a difference in the relative perceived distance (or relative perceived size) of the induction and test portions of the illusion with the retinal size of the display held constant (see Greene, Lawson and Godek, 1972; Hennessy and Leibowitz, 1972).

Conclusions

Evidence has been presented that the process involved in translating a proximal stimulus to a perception can often be expressed parsimoniously in terms of the hypothesis of perceptual interactions. Although the evidence considered is not intended to be inclusive (see Hochberg, 1968; Attneave, 1971, for additional possible examples of perceptual interaction) the number of instances in which perceptual interactions have been demonstrated requires that this point of view be considered seriously.

. From Eq. 1, a dependent perception (ψ_2) is a function not only of the relevent proximal stimulus (R) but also at least of one other (independent) perception ψ_1. According to Eq. 1, some value of both R and ψ_1 must be present if ψ_2 is to occur. Thus, for example, S' in Eq. 2 requires a value of D' as well as a value of θ, and, as discussed, if cues of D' are absent, the magnitude of D' will be determined by observer tendencies. If ψ_1 is held constant ψ_2 will vary with R. Again, the proportionality between ψ_2 and R under this condition does not indicate any determination of ψ_2 by R independently of ψ_1 i.e., the constant value of ψ_2 is a necessary condition for the proportionality. If R is held constant ψ_2 will vary with ψ_1 as is indicated by many of the examples cited. It will be noted that from this point of view R and ψ_1 are complementary rather than in opposition in their determination of ψ_2.

If the hypothesis of perceptual interactions is valid attempts to explain ψ_2 solely in terms of R under any conditions will be in error. The solution proposed by the core-context hypothesis is to specify the contextual proximal stimuli that determine ψ_1 as well as the core proximal stimulus R for ψ_2 in order to predict the value of ψ_1. A difficulty in this approach is that predictive errors will remain to the extent that observer tendencies contribute to ψ_1. As will be considered in the article that follows (Gogel, 1973) this contribution is appreciable in many situations. Also, it will be noted that the point of view expressed in Eq. 1 tends to be parsimonious in predicting ψ_2 in that ψ_2 is independent of the cues by means of which the value of ψ_1 was determined. For example in Eq. 2, for a given value of θ, a particular D' will determine a particular S' regardless of the distance cue or cues used to achieve that value of D'. This suggests an experimental criterion for the identification of an independent perception in perceptual interactions. An independent perception ψ_1 is identified if the effect of ψ_1 on ψ_2 is independent of the factors by means of which the particular value of ψ_1 is made to occur.

A present limitation in the use of perceptual interactions in order to achieve predictive parsimony and predictive accuracy is that, except mainly in the cases of the invariance hypothesis and the adjacency principle, there has been little systematic research concerning perceptual interactions. It does seem, however, that one of the ubiquitous perceptions involved in perceptual interactions is that of the perceived distance or the perceived separation of objects.

Note

Preparation of this chapter was supported by PHS research grant number MH 15651 from the National Institute of Mental Health and PHS research grant number NS 18883 from the National Institute of Neurological Diseases and Stroke.

References

Ames, A., Jr.: The rotating trapezoid, p. 222–256. In: Explorations in transactional psychology (Kilpatrick, F. P., Ed.). New York: University Press 1961.

Attneave, F.: Multistability in perception. Sci. Amer. **225**, 63–71 (1971).

Attneave, F.: Representations of physical space. Chapter in: Coding process in human memory (Melton, A. W., Martin, E., Eds.). New York: H. V. Winston & Sons 1972.

Attneave, F., Block, G.: Apparent movement in tridimensional space. Perception and Psychophysics **13**, 301–307 (1973).

Biersdorf, W.: Convergence and apparent distance as correlates of size judgments at near distances. J. gen. Psychol. **75**, 249–264 (1966).

Bonnet, C., Pouthas, V.: Apparent size and duration of movement aftereffect. Quart. J. exp. Psychol. **24**, 275–281 (1972).

Boring, E. G.: The perception of objects. Amer. J. Phys. **14**, 99–107 (1946).

Brown, J. F.: (1) The thresholds for visual movement. Psychol. Forsch. **14**, 249–268 (1931).

Brown, J. F.: (2) The visual perception of velocity. Psychol. Forsch. **14**, 199–232 (1931).

Carlson, V. R.: Overestimation in size-constancy judgments. Amer. J. Psychol. **73**, 199–213 (1960).

Carlson, V. R.: Underestimation in size-constancy judgments. Amer. J. Psychol. **75**, 462–465 (1962).

Collins, W. E., Schroeder, D. J.: Some effects of changes in spiral size and viewing distance on the duration of the spiral aftereffect. Perceptual and Motor Skills **27**, 119–126 (1968).

Corbin, H. H.: The perception of grouping and apparent movement in visual depth. Arch. Psychol. **273**, 1–50 (1942).

Coren, S.: Brightness contrast as a function of figure-ground relations. J. exp. Psychol. **80**, 517–524 (1969).

Coren, S.: (1) Subjective contour formation. Paper presented at the 12th Annual Meeting of the Psychonomic Society, St. Louis, November 1971.

Coren, S.: (2) A size-contrast illusion without physical size differences. Amer. J. Psychol. **84**, 565–566 (1971).

Day, R. H.: Human perception. Sydney: John Wiley 1969.

Epstein, W., Franklin, S.: Some conditions on the effect of relative size on perceived relative distance. Amer. J. Psychol. **78**, 466–470 (1965).

Epstein, W., Park, J. H.: Shape constancy: functional relationship and theoretical formulations. Psychol. Bull. **60**, 265–288 (1963).

Epstein, W., Park, J., Casey, A.: The current status of the size-distance hypothesis. Psychol. Bull. **58**, 491–514 (1961).

Flock, H. R.: Lightness embeddedness and contrast. Perceptual and Motor Skills **35**, 87–100 (1972).

Foley, J. M.: Depth, size, and distance in stereoscopic vision. Perception and Psychophysics **3**, 265–274 (1968).

Freeman, R. B., Jr.: Contrast interpretation of brightness constancy. Psychol. Bull. **67**, 165–187 (1967).

Gogel, W. C.: The tendency to see objects as equidistant and its inverse relation to lateral separation. Psychol. Monogr. **70**, (Whole No. 411) (1956).

Gogel, W. C.: Perception of depth from binocular disparity. J. exp. Psychol. **67**, 379–386 (1964).

Gogel, W. C.: Equidistance tendency and its consequences. Psychol. Bull. **64**, 153–163 (1965).

Gogel, W. C.: (1) The effect of object familiarity on the perception of size and distance. Quart. J. exp. Psychol. **21**, 239–247 (1969).

Gogel, W. C.: (2) The sensing of retinal size. Vision Res. **9**, 3–24 (1969).

Gogel, W. C.: Adjacency principle and three dimensional visual illusions. Chapter in: Human space perception: Proceedings of the Dartmouth conference (Baird, J. C., Ed.). Psychonomic Monogr. Suppl. **3**, (Whole No. 45) (1970).

Gogel, W. C.: The validity of the size-distance invariance hypothesis with cue reduction. Perception and Psychophysics **9**, 92–94 (1971).

Gogel, W. C.: (1) Depth adjacency and cue effectiveness. J. exp. Psychol. **92**, 176–181 (1972).

Gogel, W. C.: (2) Scalar perception with binocular cues of distance. Amer. J. Psychol. **85**, 477–498 (1972).

Gogel, W. C.: The organization of perceived space. II. Consequences of perceptual interactions. Psychol. Forsch. 1973.

Gogel, W. C., Brune, R. L., Inaba, K.: A modification of a stereopsis adjustment by the equidistance tendency. USAMRL Report **157**, 1–11 (1954).

Gogel, W. C., Koslow, M. A.: The adjacency principle and induced motion. Perception and Psychophysics **11**, 309–314 (1972).

Gogel, W. C., Mershon, D. H.: Depth adjacency in simultaneous contrast. Perception and Psychophysics **5**, 13–17 (1969).

Gogel, W. C., Sturm, R. D.: Directional separation and the size cue to distance. Psychol. Forsch. **35**, 57–80 (1971).

Gogel, W. C., Tietz, J. D.: Absolute motion parallax and the specific distance tendency. Perception and Psychophysics **13**, 284–292 (1973).

Greene, R. T., Lawson, R. B., Godek, C. L.: The Ponzo illusion in stereoscopic space. J. exp. Psychol. **75**, 258–264 (1972).

Harvey, L. O.: Critical flicker frequency as a function of viewing distance, stimulus size, and luminance. Vision Res. **10**, 55–63 (1970).

Hay, J. C., Sawyer, Susan: Position constancy and binocular convergence. Perception and Psychophysics **5**, 310–312 (1969).

Hennessy, R. T., Leibowitz, H. W.: The effect of a peripheral stimulus on accommodation. Perception and Psychophysics **10**, 129–132 (1971).

Hennessy, R. T., Leibowitz, H. W.: Perceived vs. retinal relationships in the Ponzo illusion. Psychonomic Sci. **28**, 111–112 (1972).

Hochberg, J.: Effects of the Gestalt revolution: The Cornell Symposium on perception. Psychol. Rev. **64**, 73–84 (1957).

Hochberg, J.: In the mind's eye. In: Contemporary theory and research in visual perception (Haber, R. N., Ed.). New York: Holt, Rinehart, & Winston, Inc. 1968.

Hochberg, C. B., McAlister, E.: Relative size vs. familiar size in the perception of represented depth. Amer. J. Psychol. **68**, 294–296 (1955).

Holway, A. H., Boring, E. G.: Determinants of apparent visual size with distance variant. Amer. J. Psychol. **54**, 21–37 (1941).

Horrell, R. I.: Retinal image or perceived features as determinants of error in geometric illusions? Quart. J. exp. Psychol. **23**, 97–106 (1971).

Ittelson, W. H., Ames, A., Jr.: Accommodation, convergence, and their relation to apparent distance. J. Psychol. **30**, 43–62 (1950).

Katz, D.: The world of colour. Translated by R. B. MacLeod and C. W. Fox. London: Kegan, Paul, Trench, Truber & Co. 1935.

Kilpatrick, F. P., Ittelson, W. H.: The size-distance invariance hypothesis. Psychol. Rev. **60**, 223–231 (1953).

Koffka, K.: Principles of Gestalt psychology. New York: Harcourt Brace 1935.

Kolehmainen, K.: (1) Apparent size as a determiner of figural aftereffects I. Scand. J. Psychol. **9**, 230–231 (1968).

Kolehmainen, K.: (2) Apparent size as a determiner of figural aftereffects II. Scand. J. Psychol. **9**, 237–240 (1968).

Kolehmainen, K.: Apparent size as a determiner of figural aftereffects III. Scand. J. Psychol. **10**, 71–73 (1969).

Kolehmainen, K., Cronhjort, R.: Apparent properties of inspection figures as determiners of figural aftereffects. Scand. J. Psychol. **11**, 103–108 (1970).

Kolehmainen, K., Tuomisaari, R.: The locus of visual afterimages. Scand. J. Psychol. **10**, 45–48 (1969).

Lawson, R. B., Gulick, W. L.: Stereopsis and anomalous contour. Vision Res. **1967**, 271–297.

Lodge, H., Wist, E. R.: The growth of the equidistance tendency over time. Perception and Psychophysics **3**, 97–104 (1968).

Luckiesh, M., Moss, F. K.: The dependency of visual acuity upon stimulus distance. J. Opt. Soc. Amer. **23**, 25–29 (1933).

Luckiesh, M., Moss, F. K.: The variation in visual acuity with fixation distance. J. Opt. Soc. Amer. **31**, 594–595 (1941).

Mehling, K. D., Collins, W. E., Schroeder, D. J.: Some effects of perceived size, retinal size and retinal speed on duration of spiral aftereffect. Perceptual and Motor Skills **34**, 247–259 (1972).

Mershon, D. H.: Relative contributions of depth and directional adjacency to simultaneous whiteness contrast. Vision Res. **12**, 969–979 (1972).

Mershon, D. H., Gogel, W. C.: The effect of stereoscopic cues on perceived whiteness. Amer. J. Psychol. **83**, 55–67 (1970).

Price, G. R.: On Emmert's law of apparent sizes. Psychol. Rec. **11**, 145–151 (1961).

Richards, W.: Apparent modifiability of receptive field during accommodation and convergence and a model for size constancy. Neurophysiologia **5**, 63–72 (1967).

Rock, I., Brosgole, L.: Grouping based on phenomenal proximity. J. exp. Psychol. **67**, 531–538 (1964).

Rock, I., Ebenholtz, S.: Stroboscopic movement based on change of phenomenal rather than retinal location. Amer. J. Psychol. **75**, 193–207 (1962).

Rock, I., Halper, F.: Form perception without a retinal image. Amer. J. Psychol. **82**, 425–440 (1970).

Rock, I., Hill, A. L., Fineman, M.: Speed constancy as a function of size constancy. Perception and Psychophysics **4**, 37–40 (1968).

Roelofs, C. O., Zeeman, W. P. C.: Apparent size and apparent distance in binocular and monocular vision. Ophthalmologica (Basel) **133**, 188–204 (1957).

Ross, H. E., Gregory, R. L.: Is the Weber fraction a function of physical or perceived input? Quart. J. exp. Psychol. **16**, 116–122 (1964).

Schumann, F.: Einige Beobachtungen über die Zusammenfassung von Gesichts-eindrücken zu Einheiten. Psychol. Stud. **1**, 1–32 (1904).

Seashore, C. E.: A new factor in Weber's law. Studies from the Yale Psychological Laboratory, IV, 1896.

Stadler, M., Crabus, H.: Peripheral vs. central factors in figural aftereffects: Some new results and considerations. Talk given before the XXth International Congress of Psychology, Tokyo, Japan, 1972.

Sutherland, N. S.: Figural aftereffects and apparent size. Quart. J. exp. Psychol. **13**, 222–228 (1961).

Teuber, H. L.: Perception. In: Handbook of Physiology, Vol. 3, Chap. 65 (Field, J., Ed.). Washington: American Physiological Society 1960.

Wallach, H., Frey, K. H.: Adaptation in distance perception based on oculomotor cues. Perception and Psychophysics **11**, 77–83 (1972).

Wallach, H., Yablick, H. S., Smith, A.: Target distance and adaptation in distance perception in the constancy of visual direction. Perception and Psychophysics **11**, 3–34 (1972).

Wallach, H., Zuckerman, C.: The constancy of stereoscopic depth. Amer. J. Psychol. **76**, 404–412 (1963).

Weitzman, B.: (1) A figural aftereffect produced by a phenomenal dichotomy in a uniform contour. J. exp. Psychol. **66**, 195–200 (1963).

Weitzman, B.: (2) A threshold difference produced by a figure-ground dichotomy. J. exp. Psychol. **66**, 201–205 (1963).

Williams, M. J., Collins, W. E.: Some influence of visual angle and retinal speed on measures of the spiral aftereffects. Perceptual and Motor Skills **30**, 215–227 (1970).

Wist, E. R., Susen, P.: Evidence for the role of post-retinal processes in simultaneous contrast. Psychol. Forsch. **36**, 1–12 (1973).

Index